The Modern Liberal Jungle: A Guide for Americans

JAMES B. CONNELLY

Cover design by BizzyBzzz Graphic Design

The Modern Liberal Jungle: A Guide for Americans

ISBN: 1475105436
ISBN 13: 9781475105438

Contents

Introduction

Several years ago, I spoke with a friend about a series of exchanges I had with a Modern Liberal. As usual, the Liberal's ideas and rationales were bereft of logic and coherent thought, and they were replete with appeals to base emotions, distortions of facts, and revised history. On top of this, the Liberal demanded a complete acceptance of his dogma. I told my friend that as of late, it had become rather easy to remain undaunted and avoid acquiescing to these people. In fact, I told him, if one goes on the offensive most Modern Liberals can be readily reduced to confused and impotent sputtering and mumbling about "compassion" and "caring." The Liberal in this case, I informed my friend, had resorted to regurgitating the familiar and meaningless charges that I was a brainwashed dolt of right-wing media, a dupe of corporate interests, and a right-winger who lacked compassion for the poor and disenfranchised. The charges had the effect of the proverbial "water off a duck's back."

My friend sighed and said, "I could never do that." He added that he would "wind up being made to feel stupid" from such an interaction with a Modern Liberal, apparently recalling past encounters.

I was surprised and puzzled by that comment: My coworker-friend was not only very intelligent, but he knew more than I about American history, politics, and culture. He had graduate degrees and served as a school principal. He had led and managed staff, dealt with school boards and parents, and mediated all sorts of disputes on a routine basis. By all measures, he was more capable than

I of dealing with a typical Modern Liberal.

What was the "disconnect?" Why would such an astute and well-educated person with successful leadership and life experience "feel stupid" engaging a Modern Liberal? This was not an isolated or unusual comment; I had heard variations of this from others. In my experience, most people will flee from discussions about politics or social issues with Modern Liberals. If cornered, they will generally try to change the subject; acquiesce; or tacitly agree with their ideology, proposals, and pronouncements. When these Americans do make some attempt to assert their own opinions to a Modern Liberal, many wind up feeling defeated or humiliated. Or, like my friend, "stupid."

What is going on?

The reason is not obvious at first glance, yet it is simple and, at the same time, rather complex. For most Americans, their families, work, churches, and communities are of primary importance. In contrast, most Modern Liberals actually have, from a relatively young age, been *trained*—or programmed—to politicize every aspect of life. During their formative years, Modern Liberals see significant adults, peers, and professors engaging in this politicization. They adopt the Liberal worldview and these behaviors for a variety of reasons, including a desire to be accepted, a sense of power, a need for status, or simply because they don't know any alternative.

Most Americans mistakenly assume that others unabashedly love the United States, that their fellow countrymen respect American traditions and customs, that their neighbors and friends get a surge of pride when they see the Stars and Stripes or hear the National Anthem, that most of us are generous, and that everyone realizes that our nation is special, a "shining city on a hill." But these attitudes are anathema to the worldview of Modern Liberals. Therefore, Modern Liberals will use virtually any artifice, distortion, or form of attack to promote and defend their ideology. These methods are rarely learned formally—there are no "Liberal Tactics 101" courses—but taught and absorbed in their culture.

When Americans like my friend meet Modern Liberals, they are not only confronted with people whose views of America, traditions, and the free market stand in direct contradiction to theirs, but with people who have learned to politicize virtually every aspect of life and vehemently demand others accede to their dogma.

This book is for Conservatives, Traditionalists, Patriots, and others who want to stand up to these Modern Liberals. It is dedicated to those who are saying, as Howard Beale (Peter Finch) did in *Network*, "I'm mad as hell, and I'm not going to take it anymore," who want to restore our founding values and principles, and who no longer want to be forced into what they view as a choice between capitulation or feeling "stupid."

Rather than analyzing current political platforms, this book provides the reader with conceptual frameworks and practical ideas to join the fight for our country, both before and after votes have been cast. It is divided into two sections: Part I introduces the Modern Liberals; Part II is about the "rest of us," represented by Conservatives in America. Conservatism provides a dramatic and coherent contrast to the ideology, ideas, and agenda of Modern Liberalism, and Conservatism strives to preserve what is unique and *exceptional* about America.

In both sections, the respective populations are defined, their beliefs are described, and their histories are outlined. In addition to tracing the overall origins and history of Modern Liberalism in Chapters 1 through 3 of the first section, there are two additional chapters that further explicate how they came to be: Chapter 4 is about their education—how people actually *become* Modern Liberals—and Chapter 5 describes their Marxist roots. Chapter 6 addresses the question of whether Modern Liberals really hate America. The final chapter in this section, Chapter 7, describes their tactics and propaganda.

The first three chapters of the second section, Chapters 8 through 10, clarify who Conservatives are, explain their beliefs, and outline their history. In promoting their ideology and agenda, Modern Liberals often offer Europe as a model to which America should aspire, so Chapter 11 presents a contrast of America's exceptional culture, origins, and values with those of Europe. Chapter 12 is devoted to Ronald Reagan, a man who embodied our founding principles and provided an antidote to Modern Liberalism: Ronald Reagan was an optimist, articulated the American Dream, stood resolutely against Communism, and believed in the free market; he warned Americans of the dangers of big government and reminded us that liberty is fragile and can be lost in a generation. Chapter 13, "Taking America Back," is the longest chapter. It covers methods to deal with Modern Liberals and includes suggestions to renew and restore our founding principles and American values.

A list of websites, organizations, and suggested readings are provided in the Appendix.

We are winning the battle against Modern Liberalism, but we need to be well-armed and resolute. It is my hope that the reader will become a bit better equipped to defend America against the interminable onslaught of Modern Liberalism and to encourage others to preserve the traditions and values of the "greatest country in the world."

Part I

Modern Liberals

1

Who Are The Modern Liberals?

For the average American, the message is clear. Liberalism is no longer the answer. It is the problem.

—RONALD REAGAN

I n a 1964 Supreme Court case dealing with obscenity, *Jacobellis v. Ohio*, the justices were having difficulty with definitions. Exasperated, Justice Potter Stewart said, "I know it when I see it."

Precisely defining what otherwise seems obvious can be an arduous task, and we wind up getting bogged down in details, contesting fine distinctions, and getting lost in a series of qualifiers and exceptions. Meanings can change with time and circumstance.

So, who are the people discussed in this book? Who, exactly, are the Modern Liberals?

There is a multitude of terms used to describe a set of people whom, to paraphrase Justice Steward, "we know when we see and hear": Progressives,

Left-wingers, Collectivists, Liberals, Leftists, Socialists and even Communists. Bill O'Reilly contrasts "Secular-Progressives" with "Traditionalists," John Diggins refers to the "Academic Left," and Thomas Sowell wrote a book about the "Anointed."[1, 2, 3] In *Liberty and Tyranny: A Conservative Manifesto*, Mark Levin wrote, "The Modern Liberal believes in the supremacy of the state, thereby rejecting the principles of the Declaration... For the Modern Liberal, the individual's imperfection and personal pursuits impede the objective of a utopian state...it is more accurate, therefore, to characterize the Modern Liberal as a *Statist*."[4] (Emphasis original)

These terms represent people we know when we see (or hear), but using them willy-nilly can lead to confusion. In this book, only the term "Modern Liberals" is used. This is intended to help the reader keep in mind that today's Liberals – the *Modern* Liberals – come from a tradition that is over a century old, a tradition that began 124 years before the writing of this book to be precise.

Are there unifying themes that define Modern Liberals? Most Modern Liberals will insist that they are not Statists, Collectivists, Socialists or Communists; some will resist being called Leftists, Progressives or even Liberals; and a good number will claim that they are "Centrists" or "Moderates."

So what are the unifying characteristics?

The cardinal one is that Modern Liberals believe that the building of the best possible society can only be realized via a centralized state power. In America, this centralized state power is the federal government. Modern Liberals promote this credo not only by pushing for increased federal power, but also by doggedly resisting any decentralizing of authority or local control. For Modern Liberals, decentralization and local government are anathema to their ideology and core beliefs. This becomes very clear if you advocate for the rights of states and local communities: Modern Liberals will brand you a defender of Jim Crow laws, a supporter of back alley abortions, or a hate-filled homophobe. You may be accused of being a religious "fundamentalist" who wants Creation Science taught in the schools, a person trying to stop children from being protected from pregnancy and venereal disease, or a racist who wants to reinstate segregation in schools and communities. The specific techniques that Modern Liberals use will be covered in Chapter 7, but they are all designed to promote this unifying characteristic that distinguishes Modern Liberals: Issues about education, society, the economy – in a nutshell, everything in our lives – are to be decided and enforced by a central authority.

To know if you are in the presence of a Modern Liberal, reading one of their publications, watching their news or movies, or looking at one of their websites, all you need to do is to listen to the solutions that are proposed: The solutions will be some kind of action by the federal government. They may be federal regulations, new agencies, or expansions of existing bureaucracies. The solutions might be enforcement or strengthening of existing federal laws or additional federal funding of some sort. And they could simply be more federal or national taxes.

Discover this for yourself by doing a simple experiment: First of all, virtually all news shows – Liberal, Conservative, Moderate, or otherwise – have a similar format: Topics of importance are selected and discussed, and then they are usually followed by recommendations to solve them. Choose a television program, magazine, or web site that is manifestly favored by Modern Liberals, such as MSNBC, the *Huffington Post's* website, or *Nation* magazine.

Then, when solutions are suggested, notice how these are to be carried out: Who or what is involved with each solution that is presented by the newscaster? I did this with MSNBC's Rachel Maddow Show a dozen times, and *every* proposed solution was a federal government one: federal funding, regulation, oversight, prosecution, taxation or administration. Not even one recommendation – in twelve hours of broadcasting – stressed individuals making choices or community-level decision making. None called for charities to help or for local school boards to get involved. There was not a single instance of a call to parents or citizens to do something without the aid of the federal government. Rachel Maddow typifies Modern Liberals and their agenda for America. She expresses the essence of Modern Liberalism: The federal government is needed to solve our problems, and we Americans cannot solve them without it.

An essential element in the drive to centralize power is change. The centralization of power in the state necessitates a radical alteration or end of the old order. Modern Liberals generally celebrate progress for its own sake and presume it is essential to improve society, promote fairness, and encourage prosperity. From this viewpoint, our common history, age-old traditions and established institutions retard this "progress." *True* diversity of thought cannot be tolerated by Modern Liberals because it has the potential to thwart progress as they envision it. Unless everyone shares *their* vision, they believe "progress" will be hamstrung. Modern Liberals insist that progress is necessary, but, as expected, only the types that *they* have promoted. This forms the imperative to change or "deconstruct" history and traditions in order to promote the Modern Liberal concepts of progress.

So, if you are unsure whether or not you are in the presence of a *Modern Liberal*, simply ask what the person thinks are solutions to problems in education, the economy or crime. Many self-proclaimed "Liberals" intermittently spout platitudes and clichés about people being responsible, caring and compassionate, occasionally followed by denunciations of the wealthy, corporations or capitalism. Some of them may recommend the federal government to take action. The difference between these people and the *Modern* Liberals is that they do not call for action by the federal government for virtually every issue of concern. When you get consistent responses that demand a powerful role for the federal government, you are most certainly in the presence of a *Modern* Liberal. This consistency is the tell-tale mark. Typical Americans will sometimes recommend a role for the central government for the country, but not for every major issue. In contrast, for Modern Liberals the ideal is an omnipresent federal government. As a typical example, in southern California the American Civil Liberties Union (ACLU) – that arm of Modern Liberals – maintains that parents have no fundamental right to be the sole provider of sexual information to children.[5]

And there is no end to the demands of Modern Liberals. William Voegli, author of *Never Enough*, explained that "liberalism…will always have room for one more program to address one more problem… This *lack of a limiting principle* is the defining characteristic of liberalism. Its philosophy amounts to the belief, 'Everything is good to do.'"[6] (Emphasis added)

Modern Liberals insist that the centralization of power is necessary to insure to human equality, but their notion of equality is a *forced equality*, more accurately described as radical egalitarianism. In a society where people are free – are truly free and equal *in the eyes of the law and God* – they will reap the rewards and losses of their actions and efforts, and not everyone will wind up in an "equal" condition: Differences in ability, effort, determination, morals, and backgrounds will result in differences in outcomes. Modern Liberals refuse to tolerate this kind of society and advocate for more and more of a forced equality by a central power – the federal government. Their agenda tends to focus on our economic lives, but it also filters into work, education, local communities and family.

A secondary unifying characteristic of Modern Liberalism is the belief that human reason has an unlimited capacity to comprehend, evaluate and arrange an ideal society. This leads to the premise that "experts" can discover and formulate ways to create a utopia and that they should advise and guide the central power.

The contrasting view – the one espoused by our Founding Fathers – is that reason is limited and moral guidance is essential. The American predecessors of Modern Liberals – the Progressives of the late 19th and early 20th centuries, followed by the Old Left of the 1930s through the 1950s, and then the New Left – strove to change humans and to create a perfect society. In contrast, the Founding tradition accepts human nature, adheres to limited government, and is comfortable with what is truly attainable. This is why the Founding tradition emphasizes the *restriction* of government rather than the Modern Liberals' *expansion* of it. The eventual "end state" of Modern Liberalism is Communism. The Founding tradition emphasizes the free market and individual choices, so there can be no ideal "end state." With the Founding tradition, *we have already arrived*.

Classical Liberalism of Old

It is important to focus on the ideology of *Modern* Liberals, rather than summarily applying labels. Many who refer to themselves as Liberals are simply viewing themselves as being "tolerant" in some way. These people think that being Liberal means simply not condemning differences in lifestyle, sexuality, dress or interests and they presume that Liberals are "non-judgmental." This is quite different from the Liberal who focuses on federal government solutions. In fact, if one queries the former, they are often against many federal government interventions. There is a difference between the person who says that gays should be tolerated or left to do as they please, and someone who pushes for the establishment of "Hate Crime" laws in which the federal government defines what constitutes "hate" in a crime, the FBI helps with apprehension and prosecution, and judges give harsher penalties for crimes against those in specific categories defined – again – by Modern Liberals. There is a difference between the person who says gays should not be insulted and bullied out of respect for them as human beings, and someone who wants *federal* funding in schools to promote a specific curriculum designed to normalize particular lifestyles determined to be in need of deferential treatment.

What is ironic – and another reason that the word "Modern" is affixed to Liberal – is that many of today's Conservatives and Traditionalists are remarkably similar to those who were the *Classic* Liberals of old. Richard Hudelson wrote the following in *Modern Political Philosophy*:

It is important not to confuse…classical liberalism with the political ideology known as "liberalism" in the United States in the twentieth century. In fact, the ideology of classical liberalism is closer to what today is a current of conservatism in the United States. Central to the classical liberalism of the nineteenth century is a commitment to the liberty of individual citizens… Central to classical liberalism was a commitment to a system of free markets as the best way to organize economic life.[7]

William Novak wrote that there was a "dramatic transformation in liberal ideology and governance between 1877 and 1937 that carried the United States from laissez-faire constitutionalism to New Deal statism, from classical liberalism to democratic social-welfarism."[8]

We frequently hear the term "Liberals." Our Founders were Liberals, and our Declaration of Independence was written, at least in part, on liberal principles. Nobel Prize winner Milton Friedman, the gadfly of Modern Liberals for extolling free market principles, calls himself a Liberal, but refers to it in this classic sense:

I use the term "liberal," as Hayek does – in the original nineteenth-century sense of limited government and free markets, not in the corrupted sense it has acquired in the United States, in which it means almost the opposite, in which government activity is limited primarily to establishing the framework within which individuals are free to pursue their own objectives.[9]

Modern Liberal Commandments

We are *forced* to deal with Modern Liberals because they have politicized everything, from religion and child rearing to movies, books and sex. Nothing escapes their politicization of our lives. One is asked to take a stand on everything. If one does not, one is deemed "uncaring" "cold-blooded," racist, greedy or selfish.

Fortunately, Modern Liberals are not a unified conspiratorial group, plotting and organizing a new order behind closed doors, sending out diktats to their satellite organizations. Rather, they have a shared mindset: They have accepted, and believe in, the necessity of change and progress that can only be carried out by the federal government. Most focus on only a few special issues, but no matter what the concern, they advocate for a central authority to plan a solution and then implement, regulate, fund and/or control its course.

Bill O'Reilly and Patrick Buchanan list the *commandments* that these people observe. Those listed by O'Reilly include these commandments:

> [Self] gratification is paramount,…take from the rich,…[do] not respect private property,…circumvent mothers and fathers in personal issues,…do not limit the power of government in order to promote "greater good," [and] do not acknowledge God in public.[10]

Here are some Modern Liberal commandments listed by Pat Buchanan:

> All lifestyles are equal,…all voluntary sex relations are permissible,… the Christian code is cruel and hinders human fulfillment,…public schools will be used to teach children to like all lifestyles…and Western history as a catalogue of crimes.[11]

Jonah Goldberg, author of *Liberal Fascism*, refers to them as "left wing" and writes: "I would broadly define 'left-wing' as statist, collectivist, egalitarian (within a defined group, be it based on class, race, or nationality), and hostile to tradition, religious orthodoxy, natural rights, and Lockean individualism."[12]

The Modern Liberal Worldview

The Modern Liberal ideology and agenda center on experts determining how to set up the ideal society and have their plans implemented, managed and enforced by the federal government. Here are characteristics that dominate their worldview. Some contradict others, but the minds of ideologues are rarely rational:

Radical Egalitarianism

True liberty results in inequality of outcome, and this is unacceptable to Modern Liberals. For them, *outcomes* must be the same as possible. Modern Liberals will never acknowledge that this necessitates coercion and thus destroys liberty. On the contrary, Modern Liberals are convinced that any beliefs or institutions that hint at superiority or have authorities in the family, church and teacher-student relationships stand in the way of achieving true equality by the mere fact that they adhere to a hierarchy. In addition, Modern Liberals fear that these institutions may inculcate ideas that run counter to their ideology. For example, a person's church may emphasize the supremacy of private charity over government welfare, or parents may extol the successful entrepreneur in the free market. Modern Liberals subsequently conclude that it is imperative to weaken, undermine and even eliminate traditions and institutions in our culture in order to promote *their* concept of equality.

Radical individualism

Modern Liberals tell us that the ultimate source of happiness, love, and life's meaning and purpose is the self. Instead of focusing on one's duties, obligations, promises, honor and virtue, one's priorities should be the search for the inner self, learning to love oneself, and finding *personal* satisfaction and meaning. This has created what Christopher Lasch, himself a Liberal, has called "The Culture of Narcissism"[13]

Envy

This is the cardinal source of energy for Modern Liberal activists, as well as a fount of self-pity and a sense of failure that often accompanies and reinforces this green-eyed monster. Modern Liberal envy centers primarily on the financial success of others, but status plays a pivotal role. The ultimate irony – and there are plenty of them with Modern Liberals – is that they claim they attack the rich because income inequality ostensibly creates social unrest, but *they* are the ones who foment this very unrest.

Liberty Means "Liberation"

Modern Liberals claim that they are for freedom, but they have perverted its meaning by changing the concept of liberty to that of "liberation." Liberty requires *self*-government, and the Founders knew this meant *governing the self* in order to be a responsible citizen. Modern Liberals have attempted to disconnect the inextricable links of morals, virtue, obligations and responsibilities with liberty. In reality, Modern Liberals are willing to give up political freedom in order to arrive at a society in which they can give vent to their every impulse and desire.

Government

Modern Liberals insist that federal government action is the only reliable way to better our country. They think that if individuals act freely on their own within a legal framework, it will result in chaos, poverty and gross inequalities.

Groupthink

For Modern Liberals, the group is the primary unit of concern, not the individual. Freedom and "liberation," according to Modern Liberals, are only possible within a group that adheres to specific behaviors, beliefs and values, and these are not possible when individuals voluntarily cooperate under Rule of Law as our Founders intended.

Victimology

Various groups of people are classified as victims or oppressed by Modern Liberals in order to promote their agenda. Their parents, the New Leftists, were leeches who rode on the shoulders of the Civil Rights movement and perverted its goals: The Civil Rights movement began because brave blacks wanted equal *individual rights* before the law and full access to *existing American institutions*. The New Leftists and Modern Liberals advocate for *group rights* and a radical alteration or obliteration of existing institutions. Not satisfied with labeling blacks as victims and trying to convince them that they are an oppressed class of citizens, they subsequently added women, then various ethnic groups, followed by the physically and mentally handicapped as new victims who are supposedly oppressed. Most recently, Modern Liberals have added particular sexual preferences one chooses to their list of those who need of the protection and guidance of the federal government. Over thirty years ago, George Gilder reported that 70 percent of the population became "an array of victims," fitting into one or more select groups.[14]

The Moral High Ground

Modern Liberals try to seize the moral high ground. They mouth equality, compassion and fairness, but declamations do not necessarily equate to actually practicing what they preach. The reality is quite different: Modern Liberals give less to charity than their Conservative counterparts, and they even donate less blood.[15] Modern Liberals are intolerant of different points of view, insisting theirs is righteous. Throughout all of this hypocrisy they insist that they are morally superior, but this is primarily based on platitudes and pretentious but unrealized claims.

Alienation

Modern Liberals have alienated themselves from the enjoyment of American traditions – the values, activities and ideas that define America and bring a sense of cohesiveness and unity. The typical American's enjoyment and sense of pride in our historical accomplishments are belittled and mocked by Modern Liberals. To them, flying a flag shows jingoism; to feel choked up when hearing the Star-Spangled Banner is puerile; and to express reverence and pride in our Founding is to be benighted or in denial of America's "real" history of oppression, racism, greed and genocide.

Exclusiveness

Modern Liberals consider anything not acceptable to their dogma as hateful, immoral and invalid. Rather than considering the overall consequences of their ideas and agenda in a rational and dispassionate manner, anyone who does not agree with them is brushed aside as uncaring, malevolent and reprehensible. Modern Liberals invariably reduce issues and policies to superficial choices such as caring or not caring, *as defined by them*, of course.

Control and Impoverishment by Capitalists

Modern Liberals insist that capitalists are controlling our lives by limiting our choices and conditioning us to buy their products. On top of this, Modern Liberals proclaim that free market capitalists are intent on impoverishing the mass of citizens, believing – contrary to all common sense – that impoverishing the populace somehow makes them richer. Capitalism, according to Modern Liberals, is the primary source of the world's problems, and they focus on American capitalism in particular.

"Diversity"

Modern Liberals demand that we celebrate diversity, and America has become the symbol – in their minds – of repressing diversity; ergo, the struggle to free ourselves from this repression becomes a struggle *against America itself.* The irony is that it is Modern Liberals who actually suppress differences! James Ceaser, in *Reconstructing America*, wrote that – in the mind of these people – this is really because America gives rise to and sustains technologism. In this view, everything is put into "one vast, boundless mass." According to this Modern Liberal mindset, the diverse and indigenous cultures of the world and within America must be protected from Americanization – they have to be shielded from the homogenization into one Disney World. A "politics of difference" becomes the rallying cry, and everyone who resists is vilified as being complicit in the destruction of these unique entities or has some kind of "phobia." Differences, Modern Liberals claim, are repressed in order to exclude all that does not fit the norms. Even rationalism comes under attack. A new "multicultural" history of America is what is needed, according to Modern Liberals in academia, in order to save the oppressed and marginalized and give them true freedom. They insist that America's fundamental principles are inseparable from oppression and racism, so the Founders and their principles themselves come under attack and are discredited. The most pernicious development was the slowly evolving manner in which the Civil Rights movement was perverted to represent economic redistribution. At an address to the National Black Republican Council on September 15, 1982, Ronald Reagan spoke on how it was changing the character of the American people:

> This country entered the 1960s having made tremendous strides in reducing poverty. From 1949 until just before the Great Society burst upon the scene in 1964, the percentage of American families living in poverty fell dramatically from nearly 33 percent to only 18 percent... Congress had started a binge that would slowly change the nature of our society, and, even worse, it threatened the character of our people.

But with Modern Liberals, civil rights came to be equality of results, economic results — along racial lines.

———◆———

This chapter will end with a passage from James Burnham's 1964 classic *Suicide of the West*. Burnham's analysis of the thinking of the parents of Modern Liberals, the New and the Old Left, reminds us that they are not a new breed, but one with deep roots:

> Liberals...are not subject to strong feelings of national patriotism and are likely to feel uneasy at patriotic ceremonies. These...are dismissed by liberals rather scornfully as "flag-waving" and "100 percent Americanism." The national anthem is not customarily sung or the flag shown, unless prescribed by law, at meetings of liberal associations. When a liberal journalist uses the phrase "patriotic organization," the adjective is equivalent in meaning to "stupid, reactionary and rather ludicrous." The rise of liberalism to predominance in the controlling sectors of American opinion is in almost exact correlation with the decline in the ceremonial celebration of the Fourth of July, traditionally regarded as the nation's major holiday. To the liberal mind, the patriotic oratory is not only banal but subversive of rational ideals; and judged by liberalism's humanitarian morality, the enthusiasm and pleasures that simple souls might have got from the fireworks could not compensate the occasional damage to the eye or finger of an unwary youngster. The purer liberals...are more likely to celebrate UN day than the Fourth of July.[16]

2

Beliefs Of Modern Liberals

Don't confuse them with facts...
they know what they feel.

—Anonymous

Boy, when those liberals start
mixing into policy, it's murder.

—John F. Kennedy

n order to fully understand Modern Liberalism, it helps to look at the world
from their eyes for a moment. For most of us, their psyche does not make
much sense and often seems self-contradictory; however, in dealing with

their daily assaults on our society, it is important to see how they perceive our nation and the American people. This chapter is essentially an elaboration of the previous one: It covers the fundamental beliefs that form the foundation of the ideology and agenda of Modern Liberals.

John Hawkins described seven flawed beliefs of these people:

1. They assume human nature can be changed.
2. They think that "our bitterest enemies have rational reasons for disliking us and that can easily be talked away if they realize we're good people."
3. Their lack of respect for American culture and traditions leads them to conclude that "our cultural, economic, and political norms were formed by backwards troglodytes making arbitrary decisions based on superstition and racism."
4. They consider other Modern Liberals to be on the side of angels.
5. They "believe merely being liberal makes them good people."
6. They "have too much faith in government."
7. If their programs do not work, they are considered successful if they show compassion.[1]

William Voegeli, in Never Enough: America's Limitless Welfare State, put one aspect of their mentality quite succinctly: "Liberal victories advance liberalism; conservative 'victories' postpone liberalism."[2]

John McElroy, in Divided We Stand: The Rejection of American Culture Since the 1960s, juxtaposed our two belief systems:

America's Traditional Beliefs	The Counter-Culture's Beliefs
Improvement is possible.	Improvement is impossible without government help.
Society is a collection of individuals.	Society is a collection of classes.
Each person's success improves society.	Privileges of birth determine social rank.
Every person is responsible for his own well-being.3	Those who succeed do so by suppressing others.

Psychiatrist Lyle Rossiter's book, *The Liberal Mind: the Psychological Causes of Political Madness*, is excellent for helping to understand Modern Liberals. Rossiter writes that we can know their character by what they value and devalue, and about what they are passionate. Rossiter wrote about what Modern Liberalism *rejects*:

> [Modern Liberalism] does *not* insist that the individual is the ultimate economic, social and political unit; it does not idealize individual liberty and the structure of law...it does not defend the basic rights of property and contract; it does not preach an ethic of self-reliance and self-determination...it does not celebrate...the blessings of voluntary cooperation. It does not advocate moral rectitude or understand the critical role of morality in human relating...It does not celebrate the genuine altruism of private charity.

Following is what Modern Liberals *embrace*:

> [The] liberal mind *is* passionate about...a world filled with pity, sorrow, neediness, misfortune, poverty, suspicion, mistrust, anger, exploitation, discrimination, victimization, alienation and injustice...[According to the Modern Liberals, these victims] bear no responsibility for their own problems. None of their agonies are attributable to faults of failings of their own: not to poor choices, bad habits, faulty judgment...lack of ambition, low frustration tolerance...Instead, the "root causes" of all this pain lie in faulty social conditions...[including] discrimination...capitalism, globalization and imperialism...The liberal cure...is a very large authoritarian government that regulates and manages society...[the Modern Liberal] recommends denial of personal responsibility, encourages self-pity...fosters government dependency, promotes sexual indulgence...excuses financial obligation...denigrates marriage and the family...defies religious and social tradition.[4]

Creating a New World

Our voluntary behaviors—choosing a spouse, the work we decide to do, the friends we enjoy, and our use of free time—are all driven by our fundamental assumptions and values: What is the "good life?" What is moral? What is best for our loved ones? Some of us are more aware of our core beliefs and values than others, and some of us act on them more than others do. One person may posit that education and knowledge lead to fulfillment, while another may conclude that independent economic success results in life satisfaction; one person may surmise that our spiritual well-being is all that is really important and gives purpose to life, while another might suppose that being in control of one's life here on earth is primary. In a free society, each citizen—to the extent that he is able—has the liberty to pursue his values within the frame of the law.

The beliefs and values that guide Modern Liberals in their political credo are that an "ideal" society can be developed, and that guidance is needed from experts to engineer its construction. Nobel Prize winning economist Milton Friedman and his wife Rose Friedman, in *Free to Choose: a Personal Statement*, pointed out that this is really a form of aristocracy and discrimination:

> Believers in aristocracy and socialism share a faith in centralized rule, in rule by command rather than by voluntary cooperation. They differ in who should rule: whether an elite determined by birth, or experts supposedly chosen on merit. Both proclaim…that they know what is in the "public interest" and how to obtain it better than the ordinary person.[5]

The more radical of these dreamers tried to create completely new societies such as we have seen in the French Revolution, Lenin's Russia, Hitler's Germany, Mussolini's fascist Italy, Mao's China, Pol Pot's Cambodia, Castro's Cuba, and Kim Jong-Il's North Korea. The horrific results of the calls to build new societies are now well known, and this impulse for such revolution has been tempered, so Modern Liberals now only call for incremental changes within the existing systems. But not long ago the New Left fought on city streets and campuses for a "cultural" revolution with the hope of overthrowing the existing social and political order and ushering in a new society in its wake.

Of course, Modern Liberals will never admit—to any degree—that they envision a "utopia," simply because it would imply that they are not only naïve but also dangerous and irrational. Instead, they say they are "Progressives" or "Pragmatists." They then assume that their positions will be easy to defend; after all, who can be against progress or being pragmatic?

The justifications that Modern Liberals inherited in perfecting society stem from a number of developments that were reaching their zenith in the late 19th and early 20th centuries. With the advent of the industrial revolution and the invention of all sorts of technological "miracles," many people came to fancy that science could eventually solve anything. Along with this, there was another influence adapted and blended from Hegel and Darwin: Not only life, but society itself was evolving into superior forms, and this process was inexorable; humans could not stop this "evolution." Finally, the ideas of Marx and Freud convinced people that there were *hidden* realities driving our behaviors—economic forces and the unconscious mind, respectively—that only experts were capable of understanding and interpreting. In sum, many divined that society was unrelentingly evolving, science could be used to create or fix virtually anything, and experts had uncovered the prime movers behind our history and even our emotions.

At that time, free-market capitalism was creating unprecedented prosperity, but it was not without cost. Overall, life expectancy increased, incomes went up, work days were shorter, people ate better, and infant mortality declined. But there were drawbacks: Rural life was disrupted because of mass migrations to the cities, there was an influx of immigrants, slums proliferated, and many farms foreclosed. To some, it started to seem like a failure of the "system." Those who focused on the "failures" did not recognize that most of the people who failed at farming were novices; that land speculation—mostly as a result of government intervention—drove up prices; that immigrants and country folk who went to the cities actually improved their condition; and that rural life was far from being a bucolic paradise. It would take time to absorb the mass of immigrants and rubes that crowded into the cities, and time was needed for those who remained in rural America to adapt to these changes. This era was possibly best described by Richard Hofstadter in which he chronicled how the Progressive and Populist demagogues played to the doleful longings of Americans for a pastoral, agrarian past—one that never really existed as they imagined—in an increasingly industrial and urban America.[6] The Progressives and Pragmatists thought that the evolution of mankind and society toward a paradise—according to the popular interpretations of Hegel, Marx, and Darwin—was unstoppable, so rather than wait, why not accelerate its arrival? What was needed, they proposed, was the right knowledge and methods applied correctly. Two things were essential: (1) "experts" and (2) a central power to put the plans into action and enforce them. Many agreed with Rousseau's postulate that it is imperative that some individuals in a society have to be "forced to be free."[7]

Underlying all of this was a perception that human beings are infinitely malleable, and that human nature could be fundamentally changed and perfected. John Dewey, a leading Progressive of that era who is still highly respected by today's Modern Liberals, said that in society, "social arrangements, laws, institutions…are means of *creating* individuals…Individuality in a social and moral sense is something to be wrought out."[8] The legacy the Modern Liberals inherited from their Progressive forebears is one in which they conclude that we can *create* individuals, whereas our Founders bequeathed the idea that the government is established to *protect* individuals. This is a fundamental difference between the Modern Liberals' and the Founders' idea of the purpose of government.

Visionaries like Plato, Aquinas, and Thomas More have existed for centuries, but the assumption that reason can accomplish anything, accompanied by the new conviction that science could be used to uncover hidden meanings, finally led to full-scale implementations of these visions. Marx said that the French Revolution was the first "true communist revolution." The French revolutionaries envisioned changing the nature of man, and they created a new calendar and outlawed God. In the 20th century, various planners—from Hitler and Stalin to Mao and Pol Pot—wanted to design society according to their visions. Today, because of the horrors unleashed by these utopians in the 20th century, revolutionary planning has fallen out of fashion, but we are obliged to remember that the schemes of these 20th century tyrants—before their horrors were discovered—*were embraced by the precursors of today's Modern Liberals*. They felt that Marx's underlying principles, once implemented, could lead to a society without flaws, where the malevolence of private property and individual competition are extirpated, and where man could reach fulfillment of his "true nature," as Marx termed it. Some of the results of the attempts to fulfill this "dream" are documented in the *Black Book of Communism*. The writers concluded that from Communism "the total approaches 100 million people killed."[9]

Modern Liberals will deny—or more often not even be fully aware of—this connection with their past, of their ideology's underlying drive toward utopianism, of the imperative to engineer and manage society, and of the belief that human nature can be fundamentally changed. They have temporarily given up the revolutionary fervor and now insist that they are for "progress," but the impulses are fundamentally the same: creating a new society according to a grandiose and fanciful vision. Most of today's Modern Liberals are simply conforming to the road plan created before, and they only see isolated movements, agendas, and crusades—optimum health care for every single person, a flawlessly clean environment, world peace, the complete eradication of poverty, each individual being fulfilled or the end of all prejudice—and they do not see the overall picture. As the cliché goes, they cannot see the forest for the trees.

Modern Liberals seem incapable of understanding the incompatibility of freedom and liberty with the forced uniformity and submission needed to achieve an ideal society. They somehow do not make the connection that in a society of total equality, there can be no utterances of offensive speech; they do not see that the *ignis fatuus* of an unceasing peace is one of enforced conformity and a "Brave New World" mindless capitulation to an invisible and unaccountable central authority. They are like children who put their hands over their ears, screaming to drown out what they do not want to hear when they are reminded of what happened in the Soviet Union, China, Cuba, and Cambodia. No, the Modern Liberals proclaim that the nightmares visited on those people in the 20th century were not from the "dream" itself, but from evil men who did not stick to the *plan*. They refuse to recognize that the dream itself is not possible and that it only sets the stage for the entrance of these tyrants. Rather than denying and obfuscating the connection and the legacy, they should be asking how their dream, in fact, did lead to the barbarism, enslavement, and slaughter of tens of millions. Their excuses and denials only set the stage for pursuing it yet again. Modern Liberals have reluctantly accepted that advocating quick revolutionary change will be summarily rejected; hence they now proceed in incremental steps to their Shangri-La and profess that they are simply for "Progress" or are "Pragmatists."

Some Modern Liberals are well aware of this underlying utopianism, but most are not. The leaders who are aware do not want to be discovered. The followers, unaware, cannot articulate underlying principles, so they spout sophomoric banalities about "caring" and "compassion." (This will be discussed in more detail later.) If Modern Liberals are pressed to articulate or think through their *ultimate* objectives, they will be compelled to admit that they want to construct a new society which can only be realized through an all-powerful central authority that controls virtually every aspect of our lives. Nothing short of complete uniformity and compliance with the dream will satisfy Modern Liberals. If Modern Liberals had the power, people who do not adhere to their agenda would be compelled to capitulate—for their "own good." Modern Liberals are incapable of real tolerance, because "tolerance" means putting up with something with which you do not agree or of which you do not approve. The goals of Modern Liberalism necessitate uniformity and conformity.

Core Beliefs

Let's have a look at some of their core beliefs, however incredulous they may seem. How Modern Liberals came to these conclusions will be described more fully in the next three chapters that deal with their history, their connection to Marxism, and their education. The beliefs are divided into six categories: economics and the free market, society and individuals, culture and traditions, morals and religion, government, and America.

<u>Economics and the Free Market</u>

The Modern Liberals want power to be centralized in the federal government in order to carry out their agenda. The more a central power—the federal government—controls the American economy, the more it can control every aspect of our lives. Although attacks on the free market are not really among the most vicious, Modern Liberals use them the most frequently. This is in large part because of their Marxist roots (see Chapter 5) and to support the premise that they are "compassionate" and "caring."

Their professed "compassion" can be very appealing and difficult to contradict or refute without appearing to be the opposite, and they count on this. Their so-called "compassion" is directed solely at the *enemies* of the middle class, the ones who are the beneficiaries of the labor of *others*. These are the very people who lack compassion for the rest of us. There are those who clamor for government largess, and it is supplied by taking the earnings of the middle classes. Modern Liberals call this "compassion," but they are rewarding only those who *lack* the virtues of compassion. As University of Virginia professor James W. Ceaser wrote, "Modern liberalism, in its focus on compassion, has had difficulty openly supporting and rewarding excellences."[10]

——◆——

Following are some Modern Liberal beliefs about economics and capitalism:
Modern Liberals declare that economic success is invariably a result of oppressing others. Incredible as it seems, Modern Liberals actually postulate that increasing wealth leads to increasing poverty. This thesis is seen in their

remarks about how more citizens supposedly become increasingly poor as the affluent grow richer. In *Wealth and Poverty*, George Gilder wrote what was behind the absurd idea that poverty is predicated upon others' wealth:

> [It] still shines brightly for all who seek some alternative to hard work, inequality, thrift, and free exchange as a way of escaping want. How much easier it is - rather than learning the hard lessons of the world - merely to rage at the rich and even to steal from them...Rather than wealth causing poverty, it is far more true to say that *what causes poverty is the widespread belief that wealth does* (emphasis added).[11]

Modern Liberals like the famous scene from the anti-free-market movie *Wall Street*. Michael Douglas plays the role of a villain, Gordon Gekko, an "evil" capitalist who is driven by an insatiable lust for wealth and power and who cares nothing about impoverishing and ruining the lives of decent, hardworking people. In the scene that swells the hearts of Modern Liberals, Gekko's protégé is appalled that Gekko's takeover of a company resulted in so many people losing their jobs, thus destroying their lives. Gekko, the capitalist, blithely remarks, "Well, kid, there are winners and there are losers." In the psyche of Modern Liberals, this absurdity accurately portrays entrepreneurs in the free market.

Modern Liberals believe that capitalism promotes *evil*. *Nation* magazine published an interview with two infamous and rabid anticapitalists, one questioning the other: columnist and writer Naomi Klein and filmmaker Michael Moore. After demonizing the Tea Party "hordes" and accusing them of racism and being against social programs, Klein revealed her opinion of capitalism quite clearly when admitting she was "struck" by a statement made to Moore "that it's *greed* that's evil." She asserted that greed is "the engine and the centerpiece of capitalism," to which Moore replied, "as I said...capitalism is the legalization of this greed...Capitalism...encourages it, it rewards it" (emphasis original).[12]

Modern Liberals allege that virtually all American military actions have capitalist interests behind them; they say that capitalists, somewhere, are making profits, even though they rarely pinpoint anyone or substantiate these allegations. A good number of Modern Liberals maintain that September 11 was used as an excuse to invade Iraq to get increased profits for big oil companies.

Modern Liberals have a bizarre way of perceiving who rightfully owns the money that is earned by American citizens. They believe an individual's income belongs to the government by default: They propose that by not raising taxes on the so-called "rich," the government is letting them keep more of their wealth; since the government decides how much they are allowed to have, which implies that it belongs to the government. Matthew Continetti, author of *The K-Street Gang*, described this:

> In the liberal imagination, the money is the government's by default, and the president and the Congress determine…how much to "give back to the people," referring to Obama's statement that an extension of the Bush tax cuts "would be 'giving them $100,000 for people making a million dollars or more,'" and trenchantly concludes that "this is backwards. Low taxes don't give away the government's money. Low taxes allow individuals to keep the money they've earned through hard work, sound investment, and good fortune.[13]

Modern Liberals are incredibly materialistic, even though they purport to be otherwise. They presume that the source of virtually all strife in society stems from economic inequality, and that almost all unfairness in life can be conceptualized in terms of this type of inequality. They claim that to make the people happier and more fulfilled, it is imperative to "spread the wealth around." Modern Liberals fail to understand that *earned* success leads to true happiness, not the spreading of *unearned* wealth.

Modern Liberals adduce that society, history, and politics can be most accurately understood by analyzing economic forces. As explained in Chapter 5, Marxism has played a large role in the development of this mindset: Marx interpreted history and society in terms of economic forces. For example, many Modern Liberals surmise that September 11 happened because of economic oppression and aggression for economic gain, so America is ultimately to blame because its capitalist imperialism has impoverished people who became understandably enraged at us.

Modern Liberals believe that the so-called "rich" should be punished, and that they simply do not deserve their wealth. As Peter Wehner pointed out, one Modern Liberal senator, Mary Landrieu, wanted to have taxes raised on the rich; when it was decided to keep the Bush tax cuts, she declaimed that "this is beyond politics. This is about justice and doing what's right." Wehner explains their psyche:

> Those who favor allowing high-income earners to keep more of their money are not simply wrong; they are guilty of an immoral act…mention

the wealthy and liberals don't think of creative, entrepreneurial, and hard-working people; they think of Gordon Gekko. [They are motivated by] the belief that the rich need to pay more in taxes in order to reduce inequality… even if [tax cuts] make economic sense…[it is]…an offense, and the role of the state is to narrow inequality through redistribution of income… In an effort to promote an economic theory, liberals are appealing to class resentment.[14]

According to Modern Liberals, powerful "capitalists" even dictate our very desires through their control of the media. They claim that our "fraternal" feelings to our society have been driven out by capitalist propaganda, forcing us to look at people as objects. Steven Pinker, in his magisterial tome *The Blank Slate: the Modern Denial of Human Nature*, presented research to the contrary: Throughout history, leaders have had to encourage people to look outside of their blood kin and regard the other members of society with these fraternal feelings.[15]

Many Modern Liberals postulate that success comes primarily from luck—the fortune of birth, inheritance, ability, parents, and one's overall environment. This implies that since we really have no control over what we receive through "luck," economic success is not truly deserved. This sets the stage for a rationale to appropriate wealth from those who have become wealthy.

Modern Liberals feel that many people are not compensated based on their *value* to society: A teacher, for example, will get a lower salary than a professional baseball player, even though the former is presumed to be fulfilling a more needed and valuable function—*as determined by Modern Liberal experts*—for society. Consequently, many Modern Liberals have concluded that the value of roles in society should be determined by their experts, and the people should be rewarded at levels commensurate with these values. They do not want to let the market—individuals deciding where to spend their money—determine who gets what. The allocation of resources should not be determined by the whims of the people and whom they favor; according to Modern Liberals, experts should decide who gets what.

The desire for profit in the free market led to technological improvements, and competition played a large role in this development. However, the Modern Liberals' canon will not allow them to recognize this, and it compels them to adhere to the myth that technological improvements came first. In the self-serving and convoluted reasoning of Modern Liberals, this technology belongs to society because it is only an inevitable result of the societal conditions that preceded its development. Accordingly, the benefits of any technology belong to the society. This is one of several ways that Modern Liberals have convinced themselves that the birthright of the "people" has been stolen by the capitalists.

Ralph Nader, a consummate man of the Old and New Left, articulated one of their axioms in the magazine of the far-Left academicians, *Nation*, and it is still maintained by today's Modern Liberals: "The consumer must be protected...from his own indiscretion and vanity."[16]

Contrary to common sense, anthropological discoveries, and research on numerous cultures, Modern Liberals believe that the free market is an artificial condition that has been forced on society by rich capitalists; Modern Liberals fancy that the natural inclination of human beings is a socialist economy. The truth is that human beings have struggled for centuries to *free* themselves from central control—from feudal lords, emperors, the Church, and kings—and gain control over their own lives and govern themselves. The Modern Liberal inclination to have a central power manage and control the economy is a *regression* to a primitive and barbaric past. Jim Manzi points this out:

> The right to property...appears in legal codes, myths, and stories as far back as we have writings. It is in the archeological record before that and has antecedents even in the territorial behavior of many animals... Adam Smith's famous assertion that some "propensity to truck, barter, and exchange one thing for another" is inherent to human beings...Capitalism can channel potentially destructive human characteristics—including greed, envy, and the need to establish personal and social dominance over others— into benign and socially productive work...capitalism allows expression of these urges without violence as markets transform our baser motivations into general progress.[17]

Government

In the previous chapter it was stressed that a primary unifying characteristic of Modern Liberalism is the desire to create a central power that carries out and enforces their ideology and agenda; without this, they purport, society would be cruel, harsh, and barbaric. They declare that if we do not adhere to the agenda of Modern Liberals and instead leave substantial power in the hands of individuals, communities, and states, we will return to a Dickens' era of the masses living in overcrowded and disease-ridden tenement slums, people being virtual slaves to those in control of the means of production, and most of us sending our children back to sweat shops in order to simply survive. Local and state decisions, Modern Liberals say, will result in the marginalization of people, bring back Jim Crow laws, and have children return to the factories. They assume that unless the federal government manages and regulates everything, state governments and communities will not protect the environment, the poor and the elderly will be abandoned, and companies will indiscriminately dump waste and pollute and poison the residents to increase profits. (Talk with Modern Liberals and you will see that they actually have this image!)

———————

Following are some Modern Liberal beliefs about government's role in our lives:

Modern Liberals think that by depriving individuals of power and transferring it to the federal government, they can extinguish those very problems of power. They envision that by putting more and more power in the hands of the central government we will be protected from the vagaries and dangers of those in control. As Jonah Goldberg, author of *Liberal Fascism: The Secret History of the American Left*, wrote, "There's a reason the 19th century progressives referred to it as the 'God-State'…They believed that it was the sole agency for material and spiritual redemption."[18] Modern Liberals look at the capitalists —who they imagine are in control of our society—and believe that if somehow their wealth is seized and transferred to the state, control over our lives will diminish. They fail to see that this only concentrates power all the more, and, as Nobel Prize winner Milton Friedman sardonically remarked to those who would propose this: "Where are we going to find all of these angels?" Modern Liberals fail to understand that capitalists are not one huge conspiratorial group; capitalists are competing against one another and the economic power bases change continually. One can simply look at the Forbes 400 from ten years ago to see how the list has dramatically changed: Most are either no longer on that list or are of a completely different rank.

Modern Liberals believe that money spent by the federal government is the source of all good.

Ultimately, Modern Liberals renounce the premise that there are Natural Rights, and they inherited this legacy from the Progressives in the early twentieth century. The Progressive John Dewey spoke for them when he wrote that freedom is not "something that individuals have as a ready-made possession," but it is "something to be achieved," and that "natural rights...exist only in the kingdom of mythological social zoology."[19]

Modern Liberals actually suppose that government policies can end or cure avarice and selfishness. They surmise that the free market promotes those attributes, somehow altering human nature; ipso facto, if the free market can come under strict control of the government and socialism is implemented, there will be no more rapacious greed. Ronald Suny, writer for the Leftist *Nation* magazine recently described socialism "as a noble political philosophy devoted to promoting the common good," and laments that it has been "reduced to an epithet hurled at anyone skeptical to...the idea that capitalism is intrinsic to the natural order." He reviewed the book, *There Is No Freedom Without Bread!*, in which the Socialism of Eastern Europe is extolled:

> [Socialist] regimes not only survived for forty years, but were relatively stable...people accepted the state...because of free health care, free housing, and free education...*The communists*...provided jobs in new industries and made life and livelihood more secure and predictable...Economies grew (emphasis added).[20]

Modern Liberals emphasize equality, but it is equality of outcome. At a commencement address at Howard University in 1965, President Johnson said that "we seek not just legal equality but...*equality as a result*" (emphasis added).[21] Modern Liberals are reluctant to rely on the Rule of Law, before which all are treated as individuals. Rather, they stress group rights that they call "social justice." They believe that equal political rights and equality before the law are not enough; state intervention is necessary to get equality as *they* define it. Harry V. Jaffa, distinguished fellow of the Claremont Institute, wrote about this:

> A free society, so far as possible, has a level playing field. But within the human family, there is a great variety of talents, and of energy, and of ambition. Equality of opportunity leads necessarily to inequality of results. Equality of rights leads necessarily to inequality of wealth. A war against wealth is a denial of the equality of rights. James Madison, in the

tenth *Federalist*, observed that there is "a diversity in the faculties of men from which the rights of property originate," [and] the equal protection of unequal faculties of acquiring property is "the first object of government." As Abraham Lincoln wrote: "that some should be rich shows that others may become rich, and hence is just encouragement to industry and enterprise." It is the encouragement to industry and enterprise, arising from the recognition of human equality, which makes a free society more productive, with more wealth, more widely distributed, than any other form of human society.[22]

Some Modern Liberals actually fancy—incredible as it sounds—that government should have a role in our happiness! Walter Mosley, a member of *Nation* magazine's editorial board, wrote that "Americans deserve a government agency charged with fostering the pursuit of happiness." He combines this with a typical Modern Liberal's picture of America as a nation of oppressed people:

> [Our] *happiness is kept from us* by prisonlike schools and meaningless jobs...untreated physical and psychological ailments...Many of us suffer under a corporatized bureaucracy where homelessness, illiteracy, poverty, malnourishment (both physical and spiritual)...are not only possible but likely.

Mosley continued, insisting that our founding documents support this conviction:

> Our Declaration of Independence says that the pursuit of happiness is an "unalienable right." This language seems to make the claim that it is a *government responsibility* to ensure that all Americans, or as many as possible, are given a clear path toward that pursuit (emphasis added).[23]

Concurring with this, George Lakoff, a leader in the intellectual circles of Modern Liberals, recommends that the state be the ultimate provider, not only of basic needs, but of *emotional fulfillment*: "[The] nation should provide a decent standard of living...[and]...greater fulfillment in life."[24]

Modern Liberals and their predecessors have redefined "freedom" under the new form of Socialism: freedom from want. The upshot of this is that, in order to ensure this perverted form of "freedom," central planning of the economy is required. This provides yet another rationale for attacking the free market: In this convoluted reasoning process, the free market destroys their abased idea of freedom (freedom from want) because the distribution of wealth is at the whims of the marketplace. Modern Liberals may look at liberty as freedom from poverty, but our Founders knew that liberty is freedom from despotic and predatory domination of one person or group over another. For Modern Liberals, freedom is to be unencumbered by any limits imposed by nature, and the duty of the state is the *fulfillment* of human capacities. In the words of that revered Progressive, John Dewey, "the state has the responsibility for creating institutions under which individuals can effectively realize the potentialities that are theirs."[25]

Modern Liberals presuppose that the federal government can be trusted. In fact, they assume that we can trust the government more than our neighbors and fellow citizens, never mind big business. Modern Liberals endorse government regulations and taxation to make us more moral; they uphold this despite the obvious fact that morality necessitates making a choice, and that government laws, funding, and regulations remove choices. For example, they would prefer it if we no longer have to worry about taking care of our elderly parents and grandparents because, in the world of Modern Liberals, the government will provide for their old age.

Modern Liberals do not look at the family in terms of an independent and autonomous unit in our society to be supported as such, but in terms of recipients of funding or guidance from the government. They advocate for federal government spending on families to enable government to supervise and guide family decisions. If Modern Liberals wanted to encourage family autonomy, they would recommend increased tax exemptions, for example, so that families could keep more of the money that they earn and make *independent* decisions.

Modern Liberals assume that most individuals do not make, and are not even capable of making, choices in their own best interests. Therefore, the government must aid them in their decisions. This supposition is the theme of a book that was immensely popular with Modern Liberals, *What's the Matter with Kansas?: How Conservatives Won the Heart of America*. Its author declares that the people are voting against their own best interests when they vote non-Liberal candidates into office. These Modern Liberals fail to see that one can vote for the interests of the country and not just for one's own parochial concerns.[26]

Modern Liberals hypothesize that central government—if not hindered by reactionary elements—can *guarantee* employment, ensure we all get medical treatment, and provide for our old age. They postulate that it is possible *right now*, but that the government is hamstrung by capitalists and reactionary forces.

Government regulation and management of the economy, according to the mindset of Modern Liberals, can prevent—or at least ameliorate—economic ups and downs. Modern Liberals brush aside the lessons and realities of history. Robert Schuettinger and Eamonn Butler, in *Forty Centuries of Wage and price Controls: How Not to Fight Inflation*, document how governments have tried—and *always* failed—to manage their economies by controlling prices and wages since antiquity.[27] Albert Jay Nock, dubbed by one Conservative historian as "the John the Baptist of modern conservatism,"[28] also pointed out the futility of government regulation and management:

> Price-regulation by State authority…was tried in China about 350 B.C. It did not work. It was tried again, with State distribution, in the first century A.D., and it did not work…regional planning was tried…I suppose there is not a single item on the modern politician's agenda that was not tried and found wanting ages ago.[29]

As illogical and even counter-intuitive as the idea is, Modern Liberals actually believe that the government is more efficient than the private sector.

<u>Society and Individuals</u>

In the minds of Modern Liberals, the society of a nation can be treated as a whole, not individuals acting freely and individually. Modern Liberals deny that they envisage a beneficence of the "collective," and many are not even aware that they subscribe to, willy-nilly, and support this dogma. In essence, they go along with Rousseau's declaration that man ultimately should be "forced to be free" because an individual's own will has been formulated in the "general will," or, in today's understanding, in the "collective." Ergo, since problems—problems that ordinary Americans acknowledge arise from people being different and making individual choices in a free society—are an outcome of some flaws in this entity, this *unit* called "society" must be fixed. According to Modern Liberal thinking, if it can be fixed, adjusted, or corrected, it will "progress" and move closer to their grandiose vision.

———◆———

Following are some Modern Liberals' incredible beliefs about human society:

For Modern Liberals, the definition of a social problem is a situation in which the real world differs from their theories. In other words, for Modern Liberals, the real world is wrong and needs to change.

Modern Liberals believe that people are passive entities and human outcomes do not come from choices but from material forces in the society. As Myron Magnet wrote in *The Dream and the Nightmare*, "by basing social policy on a vision of the individual self that is so utterly the creation of material forces, the liberal view makes the self so passive and shrunken as to deprive it of moral significance or dignity or even individuality." [30]

Modern Liberals conceive that society, not individuals themselves, is responsible for the people's well-being. Since society itself cannot actually rectify the mistakes that have resulted in problems, it is up to the central power—the federal government—to ensure it is done. In other words, the federal government is required to use its power to weed out and fix the *root causes* of problems, which lie in society itself, not in individuals. In the imagination of Modern Liberals, any time individuals commit acts that are disruptive to others, it is a sign that something is amiss in society, and the federal government is needed to search for the antecedents and rectify them.

Since Modern Liberals reason that society, not individuals, is responsible for people's choices and behaviors, they insist that the judicial system must requite all *inequalities of condition*. Ultimately, because Modern Liberals trust government and not the people, they strive for a "socially just" Stalinesque world, one in which the State will rectify all inequalities. Modern Liberals divine that with enough effort, they can find the sources of inequalities of nature and society. Thomas Sowell refers to this as "Cosmic Justice." [31] For example, Modern Liberals may recommend a lighter sentence for the perpetrator of a crime if he grew up in poverty or an abusive home because they believe that society was ultimately responsible for his developing into a criminal; they champion our being more "tolerant" of miscreants and derelicts because they had parents who were not emotionally supportive. Modern Liberals would even say that companies should financially compensate unproductive people of lower intelligence or ability because this is no fault of their own. Thomas Sowell writes about reality: "[P]eople are in jail because they cannot function in this society. It is not they do not choose to function, but to prey on others instead, and to commit acts that are crimes in all sorts of societies around the world"; with Modern Liberals, however, "neither evidence nor logic is asked or given for such blanket indictments of 'society' or for a nonjudgmental view of criminals."[32] Modern Liberals will never admit to some manifest realities: We can never know all of the causes; we can never know the relationship of life circumstances to present situations; and there are many costs to society in vainly attempting to administer this Cosmic Justice. As part of the attempt to administer Cosmic Justice, Modern Liberals look for someone or some group—*usually capitalists*—that they contend stands in the way of achieving *their* idea of social justice.

Modern Liberals fancy that all problems can be solved by engineering society. If the problems are not being solved, Modern Liberals usually claim that one reason is that someone or something is obstructing it. In *Vision of the Anointed*, Thomas Sowell described how Modern Liberals explain their position:

> [We] already know the answers…and the kinds of questions raised by those with other views are just stalling and obstructing progress... Intractable problems with painful trade-offs are simply not part of the vision of the anointed. Problems exist only because other people are not as wise or as caring.[33]

Modern Liberals unnecessarily add the word "social" to justice, and this is used to undermine Rule of Law. Barry Lobefeld explains how "Social Justice" in practice is really code for Communism because it ultimately necessitates that someone in a powerful central government determines what people and groups can or cannot have; these people in authority exert the power to seize rights and property from one group and give them to others who are under no obligation to earn it. "It is the choices of the masses ('the market') that create the inequalities of fortune and fame—and the only way to correct those 'injustices' is to control those choices." The object of *true justice* via Rule of Law is the individual; the object of *social justice* is society: "the very notion of 'social justice' presupposes a volitional Society whose actions can (and must) be held accountable."[34]

As Thomas Sowell put it, "Presumably, the vast ranges of undeserved inequalities found everywhere are the fault of 'society' and so the redressing of those inequalities is called *social* justice, going beyond the traditional justice of presenting each individual with the same rules and standards."[35] Modern Liberals use the term "social justice" in an Orwellian way to avoid opposition; after all, aren't we all for a just society? Michael Novak wrote that it really is never clearly defined:

> The minute one begins to define social justice, one runs into embarrassing intellectual difficulties. It becomes, most often, a term of art whose operational meaning is, "We need a law against that." In other words, it becomes an instrument of ideological intimidation, for the purpose of gaining the power of legal coercion...Most who use the term, however, ascribe it not to individuals but to social systems...Their focus is...power.[36]

As Balint Vazsonyi put it, "all 'definitions' of social justice boil down to any of the following:

> (1) Somebody should have the power to determine what you can have, or
> (2) Somebody should have the power to determine what you can*not* have, or
> (3) Somebody should have the power to determine what to take away from you in order to give it to others who receive it without any obligation to earn it."[37] (Emphasis original)

One of the leading proponents of "social justice" is the Modern Liberal hero John Rawls. His work promoted the idea that the condition of the "have-nots" should be the moral touchstone for society, not things such as the overall national wealth, freedom, virtue, true democracy, or artistic achievements. The condition of the poor, in Rawlsian theory, is the measurement of value of the nation; their condition becomes the benchmark, the standard, by which to justify the entire society. In contrast to the Founders, who deferred to men of wisdom and virtue and extolled those considered decent and honorable, Modern Liberals are driven to elevate those who are lacking in those very qualities. For Modern Liberals, the more that a group of people is lacking, the greater its moral claim on society. The handicapped, the shiftless and lazy, the drug addicts, the criminals, the disabled, the stupid, and the ignorant—those who are lowest—are elevated to a nearly sacred status by Modern Liberals.

Modern Liberals surmise that since "social justice" is not being adequately served in our oppressive nation, it should be carried out through the courts. In *Nation* magazine, Gara LaMarche wrote that *"we need a Court that force-fully* upholds...the *right* to abortion, of course. But we need a Court that is... 'empathetic' to those who have been economically marginalized...[and one that] is going to *force* the government to treat a suspected terrorist more fairly" (emphasis added).[38]

Since Modern Liberals surmise that our justice system is barbaric and oppressive, they say that methods such as "Restorative Justice" are excellent ways to deal with crime, no matter how heinous and violent. Bill O'Reilly, in *Culture Warrior*, presents an example of such a case: Under the name of "Restorative Justice," a male babysitter in his thirties repeatedly raped a child in his care for four years, from age six to ten; he was given six months to ten years but let out in six months in order to get psychological treatment! This was to "get to the source of the illness."[39] After all, Modern Liberals say, criminality is a disease and should be treated as such. Akiva Gottlieb, writing for *Nation* magazine, quotes from an article in *The New Yorker*, "crime is caused by deprivation, misery, psychopathology, and social injustice."[40] In other words, crime is a result of just about everything except individuals choosing to commit crimes.

Modern Liberals assume that legal decisions by the courts like *Miranda* ("You have the right to remain silent") have improved the criminal justice system despite overwhelming evidence that conclusively shows these have resulted in fewer arrests, fewer convictions, shortened sentences for violent criminals, and more violent crimes committed on innocent citizens.[41]

Modern Liberals do not only look at society as a unit, but, when it serves their purposes, contend that it comprises various groups. These groups are defined by Modern Liberal "experts." They can be based on race, ethnicity, and, most recently, sexual preferences; they can also be criminals, the homeless, and the poor. Thomas Sowell refers to them as the "mascots," defined and created by the "Self-Anointed" who use them only to enhance their own status and influence.[42]

Alan Charles Kors, history professor and chairman of the *Foundation for Individual Rights in Education* (FIRE—see Appendix), wrote that these Modern Liberals have concluded that

> an individual is not an autonomous moral being, but a member of a racial and historical group that possesses moral debt or credit. There is only

one appropriate set of views about race, gender, sexual preference, and culture, and holding an inappropriate belief, once truth has been offered, is not an intellectual disagreement, but an act of oppression or denial.[43]

Since these groups, according to Modern Liberals, are oppressed and victimized, they need special laws, government regulations, and funding. Modern Liberals assume—in spite of overwhelmingly documented evidence to the contrary—this will ameliorate problems with poverty, employment, education, and crime.

Modern Liberals face a dilemma with their obsession that there is discrimination and oppression everywhere, looming within almost every tradition and practice, within societal norms, and within most religions: People in the ostensibly "oppressed" groups will understandably take advantage of this and *use* the Modern Liberals' agenda to get more benefits. As Ryszard Legutko pointed out in his essay, *"What's Wrong With Liberalism?,"* "the liberals cannot reject the claims of such groups because they are paralyzed by the rhetoric of liberation and by their own conviction - which I find rather silly - that saying 'no' to these groups would amount to the renunciation of the liberal creed." They refuse to see that "[t]he effect of the increasing number of individual and group claims and the supportive toleration of those claims by liberals creates social and political chaos."[44]

Modern Liberals also believe that their select suffering groups have a *right* not to be offended; however, those in the select groups can offend those who are *not* in these groups. This aspect of Modern Liberalism dominates American campuses; as Alan Kors said, "if they belong to a protected category...they have a right to four years of never being offended...while being free, themselves, to use whatever rhetoric they wish against the bearers of such stains."[45] Jonah Goldberg, author of *Liberal Fascism*, pointed out what the typical student on American campuses is taught by Modern Liberal professors: "His ethical training amounts to a prohibition on bruising the overripe self-esteem of another person, particularly a person in good standing with the Coalition of the Oppressed."[46]

Modern Liberals incessantly refer to oppression in America. They claim that there is so much oppression —especially of the racial variety—that individuals do not really have free choice. New Leftist-Modern Liberal Peggy McIntosh wrote an article that is considered a "classic" by those in academia who are dedicated to exposing America's oppression: "White Privilege: Unpacking the

Invisible Knapsack." In it, she writes about "the myth that democratic choice is equally available to all." McIntosh characteristically uses Modern Liberal Orwellian doublespeak when she writes that "talk by whites about equal opportunity seems to me now to be about equal opportunity to try to get into a position of dominance while denying that systems of dominance exist." In other words, if one acquiesces to this Modern Liberal position, they are correct; if one does not, one is in *denial*.[47]

Modern Liberals pay homage to "therapism." Christina Sommers and Sally Satel, authors of *One Nation Under Therapy*, describe this pernicious idea as one that

> extols openness, emotional self-absorption, and the sharing of feelings. It encompasses the assumption that vulnerability rather than strength characterizes the American psyche and that suffering is a pathology in need of a cure. Therapism assumes that a diffident, anguished, and emotionally apprehensive public requires a vast array of therapists, self-esteem educators, grief counselors, work-shoppers, healers, and traumatologists to lead it though the trials of everyday life. Children, more than any group, are targeted for therapeutic improvement.[48]

It fits the assumptions of Modern Liberals about human nature because it "tends to regard people as essentially weak, dependent, and never altogether responsible for what they do."[49] On top of being a winner of the National Magazine Award and Pulitzer Prize, Charles Krauthammer is also a Harvard-trained psychiatrist. He once clearly stated: "Psychiatry has no application to politics…and anyone who pretends it does is a fraud."[50]

Modern Liberals reject the idea that individuals can, or even should be allowed to, be autonomous decision-makers. They suppose that individuals will make the *wrong* decisions, and those *wrong* decisions are the ones that conflict with the visions and plans of Modern Liberals. Modern Liberals are dogmatically against the autonomous family as a decision-making body, especially when the family independently determines when and how sex is taught to children, what moral and social philosophy is to be passed on, and whether a child can have an abortion. Modern Liberals contend that families need their "wisdom." Thomas Sowell wrote that they refuse to acknowledge

> ordinary people as autonomous decision makers free to reject any vision and to seek their own well-being through whatever social processes they

choose…Thus…they tend to conceive of the family as a *recipient* institution for government largess or guidance, rather than as a *decision-making* institution determining for itself how children shall be raised and with what values.[51] (Emphasis original)

Ultimately, Modern Liberals' social engineering is for the purpose of changing *us*. Hillary Clinton represents the agenda of Modern Liberals when she said: "We are not interested in social reconstruction; it's human reconstruction."[52] In her book, *It Takes a Village*, everything is the State; the State is needed to help citizens raise their children.

Since Modern Liberals are convinced that bigotry and oppression define the West, and especially America, in their world it would make sense that we should look abroad to find better alternatives. Modern Liberals foist this on the American public, especially on children in our public schools, with the endearing term "multiculturalism." Dinesh D'Souza, best-selling author of conservative books and an advisor in Ronald Reagan's White House, explains this mentality in his book *Letters to a Young Conservative*:

> It is impossible to understand multiculturalism in America without realizing that it arises from the powerful conviction that bigotry and oppression define Western civilization in general and America in particular…The multiculturalists look abroad, hoping to find in other countries a better alternative to the bigoted and discriminatory ways of the West…If they look honestly, they soon discover that other cultures are even more bigoted than those of the West."[53]

Culture and Traditions

American culture and traditions are powerful forces in our lives and throughout the world. These are discussed more in Part II, but suffice to say that these forces drive Americans to an instinctive distrust of government and a fierce sense of independence from it. Americans have resisted the imposition of government since our colonial era. This attitude outrages Modern Liberals. For Modern Liberals, our very culture and traditions stand in the way of their ideal of "progress"; for them, American culture and traditions are only old, outdated, and useless artifacts of a bygone era: retrograde, reactionary, and stifling. Because they believe these traditions thwart "progress," they are determined to rid our nation of them. This attitude emerged, in part, with an Italian Communist, Antonio Gramsci, who said that in order to bring about a Marxist utopia, the promotion of a worldwide *economic* class struggle should be abandoned, and the prevailing *culture* must be infiltrated. Gramsci postulated that thousands of years of religion and centuries of capitalism are too powerful to be attacked directly, so the way to achieve the dream is to undermine the institutions that support it. This can be accomplished, Gramsci maintained, by attacking the cultural traditions and beliefs themselves.

Following are some of the Modern Liberals' misconceptions about our exceptional culture and traditions that made America truly great:

Modern Liberals suppose that America has no "real" culture. To them, Europe and Third World countries have old, deep, and rich cultures. According to Modern Liberals, America's culture is only one of superficial materialism.

Modern Liberals tell people that an intelligent person, a person with an open mind, rejects American culture and traditions. In addition, if a person is intelligent and sophisticated, according to Modern Liberals, he will scoff at patriotism and displays of flag-waving.

Modern Liberals reject that America is exceptional. James W. Ceaser wrote about the process they use to reject our exceptionalism: "Modern liberalism... has also allied itself culturally with relativism, which is the application of the idea of equality to all thought. Relativism makes it harder to support standards except those that touch on equality or diversity."[54] The truth is that American exceptionalism is grounded upon an idea in the founding era: America was designed to be a nation of laws and not of men, built on the concept of individual liberty and equal justice before the law, with freedoms ranging from speech to worship, and rights from gun ownership to freedom of assembly. When Barack Obama was asked on an international stage if he believed in American exceptionalism, he replied, "I believe in American exceptionalism, just as I suspect that the Brits believe in British exceptionalism, and the Greeks believe in Greek exceptionalism." This was a typical denial of America's exceptionalism by a Modern Liberal.

Morals and Religion

Modern Liberals claim superiority and try to get an upper hand by asserting that they are more moral than the rest of us. Modern Liberals insist that their ideas show their "compassion," "caring," and devotion to "fairness"; by default, this implies that those who do not accept their doctrines lack these qualities and sentiments. Modern Liberals insist that organized religion must kowtow to their agenda and articles of faith; when it does not—as seen with Catholic Popes, for example—it is considered abhorrent, oppressive, and reactionary, and this denunciation is followed by a litany of atrocities and crimes they pronounce the Church has perpetrated. Mention the Catholic Church to a Modern Liberal, for example, and he will fulminate against "rampant" child molestations, presenting them as though they are integral to the Church, despite massive and consistent documentation to the contrary.[55] Modern Liberals have savaged the Church in myriad ways: In 1987, Abortion Rights Mobilization filed a lawsuit challenging the tax exempt status of the Catholic Church, claiming that it had violated that status by taking a public stand against abortion.[56] On March 10, 2006, Catholic Charities of Boston decided to stop placing children in adoptive homes because it was required by state law to consider gay couples as parents. Recently, in January 2012, Modern Liberals supported the Department of Health and Human Services mandate that all employers provide free access to contraception, forcing Catholic charities, hospitals, and schools to go against their fundamental beliefs. As Patrick M. Garry noted about the attitude of the New Left toward religion,

> Religion stood for everything that the revolution opposed: self-restraint, the subservience of the individual to a higher authority, the notion of sin, the individual's subjection to moral judgment, self discipline, and the elevation of virtue over self-actualization. Religious institutions, as a reflection of the larger social establishment, came to be seen as perpetrators of repression and injustice.[57]

Following are a few Modern Liberal views on morals and religion:

Modern Liberals imply that intentions in themselves, *without effort*, show morality: For example, if a Modern Liberal wants to help one of his self-selected groups that he has categorized as poor or oppressed, personal efforts are of little importance; Modern Liberals conclude that the *intent to help in itself* is sufficient to establish a higher level of morality.

The methods of help are of scant importance when Modern Liberals want to establish their moral superiority. Their methods often deprive others of property and liberty, but it is of secondary importance because the primary goal is to establish the moral dominance of Modern Liberals.

Religions that do not capitulate to the demands of Modern Liberals—such as accepting gay sex as the moral equivalent of heterosexual sex, ordaining female priests, allowing abortion-on-demand, or encouraging education for birth control—are excoriated by them as reactionary, repressive, and malevolent.

Modern Liberals deem people who do not conform to their agenda as unenlightened, immoral, and generally stupid; most likely, they say, such people have been brainwashed by some "right-wing" media outlets that are controlled by *evil* corporations.

Modern Liberals conclude that the above "unenlightened, immoral, and stupid" people need to be educated to the correct way of thinking, and this must start in public schools from a young age.

Modern Liberals actually believe that government programs, if they conform to their dicta, can turn vice into virtue and evil into good. Modern Liberals are convinced that with enough programs and the "right" training and indoctrination, human nature itself can be changed. This is not a new concept, but a legacy of their Progressive era. Ron Pestritto described this thinking as reflected in the Progressive President Woodrow Wilson: "for [Wilson], the latent causes of faction are *not* sown in the nature of man, or if they are, historical progress will overcome this human nature."[58] (Emphasis original) The more recent Leftist historian Richard Hofstadter confirmed this thinking when he wrote that "[No] man who is as well abreast of modern science as the [Founding] Fathers were of eighteenth-century science believes any longer in unchanging human nature."[59] David Horowitz, conservative author and founder of Students for Academic Freedom, used to be a member of the far Left and understands their psyches from an *insider's* point of view: "Belief in the kingdom of socialist heaven is a faith that can transform vice into virtue, lies into truth, evil into good."[60] These Modern Liberal beliefs stand in stark contrast to the wisdom bequeathed to us by our Founders who knew, understood, and accepted human nature. It was written clearly in the *Federalist 10*: "the latent causes of faction are sown in the nature of man."

America

When Modern Liberals talk about America—either its present or its past—their beliefs and ideology manifest themselves very clearly. Modern Liberals are well aware that if they give full vent to their attitudes toward the United States, most Americans will become enraged and repulsed; therefore, they will express condemnation and denigration of America to the degree to which they feel that they are in a safe environment with others like themselves. They generally "test the waters" by injecting cynical and critical comments—of increasing intensity—into conversations, such as America being a country that promotes racism, greed, or sexism, or by making casual references to the suffering of Native Americans or the Founders holding slaves. Modern Liberals follow in lockstep to the lead of American Marxist historians like Charles Beard and Howard Zinn (his pupil), and present the founding of America as one of ruling elites whose sole purpose was to consolidate and aggrandize their power, wealth, and status. If others either remain silent or show even mild encouragement, the attacks on America invariably intensify and unfold into lengthy and vicious tirades.

A significant reason that Modern Liberals' consistently disparage America is that the United States stood in the way of the "dream." The important question—do Modern Liberals actually hate America—will be covered in Chapter 6. Let's now look at some Modern Liberal beliefs about the country that gave them liberty, protection, prosperity, and Rule of Law:

Modern Liberals posit that America is too strong militarily and needs to be weaker. They assert that American hegemony—in military and law—needs to be replaced by international bodies, courts, and agencies. As University of Virginia James W. Ceaser put it, "Modern Liberalism...has grown increasingly uneasy about nation. It considers patriotism an anachronism and promotes global citizenship and education."[61] This hamstrings America for the fight on terrorism: Since Modern Liberals consider the idea of patriotism and nation to be backward, ignorant, and retrograde, they are compelled to go against such displays or expressions, thus hampering America's defense against terrorism.

Modern Liberals have created what Jeff Bergner, former staff director of the Senate Foreign Relations Committee and Assistant Secretary of State, calls "The Narrative." The Narrative is a Modern Liberal story of our country, designed to support their assumptions and dogma. According to this Narrative,

> the story of America is one of progress toward the fulfillment of the chimera of equality. The end of slavery…women's suffrage…the federal income tax [was] later used to redistribute wealth…Then came…Social Security…Medicare, Medicaid, food stamps…Each and every policy that aims to level distinctions between Americans has found its place within The Narrative…[This is] more or less inevitable, [and] labors of progressive heroes [are] exalted…Virtue belongs to those who advocate the fulfillment of equality…The federal government is the instrument for achieving the promise of equality…The Narrative opposes anything that smacks of American exceptionalism [because it] implies the inferiority of the institutions and cultures of other nations.[62]

Modern Liberals don't credit Ronald Reagan, Margaret Thatcher, or Pope John Paul II with helping to end the Cold War; they give all of the human credit to Gorbachev. The Leftist and radical anti-nuclear crusader Helen Caldicott said "[Gorbachev] is like Jesus"; Liberal columnist Mary McGrory wrote that "[Gorbachev] is a political leader to make Americans weep." Modern Liberals eschew the role of the West and of America in particular in ending the Cold War because they can then credit the victory to a devout socialist leader. Modern Liberals refuse to recognize how much the West advanced during this Cold War period, the era from Eisenhower to Ronald Reagan, the era in which the consumption of goods and services by the American family had actually more than doubled. This was the era in which the poorest fifth of our population—by 1995—was consuming more than the middle fifth of 1955.

Modern Liberals ascribe to a revision of American history as one of people struggling to rid themselves of oppression. Pat Buchanan wrote about their historical revisionism in *The Death of the West*:

> [The] cultural revolution teachers that the real heroes of history are not the conquerors, soldiers, and statesmen who built the Western nations and

created the greatest empires, but those who advanced the higher cause—the equality of peoples. Thus, the end of segregation in the South…triumphs greater than the defeat of communism.[63]

Immigrants do not assimilate into America, according to Modern Liberals; they proclaim that was a myth and wishful thinking of the dominant culture that forced conformity on unwitting and powerless people who should now be "empowered." (Modern Liberals like catchy and clever-sounding terms like "empowered.")

Modern Liberals are convinced that America is the primary danger to the world. According to Modern Liberals, America is responsible—directly or indirectly—for most wars, genocide, famine, poverty, and terrorism. Modern Liberals see America as the main threat to the world's environment. Many of them emphasize environmental issues because this touches on everything from what we wear, how we travel, and even what we eat; it also serves the additional function of being anti-capitalist because "profits" can be linked to harming the environment.

William Appleman Williams was a prominent figure of the New Left, and Modern Liberals still utter panegyrics to him. In *Nation*, one of the most influential magazines among the more academic Modern Liberals, a seven-page article was recently devoted to Williams, and it demonstrates the mindset of Modern Liberal intellectuals toward America quite clearly: "[Williams] also chose Marx, 'exhilarated' by his capacity to see in one piece of evidence a set of relationships that reveal an economic truth…[Williams hoped] that Soviet nuclear power would rescue history from the 'Puritan memory hole.'" This is followed by a celebration of even more radical historical revision, blaming America for everything, and apologizing for the USSR: "[The] United States eventually conjured up the enemy it feared; armed with the threat of containment, Stalin drove the Soviet people to the brink of collapse until he turned his country into a nuclear power." Ergo, Stalin's relocation camps and movement of peasants to build up the Soviet state, resulting in deaths of millions *is America's fault*.[64] *Nation* magazine supports that idea that the USSR's actions were reasonable responses to what its writers assert was America's drive toward overseas expansion and domination. According to Williams, as he wrote in *The Tragedy of American Diplomacy*, the days of frontier expansion were over, so America externalized this tendency to overseas expansion. Williams had no patience with the facts of the Cold War origins in Eastern Europe.

America is portrayed by Modern Liberals as a racist country, filled by those who engage in, or support, racist policies. Susan Sontag, a New Left and Modern Liberal icon, said that "the white race is the cancer of human history." In the spring of 2002, the University of Massachusetts held a conference entitled, "Abolish the White Race." These Modern Liberals and their New Leftist cohorts began a journal: *Race Traitor*; in a lead article, an author wrote: "whiteness is a structure of domination."[65] Modern Liberals profess that there is "institutionalized" racism that manifests itself in inner city poverty and an "underclass." They professed this despite the fact that this "underclass" arose *after their programs*—the Great Society—began.

Modern Liberals surmise that people in the lowest economic classes in America are "stuck," and that this condition is relatively fixed and permanent, despite the fact that numerous studies have clearly demonstrated that from 86 to 91 percent of individuals and households in the lowest quintile are out of it within a period of eight to 11 years.[66]

Modern Liberals strive to classify America's population by distinct racial, ethnic, and other groups defined and chosen by them, of course. Modern Liberals believe that America should also be organized—by the federal government—according to these categories; this, they claim, is to help set up laws, regulations, and programs of redistribution of wealth in order to ensure fairness and true (Orwellian) equality.

America, according to Modern Liberals, is an imperialist country. They claim that wherever America has a military base, it is "occupying" that country, despite the fact that the bases are there by lawful agreements with the respective host countries. As well, the soldiers, sailors, and marines at these bases must abide by, and are subjected to, the laws of the host country. But Modern Liberals say that imperialism has also taken the form of *economic* imperialism. This is a self-serving proposal because many countries, especially poorer countries, want America's products. Shortly after a McDonald's restaurant was set up in Moscow, people voluntarily lined up for hours, waiting for the doors to open, in order to bite on some of America's *economic imperialism*.

Many Modern Liberals have blamed America for the attacks on September 11, 2001. It can be very disconcerting for most Americans to hear these noxious denunciations of their country, society, free-market capitalism, organized religion, and traditional morality. Nobel Prize winner Fredrick Hayek offers one explanation; he wrote about *why* many people choose the road that Modern Liberals do:

It is tempting to believe that social evils arise from the activities of evil men and that if only good men (like ourselves, naturally) wielded power, all would be well. That view requires only emotion and self-praise—easy to come by and satisfying as well. To understand why it is that "good" men in positions of power will produce evil, while the ordinary man without power but able to engage in voluntary cooperation with his neighbors will produce good, requires analysis and thought, subordinating the emotions to the rational faculty...The argument for collectivism is simple if false; it is an immediate emotional argument. The argument for individualism is subtle and sophisticated; it is an indirect rational argument.[67]

3

The Historical Path To Modern Liberalism

[Liberalism] is an ethos that aims simultaneously at political and social collectivism on the one hand, and moral anarchy on the other.[1]

—IRVING KRISTOL

In America, the Modern Liberals' penchant to centralize authority in order to manage all aspects of our lives is incomprehensible to most people. Americans see the need for national structure—such as with the military, the FBI, protections of voting rights, and coining our currency—but we want the federal government's reach to be limited as our Constitution prescribes. Americans are unique in our inherent suspicion of government, especially in its most centralized form: the federal government.

Mark Twain once noted that in order to understand humanity, all he needed to do was to look within himself. In order to try to comprehend the mindset of Modern Liberals, it can help to look within ourselves and recognize different impulses, temptations, fears, and the will to power that we all have. Throughout human history, there have always been the impulses and temptations to create a utopian society, usually accompanied by the hubris that we are capable of it. With a bit of reflection, most of us can see elements of those impulses in ourselves. For example, many of us in our youth assumed that we could set up the "ideal" lifestyle, find the "perfect" life partner, or mold our children as we wish. Some people limit such inspirations to themselves, and others attempt to impose them on their family, friends, neighbors, or coworkers. In any case, in pursuing such lofty goals, it is imperative to meet two conditions: First, one must implement all of the plans necessary to reach them, and next, one must *eliminate* everything that gets in the way.

Working toward *improvement* is a laudable goal. With the forerunners of Modern Liberals, this dreamy vision of a utopia evolved into the presumption that we can actually create a wonderland if the federal government is empowered to implement the right "plans." The danger is that Modern Liberalism ultimately envisions *perfection* in all of society via the power of the federal government. Modern Liberals want—and imagine possible—a society of absolute fairness, complete security, economic equality, and even satisfaction of all needs and desires, and they call on the federal government to force their plans on the citizenry. One aspect of this reached a logical outcome in Sweden where the Socialists actually proposed that the government pay for prostitutes ("free sex partners") for people who were living alone.[2]

As the scholar John Diggins put it, the Left's "categorical imperative" is to strive after another world in defiance of reality. It affirms "its own vision of an 'impossible ideal' as a truth about to be realized…[The] left has sought to transform present society in the hope of realizing 'unborn ideals' that transcend historical experience."[3] Daniel Flynn, in *A Conservative History of the American Left*, wrote that

> rather than a laundry list of complaints and wishes, an attitude better captures the Left. It is, in its simplest form, scorn for what is and hopes for what could be. The ideology's appeal exists in neither the experienced past nor the concrete present, but in the imagined future.[4]

This requires ignoring the past and thus increases the chances of not creating history but reliving it. Flynn continued:

> The Left condemns itself to replicating its mistakes, its tragedies, its failures. Its past is not a road map to consult in confusing times, but a relic to be hidden away…Does it not feel better to instead foretell of the human brotherhood, heaven on earth, and perfection of mankind that will certainly follow if only everyone embraces the latest leftist panacea?[5]

Modern Liberals and their predecessors have always wanted to change the existing order. They fathom that history can be transcended and that unborn ideals can be attained, and the pattern is consistent: The past is not something from which to learn but a relic to be ignored or discarded. The dilemma is that they must treat the impossible as the possible.

The Early Stage in America

About two centuries ago, after the War of 1812 ended, America finally started to be recognized as a stable, strong, and prosperous country in its own right with an up-and-coming industrial and agricultural base. At this point, there was the inception of some "utopian" communities. Virtually all of them had the following commonalities: abolishing private property, proscribing organized religious practices, and eliminating the institution of marriage. However, they did not ask outsiders to conform to their lifestyle. Rather, they isolated themselves from mainstream society and tried to establish their own heaven-on-earths. Each had a dream, a vision, and an imagined future where humans would live in harmony, peace, and happiness in their respective communities. They fancied that humans and society could be perfected and everyone's needs met without real cost.

Robert Owen, for example, said that private property, religion, and marriage were "the most monstrous evils" and set up communities from the 1820s. He professed what all Socialist visionaries profess: Adherence to the plan would transform selfishness to altruism. But there was a problem: "Capitalism works for men who do. Socialism for men who don't."[6] In Owen's New Harmony, it simply did not pay to work.

Robert Owen has been credited with coining the term "Socialism," and it ultimately means to transfer responsibility from the individual to the society. In

Socialism, society, not the individual components, should be rewarded or punished. Everything in these communities was, of necessity, centrally planned. The distribution of goods was planned to the smallest detail. Owen's New Harmony was what we today often call a government "housing project": Nobody owned the houses in which they lived, so decay set in. It was a precursor of the New Left's housing projects that began in the 1960s. "New Harmony was a giant one, albeit a housing project on the dime of a rich guy instead of the taxpayers."[7] They wrote constitutions and separated children from their parents early on to learn the "right" thinking to fit the ideal society that was being created.

Not one of these lasted more than about four years, and the failure was never acknowledged to be a flaw in the basic premises that a perfect society can be created and human nature can be molded to fit the vision. The followers of Owen insisted that any failures were due to people not adhering to the *plan*. This presupposes that there were no flaws in the system, and that if people had followed it correctly, according to these fanciful thinkers, it would have worked. This sets the stage to attempt it again.

John Noyes founded the Oneida community in 1848, and one can visit the historical monuments and structures to this day in upstate New York. As with the others, property was communal, the society was collective, and wives were shared. There were even "Rules for Sexual Intercourse," and eugenics was practiced. They all failed, of course.

Between 1830 and 1855, several other utopian communities in America were built, based on the theories of the French philosopher Charles Fourier, a man who never set foot in this country! Fourier specified, in minute detail, a design for communal living based on the theory of the "thirteen passions." An analysis and arrangement of them, he claimed, would reorient people to the "right" interests, attractions, and passions, and this would lead to social harmony. Like those who would follow, they believed that "scientifically" designed plans could cure all social ills. The devotees also clung to its inextricable accompaniment: existing institutions and beliefs in society thwarted the realization of the dream. As is the wont of today's Modern Liberals, the Fourierists exaggerated the grimness of the present world and extolled the glories of the future. All of the 29 Fourierist communities (Phalanxes) failed. Only one made it past five years: the North American Phalanx made it to 12, but the people were hard workers and 70 percent of the applicants were rejected. The followers and disciples explained away the failures by saying that Fourierism was never really tried. This sounds amazingly similar to the Old Left, New Left, and Modern

Liberals of today who apologize for Marxist regimes, saying that they never really followed the true principles but failed only because they were taken over by reprehensible men or corrupted by malevolent influences and encroachments of capitalism. In other words, in their minds Socialism-Communism has never really failed, but has only been corrupted.

Before our Civil War, these utopian communities of Noyes, Owens, Fourier, and other dreamers isolated themselves from the mainstream. These antebellum utopians never formed or promoted "class consciousness," and they did not generally attack private property outside of their little communities. But Modern Liberals and their forebears, the Progressives, had another goal: They demanded that the federal government consolidate power and compel the citizens to *conform* to the plans. But how did this change? What happened after the Civil War to bring this about? To answer this question, we first need to review some of the developments that took place quite rapidly in America near the end of the 19th century.

The Shift to Government: Populists and Progressives

The first real attempt at changing an *entire society* in a new image of man was in France in 1789. Marx called the French Revolution the "first true communist revolution," and this was where the term "Left" originated. The goal was an egalitarian state set up by expert planners. The French revolutionaries determined that it was necessary to rid themselves of the old traditions and ways of thought in order to usher in the dream. It culminated with the "Reign of Terror" and as many as 40,000 accused prisoners were summarily executed without trial.[8]

In America, the first thoughts of compelling an *entire population* to conform to a vision began with the Progressives. Some historians say it was the Populist movement, and others emphasize Pragmatism. Some scholars have characterized the consolidation of a cultural, social, and political movement as the "Lyrical Left" that even extended into the 1930s. The central theme that has been passed on to today's Modern Liberals is the drive to have the federal government organize, manage, and otherwise *force* all of the citizens to conform to the dreams. Today's Modern Liberals refuse, of course, to acknowledge this legacy in their own history, simply because it consisted of actions such as the Palmer Raids, the Red Scare, Prohibition, forced loyalty oaths to the government, state capitalism, *real* imperialism, and racial eugenics.

These "Progressives" were not satisfied with the increase of federal power in the political arena, and they wanted to expand it to the economic one. This meant shifting more and more control of the means of production to the tentacles of the State. Progressives dreamed of some kind of "cooperative idea" to replace individual competition. John Diggins wrote about this in *The Rise and Fall of the American Left*:

> [The] American Left assumed the true freedom begins only when capitalism ends. Hence the Left was nothing if not anti-capitalist...All of the Lefts of the twentieth century...advocated various programs calling for public ownership of the means of production...Competitive individualism would be replaced by some version of the cooperative ideal in which human beings, freedom from the economic necessity of engaging in coerced labor, would realize their full nature in creative work.[9]

Their enemy was, and still is, "bourgeois" society, which led to social conformity, economic competition, and sexual repression.

Progressivism's inception, American style, was probably in 1888, when Edward Bellamy wrote *Looking Backward*. But even before Bellamy's seminal work, there were other ideas to reform via the authority of the federal government: Almost a decade earlier Henry George wrote *Progress and Poverty* and launched the "single tax" movement in which property would be taxed at its value and there would be no need for any other taxes. But this did not cohere into a national movement like Bellamy's work did. *Looking Backward* was a complete concoction of the future from a Progressive slant: The State planned and ran everything, and the nation became a paradise as a result of changed human nature by a "scientifically" engineered environment. The State was the sole capitalist and landowner, and Americans were in a giant national army. All had equal incomes. Collective kitchens and laundries were described, and there were no jails. All needs were met, and there was no war.

Not long after its publication, over 150 Nationalist Clubs sprouted up all over the country, and a primary goal was to nationalize the entire economy in steps, not by revolution. The People's Party was launched in 1891, and they were usually considered Populists. Ignatius Donnelly was inspired by the ideas of *Looking Backward*. In 1892, he penned the *Omaha Platform* for the People's Party; it included the nationalization of railroads, telegraphs, and telephones. The People's Party also wanted to see state ownership of land owned by railroads "in excess of their actual needs"[10] William Howell wrote *A Traveler from Altruia* four years after, in 1892: It was a dogged criticism of capitalism that compared America with Altruia, showing America to be a place where the people were selfish, emotionally unstable, and obsessed with money. Altruia, in contrast, was a fantasy land where income was fairly distributed, work was minimized, and everyone was equal.

Turn-of-century Progressives, especially the academic ones, learned directly and indirectly from the German school. In 1916, Teddy Roosevelt said, "I have actively fought in favor of grafting on our own social life...many of the German ideals."[11] As Ronald Pestritto documented in his comprehensive study of Woodrow Wilson's political development, *Woodrow Wilson and the Roots of Modern Liberalism*, Wilson was "both taught and influenced by German-trained pioneers of the new social sciences, and "adopt[ed] a historicism most directly attributable to Hegel...Wilson's teachers at Hopkins were all educated in Germany and in the tradition of German state theory."[12]

These Progressives, and, in turn, the Old Left, began to look abroad for inspiration and guidance. They also integrated home-grown philosophies: Darwinism—Social Darwinism—and the Pragmatism of William James blended nicely into their desire to create their new world. Social Darwinism was the idea that went beyond just the evolution of living species, including the notion that social institutions also evolve to survive. Pragmatism says that meaning can be created, reality was something unfinished, and these could be what we willed them to be. With Pragmatism, *results* were what mattered; they were the proof that the experimentation worked. John Dewey, a Progressive, said that social experimentation was needed to actualize the dream. Darwinism—applied to life forms—was already accepted as scientific truth among the intellectual Progressives, so Social Darwinism was not much of a leap. Then blend in a bit of Pragmatism, sprinkle it with Dewey's imperative to experiment, and incorporate Marxist principles, and we have the formula for the Progressive Mind. Socialist Upton Sinclair, a darling of these Progressives and the Old Left, wanted to overthrow, not preserve, the system. In his most famous work, *The Jungle*, capitalism leads to the ruin of an immigrant's life, and he becomes reborn in Socialism. (It was recently discovered that Sinclair had information confirming the guilt of Sacco and Vanzetti, the radical socialist anarchists, but he deliberately withheld the information and published the novelized story professing their innocence, *Boston*.[13] We can only speculate how much more he had falsified and distorted information over his career to advance his radical causes.)

The *Classical* Liberalism of the founding era evolved into a kind of *social* liberalism: The Progressives postulated that the social sciences had provided ways to improve people's lives, and this evolving emphasis led them from the belief that all men are *created* equal and should be treated equally under the law to the belief that it is possible—and necessary in a "just" society—to *make* everyone equal. In direct contrast to the Founders' acceptance of human nature and their structuring of government to accord with it, the Progressives began with the idea that the State could *change* human nature. The limits imposed on the federal government by the Constitution became an obstacle to be overcome.

Progressive ideas were supported by Populism. At the end of the nineteenth century, there were declining commodity prices, rising farm costs, changing rail rates, and problems with credit and banks. Populism grew as its proponents encouraged farmers to think of themselves as victims of landlords and exploitation by the wealthy. They clamored for government ownership and regulation of railroads and telegraphs, a graduated income tax, direct elections of senators, and government control of monopolies.

Around the turn of the century, Populism grew, and the Socialist Party gained strength along with it. The Socialists sponsored Eugene Debs for president in 1912. Socialism's "golden years" were from 1902 to 1912. Daniel DeLeon, a prominent Socialist, wanted his party to get power in America first through peaceful means, and then the State would be given over to the workers. As previously noted, Modern Liberals deny many aspects of their heritage: At that time, the Socialists followed racist policies, and Victor Berger, the first member of the Socialist Party to be elected to Congress, said "Socialism means segregation, capitalism means integration!" He also said: "Private ownership of industries mixes up the races...socialism would separate (them)," and "Capitalism has forced [the white man] to work side by side with the negro... In the sight of the capitalist all workers look alike." The Socialists also blamed capitalism for enticing the "lowest scum of Europe," and bringing in "Mongolian herds."[14]

These forefathers of Modern Liberals always advocated central planning, and they attacked the founding principles from early on: The Progressive president Woodrow Wilson created the American Protective League with 250,000 members: Americans were encouraged to spy on and report fellow Americans to the government. Wilson, as his Progressive inclinations led him, thought the Constitution was cumbersome. Pestritto documented this: "He complained that 'some citizens of this country have never got beyond the Declaration of

Independence'…Wilson contended that the Declaration addressed only the specific historical circumstances of the founding era, and that its principles could not be translated literally into modern times."[15] This was in line with the teachings of a major intellectual leader of the Progressive movement, Herbert Croly, who posited that the Constitution of the United States was "constraining." Croly, like most other Progressives of his time, admired Mussolini's fascist state for its efficiency. In *The Promise of American Life*, published in 1909, Croly attacked American traditions: "To achieve a better future," he wrote, Americans had to be "emancipated from their past." This book and his other one, *Progressive Democracy*, were treasured by the New Left, who used it as a rationale to "liberate" themselves, especially in the sexual realm: "Modern psychology affords no sufficient exercise for a morality of repression."[16]

The Progressives worked hard and fast to change the Constitution, which they felt restrained "progress." After the Bill of Rights was ratified, there were only two amendments added to the Constitution up until the Civil War, a period of seven decades. The Civil War necessitated three more amendments during that tumultuous period. However, during the Progressive era from 1909 to 1919, four were added. In other words, almost as many amendments were added during that ten-year period—one of relative peace and prosperity—-of Progressive dominance as during the previous 120 years!

The Progressives celebrated the Russian Revolution. In 1919, Eugene Debs said, "From the crown of my head to the soles of my feet I am a Bolshevik and proud of it." John Reed, a journalist and Communist activist of the Left, went to Russia during its Revolution and wrote *Ten Days that Shook the World*, in which he expressed the grandiose drives of these predecessors of Modern Liberals: "They were building a kingdom more bright than any heaven had to offer."[17] The pro-Communist American journalist Lincoln Steffens visited Russia after the revolution and wrote, "I have been over to the future, and it works." Another Progressive writer, Walter Lippmann, asserted that Americans were "mentally children or barbarians" and that they needed direction (from the federal government). W. E. B. Du Bois said, "I stand in astonishment and wonder at the revelation of Russia that has come to me," referring to his visit to "Holy Moscow." University of Chicago professor Paul Douglas visited Russia and reported that "there is a real community of belief, a national ideal and moral unity, which is the solid basis of the new Russia." Leftist and Progressive magazines championed the Communists. In 1918, the following was published in the *New Republic*: "[Russia is] the most democratic franchise yet devised in our world, providing for absolute universal suffrage and proportional representation." *Nation* magazine, in 1919, published this: "The franchise is more democratic in Russia than in England or the United States." Progressive Stuart Chase was a prominent American economist and Fabian Socialist whom some credit with being the originator of the expression "A New Deal." Chase was part of the Woodrow Wilson administration. He later visited the USSR in 1927 and became enamored of its planned economy. Chase subsequently wrote a lengthy article in *Harper's* in 1931 entitled, "A Ten Year Plan for America," in which he recommended a Soviet-style planned economy not just for wartime, but for peacetime as well. In *The Road We are Traveling*, Chase avoided using terms such as "central planning," "socialism," and "communism," and wrote that "we have something called 'X,' which is displacing the system of free enterprise."[18] Those who were familiar with Chase's proclivities, however, knew full well that "X" actually did mean "central planning," "socialism," and "communism." In 1928, Roger Baldwin, founder of the American Civil Liberties Union, wrote an entire book in which he offered panegyrics to the Soviet Union, entitled, *Liberty under the Soviets*: "Police brutality, such as *we now know it in America* is now rare in Russia" (emphasis added),[19] and "the most significant of all liberties under the Soviets is economic."[20] Rex Tugwell was a member of FDR's Brain Trust and was another fellow traveler to Russia who was enamored of the Soviet system; he published *American Economic Life* in 1930, in which he extolled Soviet communism and insisted that it was superior to capitalism, writing that "the *success* of the scheme seems to indicate clearly enough that *it works*" (emphasis added).[21] Tugwell wrote, "The Soviet Union is able to produce goods in greater quantities…and spread prosperity." He supported Robert La Follette who, as president of the Progressive Party, agitated for federal government ownership of railroads and electric utilities. John Dewey, the man most responsible for our children going to government schools from an earlier age (kindergarten) also went to the Soviet Union and was inspired like the others. Dewey—in the name of" social progress"—had welcomed America's entrance into World War I because it helped Americans to "march in step" and to "give up individualism."

Enter the Old Left

Progressivism became discredited shortly after the end of World War I, and many of their hopes were dashed. Then the Old Left emerged and looked to Russian Bolshevism and Italian Fascism. Also, as more Italians, Eastern

Europeans, and Jewish immigrants came to America, American Socialism incorporated Anarchism and Syndicalism: By World War I, six chiefs of state were assassinated by Anarchists, including President McKinley. A year after World War I, multiple strikes were organized, and the American Leftists, after seeing Lenin's establishment of a Communist state, wanted revolution. Lenin promoted a variation of Marxism in which revolutionary consciousness would be instilled from above, rather than wait—as Marx said—for emergence from below.

Antonio Gramsci, an Italian Communist imprisoned under Mussolini's regime, planted seeds that bore fruit later in America among the New Left in the 1960s. Gramsci saw that the dominant forces in Italy acquired their power by winning the hearts and minds of the masses, and he concluded that Communists worldwide should take that route, that they needed to articulate the desires and hopes of the people and identify with native traditions.

W. E. B. Du Bois also introduced an idea that the New Left would later incorporate: In his 1935 book, *Black Reconstruction in America* and other writings, he proposed looking at race relations from a Marxist perspective. Paul Robeson, another black American, supported this: He declared Communism to be free of racial strife and praised Stalin. Robeson said that American blacks and Russian serfs had much in common. When he went to the USSR in 1934, he said, "For the first time in my life I walk I in full human dignity."

Franklin Roosevelt, as Secretary of the Navy under President Woodrow Wilson, went along with all of Wilson's Progressive programs. Roosevelt carried on the tradition of declaring our founding principles outdated and outmoded for modern society: At a presidential campaign address to the Commonwealth Club on September 23, 1932, he referred to the rights written in the Declaration of Independence, and told his listeners that "the task of statesmanship has always been the *redefinition of these rights* in terms of a changing and growing social order" (emphasis added). However, several decades later, the Left reflected on FDR's policies and concluded that he did not go far enough. Writing for the leading magazine of Modern Liberals, *Nation*, Professor Thomas J. Sugrue wrote that

> by the 1960s...Left-leaning scholars...inspired by radical insurgencies at home and abroad, argued that the New Deal was fundamentally conservative. FDR's *fundamental sin* was that he saved capitalism from itself rather than taking the opportunity to *nationalize the financial system and redistribute wealth* (emphasis added).[22]

The Great Depression was seen by the Old Left as a vindication of their belief that capitalism led to impoverishment of the masses and that a centrally organized economy was absolutely necessary. But Americans felt their economic difficulties during the Great Depression as an individual experience, not as one of class. In other words, unemployment was felt as a personal failure by most Americans, and society was not held responsible as the Leftists had hoped.

The Old Left was convinced that that the Soviet Union was the freest place on earth, primarily because the Communists declared that they could eliminate poverty. They thought that mankind, under this system, would now evolve to a *freer* state because people would no longer have to compete in a dog-eat-dog capitalist world. Instead, the State would ensure that all primary needs would be met, and, in concert with Marx's declaration, man would thus be "truly free."[23] For example, John Kenneth Galbraith, an intellectual icon of the Old Left and New Left, said of the Soviets' overtaking of Poland after World War II: "Russia should be permitted to absorb Poland, the Balkans, and the whole of Eastern Europe in order to spread the *benefits of Communism*" (emphasis added).[24] The image of Communist Russia was inspiring and uplifting for them: These Leftists envisioned Russia as an island of human brotherhood surrounded by sea of selfish and rapacious capitalism. Many even theorized that Hitler's rise to power developed from "monopoly capitalism" and refused to acknowledge that it was really a mass movement. Some sensed that Marxism was right because capitalism must be wrong; they were considered to be "Marxists of the heart." To many on the Left, Marxism also provided an explanation to historical events and gave them some coherence. In *The Rise and Fall of the American Left*, John Diggins wrote about this mentality:

> Marxism did restore meaning and purpose to life by offering a sense of historical direction, a method of class analysis...Marxism could provide a rare glimpse of the totality of existence, an exciting synthesis that broke down the classical dualisms between self and society, idealism and realism, contemplation and action, art and life.[25]

But for three decades, these Leftists—the precursors of today's Modern Liberals—denied, apologized, and often deliberately hid the truths that were emerging, even in the early years: The Bolsheviks executed more political prisoners within one year of their takeover than the Czars did in 92 years. Soon after they seized control, the rampage started; in 1922 alone, 8,100 priests, nuns, and monks were executed. The leading intellectual magazine of the Left, *Nation*, true to form then just as it is today, denied it, asserting that the new regime was "more democratic than in…the United States." Others, like Rex Tugwell and John Dewey, praised Lenin and denied the later atrocities of his and Stalin's regimes.

Enter the New Left

Under Stalin, the Old Left continued to turn a blind eye to what was really going on in the country of their dreams. They denied Stalin's savageries and refused to accept the truth of the purges and trials. As Ronald Radosh wrote about the Old Left in his review of *The Conservative Turn: Lionel Trilling, Whittaker Chambers, and the Lessons of Anti-Communism*: "Having succumbed to the false ideals of Communism decades earlier, they felt a need to deny the truth."[26] Later, when it could no longer be denied, they desperately scrambled to find excuses for their support of what everyone came to know was a murderous regime. Many claimed that their support was really because Hitler was so atrocious that they had to stand behind Stalin. But the monstrosities that extended over decades provoked a crisis for the Old Left. In 1956, after Nikita Khrushchev denounced Stalin, the Old Left rapidly fell out of favor, and the New Left slowly emerged. The New Left disliked the Old because of its stance on the Cold War and its refusal to support Communism. Some in the Old Left tried to survive by taking an "anti-anti-Communist" stance: They felt that they could no longer support Communism, so they railed at the anti-Communists, alleging the anti-Communists were against freedoms of speech and association. These Old Leftists and the emerging New Leftists began to see that in order for them to continue promoting the "dream," the pure Marxist concept of class—the worker in relation to the means of production—must be modified. They contended that nothing in capitalism had really changed, that the New Deal "rescued" it through social security, government jobs, unemployment insurance, and unions.

The prosperity that followed World War II in the 1950s helped to kill off what remained of the Old Left, but the New Left grew stronger, especially in academia. At that time, Americans felt that they had it good, but the social scientists in the universities worked to convince them that they *never had it so bad*. Most Americans were, according to these academics, over-conforming, anguishing over being judged, and obsessively concerned with social status. This New Left resuscitated a tenet of Marx with which the Old Left rarely dealt: alienation.

They revitalized it by focusing on a humanist critique of what they insisted was a "sickness" of modern society, and they connected their "alienation" with exploitation of the lower classes. These New Leftists postulated that Americans lost freedom without even knowing it. They said that companies stifled creativity and individuality. The new suburban community of Levittown, for example—where, incidentally, Bill O'Reilly grew up—was mocked as a "low-grade uniform environment from which escape is impossible."[27] They considered the works of C. Wright Mills essential reading for the educated person, and there was a litany of attacks on the American way of life with Mills' *The Power Elite* in 1956, William Whyte's *Organization Man* in 1957, and John Galbraith's *The Affluent Society* in 1958.

The New Left came to prominence in the 1960s from a unique juxtaposition of several factors. First of all, the Baby Boomers were coming of age, and they represented the biggest proportion and number of people of such a young age in our country's history. Next, many were children of affluence whose parents wanted to give them what they themselves had lacked. Finally, a war soon to become very unpopular began in Vietnam, and the New Left used it to gain adherents and to promote their ideology. Frequently, young men initially escaped the draft by entering a college—any college—and getting student draft deferments. This resulted in an expansion of higher education all over the country, and the academics had a huge receptive audience of eager and impressionable young people: In 1960, even though the G.I. Bill had been in existence for returning veterans since 1944, there were about three million students. By 1970 this had increased to nine million.

The New Left developed a set of beliefs and values, and its paladins centered issues on poverty, blaming not only capitalism but also the culture—American beliefs, traditions, and values. The upshot of this was the shift from an emphasis on personal responsibility, self-control, and deferral of gratification to one of creating victims and of eliminating the sources of so-called "oppression." In the worldview of the New Left, people were living in poverty because of oppression in society at large, and this is predicated on our traditions, values, ideals, and attitudes. Therefore, the only way to change this, according to the New Leftists (and in agreement with the advice of the Communist Antonio Gramsci), was to put an end to these baleful institutions and beliefs and to establish new ones. So the intellectuals shifted to a criticism of the culture. Just as their predecessors did, they looked abroad, but this time to the Third World. In 1968, Dubcek proposed a new model of Socialism in Czechoslovakia, and coined the expression "socialism with a human face." For the New Left, Cuba in particular had the possibility of "socialism with a human face," and the pilgrimages—just like those of the dreamers in the 1920s and 1930s to the Soviet Union—started. They rejected the idea of a Soviet threat, and they focused on the university not as an instrument of cultural transmission, but one of changing society. This was something new in America. Previous university students were unlike this and generally supported social order. For example, during the Progressive era students actually helped the government put down Boston's general strike in 1919; in the 1930s, the 1940s and even the early 1950s, students obeyed school rules, wore jackets, and conformed to campus decorum. But the New Left students would start an upheaval of the universities that was never before seen in our entire history.

The New Leftists would never admit it, and oftentimes were probably not even aware of it, but they really exploited the poor for their own desires to free *themselves* from restraint. These New Left tutors of today's Modern Liberals said they wanted to help the poor and asserted that they were victims of a repressive, destructive, and racist society. They convinced themselves and many others that American values and beliefs were hypocritical, rigidly conforming, materialistic, superficial, and, most of all, psychologically repressive. They argued that everyone has some "authentic self." In order to get closer to this higher and nobler "true" self, it was necessary to reject the values and behaviors of the country at large. Myron Magnet described this in *The Dream and the Nightmare*:

> [By] forging your own "alternative life-style"…you would get closer to authentic selfhood by kicking free of mechanical rationality and opening yourself to altered states of consciousness…The cultural revolution… dignified the purely personal, making self-cherishing seem unselfish, almost civic-minded…The new cultural order fostered, in the underclass and the homeless, a new, intractable poverty…because the new culture that the Haves invented…permitted, even celebrated, behavior that, when poor people practice it, will imprison them inextricably in poverty.[28]

The hippies also emerged, but they were almost mutually exclusive to the New Left in their orientation: For the hippies, changing one's *perceptions* led to salvation; for the New Left, changing *institutions* was all-important. The hippies did not want to take over institutions or get an education, but the New Left developed a form of revolutionary violence with on-campus political activities that were unceasingly confrontational.

The New Leftists found leaders and inspiration from academics of the Frankfurt School, a Marxist "think tank" transplanted in America from Germany. This school turned from pure economic class divisions to employing psychology to attack the established order and married psychology to Marxism. The ruling capitalist classes, these New Leftists (and today's Modern Liberals) maintained, is a "defense mechanism" against change coming in the form of Socialism and big government. According to these emerging views of the New Left and of today's Modern Liberals, those who resist the agenda have emotional problems. The upshot of this was the elevation of self-absorption and the establishment of narcissism as a form of fulfillment. Ideas such as learning to "love the self" became a main tenet of the dogma. Psychologist Eric Fromm encouraged the "search for the self"; philosopher Herbert Marcuse borrowed from Marx and Freud and said that instead of having "surplus labor," modern society had "surplus repression." Marcuse asserted that in the past, it was necessary to defer gratification and sublimate drives into productive work because of scarcity, but that now this repression was no longer needed in a society with affluence. Others, like sociologist Theodore Adorno, attacked the established order and authority. In Adorno's 1951 book, *The Authoritarian Personality*, Adorno asserted that America was a proto-fascist state, and this could be seen in our family structure and expressions of patriotism. In his book, Adorno entreated readers to tear down all forms of established authority, discredit the value of the family, sever links to anti-Communist sentiment, and resist capitalism, which, according to this viewpoint, was based on a cruel "survival of the fittest" mentality.

As James Seaton explained in his review of *The Frankfurt School in Exile*, "According to the Frankfurt School, a socialist revolution in the West had become a practical impossibility but remained a moral necessity."[29] They created what the author of the book, Thomas Wheatland, characterized as an image of America that was "a nightmare vision of late capitalism, in which reason had become obliterated, freedom had been surrendered, and history finally be perceived as a steady descent into barbarism."[30]

These academics concluded that American society stifled creativity and individuality, and that people were misguided and mistaken in trying to adapt and be comfortable in an insane society. Books proliferated in psychology departments emphasizing how so-called psychological disorders were normal and expected responses to a dysfunctional American society. The academics wanted to "liberate" man from civilization because civilization simply was not worth the price of repressions. Man must liberate himself from family, work, church, and moral conventions. In Marcuse's *Eros and Civilization*, published in 1955, the primary enemy was work, because it negated the "pleasure principle." For Paul Goodman, who wrote *Growing up Absurd* in 1959, it was sex: adolescents needed more, there was no such thing as "abnormal" sex, and the present mores deviated from what was truly "good." Other widely-read books included *The Myth of Mental Illness*, by Thomas Szasz, first published in 1961, in which it was maintained that madness is the fault of society. Psychosis is a political statement, a protest, and society has to change. *Asylums: Essays on the Social Situation of Mental Patients and Other Inmates* by Erving Goffman and William Helmreich was published the same year, and is an excellent tract of the "counter-culture" stuff of that era: This one professed that the treatment of the mentally ill was really oppression of the powerless; behaviors were nothing but the product of the surrounding culture. Several years later, the *Politics of Experience* by R. D. Laing was published. Laing insisted—in accord with the others—that modern man had been driven crazy by our culture. Modern man, according to Laing, had become materialistic, and this wreaked havoc on his ego and alienated him: Those who are considered "sane" by society are really the insane, and adjustment to a crazy world is not sane. Ken Kesey's *One Flew Over the Cuckoo's Nest* was first published in 1962 and was made into a movie a decade later. Most people know this story. It tells the viewers that the people running the institutions are the crazy ones, and they are the ones who support the real insidious element infesting our society: conformity.

Conservative psychologists Sally Satel and Christina Hoff Sommers, authors of *One Nation Under Therapy*, explained what went on during this era:

> Colourful academic psychologists like Abraham Maslow and Carl Rogers introduced into American life their ideal of "self-actualization." Their work and that of colleagues seems at first optimistic, positive, and suitable to a dynamic and energetic society like postwar America...They were of the opinion that the vast majority of Americans led "unactualized" lives in spiritual wastelands from which they needed to be rescued. Said Maslow, "I sometimes think that the world will either be saved by psychologists - in the very broadest sense - or it will not be saved at all."[31]

The eugenics movement of the Progressives was an attempt to weed out those who would not fit in the new society. From the 1960s, psychology was used instead to weed them out: In 1964, a pseudo-psychology "insanity" tactic was used on Barry Goldwater when he ran for president: 1,189 psychiatrists said he was not "psychologically fit" to become president. One psychiatrist wrote, "I believe Goldwater has the same pathological make-up as Hitler, Castro, Stalin and other known schizophrenic leaders."[32]

At first, this propaganda was mostly limited, with academicians preaching to their inexperienced and impressionable young students in universities, but with the advent of the war in Vietnam and the ensuing doubt Americans began to have about their country's actions, it spread. Resisting the war was tied to rejecting American culture and its supporting traditions, and the educated and relatively affluent youth embraced it. These Baby Boomers were members of the largest group of young people in the history of the country, and they had the affluence and leisure necessary to participate in the "movement." The effects reverberated throughout society. The credulous participants even believed that a revolution had already started, as evidenced in Cuba, Vietnam, and other parts of the Third World, and they wanted be in the vanguard of spreading it in the West. As John Diggins pointed out, "the role of the Left was thus to align itself with the international revolution abroad by engaging in irregular warfare behind enemy lines, thereby undermining the overextended power of America's imperialistic war machine."[33] In reality, the New Left's ultimate goal was the same as that of the Old Left: rescue the Communist project from the discredited Soviet Union.

The New Left also got acolytes by proposing to save the environment. In 1962, Rachel Carson's best-selling *Silent Spring* informed people that vested capital interests were poisoning the food supply. Eight years later, Paul Ehrlich told us of a horrific future with mass starvation of millions, probably billions, of people by 1995 in *The Population Bomb*. Today's Modern Liberals have continued the tradition, forming numerous environmental organizations that must, of necessity, centralize economies and organize the lives of everyone in order to "save us" from imminent disaster.

The harangue to save society from itself culminated in the Great Society programs, one of the biggest failures in which the history of the Left is awash. Its creation was strongly influenced by Michael Harrington's 1962 book, *The Other America,* in which he claimed that Americans were unaware of a huge underclass around them. Harrington was called to the White House by Lyndon B. Johnson, and the message in his book took hold: If we change the environment, we can change the man. The mantra was that "there is literally no alternative but government intervention," and many ascribed to it. Saul Alinsky, the author of the notorious *Rules for Radicals*, helped in the project. The Great Society's monies were used to fund the leftist community action agencies that staged openly Marxist and anti-white plays, and included giving financial support to the cop killer Huey Newton and the Black Panthers.

The economic effects of LBJ's other programs ostensibly *for* the middle class were immediately seen *on* the middle class: Right after Medicare went into effect, hospital prices rose 14 percent and this rate continued, year after year, for a decade. Visits to doctors and hospitals increased. Student aid from the government increased tuition: In 1964, the mean cost for tuition, room and board was $950. By 2007, it had reached the equivalent of $10,000, more than ten-fold. The Great Society Program rarely provided jobs for the poor, and just gave them money, food, and medical care; the government assumed personal responsibility. No job? AFDC gave money. Do you have medical bills? Medicare paid for it. No cash to pay the rent? There was a rent-supplement subsidy. Need groceries? Apply for food stamps. Taking care of your children is becoming drudgery and boring? There was a Head Start program where you could dump them off on someone else. The National Welfare Rights Organization (NWRO) declared: "Poor people should be allowed to trade in [food] stamps for money," and that "homemaker services" should be provided.[34] Beulah Sanders, vice president of the NWRO, proclaimed this at a 1967 US Senate Finance Committee hearing: "We do not believe we should be forced to work. I do not believe that we should be forced to take training."[35]

But from the mid- to late-1970s, it was all coming to an end for the New Left. The war in Vietnam was over, Aleksandr Solzhenitsyn had published *The Gulag Archipelago* and was giving lecture tours in America, and the Soviets had invaded Afghanistan. Faith in government had been shaken: To those on the Right, government meant more taxes, forced desegregation, and welfare cheats; to those on the Left, it meant deceit, the draft, the "military-industrial complex," and imperialism. "Reverend" Jim Jones became one of the most famous of those who shook their faith—before they morphed into Modern Liberals—with 918 people dead his utopian community in Jonestown, Guyana. Jones had first started constructing Jonestown in 1974 for a "socialist paradise." Jones announced he would establish it as a model communist community and said, "I believe we're the purest communists there are."[36] In *Nation*, Theodore Rosak wrote about Jim Jones' work: "The temple was as much a left-wing political crusade as a church." [37]

The New Left received shocks as the "dream" vanished. The American people were appalled at the first glimpses of what the Great Society—the Old and New Left's project—brought to their television screens: Riots in Newark in 1967 with 26 dead; then the riots in Watts, Detroit, and Washington, DC. Crime rates soared: From 1960 to 1980, overall violent crime doubled, and murder rates doubled. The New Left received another blow when Ronald Reagan was elected president and a huge number of young people supported him. Not long after, with the aid of Ronald Reagan, Margaret Thatcher, and Pope John Paul II, Poland's Solidarity party grew in strength and defeated the Communist party, Hungary was freed, Romanians ousted the Communists, and the Czechs demonstrated until the Communists gave in. In 1989, students rebelled against the Communist state at Tiananmen Square in China, and the following year East and West Germany were united. The New Left saw the fall of Communism coming and scrambled. In 1988, the journal *Rethinking Marxism* was first published at that stronghold of academic Modern Liberalism, the University of Massachusetts: It announced that genuine Socialism was perverted. Shortly thereafter, yearly conferences started being held and appropriately entitled: "Rethinking Marxism." To this day Modern Liberals postulate that the "dream" was never really tried.

The Torch is Passed to Modern Liberals

The New Left entered academia en masse, and the support system carried on by today's Modern Liberals remains strongest in the universities. Universities have a plethora of Leftist journals, and programs like black studies, women's studies, and "critical studies"[38] support the Modern Liberal worldview of the oppressed and the oppressors, victims and victimizers, and a future in which Socialism replaces the free market. The universities provided a safe haven from which to heckle and revile those with whom they did not agree. Aaron Goldstein, writing for the *American Spectator*, rhetorically asked "Why Do Liberals Throw Things at Conservatives?" His answer: "Because liberals cannot bear to hear impure thoughts. They cannot countenance opinion that differs from their own. People who think differently from them must be subject to humiliation in the name of tolerance."[39]

In the 1970s and 1980s, "Western Civilization" courses came under siege. This came into the public spotlight when the controversy over courses and majors in Western Civilization were attacked by the New Left: Jesse Jackson led students in demonstrations, chanting, "Hey, hey, ho, ho, Western Civ has got to go" in an effort to end the Western Civilization program at Stanford University. In 1979, Yale University rejected a $20 million grant to endow a professorship in Western Civilization. The radicals generally got their way in academia: The universities turned to teaching students to expose the "darker secrets" of class, race, and gender. The president of the Organization of American Historians, Eugene Genovese, a former self-declared Marxist and Socialist, became its president in 1978. Genovese was followed by William Appleman Williams (whose book is described in Chapter 2) who was also a Marxist.

As previously mentioned, decades earlier, the Communist Antonio Gramsci explained "cultural hegemony" as the deliberate penetration of lower class consciousness with ruling-class values, and, according to Gramsci, the ruling class fostered a mentality of standardization, conformity to bourgeois culture, and obsession with efficiency. In this view, cinema, television, and the promotion of the idea of "Americanism" are looked at as just ruling-class instruments of cultural domination. Gramsci was prominent in originating the idea of bringing about change via "cultural hegemony," an idea that shifted the focus from the original Marxist emphasis on the economy to the culture. These New Leftists, soon to become today's Modern Liberals, adopted Gramsci's ideas and focused on the culture's "superstructure" instead of the "exploited masses." This necessitated gaining control of the means of communication rather than the modes of production as Marx had originally proposed. Following Gramsci's doctrine, these New Leftists and, later, the Modern Liberals, supported the idea that change via "cultural hegemony" required them to enter the culture itself and penetrate the fields of education, art, philosophy, and popular traditions. They turned to schools, teachers, and media in place of factories.

With control of the culture, they believed that they no longer had to wait for the dialectic to unfold; they could persuade and indoctrinate *immediately*. Today, Modern Liberal academics propose doing this by uncovering power structures in our society. Power, in their view of America, is omnipresent and creates perceptions and unconscious attitudes which they deem to make up a "false consciousness." In the past, they postulate, illusions and false reasoning set the course of the present power structures under which we now live, so they insist on locating the "sources" of power and making others conscious of them. Modern Liberal academics insist that all aspects of modern life—family, work, education, movies, television—must be probed to find these hidden modes of power and control. According to them, man has lost his freedom and *he does not know it.* The goal is to unmask the putative *concealed* power structures. With this method, for example, Modern Liberals deny that God and nature have endowed us with inalienable natural rights, simply because these are subjective human inventions.

Diggins outlines the various academic departments and how each contributes to this process: The sociology departments teach the "logic" of class conflict; in economics, they teach about the divisions/classes of labor and how the capitalists squeeze profits from them; and in the political science departments, it is the theory of the State and the promise of Euro-communism. In anthropology, the origins of property, colonization, and "dependency theory" form the core; the geography departments emphasize the destruction of the environment and the dangers of population growth; and the psychology departments teach therapy as social control and race prejudice as a function of class behaviors. The history departments emphasize the myth of the individual, and the art departments refer to the social determinants of works of art. In addition, other departments sprouted up in direct opposition to the established American society as it is, and these can be easily identified by the term "studies": Ethnic Studies, Women's Studies, African Studies, and so forth.[40]

———◆———

But Modern Liberalism is in retreat today. The New Left declared that if we got rid of "unjust laws" and pumped money into social programs and education, it would all work out. As we know, it did not. Then, in response to these abject and undeniable failures, the New Left and the Modern Liberals, as John Derbyshire aptly put it, devoted themselves "to cooking up theories about why this was so, and what might be done about it." Now, Modern Liberals still speak the rhetoric but "no longer believe any of it."[41] They failed and America turned against them. Modern Liberals still maintain power in the media, law, and journalism, having inherited it from the era of the New Left, but their theorists and intellectuals have "retreated" to the universities where they teach revised ("deconstructed") history and the underlying power structures in society.

Each generation of the predecessors of Modern Liberals was, in turn, hostile to the prevailing society at large. Each generation had two main objectives: (1) political and social collectivism and (2) moral anarchy. The Progressives rebelled against Victorian culture and "laissez-faire" competitive free markets. The Old Left fought against the "normalcy" of Harding and Coolidge, and they found inspiration from foreign sources, especially the Soviet Union. The New Left theorized that the dominant mass corporate culture alienated people from their "authentic selves" and aimed at revolution along the lines of Third World "agrarian reformers." Now the Modern Liberals strive to refine ideas they inherited from the New Left, focusing on the underlying "power structures" that they claim are manipulating and controlling us behind the scenes. They want to uncover and expose these sources of power that hinder the realization of the "dream" that has continued, essentially unchanged, for well over a century. The cultural tide has clearly turned against Modern Liberalism, so they turn to the courts. If we look at virtually every controversial Supreme Court decision in the 20th century that left the populace in an uproar, it was invariably begun by members of the Old Left, the New Left, or Modern Liberals: School prayer, deinstitutionalizing the insane, abortion, sodomy, gay marriage, flag burning, forced busing—all from their side of the isle.

Harry Stein summarized Dennis Prager's "disasters liberalism has visited upon American culture": (1) restricted speech in the name of "sensitivity," (2) revising history as therapy, (3) a decline in civility, (4) stigmatization of males as potential predators, and (5) corruption of childhood by aggressively sexualizing children.[42]

Today, we defend our country from radical terrorists. Pascal Bruckner, in *The Tyranny of Guilt: An Essay on Western Masochism*, wrote about the apparent inexplicability of the Left's (Modern Liberals') alliance with, and defense of, Islam fundamentalism. In explaining it, he reveals its fundamental driving and inextricable force: "The far Left has never gotten over Communism and once again demonstrates that its true passion is not freedom, but slavery in the name of justice."[43]

4

The Education Of
Modern Liberals

I am for socialism...I seek social ownership of property,
the abolition of the propertied class...
Communism is the goal.
—ROGER BALDWIN, FOUNDER OF THE
AMERICAN CIVIL LIBERTIES UNION

T he question invariably arises: Why do some people become Modern
Liberals? How is it that most of us —even though we may ascribe to
a few issues that generally fall into the "liberal" camp—do not push
for overall federal government control of the economy and society? Why is it
that the Modern Liberals, a relatively small proportion of the population, are

determined to have mostly non-elected experts decide what the rest of us are to do, even to the point of regulating our diets, home temperatures, and color we paint our cars? What kind of background leads people to believe that the education of our children—from rural Montana and Oklahoma to the cities of Los Angeles and Dallas, and to suburban Boston or Chicago—should be directed by experts in Washington as opposed to local governments? What have these Modern Liberals been taught? From what kind of background and environment do they come to think like this?

Nancy Morgan wrote a sarcastic and amusing article entitled "I Wish I were a Liberal." In it, she wishes she were a [Modern] Liberal because "it's ever so much easier to allow others to form my opinions for me instead of researching an issue myself"; because "I would be free to have sex whenever and with whomever I want"; "because they (Liberals) care so much"; because "any guilt I would normally feel for what used to be considered deviant, irresponsible behavior may be assuaged by merely advocating the expenditure of other people's money on whatever the cause du jour is"; and because "everyone knows they hold the moral high ground." She sardonically outlines the requirements to become a Modern Liberal: "I have to acknowledge that government is the best and only solution for any problems America has"; "I must agree that America is bad and white Christian males are responsible for all that is wrong with the world"; "I'd…have to quit judging people (except conservatives)"; and "I'd have to agree that victimhood trumps merit and that liberals know best." But what will she get in return? Well, she muses, "I'll be accepted, popular, and invited to the best parties. I'll be eligible for the right to housing, health care, a living wage (even if I don't work) and happiness. And as long as I remain a liberal, no-one is allowed to insult me."[1]

Sometimes we need to maintain a sense of humor when dealing with Modern Liberals.

Somehow Modern Liberals have come to believe that fairness, security, life satisfaction, economic opportunities, and human equality can and should be brought about by people in the central government who can determine what is in our best interests and how we should behave. From their viewpoint, most individuals make choices that are harmful to themselves, are unlikely to provide for their old age, do not properly educate their children, base their personal decisions on outmoded and worthless traditions, and are at the mercy of controlling capitalists.

Four Basic Types of Modern Liberals

There are four basic types of Modern Liberals. There is often overlap among these types, and a few are a combination of three or all four:

1. The Elite
2. The Conformists and Followers
3. The Opportunists
4. The Fearful and Insecure

The Elite

We frequently hear references to the "Elite" or the "Liberal Elite." Who are they? In general, they are the relatively wealthy and well-educated, and they have a disproportionate amount of influence on our society. Robert Bork identified them as people who are "part of the chattering class" since they are most often the people who talk and write for a living: university professors, journalists, attorneys, social workers, psychologists, and politicians.[2] They spread their ideology on television, in newspapers, and in college classrooms across the country. Their ideas filter down to public schools, popular magazines, movies, and television.

They are considered "Elite," however, not just because of their positions, wealth, and education, but something more sinister and dangerous: They are aware of the ultimate goal of a centralized state, and, for a variety of reasons, they aspire to move society toward that goal. They do not openly articulate their agenda except to other Elites; instead, they press the isolated issues, asserting that they are for the common man and fairness. For example, the founder of the American Civil Liberties Union, Roger Baldwin, stated that "Communism is the goal." Ronald Reagan paraphrased what Norman Thomas—a six-time Socialist candidate for the presidency, said:

> The American people will never knowingly adopt Socialism. But under the name of "liberalism" they will adopt every fragment of the Socialist program, until one day America will be a Socialist nation, without knowing how it happened.

The Conformists and Followers

Conformists and Followers comprise the overwhelming majority of those who can be considered Modern Liberals. These are the Modern Liberals whom we most frequently encounter in everyday life in person and on the media. They focus on countless different issues that have the common theme of the central authority managing and regulating virtually every aspect of our lives. Their "solutions" also result in usurping individual and local decision-making. For example, Conformists and Followers are adamantly against states' rights and vehemently denounce local communities making particular decisions. For them, there are no aspects of life that are to be left "undecided." One's interactions, income, education, and even the type of car one buys are to be regulated and standardized by the federal authorities, and resistance is to be overcome via court actions.

Even though these people always want the central (federal) government to decide and regulate, they differ from the Elite in two ways. First, they focus on separate issues, and are rarely aware of the overall pattern or the relation of the issues to one another. Second, they do not see the overall goal to establish an all-powerful central government, even though all of their proposals and agendas—from the environment and education to the economy and our personal lives—scream for centralized action and control and for overriding individual and community prerogatives. These Modern Liberals see one or more issues as crucial and at a crisis level. To them, our republican form of government is cumbersome, inefficient, and slow. Modern Liberals long for a faster way for the experts to implement the solutions, each leading—bit by bit—to the *ignis fatuus* of a society completely free of prejudice, inequality, and poverty, and one blessed by perfect fairness, security, and happiness.

Conformists or Followers do not discern the overall agenda in which they are participating. They are like the foot soldiers on the battlefield, knowing they are part of something that they have been convinced is grand and glorious, but really are unable to see the large picture that the generals—the Elite—see. These Conformists and Followers only fight the isolated battles, struggling for victory in their specific theater of operations. They carry out their mission, not understanding how it fits into a larger picture. In fact, if the larger picture is pointed out to them, they will deny that this even exists and proclaim that they are not part of such nonsense. F. A. Hayek, in *The Road to Serfdom*, wrote about this group:

[S]uch a numerous and strong group with fairly homogeneous views is not likely to be formed by the best but rather by the worst elements of any society...[The leaders] obtain the support of all the docile and gullible, who have no strong convictions of their own but are prepared to accept a ready-made system of values...It will be those whose vague and imperfectly formed ideas are easily swayed.[3]

The Opportunists

The Opportunists simply take advantage of openings to start their careers, gain status, get security, or make money. A typical example is the bureaucrat who checks small private businesses to ensure that they are adhering to all of the thousands of federal and state regulations.

The bureaucrats, like any other workers, want to keep their jobs and increase their incomes. They sell their services, their skills, and their knowledge—to the government. The bureaucrat, being human, simply will not want to see his source of income come to an end, especially if he has become entrenched. Accordingly, he will have a defense and rationale for what he enforces. One purpose is simply to keep his source of income, another to expand his power, and most want to feel that they are doing something useful and righteous. Few want to consciously participate in something that burdens their fellow citizens in order to advance themselves or just maintain their own quality of life. Most of these government bureaucrats simply try not to conceptualize the reality in which they participate, and they usually have convinced themselves that they are actually helping society. If they have been well "indoctrinated" from their youth and have not had exposure to alternative ways to think and live, they may actually believe that their work is significant.

However, whatever their innermost thoughts and motivations, it is imperative for them to convince the society that supports them of their necessity and importance in that society.

The Fearful and Insecure

Fearful and Insecure Modern Liberals live in a constant state of anxiety and worry. At heart, what they long for is the federal government replacing their parents. They have a need to be taken care of, or at least feel assured that they will be protected and cared for by a powerful entity. A world in which one's life is determined by one's efforts and motivation is a threatening one to them, and what are opportunities to most are seen by them as simply dangers.

University of Chicago trained psychiatrist Lyle Rossiter wrote *The Liberal Mind: The Psychological Causes of Political Madness* in which he analyzes the psychological reasons that some people become the more radical type of Modern Liberal. Dr. Rossiter maintains that their suppositions and behaviors are so extreme—temper tantrums, irrationality, intolerance, grandiosity, and a sense of entitlement, —that they can only be understood as emotional disorders:

> I attack the dominant socialist program, the modern liberal agenda's welfare statism and moral relativism, as pathological distortions of the normal social instincts...The liberal agenda's invasive social policies foster economic irresponsibility, pathological dependency and social conflict.[4]

Dr. Rossiter explains that these types of Modern Liberals have mostly dependency issues and are plagued with insecurities. They were not loved as children, so the world is a hostile place to them. They long to get their mother back and feel loved and secure, and government assumes that role for them. In addition, these Modern Liberals deplore and fear others who do not seem to have this need: People who do not want a "mommy" government and who have a sense of independence are a threat to their sense of self-righteousness and remind him—at an unconscious level—that he is really living in constant fear and that he deems himself incapable of self-reliance. The truth is that democracy frightens them. That is because, in a democracy, some things are simply left to chance. These Modern Liberals do not want to be reminded of this—again, at an unconscious level—so they will strike out at any person who recommends limited government or otherwise seems to present a threat to having an all-caring government that will "protect and defend," as they unconsciously wish their parents had.

It is quite ironic that Modern Liberals routinely profess that Conservatives are rigid, resist change, and want security. The underlying program of Modern Liberals—government management of the society and the economy—is motivated by fear revealed by their incessant demands that government protect and provide for them in case of economic instability, illness, and old age.

Motivations for Becoming a Modern Liberal

The main psychological factors that can lead one to become a Modern Liberal vary. The Elites are mainly driven from a desire for power, wanting to be part of a utopian "dream," or from a sense of frustration and personal failure. The Followers and Conformists are also motivated by those factors, but they are primarily driven by a desire to fit in and to be liked and accepted. The Opportunists are driven by what the term implies: They take advantage of available opportunities, usually as some kind of government worker. The Fearful and Insecure want the protection that they believe a mommy government can give: They want to be taken care of during adversity, and they long for guarantees of safety and security.

Of course, we all have had and seen these characteristics in ourselves and others. People want to attain higher positions and influence within their own companies and communities, and some want to start and expand a business. There are those among us who want to build the "ideal" school or find the "perfect" life partner. Many of us become frustrated, and even envious, when it seems others have richer lives, and we may feel like a failure when we do not have the success we hoped we would. Most people want to fit in and be accepted by their coworkers, friends, and neighbors. There are not a few of us who would become opportunists if it meant making a good living or having security. Finally, most of us worry about health and finances and take measures to protect ourselves from adverse circumstances.

What separate Modern Liberals from the rest of us are their goals and presumptions in response to these typical human concerns: Modern Liberals feel impotent *within the existing structures*. In contrast to us, they do not look at themselves; they shift responsibility to the existing structures. These Modern Liberals fancy that they would have power, status, acceptance, and security in a centralized State where what *they* value is deemed indispensable. They say the present system stands in the way of the utopian "dream," and they blame our culture and republic for their own frustrations and failures. Countless Modern Liberals have been convinced that they are on the side of rectitude and equality, and that to think otherwise is to be uneducated, ignorant, uncaring, lacking compassion, and having no sense of fairness. Others deceive themselves into believing that the federal government is an altruistic entity that regulates, manages, and taxes us in our best interests: Myriad government workers defend and even promote their own bailiwick in order to rationalize their own opportunism.

With a centralized power enforcing this uniformity, Modern Liberals assume that they will be valued, no longer be held responsible for any lack of achievement, can help usher in the new society, be safe, or be among those who are righteous and truly "care" about humanity. Those who dissent provide constant reminders that their ideology is not really accepted and that they may be wrong. It is precisely because Modern Liberalism necessitates uniformity that they become distraught and agitated when others do not capitulate to their demands. Modern Liberals envision nothing less than the end of traditions and free-market capitalism, which, in their minds, are the root causes of suffering and the enslavement of the multitudes, the majority of whom are—according to these Modern Liberals—not even aware how much they are oppressed.

Modern Liberal Elites

As mentioned above, Modern Liberal Elites are generally wealthy and well-educated. But not all—or even a majority—of wealthy and well educated people follow the Modern Liberal chimera of the centralized state, so how is it that some adhere to this dogma while others do not?

Let's look at one archetypical Elite, William Ayers. Ayers was relatively unknown until Barack Obama ran for the presidency. During the campaign, it was revealed that they were both members of the Woods Fund that Ayers was instrumental in starting, and for three years Obama served as president of its board of directors. Ayers grew up wealthy, and his upbringing—according to confidants—was one in which he assumed that he was a member of the ruling elite class, one of those who knew what the rest of us really need. In his youth, Ayers had a position of leadership in the Weather Underground, a radical group that broke off from the student activist movement of the New Left, the Students for a Democratic Society (SDS). This group advocated the overthrow of capitalism—specifically the American variety——and the establishment of a Marxist state. In the founding document of the Weather Underground, it was stated that its goal was to achieve "the destruction of US imperialism and the achievement of a classless world: world communism."[5] In June 1974, the Weather Underground released a 151-page text titled *Prairie Fire*, which stated: "We are a guerrilla organization...We are communist women and men underground in the United States."[6] Ayers went into hiding because of the group's bombings, only escaping imprisonment for his involvement in them because of legal technicalities (information obtained "illegally" by the FBI). The capitalist system stood in the way of his grandiose road to power and realizing the "dream," so Ayers and his counterparts concluded that it was imperative to bring it down. Todd Gitlin was the president of the SDS. He knew Ayers and most of the others who broke off from the SDS and formed the Weather Underground. What Gitlin said was chilling but most certainly not atypical of this mindset:

> They came to the conclusion which is the conclusion that was come to by all the great killers, whether Hitler, Stalin or Mao…That they have a grand project for the transformation and purification of the world. And in the face of that project, ordinary life is dispensable.[7]

So, what are we *really* talking about with such people? The motives are as old as humanity itself: power and status. Elite Modern Liberals are driven by these motives, but they feel impotent in a system of free-market capitalism and limited, decentralized government. They believe that they would be in positions of power in a centralized system in which free-market capitalism and states' rights are virtually abolished. In their visionary world, people will be made to conform to what those in positions of leadership know what is best for them. In other words, these Elite types of Modern Liberals want to create or join the power structure that a central authority can confer. These Elitists have concluded that they must endeavor to tear down the structures that limit or thwart the centralization of power: traditions, organized religion, the family, free-market economics, and states' rights. They want to increase central authority and become part of it. Better yet, these Elite believe, the centralized and collective state will be in need of people *like them*; most assume that they will have a prominent role in it. At the least, they have convinced themselves that their pronouncements and writings will align with the power structure, and that they can have high status in this new order. They proclaim that the capitalists are running the country and are responsible for any poverty, unemployment, and inequality, and they envision a government that can organize our economic and personal lives for the better. However, they ignore the central flaw in their attacks on capitalism: Even if big businesses and corporations possess incredible amounts of wealth and power, as these Elitists allege they do, they are at the beck and call of the consumer who can choose not to buy their products and services! The great railroads fell with the advent of cars, trucks, roads, and highways, and carriage manufacturers vanished into obscurity when cars became affordable to the masses. Corporations, sources of wealth, and businesses come and go.

Another drive that is quite strong with, but not limited to, Modern Liberal Elites has been well documented by insiders—former radicals and Communists like Whittaker Chambers, Frank Meyer, and David Horowitz—who have described the allure of the "dream," the "vision," and the "plan." Horowitz described how intoxicating it was to feel that one was actually part of what he and his coterie of true believers thought was the inevitable fall of capitalism and the formation of a new society. They were exhilarated at the thought that they would create a society in which one no longer had to inhibit or restrain one's carnal and emotional desires, where one no longer had to have any uncertainty about the future, where one does not worry about ever becoming poor, and when the struggle and cruelty that emanate from competition for more property and wealth are gone. Even today, some Modern Liberal Elites postulate that the dream can be achieved—"only if." "Only if" capitalism ends, "only if" property is abolished or controlled, and "only if" there is total and perfect government enforced economic equality.

Modern Liberal Elites realize that a central authority is needed to regulate the economy and enforce conformity as they deem necessary, and they want this authority to rid us of existing structures that have created the purported mess in which we now live. The pull to this dream is like that of the inexperienced and intoxicated person when he falls in love for the first time: The dream of a future ecstasy is all he can envisage, and any attempt to get him to be rational or face reality is useless. The dream is too beautiful, so who would want to return to reality?

Another strong force among Modern Liberal Elites, but not limited to them, stems from frustration and a deep sense of personal failure. These emotions can intensify the drives for power and to realize the "dream": This type of Modern Liberal refuses to face the frustrations and failures that reside in himself, the ones that are a result of his own personality and behaviors, so he envisions a new society in which he has power and he is important and successful. The present American society, he convinces himself, stands in the way of better values, fairness, and equality, so it must be toppled and replaced with the quixotic one that is real in his mind.

These irrational forces are usually not even understood by the Modern Liberals themselves. Modern Liberals who are under their spell are the ones who become the angriest and most indignant when they are asked to provide rationales for their proclamations. They will say that any outrage stems from injustice, unfairness, and poverty in society; in reality, it is from a sense of personal failure, frustration from a lack of recognition and status, and simple envy of others' success. These Modern Liberals are the most blind of all, and the desire for central control is not so much a way to establish a more equitable society as it is to destroy what they imagine stands in the way. They see evil forces—traditions, organized religions, the independent family unit, and free-market capitalism—as preventing progress toward their "dream," the future wonderland where they are valued, appreciated, recognized and successful.

No matter whether these Modern Liberal Elites desire power, envision an Eden, or unleash anger from frustration and a sense of personal failure, their response defines them: They clamor for centralizing authority to control a society in which they believe they can have power and influence, a society in which they can be part of what Horowitz refers to as the "heady dream," or where they can help to punish those who they fathom have caused their failures and prevented the world from recognizing how great they truly are.

In sum, the "Elite" Modern Liberals are those who are well-aware they want to see a powerful central authority that controls the economy, manages our society, and instructs us in how to best run our lives. They will rarely openly clarify or acknowledge their vision. Instead, they will describe how the central government—with experts running the show—is absolutely necessary for the good society, for fairness, for true equality, for security, and for eradicating poverty.

Modern Liberal Followers and Conformists

Just as the Elites, the Modern Liberal Followers and Conformists are motivated by drives for status, acceptance from peers, being part of a dream, or indignation at a system that they have been conditioned to believe thwarts their ability to achieve and to be recognized. But there are two qualities that separate them from the "Elite": First, they are rarely aware that they are promoting an overall movement for the complete centralization of power. Second, they do not consciously choose to become this way; they primarily assimilate it from their surroundings. This is a result of a very simple, yet rarely acknowledged, process: enculturation. To understand the power of this, we need to reflect a bit on how culture molds us.

When we envision "culture," we often imagine very different, dramatic, and all-encompassing ways of life. We may contrast the cultures of Southeast Asia or China with those of Europe or the Middle East, for example. But culture is also subtle and subdued, and we absorb it naturally. Reflect a bit on the life and values of typical people in rural and urban America. Consider the disparate attitudes of fellow Americans toward education, leisure time, and sports. We see that our own surrounding environment has shaped what we believe is valuable, ethical, important, and worthwhile.

This occurs everywhere and with everyone, of course, and most Modern Liberals are created by a specific type of "culture." Modern Liberal culture is usually omnipresent in the universities and can change the course of students' lives. Dinesh D'Souza described this process as a student at Dartmouth: D'Souza saw countless students being indoctrinated through etiquette and other social pressures. The young students naturally want to be considered an "educated Dartmouth man (or woman)." The professors know this and exploit it. For example, D'Souza pointed out, a student considers the possibility that Communists are involved in some untoward event. Does the professor discuss and debate this? *No.* The professor simply raises his nose and asks, "Are you from Iowa?"[8] The student wants to fit in, and the message is clear: Ignorant hicks have such ideas, and Dartmouth people don't. Another method the professors typically use is to undermine the idea of being an American and emphasize the idea that in a country of racism and oppression like America, one must aim to help others to hold fast to their racial and ethnic identity. And, as Jonah Goldberg, author of *Liberal Fascism*, wrote, "the student is stuffed to the gills with cant about the corruption of the 'system.'"[9] "Diversity" is promulgated in the universities, and Modern Liberals believe that conformity is diversity. Barton Swaim, author of *Men of Letters in the New Public Sphere*, explains this Modern Liberal mindset:

> [P]romoting diversity of opinion and shutting out contrary opinion [are] one and the same thing...The trouble with that line of thinking is that it always applies to other people, never to oneself. Its adherents naturally believe their views are in the minority...and that views they detest are everywhere prevailing. And the only way to uphold their commitment to "diversity" is to impose, within their sphere of influence, a rigid ideological conformity...[It] exists in its purest form on today's university campuses.[10]

The professors also train their students to think in terms of what Thomas Sowell aptly entitles "Cosmic Justice," in which the concept of a perfect and ideal society is deemed attainable if only the agenda of Modern Liberals is carried to completion. Cosmic Justice assumes that experts can analyze every inequality of birth, education, ability, and family, and then rectify these if only their programs would be realized. They profess that entrenched forces—free-market capitalism, traditions, and entreaties to patriotism—must stand aside. Taking a verbal stand against the existing society is cheap and easy, and these professors do not tell their students about the nitty-gritty of compromise and incremental change. Hard work pales to what the imagination can produce, and it costs nothing—but the professors never tell their students about *that*:

> The prerequisites of civilization are not an interesting subject to those who concentrate on its shortcomings—that is, on the extent to which what currently exists as the fruits of centuries of efforts and sacrifices is inferior to what they can produce in their imagination immediately at zero cost, in the comfort and security provided by the society they disdain.[11]

The students are taught this Cosmic Justice version as reality. The professors instill in them the idea that experts are capable of determining who has more "merit" and ipso facto deserve rewards if our society is truly "just." In reality, this leads to disastrous results:

> We can judge who has produced results, according to the established rules and criteria, but we cannot determine which of our fellow human beings has more personal merit. Schools have too often forgotten that limitation, and have graded students not on the quality of their work but on whether they were working up to their ability—as the teachers imagined their ability. Little Billy might make 90% on a math test while little Johnny made 50%, but both might receive the same grade if the teacher imagined that both scores represented their real ability. But, trying to reward them for personal effort, rather than their actual results, meant an utter absence of standards, contributing to the decline of American education—all as a result of trying to do what was beyond any person's power to do.[12]

A distorted and ugly version of America is promoted in the universities. *A People's History of the United States* by Howard Zinn provides an example of how Modern Liberals in academia persist in presenting America as a country formed to protect the controlling interests of a few, and is only a history of oppressed people struggling against entrenched powers for their freedom, being beaten down, and rising up again. Zinn's history of America has been thoroughly discredited by Ron Radosh, Roger Kimball, and Aileen S. Kraditor.[13,14] Eminent historian Arthur M. Schlesinger, Jr., once remarked that "I don't take him very seriously. He's a polemicist, not a historian."[15] Harvard University professor Oscar Handlin denounced "the deranged quality of his fairy tale,"[16] and even the Leftist historian Michael Kazin concluded that this book was just "bad history."[17] Yet it remains a favorite textbook of Modern Liberal professors. Modern Liberal promotion of this odious work has contributed to its having sold over four million copies, and a watered-down version, *A Young People's History of the United States*, has been published for consumption by children in America's middle schools and high schools.

Adolescents and young college students have scant foundation with which to resist this onslaught. The history that these young people have learned is a revised one, one that does not celebrate our founding principles. David Horowitz, ex-Leftist radical, author, and founder of *Students for Academic Freedom* wrote about the situation in the universities dominated by the Left: "The works of von Mises, Hayek, Aron, Popper, Oakeshott, Sowell, Strauss, Bloom, Kirk, Kristol and other antisocialist thinkers are virtually unknown on the Left—excluded from the canons of the institutions they dominate."[18] Young and inexperienced students naturally want to be on the side of virtue, fairness, and equality, and they are told that only the central government can bring this about. They are inculcated with the idea that if the federal government does not enforce the Modern Liberal agenda, the alternative is oppression, poverty, racism, and chaos. These young people naturally want to be accepted and respected by their peers and professors, so even if they see flaws and incongruencies, they usually agree and acquiesce, rather than being the one to state that the emperor is not wearing any clothes.

Few young people entering college have had exposure to the principles and history of free-market capitalism. They have been told myths about the Robber Barons and the "Gilded Age." When Jamestown and Plymouth are covered in their history classes, the failures of communal living (Socialism) in those colonies are never described, nor are the subsequent successes from switching over to a private property, free-market system. An excellent book with the title *How Capitalism Saved America* would never be considered reading material by their professors in college.[19] In fact, as of this printing, a Google search in the ".edu" (educational institutions) domain with the terms "syllabus" and the phrase "How Capitalism Saved America" resulted in four hits, while another search in the same domain that included "syllabus" and the title of the text *A*

People's History of the United States—the book written by a committed Marxist that describes America as a place of oppression by ruling capitalists (see above)—resulted in over 35,000 hits. The Modern Liberal professors teach our youth that it was the centralization of power in the government that ended slavery and brought about civil rights (both false premises). Those eager students are not taught that capitalism brought a higher standard of living, extended life spans, improved diets, freed people from having to make their children work, and enabled the masses to buy what only royalty could heretofore afford. And they never learn how the free market actually *forced* the ruling classes to give more rights to the common people.

Modern Liberals do not want to look at the history of the free market and our country to build a future: In their world, whatever binds people to such a past has to be erased or revised because it may stand in the way of their agenda. For Modern Liberals, the ideology comes first, and they accept only what supports and reinforces it. Most Modern Liberals convince themselves that this is for the good of all: People are being oppressed, Modern Liberals tell themselves, and they are obliged to speak out and help. Modern Liberals go so far as to say that many people are not even aware of their oppression because they have been brainwashed by the controlling capitalist entities. In *The Blank Slate*, a book about inherited and universal human traits, Steven Pinker describes how and why humans come to believe their self-deceptions.[20] These Modern Liberals have many.

In such an environment, an alternative is never presented. The Modern Liberal professors allege that anything other than a central power run by experts is malevolent, a system perpetuated by greedy people who want to maintain their power over the masses. Even our Constitution, according to Modern Liberals in academia, was created to solidify the wealth, land holdings, and slavery system of the Founders. History is thus presented in terms of class and racial struggles and of oppression. Those who state otherwise—that it consists of individuals making choices and great ideas being fulfilled—are said to be either dupes of the controlling powers, ignorant of the truth, or unwitting participants in the oppression of the masses. In one college textbook of Modern Liberals, *Handbook of Social Justice in Education*, a contributor wrote that "in the United States an economic war against youth, the poor, the working class, and people of color has been waged"[21]; another described "the anti-democratic foundation stones of American democracy"[22]; and yet another announced that the New Left broke the "U.S. system of racial apartheid."[23] In a book intended for college students, *Race Course: Against*

White Supremacy, William Ayers, Acting Head of the Division of Curriculum Studies in one of the most influential educational research establishments in our country, the American Educational Research Center, and his wife wrote an outline of American history in five brief pages, and it is typical to what Modern Liberals ascribe: America is the most evil civilization on the planet. According to this view, the Puritans began the "justification for anything - conquest, theft, and mayhem, ultimately mass murder," in the name of God. The Declaration of Independence is "stamped with white supremacist thinking," and "the founding fathers were fundamentally, to a man, undeniable white supremacists." In New Leftist-Modern Liberal fashion, these authors claim that the United States is to blame for the following: promotion of local wars, toleration of famine, genocide, theft of wealth from poor countries, displacement of people and forced migration (especially people of color), torture and extrajudicial killings, "savaging" the planet's integrity, and violent assaults on women's reproductive freedoms, sexuality, economic equality, and independence. According to these authors, America itself has demonized gays and lesbians, created child poverty, showed disdain for the arts and intellectual life, promoted mass incarceration, and militarized the borders.[24] This is what Modern Liberal professors are telling our youth.

For now, we simply need to know that this most common group of Modern Liberals, the Conformists and Followers, are a result of brainwashing and propaganda of their own media, social pressures, and dominance in education. Most of us have absorbed enough of our founding principles, love of America's special qualities, and distrust of federal authority to provide a bulwark to fortify us against Modern Liberal propaganda. Unfortunately, many of us are blasé or indifferent to what is happening. Modern Liberal political beliefs? Vilifications of America? Revisions of our founding? Most people either care little or do not think conflict is worth the effort or price.

Modern Liberal Opportunists

The Opportunists, as previously described, look for and use situations that will be personally profitable. In order to adjust to their situation and even advance in it, the Opportunists are obliged to at least spout the Modern Liberal mantra that justifies their position. If they have not been fully inculcated with Modern Liberal ideology, they will either become "true believers" or suffer cognitive dissonance when their outward actions and words conflict with their mindset and values. Most Opportunists are not simply crass mercenaries without any compunctions or consciences; most are like the rest of us and want to believe that they are doing something worthwhile and meaningful for others. So the process of "rationalization" usually begins: They listen for, or develop, a variety of excuses for their behaviors. They convince themselves that the government policies that they dutifully enforce are to help and protect people; they tell themselves that they make necessary bureaucratic mandates more palatable and meaningful for people; or they start to believe that these rules actually promote efficiency and make people more accountable. Behind all of these complex government regulations, this wasteful paperwork, the pointless rules and labyrinthine laws there are myriad excuses, rationales, and legal jargon that can support their enforcer—the Opportunist.

Fearful and Insecure Modern Liberals

The Fearful and Insecure find a comfortable and safe haven in the womb of Modern Liberalism. Modern Liberals promise a caring, beneficent, and compassionate government that gives guarantees and assurances to everyone. Modern Liberalism also presents the alternatives—the free market, our founding principles of limited government, states' rights, and Rule of Law—as existing in a dangerous, cold, and foreboding place of cruel capitalists, religious fundamentalists, and "right-wingers" demanding conformity. These people, in the minds of the Fearful and Insecure, lack compassion for the weak, poor, disenfranchised, and helpless. In addition to painting the nation as a choice between the dichotomy of heartless cruelty or warm compassion, the Fearful and Insecure are drawn into Modern Liberalism by another tantalizing dish that is irresistible for them: Socialism.

Socialism not only holds the promise of physical security and safety, but it also allays anxieties stemming from a fear of failure or a lack of success. The Socialism of Modern Liberals guarantees one will never have to worry about getting a job, preserving a "decent" standard of living, having adequate housing, getting excellent medical care, or winding up poor in one's dotage. Socialism tells the Fearful and Insecure that people became successful only from luck, connections, cheating, or conspiracies with other capitalists. Under the Socialism of Modern Liberals, the Fearful and Insecure are told that one no longer needs to feel embarrassment or shame for not achieving because there will no longer be large differences of incomes and "the wealth will be spread around," as one prominent Modern Liberal proclaimed in 2008 to "Joe the plumber."

Modern Liberals absorb an admixture—from a young age—of the following fallacies. These myths are accepted as axioms by Modern Liberals:

1. "Scientific" analysis and methods should be used to solve personal and social problems. This implies that there actually *are* ways of solving *all* such problems; either we have not discovered them, or there are individuals, groups and institutions thwarting their discovery and implementation.
2. Without a central organization of our society and economy, there will be chaos and anarchy. The only reason we have not already fallen into a barbaric state is because of beneficent management by the federal government.
3. Experts—especially those in the social sciences—can discover and decide what is best for the country. The plans of experts have to be implemented nationwide, not piecemeal, so that they are not sabotaged or fail. This is the reason that a powerful central authority is necessary.
4. The masses are ignorant and rarely decide what is in their own best interests. The masses simply are not capable. An entire book was written to emphasize this: *What's the Matter with Kansas?*[25]

In their education, Modern Liberals are led to believe that there are three main enemies thwarting progress:

1. *Patriotism.* Modern Liberals contend *patriotism* is a dangerous emotion. According to Modern Liberals, the emotions of patriotism trigger military conflicts, throttle open-minded thinking, allow the controlling interests to take advantage of the masses, support the "military-industrial complex," stop the diversion of wasteful monies to programs that are "compassionate," and lead to a false understanding of our *authentic* history of oppression, genocide, racism, and control of the country by the wealthy.
2. *Conservatism.* Modern Liberals have concluded that those who are not in agreement with them—especially those who identify themselves by

that odious term *conservative*—are jingoistic flag-wavers, racists, religious fanatics, mindless idolaters of the Founders, sexist, homophobic, and otherwise generally benighted dolts.

3. *Capitalism.* Modern Liberals believe that *capitalists* are rapacious, hoard wealth, impoverish the population to increase their already enormous wealth, willingly pollute for any gain, conduct war for profit, and control the ideas and desires of the masses through monopolies and advertising.

The Modern Liberals' training, propaganda and education have strong appeal to the ego. Those who join them are told the following:

1. You are well-educated, and the well-educated adhere to our truisms. You are now among those who are at the highest intellectual level. You are one of the sophisticated and enlightened.

2. You are pragmatic. You go by what "works," and do not cling to the past and outmoded ways of thinking and acting. This proves you are for progress, another mark of a flexible, emotionally healthy, rational, and well-educated person.

3. You are kind, caring, tolerant and compassionate. You *care* about people and believe in fairness and equality.

4. You are righteous. Yours is of the highest form of morality, carrying on in the footsteps of people like Mahatma Gandhi, Martin Luther King, and even Jesus Christ.

5. You have good intentions. Even if you make some small mistakes, they can be excused because your intentions are pure.

Since Modern Liberals believe that they possess these five characteristics, this of course implies that those who disagree with them are bereft of those qualities; non-Modern Liberals are uneducated, corrupted, obdurate, benighted, cruel, and intolerant.

It is informative to have a look at a leading magazine of the Modern Liberals like *Nation*. It has been in circulation since the end of our civil war, and it contains articles written by leading Modern Liberal academics today and their predecessors in the past—the Progressives, the Old Left, and the New Left. This is the *preeminent publication* of Modern Liberal academics and pundits, and their ideas are being passed down to our students in leading universities.

Each and every issue contains denunciations of capitalism and execrations of America; each one bellows for the worldwide establishment of some form or combination of Marxism, Socialism and Communism.

The title of one leading article, randomly selected from the author's book-shelf, is "Afterimages." It is about Che Guevara. In this article, the author writes panegyrics to the memory of Che:

> [Che] rushed to the docks and helped provide medical aid to the wounded and the dying...[Che has] a mythical appeal...[can] strengthen the nonreligious but barefoot Order...of the guerrillas [of today]...[Che] conducted himself like a man...He was facing death with courage and grace...[Che] conducted himself with respect to the very end....Che's charismatic appeal [through his picture]...also lies in its spirituality, in its ability to feel people's longings for a better world.[26]

Another rather lengthy article in the same issue was entitled, "The Rogue Nation Contest." This article starts off as an apparent condemnation of North Korea because it imprisoned two journalists for crossing the border. However, the emphasis shifts: It attacks the United States, excuses North Korea by comparison (the US is made to look worse than that North Korea!), and ends with this sentence: "And they call North Korea a rogue nation?" This implies, of course, that America is far worse.[27]

In another issue, again randomly selected, a full seven pages of small print was dedicated to praise for William Appleman Williams, the American Marxist who hoped that Soviet nuclear power would rescue history from the "Puritan memory hole."[27] Each week, *Nation* publishes recommendations for its activist readers entitled "Ten Things." In its September 20, 2010 issue, the recommendations included, "Know your [capitalist] enemy" and "read, or reread Marx for what is still the most thoroughgoing criticism of capitalism."[28]

Nation manifestly evinced its ideology in a cover article entitled "The Fifty Most Influential Progressives of the Twentieth Century." It reads like a list out of a Socialist or Communist party manifesto. It included Eugene Debs, *Socialist* candidate for the presidency; Lincoln Steffens, famous for his statement, after visiting the USSR, "I have seen the future and it works"; Henry Wallace, sponsored by the American Communist Party for the presidency in 1948; Paul Robeson, winner of Stalin Peace Prize, supporter of Communist countries, eulogist of the "freedom fighter" Ho Chi Minh, and singer of the Soviet

National Anthem; Saul Alinsky of *Rules for Radicals* fame; I. F. Stone, a journalist about whom recent evidence revealed spying activities for the USSR; Michael Harrington, a Communist, historical revisionist, and denier of Stalinism; Gloria Steinem, who admitted she was a Marxist from college; and Tom Hayden, who wrote the manifesto of the SDS and went to North Vietnam to help America's enemy during the war. And, of course, Michael Moore.[29]

The world of typical people deals with realities and consequences. In academia, the Modern Liberals do not, and they are training and influencing the youth of America. Robert Bork, former professor at Yale University and nominee for the Supreme Court (whose appointment Congressional Liberals stopped), wrote the following in *Slouching Towards Gomorrah: Modern Liberalism and American Decline*:

> [The] economic marketplace penalizes wrong decisions…The intellectual and cultural "marketplace"…imposes few or no penalties for being wrong, even egregiously wrong. In fact, patently foolish ideas are likely to be regarded as daring…The left-wing intellectual…can go on selling defunct ideas for decades.[30]

No matter whether a Modern Liberal is one of the elites, a conformist, a follower, or a simple opportunist, or simply clings to Modern Liberalism out of fear, once he becomes one of the pack, he participates, willy-nilly, in promoting the agenda to concentrate power in the federal government.

5

Modern Liberals And Marxism

To each according to his needs.

—Karl Marx

To each according to his accomplishments.

—Ludwig von Mises

Modern Liberals go apoplectic when they are called Marxists, Socialists, or Communists. Modern Liberals say that characterizing them thus is absurd, and that the name-callers do not even understand the labels they are using. But even if many do not understand the epithets they hurl at Modern Liberals, the question remains: Are Modern Liberals Marxists, Socialists, or Communists? Do they have proclivities in that direction? Do they ascribe to those ideologies?

There is one simple way to discern this, and I now challenge the reader of this book, including those of you who may have some Liberal leanings, to try for yourselves. It is a simple task, and it will provide insight into the psyche of Modern Liberals. Find a few books about the history of "Liberalism" or the "Left," ones that trace it from its inception in the late 19th century to the modern era. Include some books written by those of the Old Left, the New Left, or Modern Liberals, lest one accuse you of choosing biased "right-wing" sources. The more books that you choose, the better. One more consideration: Choose books that have gotten relatively good reviews from reputable sources. You will not need to buy the books or even read them; simply peruse good descriptions presented in reviews or ones that simply summarize the contents. This can be done on the Internet quite easily.

You will find that *all* of the books, no matter the background or political penchant of the authors, include the following: How the varieties of Marxism, Communism, and Socialism were promoted, advocated, and partially fulfilled among the predecessors of Modern Liberals. You will see that the history of Modern Liberals is largely one of importing and adapting varieties of these ideologies. Some of their forebears put an American spin on these political philosophies and integrated American-style Populism or Pragmatism, and others were outright revolutionary in their approaches. And some chose to emphasize a cultural approach, striving to revise history, foment racial conflict, and create a counter-cultural movement so America would be more receptive to the Marxist, Communist, and Socialist agendas. If you look at the histories of Modern Liberals—no matter who has written them—you will see varieties of these ideologies throughout the history of Progressivism, the Old Left, the New Left and Modern Liberalism.

It is critical to remember that Marxism and its varieties have adapted and been modified over the last century and a half, and today it is rare for anyone to openly identify himself as a Marxist per se. Communism has been discredited, and it is only the exotic bird who brands himself as one. But its essence remains; the forms have simply metamorphosed as they adapted. The principle aim of these ideologies—management of the society and the economy by the central government—remains the prime mover of Modern Liberalism today.

Ludwig von Mises, a free-market economist, cites three basic lies that those whom he designates as "anti-capitalists" have foisted on people; these stem from Marxism and are axiomatic among today's Modern Liberals in modified forms:

1. There is a great ideological conflict in society's economic organization. There is no conflict: People throughout the world want a government that supports a free market.
2. Socialism and Communism are different economically. The truth is that they are essentially the same: Both use large-scale planning as a means of central control, and the government regulates and manages, not individual citizens.
3. There are successful mixed economies. There is not really such a thing as a mixed economy; Socialism and free-market capitalism are polar opposites. The Socialist entities in economies always struggle for dominance. This is because the free market responds unpredictably to individuals making choices: Their voluntary purchases affects values and prices in ways that cannot be known or predicted in advance. In contrast, a Socialist economy *demands* controls of prices, production, and consumption.[1]

Marxism combined elements that form the bulwark of the Modern Liberals' ideology and that of their predecessors: determinism, science, and revolution. Simply put, Marxists initially fancied that society is evolving toward a higher form, a combination of physical and social evolution, and they proclaimed this was inevitable and unstoppable. All of this is supposedly explained "scientifically," giving it the cachet of respectability in academia. It is beyond the scope of this book to delve into the finer points of Marxist theory, its variations, and experiments with it all over the world; suffice to say that the more "pure" Marxists, Communists, and Socialists—in their theoretically ideal state—vaticinate that government itself eventually will not be needed in the upcoming utopia. They say that one-party central control is only a temporary expedient for a Socialist order (Marx's "dictatorship of the proletariat") to rid society of its control by the capitalist ruling class, and to awaken the consciousness of the oppressed masses so that they can clearly see the values that have been imposed on them by the capitalist oppressors. The only reason that these programs failed to achieve a paradise, proponents assert, is because evil men like Stalin, Mao, and Pol Pot usurped power and corrupted the dream. Of necessity, Modern Liberals deny that they ascribe to any "pure" Marxism, and they distance themselves from any connection to these Socialist tyrants whose programs resulted in poverty, misery, starvation, and death. "Pure" Marxism, they postulate, can never work, but Socialism can, they insist, and they then allege that the murderous despots did not install "true" Socialism, but were simply ruthless men running murderous regimes.

But the "dream" of Modern Liberals is essentially the same: the construction of the ideal society planned by experts and enforced by a central authority. Conformity is essential in order to prevent a corruption of the dream; thus the demand for the central government and the federal courts to set up laws and regulations on a national basis, and an unwillingness to let states and local communities determine things for themselves. When communities do not go along with the agenda, Modern Liberals perceive them as a threat. Thus the attack on the system is two-fold: to establish laws and regulations on a national level to enforce conformity, and to eliminate traditions, institutions, individualism, and local control that resist the "plan."

The "mildest" form of this ideology is Socialism. Marxism and Communism have become pejoratives, and Modern Liberals obfuscate and spin in any way they can to avoid being associated with either of those. Even the term "Socialism" standing alone has a slew of unfavorable connotations, so Modern Liberals imbue it with something that cannot be rejected: Democracy. Accordingly, Modern Liberals clamor for *Democratic* Socialism, and proclaim that it is successful in Europe. Modern Liberals also aim to convince their fellow citizens that Socialism is already servicing us in ways that we welcome and desire: public education, social security, the military, and the police. But they conveniently obscure the essence of Socialism: control of the *means of production.* Asking our government—as prescribed in our Constitution—to protect the lives and property of its citizens is not Socialism; it is citizens supporting what is necessary to keep and defend our republic, and the Founders created it to ensure our liberty and our prosperity.

But what is Socialism? The most hardcore Communists in the former Red China, the Soviet Union, and North Korea referred to themselves as "Socialists." Kevin Williamson wrote about this in *The Politically Incorrect Guide to Socialism*:

> Socialists invariably maintain, in essence, that all the bad stuff done in the name of socialism is communism, and all the good stuff is socialism. Free healthcare? That's socialism. Political repression? That's communism. Public pensions? Socialism. The Gulag? Communism...Whether one describes a particular arrangement as socialist or communist, one is talking about different expressions of a single phenomenon...The great

communist leaders regularly describe themselves, their work, and their philosophy as *socialist*."[2]

When Paul Sweezy, a prominent Marxist economist and founder of the *Monthly Review* ("a leading voice of independent Marxian socialism"[3]) and Socialist coeditor Leo Huberman were asked to explain the difference between Socialism and Communism, they gave the following response:

> Socialism and communism are alike in that both are systems of production for use based on public ownership of the means of production and centralized planning. Socialism…is the first form of the new society. Communism is a further development or "higher stage" of socialism… Socialism is…the necessary transition stage from capitalism to communism.[4]

Comrades Sweezy and Huberman also explained that the Communists want to change the basic structure of the capitalist state, while the Socialists want to have the State appropriate (confiscate) the existing means of production.

There are all sorts of fine points, such as the degree of State ownership, which services and goods are in the government sector, and how much the State manages the setting of prices, dictates output quotas, and controls through regulations, but as Williamson wrote, "when it comes to the deep structural issues in the economy—investment, infrastructure, large-scale property rights, capital markets, trade, etc.—socialism and communism are, in the analysis of America's leading Socialist thinkers, *identical*"(emphasis original).[5] Adam Shaw wrote in *American Thinker* that "there are as many exact definitions of socialism as there are Socialists. Yet they do have common characteristics. Love of big government, nationalization of industry, massive taxation, wealth distribution, etc. all point toward socialism."[6]

Modern Liberals would have us believe that *anything* and *everything* government funds or manages is Socialism. Of course, we must understand that the governments of all nations should support some services that are extremely difficult for the private sector to provide, such as a court system, national defense, disaster relief, and the police. An essential factor that plays a role in these government services is that they are *not* limited to certain persons, and others do *not* then get excluded or unable to get these services if someone uses them. Hopefully, with government services such as the military and the police, *everyone* is protected and the courts are open to all; both are free in the sense of individuals not "buying" these services for personal consumption and using them does not reduce what is available to others. If one person gets police or court services, for example, they are not "consumed" or "bought" in the sense that there is a limited amount for sale; a person getting helped by the police does not reduce the amount of help or raise any personal cost for the next person who needs assistance from the police. In contrast, in the private sector, when someone buys an airline ticket, for example, someone gets "excluded" because there is one fewer ticket; and when one pumps gas, there is that much less gas for others. In addition, in the private sector some people can buy more than others.

But still, how is this government provision of services different from Socialism? Socialism is not the provision of services per se, but it is the central planning, management, and control of the economy. This ranges from the government organizing the overall economy to the nationalization of industries; it can include government ownership, government direction of companies, government provision of goods or services, and government management of what are typically private market activities, such as setting the price of oil and subsidizing farm production. Today, few Modern Liberals openly assert that they want to control the entire economy and centrally manage it; rather, Modern Liberals want to direct the economy—as much as possible—*as if* the government owned the means of production. Under this kind of Socialism, the government does not have to *own* the means of production, but it can micromanage, direct, and *regulate* it.

———◆———

Another aspect of Socialism—in contrast to capitalism—is that Socialism adds a moral dimension. Socialism bases its rationale to manage the economy on its beguiling claims for equality and fairness: This justification is used to set prices, control and regulate production, and even nationalize industries. Venezuela's Hugo Chavez, for example, asserted that he would help the people by nationalizing the oil companies; this resulted in drops in production and prices. In order to help ensure everyone would get adequate food, Chavez professed, he ordered the military to seize control of all Venezuela's rice processing plants in February 2009; it resulted in farmland laying fallow and food shortages. An essential difference between a free-market economy and a Socialist one is who determines what is of value: In a Socialist economy, the government decides what is "good" and "important"; in a free-market economy, the *citizens* decide. In a free-market society, an athlete may have a higher income than a teacher or a pharmacist; this is determined by the choices consumers make. In a Socialist society, remuneration is determined by experts in government deciding what to value.

Modern Liberals promote centralized control of the economy via direct government management, regulation, or outright ownership. It invariably starts out small, but they always press for increased control. For example, only the naïve would suppose that Modern Liberals would stop at having single-payer health insurance or a variation of it. If this gain is solidified, they will move to the next step: socialized medicine. Check this yourself by asking a Modern Liberal a simple question: If single-payer health insurance got instituted, would he promise to *completely stop* any more requests for government involvement in health care? You will not get a straight answer because the truth is that they simply will not admit to it. And this is with every aspect of our lives. Modern Liberals want to mandate and regulate the size of our homes, sex education in the schools, and even the temperatures in our houses and the color we paint our cars! They have tried to make inroads into micromanaging our diets, using the clarion call to "save the children" from the obesity epidemic by taxing high calorie foods, requiring restaurants to write calories and grams of fat on their menus, ordering local schools to adhere to specific dietary rules, and having social workers supervise the food choices of the poor. In Alabama, one Modern Liberal legislator actually tried to get a law passed that required waiters and waitresses to inform customers if the food that they ordered exceeded a specific caloric level.

Modern Liberals know that most Americans are against the federal government controlling our entire economy, as they are also against the idea of the government nationalizing our industries. Most of all, it is the extremely rare American who would call for a revolution to install a centralized government to replace our republican form. Hence, Modern Liberals realize that they have the onus, for the time being, of finding a compromise with capitalism and federalism, so they proceed in an additive fashion, increasing federal government control, management, and power in whatever forms they can, playing on the public's fears, promising people security through Socialism, and contending that any and every problem—from racism and poverty to unemployment and slums—stems from capitalism. The promise of security is one of their most powerful weapons.

It is imperative to keep in mind, however, that except for the "Elites," most Modern Liberals never make a systematic and disciplined study of Marxism, Communism, and Socialism; they do not study the theories that have resulted in the deadly experiments that were inevitable outcomes of these pernicious ideologies. Modern Liberals rarely study their credo in a formal fashion, but rather assimilate it through their culture. As David Conway wrote in *A Farewell to Marx: an Outline and Appraisal of His Theories*, these people absorb the theories of Marx "in the same way that young people often become smokers: that is, through imitation or cultural osmosis."[7] What they learn, for the most part, is just a cursory overview of the theory and history of these ideologies: They learn the values, beliefs, and attitudes that were articulated by Marx and his apostles, but in an indirect, diluted, and "Americanized" form. Countless erroneous beliefs of Marx have been absorbed by the culture at large, but for Modern Liberals, they form the basis of the rationale for centralized government power, usurping private property rights, antagonism to free-market capitalism, abolishing traditional institutions, and rewriting history to affirm their ideology.

What Marxist beliefs have permeated the psyche of Modern Liberals and their progenitors? Let's have a look at some that were clearly articulated by Marx and have metamorphosed and been promulgated, especially in academia. It is a human tendency to assume that most of our present beliefs and concepts have always existed; however, it is imperative to remember that when Marx's ideas were first introduced, they were new and provided some answers—via the new God of science—to explain society's upheavals and dramatic transition to an industrial society. In 19th century Europe, it appeared that people were becoming impoverished and living in filth and disease in overcrowded cities as a consequence of industrialization; the reality was that things were actually improving overall. In America, as in Europe, rural communities and their traditions were being disrupted and even destroyed with mass migrations to the cities from the countryside. A multitude of farms failed in America, but contrary to popular belief, this was not caused primarily by industrialization; people went to cities for the most part *because* the farms were failing and they wanted to escape the widespread poverty in the rural areas. On top of that, after the Civil War, America was dealing with the rebuilding and rapid industrialization of the entire country: Trains transported people and goods rapidly, oil was used for light and heat, and the cities pullulated with immigrants—with their foreign languages, customs, cultures, religions, and ideas.

Science seemed to be able to solve the practical problems of construction, transportation, and energy, so many concluded that it could be applied to society. The *Communist Manifesto* was first published in America in 1871 in Woodhull and Claflin's *Weekly*, a radical magazine that promoted causes such as a single moral standard for men and women, legalized prostitution, Socialism, women's suffrage, free love, and vegetarianism. Marxism seemed to provide some answers. After 1917, the Progressives and the Old Left looked across the Atlantic Ocean and were inspired by what they were convinced was the creation of a dreamland in Russia. Shortly after, Mussolini's regime brought the highest praise from them, and the Old Left envisioned it as a model for America: The term "Fascism" initially had a favorable ring in their quarters until "Uncle Joe" Stalin denounced it, and then the Old Left followed in lockstep, taking their marching orders from Moscow.

But, as outlined in Chapter 3, Stalin's regime became discredited, and the Old Left concluded that classical Marxist *economic* class war was not to be.

So the Left in America picked up on the idea—mainly from the Italian Communist Gramsci—that worldwide "revolution" was not happening because Christianity and Western culture had saturated the souls of man for 20 centuries, blinding them to their true class interests. In order for the revolution to succeed, Gramsci asserted, the emphasis had to change: It needed to focus on freeing people from the chains of Christianity and other Western traditions and values. Gramsci outlined eleven ideas, most of which Modern Liberals embrace today: (1) Change the popular consensus, (2) destroy Christianity, (3) attack the traditional family, (4) change the social mores, (5) change the basic culture, (6) instill Leftist values, (7) get control of the military and courts of law, (8) restrict freedom, (9) socialize the economy, (10) erase American sovereignty, and (11) embrace a world without borders. In concert with this, the Hungarian Marxist George Lukas presented a thesis that took root: "Worldwide overturning of values cannot take place without the annihilation of old values and the creation of new ones by the revolutionaries."[8] He and other German Communists set up the Frankfurt School in 1923. They were driven from Germany with the rise of Nazism, and many came to America. By the 1960s, they were able to reinstate Marxism in cultural terms in American universities, aiding the inception of the New Left, the parents of today's Modern Liberals. The enemy for the first Marxists was only capitalism; it still remains an adversary for Modern Liberals, but Western *culture* has now superseded it. The Frankfurt School, replanted in America, focused on the social sciences. One quite effective technique was branding dissenters as having emotional problems; another tactic was revising American history. References to earlier teachings of Freud were incorporated: The idea was promulgated that there are forces that we cannot see, and these forces bring about changes in people and society. Accompany this was a faith that experts—primarily social scientists—are able to analyze and interpret these unseen forces. With Freud, the unconscious drove much of our behavior, and it is inaccessible to our conscious mind without expert analysis; with Marx, it was the underlying economic forces that needed explanation and interpretation.

Before Marx's ideas and their accompanying interpretations took hold, people recognized personal and moral aspects to poverty; Myron Magnet described this in *The Dream and the Nightmare*:

> [The] poor were either "deserving"—widows, cripples, sober workmen looking for a job, all proper objects of compassion and charity—or "undeserving" drunkards, vagabonds and others able but unwilling to work and therefore worthy only of ostracism and contempt.[9]

After the ideas of Marx and Freud took hold, people's behaviors and circumstances were conceptualized as only the outward manifestations of "unseen" forces driving our society, history, and economies.

Marx's ideas and subsequent modifications have left a legacy that is with us today and permeates the dogma of Modern Liberals. Marxism is awash with flaws that are well described by Sowell[10], Conway[11], and Kolakowski[12], but there is a major overriding one: Marx disregarded and denied the natural human universal and inherent desire for property, status, and power. Marx envisioned a world where people would all become more "fully human," and he prophesized that this would happen when private property was finally abolished. Marx's description of the evils of private property and the alternatives were welcomed by the forerunners of Modern Liberals and passed on, and they are with us in various forms today. Modern Liberals adamantly cling to these falsehoods, even though they may never have read a word or even interpretations of Marx's writings.

Let's take a look at these beliefs, keeping in mind the historical perspective that before Marx these were *not* beliefs about society, government, nations or economics. Marx, when referring to the owners of property who made up the ruling class, primarily used the expression "the means of production" which referred to "property." That term will be used for brevity's sake. Listen for the echoes of these Marxist beliefs in Modern Liberals today.

MARXIST THEORIES ACCEPTED BY TODAY'S MODERN LIBERALS

All property was obtained through violence and/or theft

Mario Puzo, in his book *The Godfather*, began with a statement: "Behind all great fortunes is a great crime." Without proof—in fact with proof to the contrary[13]—Marx postulates this as a fact, and it remains today. Marx: "In actual history, it is a notorious fact that conquest, enslavement, robbery, murder, in short, force, play the greatest part [in the formation of capital]."[14] Think of how Modern Liberals discuss prosperous families: Most of them will be accused of having a history of some kind of crime or violence in acquiring their fortunes. Modern Liberals routinely accuse our Founding Fathers and their predecessors of greed and plunder. In revising history, Modern Liberals imply or state outright that successful entrepreneurs must have cheated and lied along the way. This provides a rationale for two things: First, a justification for not being successful oneself; second, a basis from which to "rightfully" confiscate what they assume was originally stolen or obtained illegally. In 1913, the Progressive academic icon Charles Beard wrote *An Economic Interpretation of the Constitution of the United States,* in which he provided a Marxist interpretation of the founding that was influential for decades. Beard was in agreement with Marx because he proposed that that social progress overall is the result of contending class interests in society. Beard postulated that the structure of the Constitution of the United States was motivated primarily by the Founders' personal economic interests. He wrote that the Constitution was written by "cohesive" elites who sought to protect their personal property and their economic standing. This book has been thoroughly discredited and debunked since then: the founding scholar Forrest McDonald, for example, showed that there were over three dozen different types of interests over which the delegates to the Constitutional Convention bargained. Despite this, the influence of the economic class interpretation of our country's origins echoes today among Modern Liberals.

The owners of the means of production—capitalists—increase profits by squeezing labor

Marx prophesized that with capitalism, it is inevitable that competition increases, and this results in developing more efficient techniques of production. However, even though technology and new methods of production increase efficiency, they can only go so far. After the capitalists reach their peak production efficiency, it becomes difficult to increase profits, so they seize profit from labor. The capitalists squeeze labor by increasing work time, commanding more effort for the same pay, or simply paying less. Marx said that capitalism is based on exploitation of workers by the capitalists' appropriation of the "surplus value" of their labor. The rate of "surplus value," according to Marx, is "an exact expression for the degree of exploitation of labor-power by capital, or of the worker by the capitalist."[15] We hear the echoes of this in a variety of forms from Modern Liberals: They say that the capitalists' profits are unreasonable and they are not improving the lives of their workers; they cite statistics that the CEOs are making x times the amount of the average worker; and they promulgate the myth that companies outsource only to get cheaper labor. Modern Liberals also allege that today's capitalists actually *want* unemployment and benefit from it because, they adduce, it drives wages down. This falsehood stems from the group that Marx designated as the *disposable reserve army*; this is "a mass of human material always ready for exploitation by capital."[16] Marx said that the capitalists wanted to have poor and unemployed people because this would not only help to keep down the wages, but it would make the masses afraid to revolt because they could easily be replaced by people in this "reserve army." Modern Liberals incessantly blame the affluent capitalists for unemployment, aligning with what they have absorbed from Marx's teachings over the past century and a half. It echoes of Marx: "In proportion as capital accumulates, the situation of the laborer, be his payment high or low, must grow worse."[17] Marx's words can be heard—in the modernized version, of course—when today's Modern Liberals speak about the rich getting richer. With Modern Liberals, we hear Marx's original statement rephrased when he wrote that the striving of the moneyed class for more wealth results in the "accumulation of misery, the torment of labor, slavery, ignorance, brutalization, and moral degradation…on the side of the class that produces its own capital."[18]

Monopolies are created to control the market and raise prices to increase profits at the expense of the "common man"

Marx professed that the creation of monopolies is an inevitable outcome of capitalism. The owners of the means of production, Marx said, eventually join forces because in capitalism, large-scale production increases efficiency and this increases profits. Marx basically said they will—indeed, *they have to*—keep increasing their fortunes: "It is a law…that the minimum amount of capital which the capitalist must possess has to go on increasing."[19] Marx also stated that "the development of capitalist production makes it necessary constantly to increase the amount of capital…[The capitalist] can only extend it by means of progressive accumulation."[20] The predecessors of the Modern Liberals, the Progressives, took it a step further: They promulgated the myth that capitalists, once they dominate an industry, will raise prices and the consumers will be at their mercy. This is blatantly false. First of all, monopolies in the private sector—ones not in collusion with the government—*lower prices* for the consumers. We can look to the past to see how oil prices dropped and how cars became affordable for the common man with the advent of mass production, or we can look to the present and see how computers and hand-held calculators are owned by virtually everyone who wants to buy one. Burton W. Folsom, in *The Myth of the Robber Barons: A New Look at the Rise of Big Business in America*; Thomas DiLorenzo, in *How Capitalism Saved America*; and Dominick Armentano in *Myths of Antitrust: Economic Theory and Legal Cases*, are among many who have demonstrated clearly that large-scale businesses that are private and not in collusion with the government actually lower prices and improve quality for the consumers.

Socialism is more efficient than capitalism

We see Modern Liberals attack capitalism with unrelenting fury whenever there are downturns in the economy, declaring that capitalism does not work. Marx said that capitalism is a necessary step in the drive to increase production, but that it reaches a stage in which it cannot increase its productivity and efficiency. Socialism, Marx proclaimed, is the next stage. This is, for Marx and Modern Liberals who have absorbed his ideas, *fact and not theory*, and Marx explained it through "historical materialism." This theory—or *fact* for Marx and his adherents—holds the following precept as articulated by Marx:

> Capitalism is destined to be replaced by Socialism because the economic fluctuations to which capital is subject reveal that capitalism is incapable of maintaining full use of the resources of an advanced industrial society.[21]

In addition, Marx points out, capitalism will be inefficient because the capitalists have to force labor to work at jobs that are "alienating," and the workers do not fully focus on their work (as they would under Socialism, of course), so managers are necessary to keep the workers in line. According to Marx, this managerial class would no longer be needed under Socialism, thus reducing that cost. In addition, according to Marx, the capitalists invariably waste profits advertising and creating unnecessary need; under utopian Socialism, people would focus on what they really need and what is more human. Today, we hear the echoes of this when Modern Liberals speak of alienated workers and those who have no choice but to accept unwanted jobs for survival. Modern Liberals also allege that advertisers convince the unwitting public to buy unnecessary products only to increase the profits of the capitalists. Of course, this implies that advertising and even the amount and type of what is produced should be regulated and controlled by the federal government.

Socialism is inevitable; Socialism is the future

Marx postulated the historical inevitability of Socialism superseding capitalism. According to Marx, capitalism is only an intermediate stage before Socialism. To believe otherwise, Marx declared, is simply an error; the error is having "viewed the capitalist order as the absolute and ultimate form of social production, instead of a historically transient stage of development,"[22] and Modern Liberals concur. The capitalists will try to prevent this, Marx prophesied, but they will eventually vanish or be overthrown. Marxists of the Old Left ascribed to the notion that Nazism was really the death throes of capitalism, the last attempt of capitalists to resist the coming Socialist revolutions. Today, we hear Modern Liberals proclaim that the more advanced nations of Europe have successfully embraced Socialism, and that capitalists and reactionaries—especially in America—are in a futile struggle to try and stop the steadily encroaching Socialism. *Newsweek* magazine recently (February 16, 2009) had on its cover the title of its lead article: "We are All Socialists Now." Resistance, Modern Liberals declare, is not only futile; it is retrograde. The truth is that Socialism is a regression to a more primitive form of organization, dressed up in the rhetoric of "science" and "progress." If we look at the past, from ancient Egypt and China to 20th century fascist Japan and Nazi Germany, we see the centuries-old drive to centralize control of the economy. People have fought and died to raise humanity out of that pit and to create structures that allow the common man to participate in free and voluntary exchanges with his own property. Socialism's central planning of the economy is a historical regression. The earliest forms of Socialism as an "ism" appeared in France and other places before Marx, but the central themes go much farther back. Western civilization contributed something unparalleled in the past several centuries: The individual is emphasized, not the State. The State serves individuals in that it sets up a framework within which individuals are free to make choices. This was progress toward modernity and its accompanying liberty. Pure "individualism" results in anarchy, of course; ergo, a set of laws that limits government to primary functions is where true freedom lies. Earlier in the history of man, there always was the all-powerful centralized state where life was predictable and the economy was controlled. Socialism, in its essence, is a throwback to those more primitive times.

There is already enough wealth for everyone, but the capitalists are hoarding it

Marx asserted that society—even in his time—had sufficient wealth to guarantee that the needs of everyone could be met, but that the owners of the means of production were unwilling to share it. In addition, Marx asserted that even more could be produced if the means of production were out of the hands of the inefficient and wasteful capitalists. Again, we hear the echoes of this in Modern Liberals when they are asked from where they will get funds for their programs: They answer that the well-to-do are holding on to the money, and if the bounty would be shared (i.e., "redistributed") everyone could have full health care, poverty would be eliminated, education could be "free," and the standard of living could be raised. Since the well-heeled are not willing to share of their own volition, Modern Liberals profess, their profits, income, and inheritances must be heavily taxed. All of these declarations mean that they actually assume that all the wealth needed to realize their fantasies is already available. Modern Liberals allege that people are poor—and stay poor—because the wealth is being somehow confiscated and hoarded by the rich capitalists. This flies in the face of the fact that virtually all people in the lowest economic quintile raise themselves out of it within ten years, along with the fact that these "rich" people are the ones creating the prosperity of the masses through investments and starting up new businesses.[23]

The ruling classes establish our desires and values

Marx thought that those in control of the means of production are also in control of the information the masses get, so they establish values that will support their power:

> The class which is the ruling material force of society is…its ruling intellectual force…The class which has the means of material production at its disposal, consequently also controls the means of mental production, so that the ideas of those that lack the means of mental production are on the whole subject to it…Their [the controlling capitalists'] ideas are the ruling ideas of the epoch.[24]

Religion is a typical example: The ruling classes encourage people to believe in God, Marx postulated, because the masses will then be less pre-disposed to strive to fulfill their full potential on earth, they will look for-ward to an afterlife, their impoverished condition will be endured more readily and easily, and they will be much less likely to rise up against their capitalist oppressors. In a similar manner, Modern Liberals claim that rich capitalists control the media and advertising and thus have established the values of the masses, and they say that the capitalists influence and control our desires in this way. Modern Liberals do not look at advertising as providing informa-tion and increasing choices that people are free to accept or reject; Modern Liberals imply that people are really not in conscious control of their choices. By professing that the masses have been brainwashed and really have limited choice, Modern Liberals have a justification for central government control of the media and means of production.

History can be "correctly" understood by viewing it in terms of classes struggling against one another

Marx viewed class struggle in terms of economic classes (generally bourgeois and proletarian), or between those who controlled the means of production and the workers. "Class" is defined by Marx as people who are in similar groups in the production of something. "Class-divided societies" are those in which some do and some do not control means of production, and Marx presumed this is how history can be explained and understood. For example, according to this worldview, in Greece and Rome there were slaves and owners, and the masters used the slaves' labor-power; and in feudal society there were lords and serfs, and the lords confiscated their production but allowed some land or time to be used for their own consumption of the fruits of their labor, leaving the serfs little control. Today, these people say, there are capitalists and wage-earners: The wage-earners have control over their labor and can withdraw it, but they do not control the means of production. When early Marxists saw that the proletarians were not forming a sufficient cohesive class consciousness to rise up, later Marxists transitioned "class" struggle from purely economic classes into new classifications such as race and ethnicity. These new "groups" retained the relation of economic classes: The Marxists said factors such as racism and ethnicism were the primary *causes* of poverty and economic inequality. It was postulated that capitalism was supporting racism to maintain cheap labor. The New Leftists and Modern Liberals increased the number of categories of the "oppressed": They added women, then the mentally and physically handicapped, and most recently those with specific "sexual preferences." It reached an ultimate absurdity: Over 70 percent of Americans now qualify for special status as some kind of "oppressed victim" in our society. When listening to Modern Liberals, one quickly notices their incessant references to groups supposedly struggling against the ruling classes, aligning with Marx's interpretation of history as one of class struggle.

In order to preserve the Marxist idea of class struggles, Modern Liberals often use "deconstruction" to analyze and explain how our very language reflects, preserves, and reinforces class structures. Deconstruction purportedly analyzes structures of control and power. For example, patriarchy, according to this notion, is supported in the Bible with linguistic references to God as a male: *He* created the world. Another example is when people make speeches they may refer to "mankind" which ostensibly supports this idea. This is basically a kind of intellectual relativism which denies that truth can exist independently of race, nation, and class. Modern Liberal academics simply expanded and applied this to more and more groups to *deconstruct* the idea of the universality and unity of human reason. This led, in turn, to political correctness in universities which has resulted in the suppression of intellectual freedom accompanied by increased intolerance. This doctrine is tyrannical because people are required to conform to the ideas and dogma of those who are supposedly "free" of these cultural biases and able to analyze and uncover (deconstruct) the "truth" of the underlying structures. Once again, we see Modern Liberals—this time in academia—bellowing for "experts" who are needed to analyze our biases and guide us in unearthing sources of oppression and power.

Socialism will make people more "human"

Marx deemed that property and competition for it made men ruthless, led to war, and turned people away from high culture; he contended that in a capitalist society, people even choose friends and marriage partners on the basis of how that will help their economic status. Modern Liberals incessantly complain that conflict among individuals and nations are the result of capitalist competition, greed, and impoverishment; even the terrorist attacks on America, they claim, were a result of economic imperialism, the impoverishment of Third World countries, and the rapacity of the "military-industrial complex." Modern Liberals denounce America as a crass and materialistic nation with people interested only in making profits. In addition, Modern Liberals, along with Marx, contend that laborers are really alienated from work and the capitalists are not interested in the humane aspects of labor; the capitalists, they conclude, are only concerned with increasing their fortunes. Marx referred to the full actualization of human potentialities as "human essence." He initially wrote that the workers under Communism would be able to change jobs when they are so inclined. Marx later realized that this fanciful thinking would not be possible in a complex economy, so he modified it and asserted the following:

I. There will be much more free time from reduced labor hours. This free time will enable the workers to actualize themselves.

2. The free time will come because Socialist production is more efficient. Socialist modes of production are scientific; they do not deal with as much overhead as capitalism and are less wasteful of labor time and resources.
3. The workers will be more focused with their work because they will be happier. This will result in their being more productive and efficient. Thus, fewer hours of labor will be needed.

In implicit agreement with these Marxist principles, Modern Liberals make incessant references to how wonderful Socialism is in Europe and how perfectly it is working there. Their proof? All of their free time! They get six weeks off a year! They work shorter hours. According to the Modern Liberals, Europeans are happier than we are! Their utterances align perfectly with Marx's method for eliminating the "alienation" of workers in a complex economy. Marx wrote: "[In] the true realm of freedom…the reduction of the working day is the basic prerequisite."[25]

Labor creates value and is not getting paid accordingly

Marx had complex theorems and formulas to analyze and explain how labor creates value and how the capitalists live off surplus labor: "[That] which determines the magnitude of the value of any article is the amount of…labor time socially necessary for its production."[26] Today's Modern Liberals cling to this basic premise and say that—even though the standard of living is improving with each generation, and even with each decade—those in control of the means of production, the CEOs, and the owners and stockholders of companies are taking more profit than they "should." This aligns with the Marxist idea that they are confiscating too much of the "surplus labor" of their oppressed workers and has two implications: First, "too much" can be somehow defined and determined, and second, if it is "too much," it should be confiscated and redistributed or it must be "shared" with the workers.

Capitalism makes people greedy

We hear this from Modern Liberals all the time as one of their primary justifications for government ownership or increased control of the means of production. As explained in Chapter 13, with people in a free-market economy, anyone who starts a business has to conceive of what others need and want, there is mutual cooperation in voluntary exchanges, and trust is implied when one receives a product or pays with a check or promise to pay in the future. But Marx looked at this exchange in a perverted fashion, just as today's Modern Liberals do: Marx wrote that a capitalist "places himself at the disposal of his neighbors' most deprived fancies, panders to his needs, excites unhealthy appetites in him, and pounces on every weakness."[27] Marx professed that capitalism forces people to look at others as only a means to one's own ends. Capitalism, according to Marx, creates a society of latent hostility of people toward one another. Marx wrote that it "dissolves the human world into a world of atomistic individuals confronting each other in enmity," and wrote that capitalist society harbors "the intention to plunder, to deceive...Since every self-interested person seeks to outdo the other, we must necessarily strive to deceive the other."[28, 29] Modern Liberals, when they denounce materialism, sound just like Marx a century and a half ago who wrote: "The more you *have*, the greater is your *alienated* life...All passions and all activity are lost in *greed*."[30]

Since society first owned all property and it was stolen by the capitalists, society has a right to reclaim it

Marx declared that all ownership of the means of production was initially gotten through theft or violence. Ipso facto, the very basis of the present ownership is not valid; the predecessors of today's capitalists, according to Marx, all acquired property that was stolen or commandeered from the society at large. Modern Liberals accept this Marxist idea and make references to how the capitalists are thieves, got their property through machinations, bribery, and collusion among themselves, and are outright criminals. Modern Liberals advocate nationalization of industries but in a stepwise fashion: confiscatory capital gains taxes, heavy regulation, and high rates of inheritance taxes. Some Modern Liberals even go to the point of saying that all inheritance over a specific amount should be taxed at 100 percent! Modern Liberals would advocate—as they did in the past for the transportation, communication, medical, and energy industries—for complete nationalization and control of our economy by the government, but the horrors of these practices in places such as Russia, China, and Cambodia are still fresh in our minds, so they restrain themselves for the time being.

Religion is an opiate of the masses

Modern Liberals completely misunderstand Marx on this one, and they only think about and support that statement to use in their attacks on organized religions that do not go along with their agenda. It is important to note that Modern Liberals do not attack all religions; they only attack those that do not align with their ideology and those that inspire public expression of religious sentiments. Moreover, Modern Liberals limit those attacks to Christian denominations.

Marx first said that the owners of the means of production encouraged religious beliefs in order to support capitalists' control: According to Marx, the capitalists encouraged beliefs in an afterlife because these beliefs would make it easier for workers to endure earthly oppression and poverty; religion would also make them feel more guilt-ridden, thus obviating the desire for revolution; religion would reinforce the general deference to authority and power; and, most of all, religion would negate the desire to achieve full humanity on earth by telling people that they are evil and by promising paradise in the future. Religious belief, Marx alleged, was simply *a symptom* of exploitation under capitalism: "Religious suffering is at one and the same time the expression of real suffering and a protest against real suffering. Religion is the sign of an oppressed creature...*It is the opium of the people*" (emphasis added)[30] Marx did not advise abolishing religion; this idea is a perversion of his original thesis. Marx said that religion would simply disappear under Communism because under Communism people would no longer be alienated and they would cooperate and attain their full humanity. When they focus on their true humanity in the Communist utopia, the false beliefs that were there to maintain the power of the capitalists would simply wither and die. Today's Modern Liberals denounce religion and God because they stand in the way of devotion to the State. In this, they follow Marx, who wrote that "for man the supreme being is man, and thus with the categorical imperative to overthrow all conditions in which man is a debased, enslaved, neglected and contemptible being." Religion was one of those "conditions" for Marx, and it is for Modern Liberals.

In addition, since Modern Liberals have switched from perceiving society purely in terms of economic classes and include attacks on the prevailing culture, some religions have become their enemy. The religions that thwart the advance of their agenda are those which are most viciously attacked. For example, Modern Liberals want full acceptance, by the entire society, of homosexual sex. The Catholic Church maintains that these people are loved by God, of course, but that homosexual sex is a sin, just as adultery between married people and premarital sex are sins. So the Church is attacked viciously at every opportunity.

———————

In reality, forces of the free market are impersonal and anonymous. People buy and sell virtually anything, create and distribute products, and request and purchase services: All of the millions and even *billions* of exchanges and transactions affect supply, needs, work, production, and prices. The results of these daily interactions are, in reality, impossible to predict, control, or manage. Some people, however, feel compelled to control that which they cannot. With the advent of academicians saying that new scientific principles could be used to guide and develop new social and economic structures, the temptations to try to control are great.

The Socialists-Marxists told people that they would bring a *new* kind of freedom, one that would liberate people from economic burdens and usher in a *higher form*: freedom from economic need. In reality, it is only a justification to redistribute wealth. This promise of a new kind, a superior kind, of freedom was excellent propaganda. The irony, however, is that the promise was built on the very traditions that Modern Liberals and their predecessors would tear down if they could—the society that established a framework where true liberty could flourish and allow people to prosper by making individual choices under Rule of Law and protections of private property.

Marxism has been revised over and over in the past century and a half; it does not survive as a system of economics, of course, but as an analysis and dogmatic view of society. And Modern Liberals embrace it to this day.

6

Do Modern Liberals Really Hate America?

Nowhere at present is there such a measureless loathing of their country by educated people as in America.

—Eric Hoffer, author of
The True Believer

For many of us, it appears that Modern Liberals actually hate and revile America. After the September 11 terrorist attack that resulted in more deaths to civilians than to soldiers at Pearl Harbor, we were shocked at the ugly aspersions and accusations being hurled at America—by Americans! Most of us are familiar with the more infamous one: "The chickens have come home to roost."

Universities are a stronghold of Modern Liberalism, a place where they speak their minds quite candidly. The halls of academia are the places where the loathsome denunciations of America by Modern Liberals go largely unchallenged, where a college professor can ask, "What has America done to make itself this kind of target?" After September 11, a torrent of blame and excoriations of America poured out from our centers of "higher learning." Following is a small sample:

University of Massachusetts journalism professor Bill Israel said "[the attack was] the predictable result of American policy."

In Marquette University, students were banned from having a moment of silence around an American flag; it was feared it could alienate foreign students.

At Florida Gulf Coast University, a librarian banned students from wearing "I'm proud to be an American" badges, ostensibly in the name of "tolerance and civility."

At Central Michigan State, flags or pictures that were pro-American had to be taken down.

At San Diego State University, when an Ethiopian student reported that he heard Arabic speaking students praising Osama bin Laden for killing Americans, he was put on "warning."

At Arizona State University, students were banned from hanging an American flag in the cafeteria.

John Hopkins professor Charles Fairbanks openly supported our war on terrorism; this resulted in his being fired from his position in an institute.

In New York, a professor lost a friend on the terrorist flight and she wanted to hang a flag in his honor. The dean himself took it down after she refused to do so.

Yale university professor Paul Kennedy said that American culture had provoked the hatred that was behind the attacks.

In discussions of the attack at Brown University, professors were required to ask students why they thought America was hated.

At the University of Wisconsin students broke into singing "The Star Spangled Banner," but protestors cut them off with an Iraqi song.

But not all indictments of America after September 11 came from the universities. Susan Sontag, still an icon of Modern Liberals, said that September 11 was "not a 'cowardly' attack on 'civilization' or 'liberty' or 'humanity' or 'the free world,' but it was an attack on the world's self-proclaimed superpower, undertaken as a consequence of specific American alliances and actions...[The terrorists] were not cowards."

Playwright Harold Pinter said that September 11 was "a predictable and inevitable act of retaliation against the constant and systematic manifestation of state terrorism on the part of the United States."

In Berkeley, an omphalos for Modern Liberalism activism centered at the University of California, fire fighters were ordered to remove American flags from their trucks; the department feared locals would attack and damage the vehicles.

David Westin, president of *ABC News*, told the newscasters not to wear American flag pins on camera because that would be "taking sides."

Soon after the strike on our country, Michael Moore wrote in the *San Francisco Chronicle* how "the American flag stands for intimidation, censorship, violence, bigotry, sexism, homophobia...Who are we calling terrorists here?"

Can we conclude that most Modern Liberals actually *hate* America? If we approach the idea of "America" as a place consisting of fifty states, a recognized sovereign nation, or a land mass covering four million square miles, the answer certainly is *no*. However, if we look at America as an idea, what it symbolizes, its realization of specific founding principles, the reasons for its exceptionality, and its unique traditions—covered in Part II—the answer becomes a resounding *yes*. For example, President Obama exemplifies and typifies the attitude of Modern Liberals about American exceptionality, and Charles Krauthammer described it:

> Obama drew the picture of an America quite exceptional—exceptional in moral culpability and heavy-handedness, for dismissiveness and derisiveness (toward Europe), for maltreatment of natives, for torture, for Hiroshima, for Guantanamo, for unilateralism, and for insufficient respect for the Muslim world.[1]

Krauthammer went on to describe the mindset:

> [The] New Liberalism [is] rooted in the conviction that America is so intrinsically flawed, so inherently and congenitally sinful that is cannot be trusted...America itself is corrupt—in the sense of being deeply flawed, and with the history to prove it.[2]

117

Daniel Flynn writes why these people hate America:

America stands as a massive refutation of every pet theory that the Left has ever held. Capitalism is a failed economic system, the Left incessantly pronounces [but] the most free-market nation on earth is also the richest. America, their mantra goes, is a racist country. Yet immigrants of color flock to our shores and borders...The United States, they continue, subjugates women. Nowhere in the world, however, is the status of women as high as it is in America and the West...The Left condemns Christianity...as intolerant. In America...people can practice any religion they want—even ones that are inherently hostile to Christians...Rather than revise their inept theories, the Left lashes out at the nation that disproves them.[3]

The source of this hatred is quite simple (see Chapter 4). The simple fact is that to Modern Liberals, America—as a principle and idea—has stood in the way of the realization of the "dream" for almost a century. Many of the original antebellum Socialists set up their communities and their utopias and tried to live out their fantasy of a nirvana without private property, marriage, or capitalism, but they isolated themselves from the mainstream of society. People were not forced to stay. If they shared children and wives, the rest of the country did not have to follow suit. And if someone left, it was a short walk or horse ride to the outside society. If they failed, it did not affect the rest of the country.

After the Civil War, inspiration came from abroad, mostly from Germany. Bismarck made the first grand attempt at Socialism on a national scale, motivating Progressives in America. The post-Civil War progressives were naïve, postulating that scientific management could create a Shangri-La, and that a central power was necessary to carry this out. Then, with the grand experiment of the largest nation in the world—Russia—it seemed possible. The dreamers, the power hungry, the frustrated, and the fearful wanted to replicate this in the United States. As suggested in the "challenge" proposed to readers in the last chapter, take a look at *any* history of the Left—one that begins from the late 19th century—and you will find that Bismarck's state Socialism and the Russian Revolution were powerful influences on the precursors of Modern Liberals, the American Progressives.

But something stood in the way. After the Russian Revolution, the Progressives and the Old Left envisaged a burgeoning paradise in Russia that would be a model for the rest of the world. To the consternation and frustration of the Old Left, America did not even recognize the USSR as a sovereign entity for almost two decades. Franklin Roosevelt finally did because of pressures from the rising Nazi state, but even then there were those who advised against its recognition because they knew that the dream was really a nightmare.

Using hindsight, Modern Liberals today propose that Communism was a doomed system, destined to fail. Modern Liberals cherry-pick some events and omit or deny others, selecting and negating whatever helps to promote their ideology. Modern Liberals deny that their legacy is one in which their fore-runners welcomed and celebrated Communism. They assert that Communism never really became a danger anyway, but was only presented as such by fear-mongering "right-wingers" and capitalist supporters of the so-called "military-industrial complex." Modern Liberals and their New Leftist parents insist that those who believed Communism was a threat to liberty and civilization were "paranoid."

The fact that the grandparents of Modern Liberals, the Old Leftists, wanted some form of a Communist nation is irrefutable. Modern Liberals claim that their predecessors were ignorant of the realities in the USSR, misguided, or a tiny minority. But the leading journals and magazines of the Left of that time wrote panegyrics to Russia's new political system, tried to begin a revolution, and promoted candidates who were Socialists, sympathetic to the Soviet state. The American Communist Party even supported and financed a candidate for the presidency in 1948. Modern Liberals not only *deny* that their grandparents in high-level government positions—like Alger Hiss, Julius Rosenberg, Lawrence Duggan, and Harry Dexter White—were spies for the Soviet Union, they actually still support, protect and eulogize them!

But was there a danger of Communism spreading? Was this fear of Communism just "paranoia" as the New Leftists and Modern Liberals pro-claim it was? Modern Liberals sometimes go so far as to suggest that the American Communists were only reformers who later helped in the Civil Rights Movement, but that is to deny history. The history of the Communist threat to the free world is not one open to interpretation, and it is not dis-torted for purposes of propaganda. Simply take a look at world maps from 1922 until 1989 and see the obvious. Below are four world maps from that era: 1922, when the Soviet Union was officially formed, almost five years after the revolution itself; 1945, when World War II ended; 1965, at the highest point in the presidency of Lyndon Johnson; and 1989, just barely more than two short decades ago.

The Spread of Marxist-Communist Regimes: 1922 to 1989

Map 1: 1922

Map 2: 1945

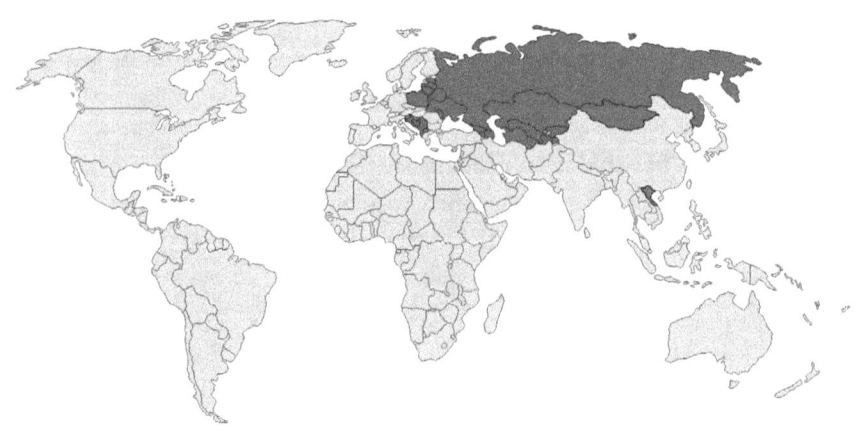

Map 3: 1965

Map 4: 1989

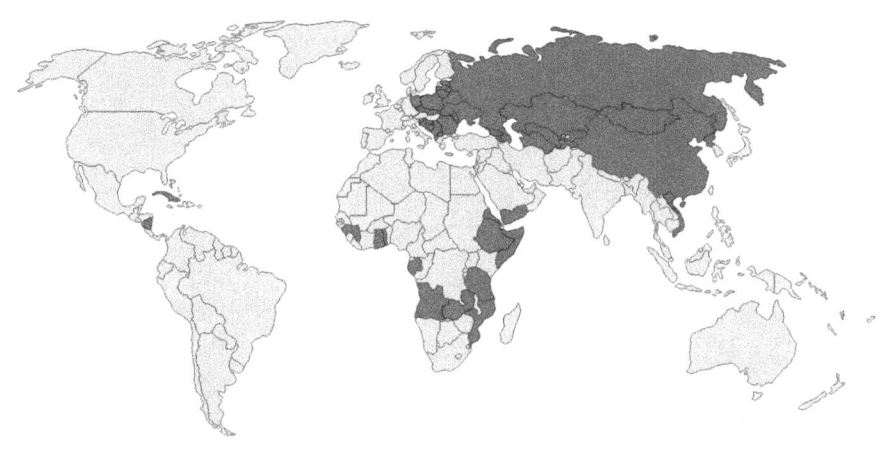

A cursory glance at these maps unmasks the undeniable reality. Today's Modern Liberals say that by the 1970s, Communism had reached its zenith and its decline began. The truth is that their parents and grandparents said this *after* the USSR formally renounced Communism. If we take a look at what the Old and New Left actually said as late as the 1980s, we see how they conveniently dissemble about their own history:

> Sovietologist Seweryn Bialer, 1982, *Foreign Affairs*: "The Soviet Union is not now nor will it be during the next decade in the throes of a true systemic crisis, for it boasts enormous unused reserves of political and social stability."

> Arthur Schlesinger, Jr. 1982: "Those in the United States who think the Soviet Union is on the verge of economic and social collapse [are] wishful thinkers who are only kidding themselves."

> John Kenneth Galbraith, 1984: "That the Soviet system has made great material progress in recent years is evident both from the statistics and from the general urban scene...One sees it in the appearance of solid well-being of the people on the streets...and the general aspect of restaurants, theaters, and shops...Partly, the Russian system succeeds because, in contrast with the Western industrial economies, it makes full use of its manpower."

> Paul Samuelson, Nobel Prize winner, 1985: "[T]here can be no doubt that the Soviet planning system has been a powerful engine for economic growth...The Soviet model has surely demonstrated that a command economy is capable of mobilizing resources for rapid growth."

> Lester Thurow, MIT economist, 1988: "Can economic command significantly...accelerate the growth process? The remarkable performance of the Soviet Union suggests that it can...Today the Soviet Union is a country whose economic achievements bear comparison with those of the United States."

The horrors under the Communist regimes were denied by the Old Left for years, but little by little they could no longer suppress, excuse, or distort the realities of the regimes. In *The Black Book of Communism*, Kramer, Murphy, Werth, and Panne document that the murderous Communist regimes were responsible for up to *100 million deaths*. Modern Liberals and their precursors try to distance themselves from all of this by making two claims: The first and most ridiculous is that their predecessors had no connection to the Communists and never gave them any support. The second is that "Communism" itself did not lead to this, but it was evil men who seized power. But the starvation, impoverishment, failure, and deaths that always ensued after a Communist government got into power rendered their assertions hollow. Today anyone who advocates a Communist paradise can be found only in universities and on the fringes of society.

Hatred of America by the progenitors of today's Modern Liberals rarely existed during the first decades of the rise of Fascism and Communism. There were some who held this animosity, and they even existed among the dreamers that predated Marx and the Civil War, but they were few and insignificant. It was not until after Communism actually started its successful spread after World War II that the vilification and denunciation of America began in earnest. The United States stood in the way of the dream. America was there, again and again, blocking Communism's spread and holding back expansion with its military and its leadership in alliances such as NATO and SEATO. It is virtually certain that if America did not support Europe with the Marshall Plan, the policy of "containment," and America's organizing and leading NATO, the Communists would have spread from Eastern Europe to Western Europe; in fact, Stalin and his lackeys to the west had a post-war plan to do exactly that. If it were not for the United Nations, led by America, the North Koreans would have easily overrun the southern part of the peninsula, and they most certainly would have advanced into Japan as well.

We can only guess what "might have" happened if America had never gone to Vietnam, and scholars and laymen alike speculate about whether we should have used greater force in the beginning, invaded the north, or never have gone there in the first place after France decided to abandon its colony. We should heed, however, the words of the prime ministers of Singapore and Thailand when they said that American's presence prevented a Communist takeover of Southeast Asia; we should remember Australia's willingness to send troops out of the same concerns; and we should not forget the Communist overthrow of Laos, the boat people, the re-education camps of Vietnam, and the Killing Fields of Cambodia.

Even with what could possibly be considered the most murderous regime of them all, the Khmer Rouge in Cambodia, the predecessors of Modern Liberals adhered to the same pattern: In the beginning, Pol Pot was described by the New Left as an "agrarian reformer." With the first accusations of his genocide, the parents of Modern Liberals denied it completely. Then, after the murders of millions—some for wearing glasses and others for having too much education—no longer able to deny it, the forefathers of today's Modern Liberals did what they always do: They distanced themselves from the issue and said it was America's fault. They asserted that the Khmer Rouge had been driven to near insanity by the bombing of their country by America, and this resulted in their murderous rage, implying that it never would have happened if it were not for the United States.

America also stood in the way of the "dream" because it presented the contrast to Communism, a contrast to the truth of the Communist world. The Communists had to close their borders, not to people who wanted to go in—they were rare—but to those who wanted to leave. And those who did manage to escape told the stories of the oppression, brutality, and misery behind the barbed wires and machine gun turrets on the Communist sides of the borders.

America's obstructing the dream was the fount of most animosity toward America. After the murderous regime of Stalin could no longer be denied, almost all of the Old Left became disheartened and few could continue to support Russia. After Khrushchev denounced Stalin's murderous rampages, the Old Left fell into disarray. David Horowitz, a former Communist whose parents were party members, recalls those days when he witnessed "[the] 'Khrushchev divorces,' of 1956—the twenty-year marriages in our parents' generation that ended in disputes between the partners over the 'correct' political position to take toward his secret report on the crimes of Stalin," where one spouse wanted to still pay homage to Stalin's regime and the other acceded to the truth and gave up the anti-American struggle.[4]

Some of the Old Left started the "anti-anti-Communist" idea: They wanted to keep the dream alive and had some hope for China, but they were afraid to openly support another Communist regime. So rather than openly back Mao, they simply contended that "anti-Communism" in America was going too far, ostensibly endangering our right to free speech, whipping up Americans into a near frenzy, and putting us in danger of starting yet another world war. Thus, they generated an "anti-anti Communist" movement. (Today, Modern Liberals apply the same tactic with "anti-anti-terrorism.") All the while, American KGB agents were giving as much military and strategic information as they could to Russia and China, stealing nuclear secrets from America, and trying to influence American policy to benefit the Russian and Chinese Communist regimes.[5, 6]

Fortunately, this alleged anti-Communist "fever" actually helped to thwart Soviet-sponsored American Communism. The Soviet Union pulled back virtually all of its operations within America and withdrew most of its support of the American Communist Party.

Enter the New Left: They were contemptuous of what they saw as the apathy of the Old Left, and they were young and enthusiastic. These New Leftists needed new heroes and new causes. One was the Civil Rights movement, which provided an opportunity to brand America as a racist and oppressive society. Another was the war in Vietnam that could be used to renew Lenin's thesis about the next level of capitalism: imperialism. According to Lenin, Marx did not foresee the stage of imperialism. Imperialism, according to this interpretation, was an intermittent stage in the transition to world-wide Communism. The capitalists, according to Lenin's interpretation, seized the cheap resources and labor of poor nations and "bought off" the workers in their home countries to prevent worker revolts. The New Left described America's involvement in Vietnam as "Capitalist Imperialism": They asserted that those in charge of this American imperialism wanted to stop an agrarian reformer (Ho Chi Minh) in a small and defenseless country of peace-loving farmers from carrying out the will of his people and expelling the exploiters from their land. The American imperialists wanted, the New Leftists declared, to impose their will and squeeze profits from yet one more colony of the "American Empire."

These parents of today's Modern Liberals, some of whom *became* today's Modern Liberals, concluded that new weapons were needed to topple this "capitalist-imperialist" American regime, the one that was preventing the "dream" from being realized in an agrarian land of peace-loving and exotic people, so they started attacks on the culture and traditions of America itself. New histories of America were written, based on the idea that America was built on a foundation of racism, genocide, and greed, all to enhance the power of the ruling class. William Appleman Williams promoted this idea and presented a rather sophisticated theory that soft-pedaled this denunciation of America itself: According to this Marxist icon of the New Left, America used to have a frontier, and this led to America's becoming a capitalist, acquisitive, and combative nation with a history of increasingly appropriating more land and resources. But, according to Williams, America had reached its shores, and since there was no more land to seize on the continent, it continued abroad with its rapacious appetite. In reality, Williams was simply joining the "Blame America" club that accused America of every world problem and would not admit that the truth was elsewhere: that America was thwarting the Communist "dream" all around the world.

From the late 1950s, anti-Americanism became a "badge of authenticity" among intellectuals. A decade later, to speak of the "American way of life" invited condescension among New Leftists. For them, being "educated" meant rejecting traditional values. Roger Kimball, contributing to a chapter in the book *Understanding Anti-Americanism: Its Origins and Impact at Home and Abroad*, wrote the following:

> What we might call contemporary anti-Americanism…was born in the aftermath of the Second World War…The image of America as essentially evil and corrupt was widely taken up and parroted by American intellectuals in the 1950s and 1960s. More and more, anti-Americanism became a necessary badge of authenticity for writers and intellectuals…It is nearly impossible for anyone with a college education to speak of "the American way of life" without irony or condescension…It is now practically taken for granted that going to college involves not so much the "questioning" as the repudiation of traditional moral and political values.[7, 8]

With the help of dogmatic Marxists-turned-sociologists and psychologists, the New Left proceeded to attack American culture and history itself, hoping to undermine the foundations of what they believed stood in the way of achieving paradise on earth. American culture itself was not only racist and oppressive, they said, but it was stifling, ignorant, and repressive for the middle class, who incorrectly assumed that life was good. Life was not good, the New Left postulated; those who were participating in the capitalist machine were not even aware of how they were held back from being "fully human," from realizing their "full potential," and from achieving the bliss of "self-actualization" which would liberate them from their bonds. Americans had been brainwashed, they insisted, by the capitalist system itself, inculcated with what really made them miserable. Just as the early utopian thinkers, as well as Marx and Engels themselves, asserted, the New Leftists said that the ties of family, religion, materialism, and capitalism prevented people from becoming what they *could be*, and obstructing the realization of the dream. And America exemplified the worst of it all: Americans were "clinging to their Bibles and their guns," they were materialistic and greedy, and their culture nourished this. It was imperative, these New Leftists concluded, to change the culture. They depicted capitalism as enslaving people's very souls with the materialist ethos it created; the New Leftists claimed it was degenerating art, literature, and high culture. Poverty—even though it has always existed—was presented as the ineluctable outcome of the failure of capitalism. The desire to "get ahead," they maintained, was only a mindless rat-race. Patriotism was no longer an expression of one's love of country: For the New Left, it meant imperialism, hate, and war-mongering. The New Left proclaimed that a new history and culture had to be created.

It was easy for the New Leftists—born into affluence that they took for granted—to vilify the very prosperity they enjoyed. After all, it provided them—and there were masses of these Baby Boomers—with the leisure and means to envision a new society. And the Old Left was there for them, in the colleges and the universities, to tutor and encourage them. The Elites, especially in the universities, had a huge captive audience of idealistic young people to convince that America is evil, immoral, and oppressive. These Old Leftist professors played on their students' naiveté, youthful idealism, and lack of real life experience. The professors would conjure up a worldly Arcadia, a visionary society free of racism, a place where poverty has been eradicated and where there is complete cooperation and no more cutthroat competition. They presented as real a nation where its citizens' desires—especially sexual—are fulfilled with little effort and no payment, and a land where there are no individuals living in opulence by feeding off the labor of others. This Shangri-La was always presented to these young people *as a reality,* and they were shown how their country not only fell far short of this, but how its traditions, values, institutions, and free market thwarted its realization. Young people were told that this world is attainable if only certain forces, people, and structures would not prevent this utopia from coming into being. In short, the dream was presented as a reality that was being thwarted by the existing structures of capitalism, racism, sexism, and a host of other "isms" and entrenched interests.

Paul Hollander, in *Understanding Anti-Americanism,* described the psyche of these New Leftists and Modern Liberals:

> [It has] ever-escalating utopian expectations that can never be fulfilled...No matter how successful America is at delivering freedom and material prosperity to large numbers of people, it will always fall short until *every* human on the planet is well fed, secure, attractive, healthy, and

brimming with self-esteem…When coupled with a distortion of the historical evidence, this utopian standard drives much of anti-Americanism… Thus critiques of core attributes of American life and ideals can be fairly characterized as anti-American when they are unsupported by evidence or are based on unrealistic expectations…[This] criticism of America…distorts the historical record, holds American behavior up to impossible utopian standards not imposed on other peoples, and attacks ideals and traits quintessentially American, will perforce be anti-American.[9]

So, for more than four decades, from the end of World War II until the Soviet Union announced that it was no longer Communist, America was there, standing in the way of the "dream" of worldwide Socialism. In 1945, Russia overtook Eastern Europe and planned to extend its reach to the Atlantic Ocean, but there was America with the Marshall Plan and NATO. Mao overtook China, and America supported his Chinese rival Chiang Kai-shek and then protected Taiwan from being taken over by Mao's army. Communist North Korea invaded the southern part of the peninsula, and America was there, once again. Then, in order to contain the Communists in Asia, SEATO—the Southeast Asian Treaty Organization—was formalized on September 8, 1954, in Manila, as part of the Truman Doctrine of creating anti-Communist bilateral and collective defense treaties. Later, America supported the anti-Communist regimes in Vietnam, first with funds and advisors, and then with our own men and women. America went wherever the Communists tried to extend their power and influence—funding Turkey, sending military equipment to outposts in Africa, helping the Afghanistan freedom fighters resist the murderous Soviets, and funding anti-Communist regimes throughout Latin America. America first slowed down the spread of Communism, then it contained it, and finally, under Ronald Reagan's leadership, America started pushing it back, beginning with Grenada in 1981, for the first time in the entire history of Communism. And the Old Left, the New Left, and Modern Liberals grew to despise America for this.

Of course, Modern Liberals do not declare, "America stood in the way of world Communism, therefore I hate America." What happened was that a *culture* developed from the original frustrations of the Old Left toward America for thwarting the dream, and their progeny simply absorbed and modified it. The Elites of the Old Left despised *the idea* of America because it stopped the march of worldwide Socialism; they passed on this hatred to the youth—the New Left—where it intensified. They created an image of America as steeped in racism, oppression, and imperialism. They told one another and our young people that America is a country founded on genocide, rapaciousness, subjugation, and greed, and that this was going on even before its founding. William Ayers is today's archetype Modern Liberal: Ayers was a student who absorbed the New Left ideology and became a university professor of some note. Ayers wrote that he realized America "is a society built on a solid—and shaking—foundation of racial subjugation."[10] Many naïve students of that era—the Baby Boomer generation—were away from home for the first time and in awe of their professors; they began their college educations in an environment of anti-Americanism that was inflamed by the fear of having to fight in the jungles of Vietnam.

America also stands for and represents something that is the antithesis of the dream: free-market capitalism. As discussed in Chapter 2, Modern Liberals and their predecessors abhor free-market capitalism for a variety of reasons, and this animosity is most virulent on campuses across America. It is in the colleges and the universities that we run across the most frustrated and angry Modern Liberal Elites. These well-educated Elites look around and see that Americans—and even their own students—admire the individualist, the successful entrepreneur, the self-made man, the capitalist, *and not them.*

Modern Liberals look to Europe as a model that America should emulate, and their "Europe-worshipping" provides another source of anti-Americanism. European anti-Americanism is centuries old, predating our founding. In *Reconstructing America*, James Ceaser, a professor of politics at the University of Virginia, described layers of anti-Americanism that have spread from Europe and infected the Left in America.[11] One is the "degeneracy thesis" that was prevalent during our colonial era. According to this, everything in America was deemed inferior and in decline. At first, this only applied to the vegetation, animals, and people in the New World, but it soon shifted to the intellectual arena: The political system of America and the overall quality of life were considered inferior. For example, Europeans concluded that the premises of the Constitution were absurd because nothing based on rational science could endure. When it *did* endure, it was at the cost of what was deep and profound, according to European thinking: It was not a genuine culture, and there was no real community, no real Volk; there was nothing but money and materialism, and this led to a stultifying conformity. Another explanation was along racial lines: They viewed Americans as people who were breeding the white race out of existence; Americans were creating a new race which was no race at all.

Later, in the late 19th and early 20th centuries, America was seen in Europe as a source of the techniques of mass production and the deadened mentality that supposedly accompanied it: According to this view, in America everything in life would be reduced to what could be calculated. Many in Europe feared that this mentality would infect them and result in a spiritual emptiness. For Americans, Europeans thought, nature is nothing more than something to use. This was typecast as "technologism." Europeans felt they were caught in the middle between the USSR and America in this technological frenzy and organization of man, and the European intellectuals concluded that America was the worse of the two: The Marxists, they reasoned, at least had a sense of history, but the materialist Americans had none. During the Cold War, Leftist Europeans were convinced that America was sapping Europe's very soul, but they were also afraid of the Russian Bear to the east, so they tolerated America's presence. But when Communism died, anti-Americanism reared its ugly head once again. Today, European politicians use anti-American sentiments to gain influence and popularity, but there is an interesting irony that exposes the hypocrisy: A major charge levied by European Leftists and Modern Liberals against America is that the United States is *not being modern enough* (with health care, criminal justice, religion, welfare, and attitudes toward sex), and, at the same time, it is criticized for *being too modern* (with technology, fast food, and conveniences).

Today, few Modern Liberals are aware of these roots of their hostility and contempt toward America, and they continue blaming America for every possible ill in the world, declaring it engages in "economic imperialism," and insisting that the ostensible evils of big business and multi-national corporations stem from Americanism itself. Professor James Seaton described it well:

[A] significant current in contemporary liberalism…finds it difficult to imagine that any opponent of the United States could possibly be guilty of more than excusable errors, since it is American military and economic power that is the source of all real evil in the world.[12]

We often find writings in publications of the "Elite" Modern Liberal media that support—or at least sympathize with—America's avowed enemies, past and present. For example, Michael Straight was the editor of the *New Republic*; he admitted to being a Soviet agent in 1983. I. F. Stone, the former editor of *Nation* magazine, was a KBG spy and was a hero to the Old Left and New Left. In a recent article in *Nation* magazine, it was asserted that Stone was intrepid and independent, and that "I. F. Stone was…a great reporter"; any complicity with the USSR was denied and they referred to "the smear that…[Stone] was on Moscow's payroll."[13] But released KGB files have conclusively established that Stone was a full-fledged KGB agent from 1936 to 1938 (his code name was "Pancake"). Stone was a recruiter for the Communists and worked with an American Communist, Victor Perlo, who was the head of one USSR espionage ring in America.[14] Recently, Alexander Cockburn of *Nation* magazine chided America for investigating, finding, and arresting five Cuban government agents on charges of espionage and conspiracy to commit murder *in America*. This action was compared to those of North Korea, and Cockburn implied in his last sentence, "And they call North Korea a rogue nation?"—that America was more of a "rogue" nation than that of Kim Jong Il.[15]

The relaxed attitude Modern Liberals have toward the enemies of America—past and present—clearly reveals their hatred. A threat to America's very existence does not seem to bother them; basically, it sounds like Modern Liberals really do not care if America is destroyed. In *Slouching Towards Gomorrah: Modern Liberalism and American Decline*, Robert Bork described it:

> Modern liberalism forms what Lionel Trilling called an "adversary culture." The components of this culture…are alienation from the American system and lack of concern about threats to the American regime.[16]

John McElroy, in *Divided We Stand: The Rejection of American Culture since the 1960s*, commented on the attitude of Modern Liberals toward America:

Anti-Americanism reveals itself in four ways: (1) the totality of its condemnation...(2) its magnification of the smallest wrongdoing...(3) its invention of offenses supposedly attributable to the United States...and (4) its indifference to offenses committed by countries, organizations, or persons hostile to the United States.[17]

7

Tactics And Propaganda Of Modern Liberals

If we forget what we did, we won't know who we are...I am warning of the eradication of...the American memory that could result, ultimately, on the erosion of the American spirit.
—Ronald Reagan, Farewell Address
to the Nation

To destroy a people, you must first sever their roots.
—Aleksandr Solzhenitsyn

We encounter the tactics of Modern Liberals in our everyday lives—appeals to base emotions, labeling and name-calling, distortions, historical revisionism, skullduggery, and intimidation. A few Modern Liberals have assiduously studied their craft, but most simply parrot dogma that they have mindlessly assimilated. Chapter 13 of Part II details how to respond to, confront, and combat Modern Liberals, beating them back with their own methods; this chapter simply describes their tactics.

Modern Liberal tactics described in this chapter will be familiar to many readers. Their strategies are used to exact agreement to their policies, programs, and doctrines, and also to stifle and shut down any dissent. The descriptions do not simply cover today's specific political issues; such issues are in constant flux and change from week to week or month to month. Rather, the focus in this chapter is on the deeper and *permanent* Modern Liberal agenda. : For Modern Liberals, the overriding drive is the centralization of authority to control and manage our economy and society. This is necessary, in their worldview, in order to impose their visions on the rest of us. This is the enduring legacy from the Progressives, the Old Leftists, and the New Leftists: They wanted the central authority—the federal government—to set up and impose the visionary programs developed by their "experts." In the minds of today's Modern Liberals, similar to the "Borg" of *Star Trek* fame, "All resistance is futile," and the Borg will prevail.

The agenda of Modern Liberals—shifting power and control over our lives to the federal government—requires the repudiation of virtually all the traditions, beliefs, and values on which America was founded, especially the concept of limited self-government and the preservation of private property. Natural law—the idea that rights are inherent in humans themselves, given to us by nature or Almighty God—is anathema to Modern Liberal ideology, in which the *government* bestows rights, rights that change depending on the circumstances, and rights that can be taken as well as given, by the *government*.

Pat Buchanan imputes a "catechism" to Modern Liberals in which there is no God and no absolute values. Following are the three primary commandments:

1. All lifestyles are equal. Discrimination against any "alternative" lifestyle is a crime.
2. "Thou shalt not be judgmental." Christianity is cruel and impedes human fulfillment. Full sexual freedom—all voluntary sex relations are permissible and all are morally equal—is enshrined.
3. Public schools are to be used to teach our children to like all lifestyles and to believe that Western history is a catalogue of crimes. The children must

be told that, for example, in the words of the Modern Liberal icon Susan Sontag, that "the white race is the cancer of human history." These young minds must be taught James Baldwin's proclamation that "there is not...a single American institution which is not racist" and Jonathan Culler's dictum that "the Bible is a powerfully influential racist and sexist text." The new history that Modern Liberals want to teach is that the real heroes of our country are not our Founding Fathers, entrepreneurs, explorers, and statesmen, but that the real heroes are the ones who advanced equality. [1]

Modern Liberals, like their forefathers, usually hit hard and fast with their programs, before Americans have much time to reflect. They slam us with issues such as gun control, abortion, and global warming, often able to get judicial and Congressional action in motion quickly. Steven Haywood wrote about Modern Liberal tactics in *The Age of Reagan*:

> [They pursue] liberal ends by undemocratic means—chiefly judicial incrementalism and bureaucratic stealth—because they were too unpopular with the public ever to be accomplished out in the open. [2]

But after a bit of time, the American people finally realize what has happened and react.

Balint Vazsonyi escaped communist Hungary and came to America where he became a world-renowned concert pianist, the director of the Center for the American founding, and a writer for the *National Review*. In his insightful book, *America's 30 Years War*, he included three sections describing the "Lethal Weapons" of Modern Liberals: "Words," "Statistics" and "Branding." The tactics of Modern Liberals in this chapter are divided along similar lines but into four categories, starting from the least to the most truculent and forceful: (1) emotional appeals, (2) distortion and manipulation of information, (3) personal attacks, and (4) labeling.

Emotional Appeals

Appeals to emotions are among the most effective tactics of Modern Liberals, simply because most people—if caught unaware and taken off guard—find these disconcerting and difficult to obviate.

Modern Liberals are under the illusion that they are morally superior. They justify this by declaring that they "care" about the poor, the oppressed, and the unfortunate, and that they have "compassion" for the most helpless and weak in our society. Some even profess to be similar to Jesus himself. In fact, most Modern Liberals say that Jesus would approve of their agenda and of their Socialism. This tactic is used because by asserting that compassion, caring, and ostensibly "Christ-like" feelings are the benchmarks of righteousness, Modern Liberals imply that people who dissent are bereft of those qualities. As Myron Magnet astutely observed, these "became the touchstones of moral worth, displacing considerations of justice and responsibility. But 'compassion' or 'caring' proved a barren value, for no amount of it made the condition of the lowest of the excluded get better."[3] Alan Bloom identifies this as "conspicuous compassion."[4] Modern Liberals have a proclivity to ostentatious displays of rectitude. Thomas Sowell aptly described the difference between Modern Liberal displays of righteousness and being truly moral:

> Sanctimoniousness is easy. There are editorial writers who are sanctimonious every day of the week, without any visible sign of fatigue. As far as they are concerned, those who disagree with them are not merely in error, but in sin. Morality means being hard on yourself. Sanctimoniousness means being easy on yourself—and hard on others...Morality isn't nearly as much fun.[5]

The intellectual Lionel Trilling, a Liberal himself, wrote a trenchant comment about their hypocrisy: "We who are liberal and progressive know that the poor are our equals in every sense except that of being equal to us."[6]

Intentions take precedence over outcomes for Modern Liberals; if their heart was in the right place, they think that they cannot be criticized for their policies, which have resulted in more violent crime, increased poverty, accelerated drug usage, and higher rates of unemployment. After all, Modern Liberals say, they tried to eradicate these; that was their intent, so they deserve adulation for that.

Modern Liberals profess that they are nonjudgmental. Tolerance, to them, is a total acceptance of everything that *they* determine should be accepted. Budziszewski, in *The Problem With Liberalism*, wrote about this:

[The] moral error of political liberalism [is] neutralism…According to this notion the virtue of tolerance requires suspending judgments about good and evil…If you really believe that the meaning of tolerance is tolerating, then you ought to tolerate even intolerance.[7]

Budziszewski goes on to describe "selective neutralism [that] remembers itself only long enough to condemn…(the Liberal inserts what he dislikes there)." In other words, Modern Liberals are hypocrites in that they deem themselves to be nonjudgmental and tolerant: They demand that one should never be "judgmental," but that only applies to what *they want* others to accept and celebrate. When others speak out against their special causes, then the nonjudgmental "neutralism" ends and harsh denunciations in the name of "tolerance" ensues:

If you really believe that the best foundation for tolerance is to avoid having any strong convictions at all about right and wrong, then you shouldn't have a strong conviction that intolerance is wrong. If you really believe that when you do have strong convictions you should refuse to express or act upon them, then your tolerance should be a dead letter; it should be one of the things you are pusillanimous about.[8]

It is incumbent on Modern Liberals to keep class antagonisms and grievances alive in order to maintain their very existence. One inextricable part of their credo is fomenting class hatred. The power and importance of Modern Liberals would diminish if they lost their assurance that they are needed to "right wrongs," so they must keep screaming and yelling about "injustice" and "oppression," inventing new ones as needed. The result is that Modern Liberals will always be at odds and in conflict with the existing culture and common sense.

Modern Liberals fancy that they evince their virtue and superiority through their passion and activism. Dissent attests to their patriotism and love of country, they maintain. Modern Liberals even impute one of our Founders with having said "dissent is the highest form of patriotism," mistakenly attributing this to Thomas Jefferson or Thomas Paine. The truth is that it was postulated as a question in the 1961 publication, *The Use of Force in International Affairs*: "If what your country is doing seems to you practically and morally wrong, is dissent the highest form of patriotism?" More specifically, New York Mayor John

Lindsay said it in 1969, and the Marxist radical Howard Zinn, hero of Modern Liberals, said it on July 3, 2002 in an interview with Sharon Basco: "I would argue that dissent is the highest form of patriotism."[9]

The ideas or conclusions of Modern Liberals are presented nonchalantly as those any "thinking person" would have. Modern Liberals tell everyone that the more intelligent and educated people are cynical about America and can see through the pro-America and "America-First" slogans. In other words, according to Modern Liberals, people who see displays of patriotism and love of country as propaganda are more sophisticated, and those who do not see this are brainwashed pawns of the entrenched power structures. Daniel Flynn encapsulated this mindset in *Why the Left Hates America*:

> For much of the Left, anti-Americanism is an article of faith. Whatever denigrates the society they hold in contempt, even lies, is encouraged. Whatever places the country they dread in a positive light, even truth, is denied. The overall "truth" that the United States is the national equivalent of a moral leper is deemed more important than "minor" truths that contradict this thesis. Above all else, the goal is to debate the country that embraces the policies that their theories vehemently oppose.[10]

Modern Liberals proclaim that they simply want people to always be *sensitive* to the needs of others; they, of course, know who are in most need of having their sensitivity increased and who most need to receive the benefits of a more sensitive populace. In addition, they know best how to help people become more sensitive. Daniel Flynn pointed this out in *Why the Left Hates America*:

> The familiar buzzwords of "sensitivity" and "civility" are meant to apply to the conduct of their adversaries...[Modern Liberals are] absolved from any obligation to conform to such niceties.[11]

America bears the onus of rectifying past sins, according to Modern Liberals. They postulate that America has innumerable sins and it can never fully redeem itself, but it must endeavor to do so. Lisa Fabrizio used the term "Progressives" when she wrote the following:

They have encouraged us to revile our predecessors as bigoted, hateful empire-builders, driven by a misguided reliance on religion; and reduced our defense of freedom around the world to a pathetic form of misplaced patriotism.[12]

Modern Liberals emphasize the "non-American" origins of people. They encourage people to emphasize the others' cultures rather than their American identity. In order to discourage people from seeing themselves as Americans, Modern Liberals promote teaching children in school to focus on their racial and ethnic origins. Modern Liberals discourage and humiliate people who characterize themselves as purely "American" because national identity increases internal cohesion among a people, and this hinders Modern Liberals' emphasis on differences among us. Modern Liberals present multiculturalism as promoting fairness, giving restitution, and making up for the suffering in the past; the truth is that it is a method for dismantling American traditions and patriotism. They conveniently forget George Washington's admonition in his farewell address:

> The name of American, which belongs to you, in your national capacity, must always exalt the just pride of Patriotism, more than any appellation derived from local discriminations.

Modern Liberals will contend that one has to "do something," and they ignore the admonition to "do no harm, and help where possible."[13] If one accepts that there will always be some people in poverty, that we have limited resources, or that programs—especially ones that have not been verified to be effective—will bring increased burdens on taxpayers, Modern Liberals will invariably scream: "You mean you think we should do *nothing*?" Ultimately, as Budziszewski wrote, Modern Liberals are going by the adage, "Better to harm magnificently in the name of help, than to help but a little."[14]

Modern Liberals frequently use lofty slogans, like "equality," "peace," and "social justice," implying that unless you conform to their agenda, you lack those qualities. For example, Modern Liberals pervert the concept of "fair." Actually, fair play means self-restraint, not taking advantage of weaker people, but for Modern Liberals, it means *not being satisfied with one's position in life*. In the minds of Modern Liberals, "unfair" treatment has invariably originated from the past, nature, other persons, or fate. If Modern Liberals convince themselves that there has been "unfairness," then they conclude that the group treated "unfairly" has special rights or entitlements—an entitlement to health care, housing, higher education, or even lighter criminal sentences.

Modern Liberals are extremely judgmental of America, and they usually center their excoriations on free-market capitalism. Modern Liberals use moral standards that are quixotic and absolute: America will be sure to fall short, and they count on it. However, the same Modern Liberals do not place Socialist regimes in this context. With their beloved Socialist countries, they switch to an *historical* perspective, placing them in "context." In short, Modern Liberals use utopian standards to judge capitalist regimes, and they look at Socialist countries with the "relative" judgment of historical perspective.

Modern Liberals vaticinate that the future of capitalism is doomed; they conclude that the free market will inexorably worsen the conditions of mankind. Modern Liberals claim that the Socialist regimes can and do improve as they progress into different stages, such as "Democratic Socialism." For example, they summarily condemned the former Chilean dictator Pinochet for his forays into free-market capitalism while they held out hope for Cuban dictator Castro's Socialist regime—"Socialism with a human face." But fifteen years after each rose to power, there was an essential difference: Pinochet consented to hold a presidential referendum, which he lost, while Castro rejected every appeal to do the same.

Modern Liberals promise security with their Socialist programs, and this is one of their strongest weapons in recruitment. As Hayek wrote in *The Road to Serfdom*, there is danger when "the striving for security [becomes] stronger than the love of freedom. The reason for this is that with every grant of complete security to one group the insecurity of the rest necessarily increases."[15]

When Modern Liberals and their parents, the New Leftists, are on the defensive, they maintain that they want to solve problems for the average person; however, when they are in power, they attack the culture. Jonah Goldberg pointed this out in *Liberal Fascism*:

> [W]hen conservatives have the upper hand on a cultural issue, liberalism is all about "solving problems" for the average Joe, about paychecks and health care. But on offense, it's about racial quotas, mainstreaming gay culture, scrubbing the public square of Christianity...It was only when the National Socialists had the upper hand that they dropped their economic arguments in favor of imposing a new cultural order.[16]

Modern Liberals give what sound like apocalyptic warnings that we have to solve one imminent crisis or another. This is very noticeable in the environmental movements. Richard Ellis, in *The Dark Side of the Left*, explained the method:

> If people can become persuaded that nature is fragile and that the slightest misstep may result in cataclysmic consequences for the human species, then it becomes difficult to resist arguments and policies that would rein in the acquisitive entrepreneur in the name of the collectivity.[17]

In other words, it provides an excuse to attack capitalists and shift complete control of our economy and society to a central power.

Distortions and Manipulation of Information

Modern Liberals cherry-pick and manipulate numbers and data. For example, if we take an honest look at the results of any president's policies, we cannot begin from inauguration day, but should start from one to two years *after* he assumed office, simply because it requires time to see the effect of his policies. This principle applies to any president, including the sitting one at this printing: Obama was of course not responsible for the economy on February 1, 2009. Recently, Modern Liberals have intensified their scathing attacks on Ronald Reagan and distorted the record: Modern Liberals "analyze" the Reagan economic record beginning three weeks *before* he took office, from January 1, 1981. Honest analyses (examining the data *after* his policies had time to go into effect) produce different results: Real economic growth, for example, averaged 3.2 percent during the Reagan years versus 2.8 percent during the Ford-Carter years and 2.1 percent during the Bush-Clinton years. (More is presented on this in Chapter 12.)

Modern Liberals cherry-pick specific policies or programs of other countries and present them out of context. For example, when health care is demanded, Modern Liberals will state how it is "free" in a number of countries. They will omit, for example, that the government is beginning to restrict treatments in Britain, or that in France people pay 18 percent of their *pretaxed incomes* for the "free" care, and it is growing more expensive.

Modern Liberals want State Socialism, and this is the legacy from their ancestors, the Progressives. Now, they modify the word—government regulations, progressive taxation, protecting the environment—or combine it with other terms—Democratic Socialism or Market Socialism—in order to make it appear that they are not promoting State Socialism. By playing these word games, they presume that they can distance themselves from the realities of past Socialist regimes of Lenin, Stalin, Mao, and Pol Pot. David Horowitz wrote about this in *The Politics of Bad Faith: The Radical Assault on America's Future*:

> [T]he socialist idea is still capable of an immaculate birth from the bloody conception of the socialist state; these people hope to evade the lessons of the revolutionary experiment by writing the phrase "actually existing socialism" across its pages, thus distinguishing the socialism of [their] faith from the socialism that has failed…[They] prefer…to regard the bankruptcy and the moral debt as accruing to someone else.

Horowitz aptly characterizes this as a "shell game."[18]

Modern Liberals distort and pervert values in order to get their pet agenda accepted. Consider tobacco and condoms: In the world of Modern Liberals, the druggist who sells children cigarettes is considered vile and should be prosecuted for endangering their health and morals, yet they recommend having condoms not only sold legally to children, but even distributed free to these same young people. Consider blasphemy, vulgarities, and obscenities: For Modern Liberals, these are fine on television and defended as free speech, but ethnic humor is condemned as immoral hate speech.

The Modern Liberals in academia have special methods that they use to attack our society, our republic and the free market: determinism, presentism, and deconstructionism. When Modern Liberals "discuss" history, they proceed from a perspective of historical determinism. This is really a modified and updated position of the determination espoused by Karl Marx. Modern Liberals, usually unwittingly, regard historical determinism as an axiom, just as Marx did. This theory provides a satisfying explanation of history for them by presenting all developments as being political positions that were historically predetermined by changing events and forces. This accomplishes two goals for Modern Liberals:

1. We no longer need to consider our founding or our Founding Fathers as unique or enduring; they were just inevitable products of their time.

2. Modern Liberal pronouncements are presented as simply statements describing an inevitable future. For example, Modern Liberals announce that Socialism is part of this future, and to resist it is

retrograde and only postpones the inevitable. Modern Liberals claim that their other programs—central control, the end of religion, alternative family structures, and internationalism—are all part of what is being determined by history. They sound like the Borg in *Star Trek*: "Resistance is futile."

Another slick method Modern Liberals utilize in their "discussions" and pronouncements regarding history is "presentism." "Presentism" is judging past events, ideas, and people by our current standards. In other words, it is reading history backwards. Modern Liberals take a contemporary outlook, like today's view of equality, use that as a standard, and *then* go backwards. This present standard is then looked at as basically always having been with us but having been blocked by certain forces in the past. For example, they will say that some people were *denied* the right to vote during our founding era; thus, rather than acknowledge that the West was the first in the entire history of the world to formally denounce slavery after thousands of years, rather than pointing out that our Constitution was the first written document formally declaring all men equal was created, and rather than stating that America enfranchised more people than ever before in history, today's standard is used to vilify our past. In addition, Modern Liberals judge only selected groups—most often our Founders—by ethical and moral standards that took centuries to formulate. Modern Liberals demand omniscience from these people: our Founders should have reached forward in time and invented the standards by which we have arrived two or more centuries later. Moreover, Modern Liberals show their hypocrisy by refusing to apply this "presentism" to their more recent heritage—eugenics, racist policies, and reverence of Mussolini and Stalin.

Deconstruction is a convoluted and subversive technique used by the more academic Modern Liberals to change the meaning of texts. It is used to attack capitalism as well as Western values, traditions, and institutions. For example, the Bible is deemed "sexist," and Shakespeare's *Tempest* is presented to demonstrate the relation between the colonizers and the colonized. Lincoln's *Gettysburg Address* contains the phrase "Our fathers brought forth…," and the deconstructionists proclaim that this reveals an acceptance and verification of a system of oppressive patriarchal authority in our nation. "All men are created equal," according to these Modern Liberals in our colleges and universities, really excludes females and numerous others, and they say it deliberately promoted equality only for a selected few.

Modern Liberal academics analyze normal social relations and denounce them as relations of power in an attempt to persuade people to view human interactions in terms of the oppressed and the oppressor, to envision society as a place where people are controlled or in control, and look at the world in terms of victims and victimizers. This process also helps Modern Liberals to disrupt and destroy age-old established relationships, such as the ones between husband and wife, parent and child, and teacher and student.

Modern Liberals change the locus of responsibility from the individual to society: In the past, Americans knew that people *chose* to commit crimes and that they deserved just punishment. Modern Liberals shifted the onus to society and claim that it is the responsibility of society to prevent crime. Along with this, Modern Liberals blame existing institutions for poverty and other social ills; they despise the free market because in it one cannot blame society for one's failures. This has run through the psyche of Modern Liberals and their predecessors for a long time. Ludwig von Mises wrote about this over a half-century ago:

> [An anti-capitalist] can ascribe adverse fate to conditions beyond his own control...It is not of his doing, and there is no reason for him to be ashamed...It is quite another thing under capitalism. Here, everybody's station in life depends on his own doing.[19]

Modern Liberals look at the results of individual behaviors in these terms: If the results are unfavorable, they profess that it is because of conditions that preceded them, so society is responsible. In other words, in the minds of Modern Liberals, failures are from social disadvantages. On the other hand, if the results are favorable, like economic success, they claim that is was from privilege or luck. Thomas Sowell put it well:

> Widespread personification of "society" is another verbal tactic that evades issues of individual responsibility. Such use of the term "society" is a more sophisticated version of the notion that "the devil made me do it."... It is used as a magic word to make choice, behavior and performance vanish into thin air...[R]esults after the fact can then be equated with conditions existing before the fact. Success thus becomes "privilege" and failure "disadvantage"—by definition.[20]

Modern Liberals constantly contradict themselves. Even though they maintain that society and its structures are responsible for how people behave, Modern Liberals often insist that social problems are the result of intentional actions by individuals or entities they abhor such as capitalists, conservatives, organized religions, and the military. Thus, according to the irrational and convoluted interpretations of Modern Liberals, any diversion from unmet ideals is because either the federal government has not enforced the Modern Liberal agenda, or because someone, or some cabal, is hindering it from coming to fruition.

Modern Liberals invariably say that free-market capitalism promotes greed. The putative rich are presented as having gained their fortunes in ways that "honest" and "decent" people do not—through theft, bribery, cheating, or abuse of labor. And Modern Liberals allege, without substantiation, that many affluent people have never worked for their wealth but simply inherited it, implying that they do not deserve what was passed on to them. In Modern Liberal mythology, the *system* of capitalism itself is often blamed. Capitalism, Modern Liberals conclude, brings out the worst in people and can only be restrained through more control by central authorities that have the best interests of the people in mind. This nonsense will be covered in more detail in Chapter 13, but suffice to say that the truth is that the free market necessitates business to search for what others want and need, and then deliver it to them as cheaply as possible. One only hears the charge of "greed" from Modern Liberals when they disparage those whom they arbitrarily brand as well-to-do. These Modern Liberals refuse to acknowledge that acquisitiveness is part of human nature. In a television interview with the New Leftist Phil Donahue, Milton Friedman once made a statement about greed which drew laughter from the audience: "It's always *the other guy* who's greedy."

Many Modern Liberals declare that the rich get richer at the expense of the poor. The growth of affluence is presented as a "zero-sum" game in which anyone who becomes prosperous means someone else, somewhere, suffered a loss. This is understood as an axiom by Modern Liberals, despite the simple and obvious fact that Americans are living better than a generation ago. For example, houses have doubled in size, most people now have air conditioning, the majority of families have at least one computer, and middle-class teenagers own more cars than before.

Modern Liberals use what Thomas Sowell calls "all or nothing" responses to "deny whatever needs denying." This tactic "enables virtually any general statement, however true, to be flatly denied, simply because it is not 100 percent true in all circumstances."[21] Modern Liberals use it to deny there is true liberty, for instance, or that there is a free market. When a reasonable person praises the benefits of the free market, Modern Liberals will say, "Show me a completely free market." This method also entails searching for any minute flaw or infinitesimal error and blowing it out of proportion. Modern Liberals take this and contend that because of the "problem" they uncovered in a person or idea, everything related to the person or idea is to be summarily rejected without exception or qualification. For example, the Nobel Prize winning economist Milton Friedman—the bugbear, the bête noire, and the nemesis of Modern Liberals—once visited Pinochet while he was in Chile at the behest of Chilean students who asked him to give a lecture about free-market principles at their university. During the entire time Friedman was in Chile, he met with Pinochet *once* for a couple of hours on one day and discussed the benefits of the free market in one sitting. Pinochet afterwards implemented only parts of Friedman's ideas. He also set up a dictatorship. Simply because Friedman spent a couple of hours with Pinochet—at *one* meeting—and Pinochet later went on to implement some dictatorial policies, Modern Liberals claim that Friedman's policies are responsible for the tyranny. According to Modern Liberals, because Pinochet implemented several free-market ideas espoused by Friedman, *everything Friedman ever said and wrote* should be completely rejected. The real purpose for their irrationality is quite manifest: It is the attempt to reject anything and everything that could promote free-market capitalism.

Modern Liberals assume cause and effect relationships, but they refuse to really look at obvious outcomes of their policies. For example, their parents, the New Leftists, proclaimed that poverty was the *cause* of crime; money was pumped into poverty programs but crime increased. Modern Liberals and their parents also said that sex education would decrease unwanted pregnancies, but they refuse to discuss the outcome: Pregnancies actually *increased* after their programs were foisted on the schools across America. In *Visions of the Anointed: Self-Congratulations as Social Policy*, Thomas Sowell presented numerous studies that document that decreases in violent crime, venereal disease, and unwanted pregnancies were forthcoming *before* their programs were put into effect.[22]

Modern Liberals propose that the "root" causes—"root" being a favorite qualifier of theirs—of wars, genocide, and terrorism are primarily from resentments toward America. These resentments, Modern Liberals presume, are normal responses to America's imperialist and other war-like policies, either directly or indirectly. The genocide of the Khmer Rouge, for example, was because Americans bombed Cambodia, driving them into a killing frenzy; Modern Liberals blamed the attack on the World Trade Center towers on America's activities abroad.

Modern Liberals assert that they can identify the historical antecedents for any problems. Invariably, they choose only those that fit their dogma and support their agenda. Modern Liberals purport to be able to disentangle all history and point to isolated causes that resulted in what they claim to be present-day "injustices." They also fantasize that they are omnipotent and can redress the "injustices of history" for virtually any group of people. Modern Liberal hubris knows no bounds.

Modern Liberals create special targets to attack. The most common include businessmen, doctors, and law enforcement. Modern Liberals encourage lawsuits against these people. For example, they say that businesses should prevent all possible harms to consumers, and they proclaim that "unlucky" accidents do not happen and someone else is culpable.

Modern Liberals strive to infuse their political tenets into every aspect of our lives. Robert Bork explains this well in *Slouching Towards Gomorrah: Modern Liberalism and American Decline*:

> The search for a "politics of meaning" is a feature of modern liberalism...Modern Liberalism...is frustrated by the structure of American government, the party system, and most Americans' distrust of excessive zeal. The notion that politics is a necessary means of finding meaning in personal life also necessarily leads to the politicization of all areas of life and culture, summed up by..."the personal is political and the political is personal." Politics is always and inevitably about power.[23]

Modern Liberals extend their concept of "rights" into every sphere in order to promote their agenda. Sometimes, they simply profess that something is a "right" and expect confirmation. If one disagrees, one is considered to be *taking away* that right. This is nowhere more obvious than in schools. In 1975, for example, a principle suspended nine students for spiking punch at a high school dance. With the aid of the American Civil Liberties Union, a far-left organization that was founded on Communism[24], it reached the Supreme Court where it was determined that the students were deprived of "due process," and their civil rights were violated. In this case, the New Left succeeded: The authority of local schools moved from the schools themselves to the federal level, to the central authority.[25]

Modern Liberals scream "rights!" Rights to housing, to jobs, to a standard of living, and to a "livable wage." If they convince enough people to even reluctantly assent that something might be a "right," they then say that not enforcing and funding this "right" is a *denial* of basic human rights. A moral principle is assumed, but it is never explained, discussed, or analyzed. Modern Liberals also profess that the people who get a "right" also want all those in their group to have it.

Modern Liberals present visionary ideals and America always falls short. In other words, *perfect* solutions —impossible ones—are presented as reality and used as benchmarks to see if America "measures up." Of course, no nation can meet these grandiose fantasies, so this forms a basis by which they can criticize and revile America, its institutions, its traditions, and its very founding.

Modern Liberals use the lives of the poor, criminals, single parents, and drug users as the touchstone by which to judge society. It does not matters to them if a policy—such as tax breaks for families or free trade—benefit the society in the aggregate; for Modern Liberals it only matters if the poorest of the poor have benefitted. Modern Liberals use them as a point of reference, and this view has been promoted by one of their prominent legal Elites: John Rawls. His ideas, especially his farcical thought-experiment, the *"original position,"* provided a rationale to use this benchmark. It makes the condition of the poor the means of justifying the policies and beliefs of a society, instead of the overall national wealth, freedom, artistic achievement, virtue, or true democracy. This dogma of Modern Liberals has already shifted some of our values: It is no longer a "stigma" to have children while unmarried; and many have come to acquiesce to the idea that society should be required to support these children and their mothers. Another example of this shift is that a poor person who does not work is considered in need of sympathy and compassion, and that idleness stems from the structure of society, not the individual choosing the way he lives. As Myron Magnet observed, because of the policies of the New Left, there now exists "the idea that society ought to give an income to the single mothers of illegitimate children and set them up in apartments, without a hint of stigma."[26]

Modern Liberals often deem that people should actually be rewarded by virtue of the group into which they are born. Jonah Goldberg wrote about this in *Liberal Fascism*:

Mainstream liberalism is joined at the hip with racial and sexual-identity groups of one kind or another. A basic premise shared by all these groups is that their members should be rewarded simply by virtue of their racial, gender, or sexual status. In short, the state should pick winners and losers, based upon the accidents of birth. Liberals champion this perspective in the name of antiracism...[L]iberals still believe that the state should organize society on racial lines.[27]

Modern Liberals deem themselves to be the voice of selected groups. Modern Liberals assume that they know what these selected groups think and desire. Thomas Sowell refers to this as part of "the shifting viewpoint" tactic: "[The anointed ones] evade responsibility for one's conclusions by shifting to someone else's viewpoint."[28] For example, they may say gay marriage can be compared to Civil Rights for blacks, but they ignore the fact that more blacks than whites are *against* legalizing gay marriage.

If someone clashes with Modern Liberals when discussing the groups that they have singled out to promote their agenda, he is told that he cannot possibly understand unless he is a member of that group. With this tactic, Modern Liberals preempt any criticism and debate, and they unwittingly deny our common humanity.

Modern Liberals present an image of a sea of millions of homeless people, impoverished because of an "uncaring" society run by *capitalist greed*. Mitch Snyder, the most influential spokesman for the homeless, testified before Congress that there were over three million such people, but it was a patent fabrication: The actual number was one-tenth of that. Robert Hayes, head of the National Coalition for the Homeless, blames deindustrialization and gentrified housing in the cities for homelessness, again refusing to put blame where it should be put: on the policies and morals of the New Left.

Modern Liberals and their New Leftist parents proclaim crises when they really do not exist. Thomas Sowell documents a number of these fabricated "crises": Before the programs of the Great Society (better understood as the *Ungrateful* Society), for example, poverty was actually declining; venereal diseases were also declining when the New Left said there was a crisis and sex education in the schools would help reduce the escalating rate. The same happened with teenage pregnancies: In 1963, before the New Left's programs, the rate of illegitimate births was 6.5 percent of all births. After their programs were in effect for over three decades, it reached almost one-third of all births, at 33.2 percent by 2000.[29] Before their programs started crime rates were decreasing, but the New Left declared a crisis, got funding, and the crime rates soared. Murder rates doubled from 1961 to 1971, and violent crime overall tripled from 1960 to 1976—all after the New Left convinced government policy makers to pump *trillions* of dollars into programs designed to ameliorate and extirpate the "root" causes.

"Hate crime" is a favorite deception of Modern Liberals, and they have managed to get a federal law passed to enforce this. The truth is quite different from what they present. For example, white criminals chose blacks as victims in 3 percent of violent crimes, while blacks chose whites in 50 percent of them. White on black rape approaches 0 percent, but black on white is 28 percent, and blacks commit 90 percent of interracial crimes. Yet, white on black crime is considered to be a "hate crime," and the power of the federal government is there not only to help in the investigation and arrest, but the courts are expected to give harsher penalties for the same crime if it is classified as what Modern Liberals have designated to be "hate." In order to discern how dangerous and pernicious this concept of viewing crime is, one only has to recognize something that is essential to be a hate crime: Only specific groups can commit specific crimes!

Modern Liberals will use—just as their predecessors did—any vehicle to destroy traditions. One of them is modern art. Wheeler Williams, a recipient of the Gould Medal in Paris, past president of the Fine Arts Federation of New York, and longtime president of the National Sculpture Society, said that the purpose of modern art "was to destroy man's faith in his cultural heritage." [30] We see that many artists of the "modern" genre are from the Old Left, the New Left, and Modern Liberals. Examples are Andres Serrano's *Piss Christ* in which a crucifix was placed upside-down in a glass of urine, or Robert Mapplethorpe's *Self Portrait with Whip* which was a picture of himself with the end of a whip in his exposed anus.

In educating our children, Modern Liberals are especially vicious in their attacks on our history and culture. They are willing to use the horrors of the Holocaust, Nazis, and Fascists to make invidious comparisons with American actions. For example, they profess our early treatment of Native Americans was similar to the Holocaust and Nazi concentration camps. In school textbooks written by Modern Liberals, they use the word "concentration camps" when discussing the internment camps of the Japanese-Americans during World War II. In the teachers' book, *Teaching for a Tolerant World*, the Holocaust appears in articles about gays, Africans, and others to build this association. Outside of the classroom, Al Gore used this comparison, comparing global-warming skeptics to Holocaust deniers. Clinton branded the Texas 2000 Republican platform a "fascist tract." Jesse Jackson has said that opposition to his agenda is "fascist."

Modern Liberals are rarely willing to defend their fantasies; they simply declare that these dreamlands and Shangri-Las are real and oblige others to prove them wrong.

Modern Liberals have managed—to a degree—to change the idea of family from one of responsibility, love, and duty to one of personal gratification.

Modern Liberals, like all their predecessors, *use* children as an excuse to promote their programs and their agenda, and this is one of their most potent weapons. For example, in 2000, Hillary Clinton advocated for gun control, saying, "No longer will we be silent as the gun lobby refuses to put our children's health and safety first."

When Conservatives make mistakes, Modern Liberals vilify them, of course. But when Modern Liberals or their predecessors are the villains, they shift the blame elsewhere. The Liberals escalated the war in Vietnam, for example, but they blamed America itself for being "imperialist," "aggressive," and "capitalist." The Tuskegee syphilis experiments—a program in which syphilis was left untreated among blacks to study the course of the disease—were carried out by *Progressives*, but after these horrors were exposed, the New Left and the Modern Liberals said they were carried out by southern racists.

Modern Liberals assert that Conservative talk shows and television broadcasting are simply indoctrination tools of the "far right" and corporate interests. Ipso facto, anyone who listens to them is simply being inculcated with lies and propaganda, and he is a dupe of vested economic interests. This technique often catches people off guard by alleging that all of one's ideas came from these shows. The purpose is clear: Modern Liberals want you to appear to be a mindless stooge or coerce you into indirectly taking a position *against* the broadcasts. In other words, their game is to embarrass you by inference or get you to state that you are *above* listening to these talk show hosts, giving tacit acceptance of the Modern Liberals' derogatory stance against them.

Modern Liberals contend that they represent the "center" politically or that they are the "moderates" in America. The obvious purpose of this is to make the true center appear to be on the right, and to make Conservatives—the ones who want to adhere to our Constitution and founding principles—to appear as extremists. This serves another purpose: "normalizing" the ideas of Modern

Liberals. They proclaim that a policy or agenda of theirs has already gained public favor, when, in fact, it has not.

Modern Liberals have several methods of "normalizing" their ideology. Thomas Sowell presented a two-by-two matrix showing four methods the "anointed" use to normalize their belief system and impose their agenda on the public. The first two deal with existing policies: In the first, if the "anointed" *approve* of an existing policy, they say we are obliged to live with it because it is part of our society and here to stay. With this method, they attempt to persuade Americans that the ideas of Modern Liberals are not new ones but are old ones. With abortion, for example, Modern Liberals claim that abortions were always going on but were hidden (already part of our society). They insist its legalization simply makes it safer, implying that the primary reason they want it legalized is to "protect" women. In the second method, if there is an existing policy that the "anointed" *do not like*, they profess it is outmoded. For example, in 2008 and 2010, the Supreme Court ruled in favor of the Second Amendment right for individuals to possess a firearm. Modern Liberals claim this is barbaric and that modern and "civilized" countries do not abide by such abominations, and that it reflects badly on our country.

The next two methods focus on policies that are not yet in place: With policies that are not yet in place, but that Modern Liberals *want*, they say that their agenda is inevitable and inescapable and to resist it is absurd. This is especially effective with their push for universal (government controlled) health care. Modern Liberals say America is backwards in its approach to medical care. They proclaim that all "civilized and modern" countries have had this socialized medicine for decades, and they do not want the United States to remain retrograde and backwards. If they *do not like* the policy that is being considered, they categorize it as unrealistic and impractical. For example, in order to provide free condom distribution in the schools, promote sex education, and have abortions without parental consent, Modern Liberals will try to eliminate any proposed abstinence programs that are not yet in a school curriculum. They allege that most middle and high school students are "doing it anyway" in this modern age (inevitable and inescapable factors), and to think that we can teach them otherwise is archaic, futile, and potentially harmful (unrealistic and impractical factors). The goal is also to demoralize those who have higher hopes for these students and get them give up their aims by convincing them that the battle has been lost.[31]

Modern Liberals summarily discount and reject the results of any polls, study, or research that do not align with their policies and agenda. If you present data and information that refutes or contradicts Modern Liberal assumptions, following are some ways that your facts will be rejected:

1. Modern Liberals will claim that you have not presented sufficient data: They will badger you for more data, but there will *never* be enough. If you provide more, they will just ask for even more.
2. Modern Liberals will deem the information outdated and insist you get newer information.
3. Modern Liberals will contend that your sources are biased.

Be forewarned that there is virtually never any point in trying to meet their demands for data or facts; Modern Liberals will simply reject anything you present or conjure up new ways to discount it. One exchange this author had with a Modern Liberal was characteristic: The Modern Liberal said that the sources were biased. However, the Modern Liberal did not look carefully: The source was the US Census data with the complete ".gov" (government site) link. When confronted with that fact, the Modern Liberal continued to stand his ground, saying that *the selection* of this particular information was biased. I asked him to find other sources that refuted the data, but he instinctively resorted to both personal attacks and name-calling. These tactics are discussed next.

Personal Attacks

Modern Liberals are quick to typecast anyone who disagrees with, or even questions, them as "intolerant." To Modern Liberals, "intolerance" does not mean putting up with something you do not like; it means not kowtowing to *their* values. Modern Liberals abhor *real* tolerance because it denies that they are the voice of the downtrodden and oppressed, the liberators, and the truly tolerant. Tolerance means to endure something *one does not like* or of which *one does not approve*. To Modern Liberals, tolerance means fully assenting to what they deem "worthy" and even celebrating it. If someone rejects their misconception and distorted ideas of tolerance, that person is branded as contemptible, having a false consciousness, or being a reactionary who wants to bring back an ugly American past.

Modern Liberals characterize those who criticize obviously outrageous behavior as being "judgmental." For example, if you identify patently irresponsible behavior—such as drug addiction or impregnating a woman and abandoning her—for what it is, you are typecast as "judgmental" by Modern Liberals.

People whose convictions run counter to Modern Liberal dogma are accused of having psychological disorders. This tactic arose from the Frankfurt School in the 1960s: People whose ideas do not align with those of Modern Liberals are not just in conflict with political or economic issues but have emotional or attitudinal pathologies. In *The Dark Side of the Left*, Richard Ellis described this attitude among Modern Liberals: "Differences of opinion and interests are seen as evidence of deviancy or a vestigial selfishness that needs to be stamped out by the authorities."[32] The Serbsky Institute in the USSR classified political dissidents as insane and put them into a hospital for "treatment." Modern Liberals may declare that people like you have "anger issues," are "in denial," or are "repressed." The Modern Liberal will profess that you are "fearful," are "frustrated," or have "unmet needs" so you follow your religion, outmoded dogma, and obsolete traditions. (Or maybe you cling to your "gun and Bible," as one well-known Modern Liberal professed.)

If you do not aspire to find the ostensible "root causes" of problems, you will be condescendingly considered backward and unenlightened. The "root causes" of all problems, according to Modern Liberals, reside in society, not human nature or individuals, and they always find these root causes in society's "oppressive" structures. And since Modern Liberals postulate that we must ameliorate the situation, it follows that we need to engineer society to rid ourselves of these oppressive structures, no matter how much it costs. If you refuse to accept or acknowledge these root causes after Modern Liberals have declared them, you are part of the problem. But Myron Magnet pointed to the example of New York Mayor Rudolph Giuliani's *ignoring* "root causes" of crime and instead attacking crime itself: This resulted in New York's becoming one of the nation's safest big cities after only five short years. "[Guiliani's] real-world success left in tatters the cultural revolution's orthodoxy that society can't cut crime without curing its 'root causes' of inequality and racism."[33]

If you say that something like drug addiction or poverty may be the result of individual irresponsibility or poor choices, Modern Liberals classify you as one of those who is perpetuating and supporting a system that keeps you rich, comfortable, and well-off.

If you do not agree with the vicious attacks of Modern Liberals on the affluent and do not assent to laws designed to tax them heavily, you will be branded as a person who wants the rich to get even richer at the expense of the poor and the middle class.

Many Modern Liberals are adept at creating nonexistent connections and associations. For example, if you dispute the benefits of their agenda to social-ize medicine, you are typecast as a person who does not care a whit about the elderly and sick children. Thomas Sowell, in *The Quest for Cosmic Justice*, wrote about the associations held by people with these special "visions":

> [When they] encounter someone who is clearly out of step with this vision, it is all too easy to dismiss his views on one issue by referring to other issues in which he is also out of step with the vision. Thus his views on national health insurance may seem suspect or not to be taken seriously because "What can you expect from someone who is against affordable housing for the poor?"...The prevailing vision not only does not require evidence, it becomes a substitute for evidence in condemning alternative views, so that the real criterion is not which theory better fits empirical facts but which theory better fits the prevailing vision.[34]

When Modern Liberals profess that they and their programs show one or more of the three big "Cs"— Compassion, Concern, and Caring— they imply that any objections mean you are the opposite.

When Modern Liberals insist there is a crisis or problem in need of imme-diate attention and you dispute this, they proclaim you are uninformed, irre-sponsible, or are operating from sinister and malevolent motives.

If you allude to any positive aspects of the past, Modern Liberals mock-ingly say that you want to return to a "golden age" that never really existed.

Labeling and Name-Calling

Modern Liberals excel at demonizing people who object to their agenda, and they have a multitude of disparaging sobriquets from which to choose in their lexicon to brand individuals or their ideas. For example, if you invoke love of country or declarations of patriotism, you are likely to be branded as benighted, a jingoist, a war-monger, or as simply unenlightened. Any opposition to the anti-free market agenda of Modern Liberals is considered by them to be a demonstration of intolerance, selfishness, avarice or ignorance. If you question any part of Modern Liberal programs for the putative "poor"—whom they profess to rescue—you will be branded as a person who wants to keep them permanently in abject poverty.

F. Scott Fitzgerald's comment about the Old Left whom he encountered is quite apropos:

> [W]hatever you say, they have ways of twisting it into shapes which put you into some lower category of mankind…and disparage you both intellectually and personally in the process.[35]

There are a whole slew of other monikers that Modern Liberals use for people who oppose them. Here are a few of the charges to which you may be subjected if Modern Liberals take exception to you:

You are insensitive.
You lack compassion.
You are a racist.
You are a liar.
You are a homophobe.
You supported George W. Bush's policies.
You are a dupe of the right-wing media.
You think what [insert any Conservative radio talk show or television host here] tells you to think.

Modern Liberals state—with conviction—the myth that Nazis and Fascists were right-wing. The purpose is to get people to believe this; then, if you disagree with their agenda, Modern Liberals reflexively designate you as "right-wing," essentially branding you as a Nazi or a Fascist. However, they can be reminded of something that George Strasser, the main Nazi party organizer in the 1930s, said: "We are socialists. We are enemies…of today's capitalist economic system."

Noemie Emery, columnist for the *Washington Examiner*, wrote about their other imputations:

> [T]hose on the left have conflated resistance to their agenda—high taxes, extravagant spending, laxity on crime, what have you—with motives of a dark nature: racism, nativism, fear of "the other," and various species of "hate." Ronald Reagan's election in 1980…was described as the bigots' revenge for the civil rights era. The midterm elections of 1994…were seen as a Confederate renaissance.[36]

If you support the Tea Party in any form, you are branded as ignorant, racist, an astroturfer, a Kool-Aid drinker, or a hypocrite. These Modern Liberals forget the ugly origin of the "Kool-Aid drinker" charge: It was from the Jamestown massacre, where over 900 people died from drinking Kool-Aid that contained cyanide. The people in Jamestown were devotees of a forerunner of Modern Liberals, Jim Jones. Jones was a self-admitted Marxist who believed he could begin a Communist revolution through organized religion. It is quite ironic that Modern Liberals apply this nomenclature to those who are the opposite of these Kool-Aid drinkers.

Modern Liberals want rule by experts or by the "Elite" with whom they associate themselves, and they disdain, mock, and disparage the average American. Matthew Continetti, author of *The Persecution of Sarah Palin: How the Elite Media Tried to Bring Down a Rising Star*, wrote about it:

> Elites regard challenges to their authority with condescension and contempt. They routinely underestimate the capacities of populist leaders. They mock their enemies as uneducated provincials who lack expert knowledge and therefore have no place in interfering in politics [because] the elite's greatest fear is that their supposed intellectual inferiors *might rule them* (emphasis added).[37]

Modern Liberals cannot understand Irving Kristol's remark in *Neoconservatism: The Autobiography of an Idea*: "The common people in such a democracy are not uncommonly wise, but their experience tends to make them uncommonly sensible."[38]

Modern Liberals suppose that if a person is a Conservative or supports such principles, he must be a Republican or aligned with a specific candidate or politician. This is absurd: First, the views of a party change, and second, to reduce another's philosophy to isolated political components is to ignore fundamental principles and the essence of the beliefs. Policy is simply the outworking of the core of principles, ideas, and philosophy, but Modern Liberals cannot, or refuse to, acknowledge this.

If you make reference to the Constitution or the founding principles, Modern Liberals will proclaim that you are a reactionary who wants to revive a past awash with racism, sexism, and genocide.

If you allude to states' rights, Modern Liberals will say you are a racist who wants to bring back Jim Crow laws, oppress gays, and submit women to dangerous back-alley abortions.

Modern Liberals are quick to attack people who are religious or even have some religious convictions. If you disagree with any Modern Liberal program based on what they perceive as religious connection—like states determining abortion laws or the Catholic Church teaching that homosexual acts are a sin—you will be branded as a member of the "religious right" or a "fundamentalist." Mention the name of David Barton, a scholar who teaches about the religious underpinnings of our country, and you will be deemed a fanatic who believes a "known liar."[39]

Meanings and uses of words are deliberately distorted and used as labels by Modern Liberals. "Imperialism" is a favorite. McDonalds' setting up a store in a Third World country is presented as a form of "economic imperialism," despite the fact that after Communism ended in the USSR and a McDonalds was set up in Moscow, Russians lined up for blocks to get hamburgers—made by American "imperialists"—*voluntarily*. Modern Liberals use words like Humpty Dumpty does in *Through the Looking Glass*: "Words mean what I choose them to mean." For example, Modern Liberals assert that burning a flag is their right to "free speech," but they proclaim that the KKK's burning a cross somehow is not "free speech." Modern Liberals try to redefine patriotism as *anti*-American. With the issue of abortion, Modern Liberals and their precursors claim *what* is chosen as *a right* to choose.

Modern Liberals have special terms they like to use. Examples are exploitation, diversity, full access, *peace* movement, public service, greed, imperialism, ruling class, poverty, perceptions, root causes, old fashioned, and stereotyping. Gary Younge, writing for *Nation* magazine and disparaging those not in accord with far-Left positions, used a plethora of special terms, saying dissenters have a "peculiar blend of paranoia, mania, fantasy and misanthropy," and also added the labels of "birthers, Swiftboaters, climate change skeptics, Obamaphobes and Palin-tologists."[40] The tacit implication is that if you are not in agreement with Modern Liberals, you possess the negative qualities of the terms. For instance, if one criticizes the peace or environmental movement for the extremism of either, then one is, by implication, against peace or protecting the environment; or, conversely, one supports war or is complicit in raping and destroying the environment. Thomas Sowell, referring to Modern Liberals as the "anointed," points to three additional reasons for these buzzwords:

(1) Preempt issues rather than debate them.

(2) Set the anointed and the benighted on different moral and intellectual planes.

(3) Evade the issue of personal responsibility.[41]

So beware: If you disagree with Modern Liberals, you will be badgered to show "compassion" by supporting their agenda, bombarded with distortions and deceit, accused of being a dupe of corporations and the wealthy, portrayed as mindlessly parroting right-wing media, diagnosed with an emotional disorder, branded heartless and cold-blooded, or, worse yet, typecast as a Fascist or a crypto-Nazi racist.

Part II

The Rest of Us

8

Who Are The Conservatives?

Conservatives are chained to reality.

—William F. Buckley

Lincoln was once asked, "*What is conservatism?*" He replied: "Is it not adherence to the old and tried against the new and untried?"

The term "Conservatism" will be used to describe the alternative to Modern Liberalism for two reasons: First, Conservatism provides a direct contrast to Modern Liberalism. When the Conservative position is presented, Modern Liberalisms' tenets manifest themselves clearly. Second, Conservatism reflects the hopes, dreams, beliefs, and sentiments of most Americans. Numerous polls have shown that people who consider themselves strongly or moderately Conservative outnumber their Liberal counterparts by at least two to one, or 40 percent to 20 percent, and the gap is increasing.[1] The remaining 40 percent consider themselves Moderates, are undecided, or simply do not know. It is the author's contention that most of those 40 percent adhere to fundamental Conservative principles and sentiments: They respect and admire our Founders and Constitution, they find inspiration in the idea of "America," they have solid patriotic impulses, and they want to preserve America's unique traditions and spirit. In short, these people are unabashedly *proud* to be Americans.

Lately, however, the Modern Liberal propaganda machine has managed to pass on the myth that Conservatism supports a corporate state that is designed to benefit the so-called "rich." Part of the purpose of this book's second section is to unmask these fallacies, distortions, and misperceptions.

Conservatives connect with the sentiments of everyday Americans and come from a tradition of wanting to preserve America's uniqueness. In contrast, Modern Liberals are estranged from our mainstream. Modern Liberals advocate conciliatory pacifism, persist on deferring to international opinion, teach that America was built on a foundation racism and greed, promote Socialism, insist that the United States must make up for its nefarious deeds at home and abroad, and demand the adoption of European lifestyles, values and policies.

Modern Liberals take our prosperity and liberty for granted; Conservatives remember what it took to attain these blessings. Since Modern Liberals take these things for granted, they do not realize how fragile they are. Modern Liberals insist on building a "better" system, but in order to build this "better" system, they are intent on tearing down the one in which we live. Conservatives, in contrast, want to preserve and revitalize the system—the founding principles—that made America great. Conservatives often ask: What would our Founders do?

Conservatives' expressions of their love of country align with mainstream America and it is uncomplicated: Americans admire and savor the country as it is, even with its imperfections and quirks. History, to Conservative Americans, is a source of pride and respect, despite past mistakes. The sight of Old Glory waving in the breeze gives them an instant feeling of exaltation, whereas among the Modern Liberal crowd it often evokes embarrassment, shame, and discomfort.

Among the broad grouping of Conservatism, there are Social Conservatives, Neo-Conservatives, Paleo-Conservatives, Traditionalists, the Religious Right, Libertarians, and others. These different Conservatives often clash with one another, but there are unifying themes among these seemingly disparate groups. A cardinal theme that unifies all of these variations is our primary weapon—a *powerful* weapon—in the fight against Modern Liberalism. It is the tool that brings down their edifice and threatens the very core of their ideology: *the Constitution of the United States of America.*

A small fraction of Americans—slightly over 2 percent—actually want to get rid of our Constitution. They are certainly not in the Conservative camp, nor are they likely to be in the other 40 percent who are moderates, indifferent, or undecided. They are among Modern Liberals. No Modern Liberal in a position of political power would dare to advocate this openly; people who do promote this idea often keep it to themselves or are relegated to the fringes of society, or they are ensconced in the history and political science departments of universities.

Modern Liberals usually claim to respect and admire our Constitution, but this is a sham, a pose. Their deception is clearly revealed in the following:

1. Modern Liberals insist that our Constitution is a "living document," and this is an excuse for turning it into whatever Modern Liberals want it to be. The "living document" view *must* maintain that there is no permanence in the Constitution, that its meaning changes with the times, and that there are no eternal truths. It also supports the idea—contrary to the very basis of Original Intent —that the government does not *secure* rights that are inherent in humans, but that government *creates* and *grants* rights.

2. Modern Liberals claim that our country was founded on—and its documents created by men who emphasized—greed, genocide, racism, and sexism. This forms a rationale, for them to reject the founding principles and their principal document: our Constitution.

3. Modern Liberals will also say that the Constitution is of another era, that it is outdated and an anachronism. The Modern Liberal legacy of, and belief in, Progressivism contends that modern man is more intelligent, knowledgeable, and advanced in understanding human nature, society, and politics than our Founders were. This in itself—if one comes to believe it—would render the Constitution obsolete, and it denies that there are any permanent values, even though our Constitution is based on "enduring values." Without an acknowledgement of the "enduring values," our Constitution can be—and is *compelled* to be— rendered obsolete. Modern Liberals will claim that the Founders could not imagine the modern state, thus rendering the principles on which the Constitution was based as archaic and in need of revision and overhaul. In a word, for Modern Liberals, the Constitution is an outmoded artifact of another time. Modern Liberals claim to be for progress, and the rudder for steering society must truckle to the ever-changing flow of its river.

In contrast, Conservatives know that the enduring principles in our founding apply perfectly today, and its eternal truths remain our guide. An essential one is Natural Rights: The government does not *give* rights; our rights are *inherent* in us as part of our nature. The Constitution is very specific about this; it states that our rights are *secured* by the government, not *given* by the government. Rights cannot be created because they are already there, an inalienable part of us. Every American either knows this or should know it.

Modern Liberals believe that the government can actually create rights and that new ones are needed with the changing times, such as a right to a job, a right to a specified level of income, or a right to medical care. Conservatives know that our society may *choose to provide* such things, but these are not inalienable rights. On the contrary, they are privileges that come from the prosperity that is a result of liberty. And just as with privileges, we must appreciate them and understand that we can lose them. But we never lose our Natural Rights. A government may fail to secure them, but they are always there and are secured to the extent that the citizens are in control of their own government.

Those in the Conservative camp—on average—lead the "good life," and Modern Liberals remain incredulous of this. A Pew Survey turned up these findings:

1. Conservatives are happier than Liberals.
2. Conservatives are more knowledgeable about politics and world affairs.
3. Conservatives are more generous.
4. Conservatives give more blood.[2]

Peter Schweizer, in Makers and Takers: *Why Conservatives Work Harder, Feel Happier, Have Closer Families, Take Fewer Drugs, Give More Generously, Value Honesty More, Are Less Materialistic and Envious, Whine Less...and Even Hug Their Children More Than Liberals*, documents that Modern Liberals are overall more selfish, more concerned about money, less hardworking, less satisfied emotionally, less honest, and less knowledgeable about politics than Conservatives. In his social survey, Schweizer found that Conservatives donate more money and volunteer more time to charities than Modern Liberals do. Even after eliminating church activities, Conservatives still volunteered for charitable work more frequently than Modern Liberals. Conservatives are more likely than Modern Liberals—55 percent to 20 percent, almost triple—to say that they get happiness by putting another person's happiness ahead of their own, and similar data were obtained in response to questions about caring for a seriously ill parent or spouse.[3] In *Who Really Cares?*, Arthur C. Brooks calculated the annual giving gap between religious Conservatives and Liberals at $2,210 to $642.

According to the "National Generosity Index" in the *Catalogue for Philanthropy*, red states were ranked the highest. The blue states, such as Rhode Island, Massachusetts, New Jersey, Connecticut, and Wisconsin were on the bottom of the Index.[4]

Conservatism has well thought-out philosophical premises, not shallow and pretentious ones like we find in Modern Liberalism. These conclusions are rooted in attitudes about the past rather than some fantastic and improbable expectations about a future. Conservatives do not expect to make people act dramatically different than in the past eons. David Horowitz explained:

> [Conservatives] like to see social arrangements that are relatively more benevolent and measurably more humane...Unlike radicals, conservatives do not pretend to be able to shape the social future by bending it to their will. They do not offer plans designed to remake human beings by inducing them to act in ways that are dramatically different from how human beings have acted in the past. The "first principles" of conservatism, then are propositions about the existing social contract, about the nature of human beings in a social context, as established by historical experience. They are propositions about limits...It is this attention to practical experience and emphasis on workable arrangements that explains why conservatives can be liberal and tolerant toward their opponents in ways that progressives cannot.[5]

Conservatives accept the past but they also accept human nature and its limits; this is one fundamental reason that Conservatives are far more tolerant than Modern Liberals.

Conservative roots run deep; Conservatives do not hesitate to draw on accumulated wisdom, just as the Founders did when they referred to the Bible, the Greeks, the Romans, and the Whigs when formulating their arguments for the best government. The "thoughts" of today's Modern Liberals are superficial. Ryszard Legutko wrote about this in *What's Wrong With Liberalism?*:

> The picture of man and the world, in the understanding of our relation to God, to nature, to one another, was all formulated outside the realm of

liberal thought…The lack of weight which one feels whenever one reads liberal works is an obvious consequence of the thinness of liberal assumptions, from which one cannot derive any profound insights…The root of the problem lies in the program of consistent reductionism which closes the liberal mind to the issues that men have always thought constitutive of the human condition.[6]

Conservative beliefs are those of the majority of Americans, and that is why Modern Liberals have to go to the courts to get their agenda enforced. Modern Liberals have to override what the people want as expressed on ballots. Most Americans simply do not want the changes the Modern Liberals demand. Bill O'Reilly's words in *Culture Warrior* ring true:

> Most regular Americans do not want drastic change in the country and therefore lean toward the traditions…[T]he mass of Americans are not yet enlisted in the cultural war; they are a sleeping giant that, if awakened, could easily defeat the S-P [Secular-Progressive] opposition.[7]

Americans respect and enjoy traditions. In December 2005, House Resolution 579 was created in response to the attacks of Modern Liberals on one of America's most celebrated traditions: Christmas. This resolution was set up to protect the symbols, traditions, and the national holiday of Christmas and to denounce attempts by Modern Liberals to ban references to it. This resolution was entitled: "Expressing the sense of the House of Representatives that the symbols and traditions of Christmas should be protected." 401 were in favor, and only 22 opposed it. Specifically:

> The House of Representatives (1) recognizes the importance of the symbols and traditions of Christmas; (2) strongly disapproves of attempts to ban references to Christmas; and (3) expresses support for the use of these symbols and traditions, for those who celebrate Christmas.[8]

9

Beliefs Of Conservatives

The facts of life are conservative.
—Margaret Thatcher

The name of American, which belongs to you. . .must always exalt the just pride of Patriots more than any appellation derived from local documentation.
—George Washington

Russell Kirk is considered by many to be the father of American conservatism. In his seminal work, *The Conservative Mind*, Kirk articulated ten Conservative principles:

1. Conservatives believe that there exists an enduring moral order.
2. Conservatives adhere to custom, convention and continuity. Conservatives prefer the devil they know to the devil they don't know.
3. Conservatives believe in what may be called the principle of prescription.
4. Conservatives are guided by their principles of prudence. (The devil always hurries.)
5. Conservatives pay attention to the principle of variety.
6. Conservatives are chastened by their principle of imperfectability.
7. Conservatives are persuaded that freedom and property rights are closely linked.
8. Conservatives uphold voluntary community and oppose involuntary collectivism.
9. Conservatives perceive the need for prudent restraints upon power and human passions.
10. Conservatives understand permanence and change must be recognized and reconciled in a vigorous society.[1]

Conservatism is openness to reality. Russell Kirk wrote the following:

[C]onservatism is the negation of ideology: it is a state of mind, a type of character, a way of looking at the civil social order. The attitude we call conservatism is sustained by a body of sentiments, rather than by a system of ideological dogmata.[2]

Jonah Goldberg agreed:

Conservatism is neither identity politics…nor right-wing Progressivism. Rather, it is opposition to all forms of political religion. It is a rejection of the idea that politics can be redemptive. It is the conviction that a properly ordered republic has a government of limited ambition…The conservative understands…that progress comes from working out inconsistencies within our tradition, not by throwing them away.[3]

We Americans are not, despite Modern Liberal claims to the contrary, against government, nor do we hate government. Rather, we want government to be limited to its role as prescribed in the Constitution. Conservative principles provide a framework and a guide with which to illuminate and reference

America's history, principles, traditions, and values. If these beliefs and postulates are outlined—those to which virtually all Americans adhere—it becomes obvious that ours are in direct opposition to those of Modern Liberals.

Freedom for Americans ultimately means being free of arbitrary actions of those with political power. Our heritage from the Greeks fostered ideas leading to liberty: republican government, Rule of Law, independence of courts, and freedom of speech. All of this was to restrain those in power and render individuals free from their arbitrariness. Around the mid-nineteenth century, the idea of liberty was firmly rooted and nobody foresaw a movement against it. The ancestors of Modern Liberals, however, introduced *their* concept of "true" freedom and proclaimed "economic freedom." But we know their other names: central planning and Communism.

We Americans acknowledge that no authority or coterie of experts can ever say with certainty what is best for individuals. We know that whenever anyone professes to know what is best for everyone, an insistence to enforce government diktats will follow and liberty will be lost. In others words, when people are in charge of their own lives, they are enjoying real liberty. Modern Liberals and their predecessors are convinced that "experts" should rule and be given the power to compel compliance. We Americans believe that people should be free to choose their own way of life, making mistakes along the way, as well as choosing what makes them happy.

Conservatives want to preserve our Constitution, the oldest written one in the world. In 1878, William Gladstone described it as "the most wonderful work ever struck off at a given time by the brain and purpose of man." Patrick Allitt, author of *The Conservatives: Ideas and Personalities throughout American History*, wrote, "The document we now know as the Federalist Papers [the 85 essays promoting the ratification of the Constitution, published serially in a newspaper and journal] was the new nation's first conservative classic."[4]

In *The Progressive Movement and the Transformation of American Politics*, Thomas West and William Schambra wrote:

> [T]hat linking the conservative resurgence to a recovery of the Constitution was in fact a critical part of its ability to flourish in a way that conservatism had not otherwise managed earlier in the 20th century... Attention to constitutionalism sustained conservatism's appreciation for the central place of individual liberty in American political life, [and] the con-

stitutional idea of equality helped us resist the liberal shift from equality of opportunity to equality of results.[5]

West and Schambra remind us of how decentralism is essential:

> [A] recovery of the Constitution's concept of decentralist federalism informed conservatism's defense of family, neighborhood, local community, and local house of worship; that is, it gave us a way to defend local community against Progressivism's doctrine of national community.[6]

The idea that "all men are created equal" means that they are equally endowed with unalienable rights: Nature does not decide who is to govern and who is to be governed, as the divine right of kings once had it. And our Founders declared that these rights are not from some legal privilege or the good graces of a ruling class; the fundamental rights of humans exist by nature, and these are prior to government and manmade laws. It is only because these individual rights are left unsecured that governments are instituted among men.

People tend to forget that our Constitution is inextricably connected to the Declaration of Independence, essentially elaborating and codifying its basic premises: The government does not create, grant, give, or bestow rights, but "secures" rights, rights that are already there and inalienable in *all* people. This is stated clearly in the Declaration: "that *all* men are created equal, that they are endowed by their Creator with certain unalienable Rights...That to *secure* these rights, Governments are instituted among Men..." (emphasis added). Our Constitution affirms this: "We the people...*secure* the Blessings of Liberty to ourselves and our Posterity" (emphasis added). Charles R. Kesler, senior fellow of the *Claremont Institute*, explained this well in his call for America to return to our Constitutional principles:

> For the Framers, rights were attributes of individual human beings who had been endowed with them by nature and nature's God. The same government needed to secure these rights could possibly threaten them, so a constant vigilance was called for to keep government limited to its just powers.[7]

Conservatives emphasize the Constitution's original intent ("Originalism"). This directs us to try to determine what the actual authors of the document, our Founders, meant and what they wanted to achieve. Professor of Law Daniel

F. Forte contributed a chapter to *The Heritage Guide to the Constitution* entitled "The Originalist Perspective." He began: "Written constitutionalism implies that those who make, interpret and enforce the law ought to be guided by the meaning of the United States Constitution—the supreme law of the land—as it was originally written."[8] "Original Intent" is found within the Constitution and the ten amendments (the Bill of Rights). Without this, the public is at the mercy of the whims of the factions of politicians, intellectuals, or ideologues. "Originalism" restrains and limits any single generation from ruling out of the passion of its times. The Constitution, as originally intended, leaves people basically in charge of their own lives; they can make errors and correct them—that is the premise of limited government. It is not, despite what Modern Liberals profess, a "living document" in which the original principles change with the fashions, fads, and evanescent whims that prevail at any time. Rather, it is a statement and a framework *for things that are permanent*. Amendments are there to help adapt it to the changing times, but its "original intent" remains. There is an inherent danger in the belief among Modern Liberals that it is a "living document": This premise allows Modern Liberals to extend the authority of the government beyond the Constitution. The cardinal reason that Conservatives seem to want less government involvement is based on Constitutional principles. And there is something else that is very important: the emphasis on Rule of Law by Conservatives. Rule of Law is an inextricable part of Originalism. Originalism means that the nation adheres to the Framers' original intent and not to men's arbitrary whims and caprices. It means that individual judges do not modify the law in order to achieve specific outcomes as Modern Liberals would have it; it demands that we follow the law.

We Americans adhere to Rule of Law, not the Rule of Man. Adherence to Rule of Law is essential to our way of life. As Friedrich Hayek wrote in *The Road to Serfdom*:

> Stripped of all technicalities, this means that government in all its actions is bound by rules fixed and announced beforehand...Under Rule of Law, the government is prevented from stultifying individual efforts by *ad hoc* action...the individual is free to pursue his personal ends and desires, certain that the powers of government will not be used deliberately to frustrate his efforts.[9]

With Rule of Law, the "rules" are set in advance, so the individual can plan accordingly. A baseball game can provide an analogy to the Rule of Law in our lives: In a baseball game the rules are established beforehand and everyone knows them. The outcomes of the game are unpredictable, but those rules apply equally to every individual who plays. Some players will get more hits and runs, and others will strike out more often; three strikes is an out and four balls is a walk—*for every single player*. The fact is that, like life itself, adhering to Rule of Law will result in inequalities of outcomes—among individuals. This unpredictability frightens Modern Liberals, and they advocate for State planning. Planning sounds reasonable: We all plan in our lives, from a road trip and our finances, to our weekends and daily life. To not plan seems chaotic. In addition, most political actions can really be considered a kind of planning. The difference between the Conservatives' view of planning in the economy and that of Modern Liberals is that Conservatives want a legal framework so that the individual can plan within it; Modern Liberals want a plan for the collective: the whole society or a large segment of it. Modern Liberals want the entire population to be made equal. The Conservatives' plan would be one in which a strict and dependable legal framework—Rule of Law—is set up within which people can choose what they want as individuals. This system must be open to improvements and modifications, of course, but the basic framework is there so that individuals can make choices and not be subjected to the whims of planners but only to the less arbitrary whims of nature. Individuals would not be at the mercy of any government power, but to the anonymous movement of the economy, which really is a result of day-to-day choices of one's fellow citizens.

Americans also reject that perversion of Rule of Law which Modern Liberals venerate: "social justice." Social justice has no basis in law. Social justice undermines law and hence undermines and destroys justice. Modern Liberals' so-called "social justice" undermines law by creating "group rights" and aiming at outcomes for specific groups. The establishment of rights and outcomes is really the government making moral decisions: If the State creates rights and aims to get specific outcomes for selected groups, then it must, perforce, make the accompanying moral choices. Referring again to the baseball game, imagine if rules were arbitrarily changed because it was claimed that some people have an unfair advantage or a disadvantage. In the world of Modern Liberal "social justice," various accommodations and adjustments would be made to ensure their concept of "fairness" is enforced: With the faster runners, the bases are moved farther apart so they do not have an "unfair" advantage; for the weaker hitters, the pitcher stands closer to home plate and throws slower to make it "easier"; and to help those who do not throw the ball so well, extra players are put in the outfield to compensate. This is the kind of world that Modern Liberals would create. Rule of Law establishes laws that apply to everyone, and, as John Adams put it, we have a "government of laws and not of men."

"Natural Rights" form the central premise upon which our country was founded, the clear statement that our rights are "inalienable"; Rule of Law is the means by which we maintain our Natural Rights. This actually leads to a common American identity: Individual rights stress similarities among human beings, group rights stress differences; individual rights promote equality, group rights stress inequality; individual rights focus on each person as an individual, group rights promote stereotypes; and individual rights are inalienable, while group rights are created by Modern Liberal activists. Individual and group rights are mutually exclusive; we cannot have it both ways. Hayek explained that "to produce the same results for different people, it is necessary to treat them differently."[10] Promoting group rights to achieve "social justice" instills fear among those who have not been chosen to have the unique or extra rights. Group rights grant unearned benefits, mostly from the labor of others. Conservatives know that the attempts of Modern Liberals to force their vision of social justice on the population only results in conflicts among groups. For example, Modern Liberals claim that the government can provide "free" medical care, simply by taxing (i.e., confiscating) some wealth of the affluent, who do not need it anyway. Conservatives are aware of what Mark Levin wrote in *Liberty and Tyranny: A Conservative Manifesto*:

> [T]he individual knows better how to make and spend that which he has earned from his own labor and provide for his family than do large bureaucracies populated by strangers who see classes of people rather than individual human beings.[11]

Charles R. Kesler wrote about the Modern Liberal version of rights: For Modern Liberals, "rights reflect society's stage of evolution and become real only when they are actualized, i.e., granted and enforced by government." Therefore, according to Modern Liberalism, "the more power given to government, the more rights it can and will give to the people."[12]

These Modern Liberal beliefs concerning our Constitution started from the Progressive era, and they were stated clearly by the Progressive President Woodrow Wilson: Wilson explained that the foundation of the Constitution—primarily the concept of Natural Rights—was no longer appropriate and that an administrative state was necessary in the modern age. According to this thinking, we have outgrown that historical period in which we worried about King and Church. Progressives fantasized that we had our rights secured and no longer had to live in fear of losing them as the Founders did. Wilson and his cronies concurred, and claimed that we had evolved and were obliged to deal with new forces. John Dewey went so far as to say that the Founders were actually rather primitive and even amoral because they only emphasized the Natural Duties that emanated from the concept of Natural Rights. The Founders conceived that individuals are free to pursue their own concerns and government should respect this, but for Dewey, these "negative rights"—freedom *from* government by restraining its powers—were empty; negative rights did not encourage active government, which was needed to actualize what Dewey called people's *spiritual potential*. The government, Dewey proclaimed, should expand to distribute resources so these "potentials" could be realized, and *new rights* should be created. In addition, according to this view, since society and the administration of the nation had grown very complex we needed experts to administer it. Progressives popularized the idea that appointed experts should run the administrative agencies; they are not elected, so this supposedly keeps them from political partisanship. The historical forces are different now, they say. As Ronald Pestritto pointed out in his scholarly work on Wilson's political thought, *Woodrow Wilson and the Roots of Modern Liberalism*, Wilson surmised that there should be "governance by educated experts" in civil service because they "will thus be in the best position to adjust governmental policy to the evolving will of society."[13] The Progressives—and today's Modern Liberals—presume that things change and that there are no eternal truths. The rest of us know that *permanent* truths were articulated by the Founders and written in the Constitution; they have always been there.

Since Modern Liberals proclaim that government exists to create and bestow rights, they contend that the government bears the onus to protect those rights. Modern Liberals look primarily at the rights that government not only created but now also exists to *protect*, while Conservatives—although they keep the protection of *existing* rights in mind—look primarily at the *exercise* of rights by private citizens. In the case of jobs, for example, Modern Liberals first ask government to create the "right" to have a job. Then, they look to the government to protect rights of citizens to have jobs. This becomes a directive for the government to create jobs, or further still, provide the *results of a job* (i.e., give unchecked welfare benefits). Conservatives, on the other hand, simply want a society in which people exercise their own rights to work with minimal or no government interference, compulsion or competition.

Conservatives see the drive to central planning of Modern Liberals, and they know the dangers, just as Fredrick Hayek described in *The Road to Serfdom*:

> [Economic and other] planning leads to dictatorship because dictatorship is the most effective instrument of coercion and the enforcement of ideals and, as such, essential if central planning on a large scale is to be possible.[14]

We Americans are for liberty, but as the Founders envisioned it, with virtue and responsibility. This is the burden of liberty. Our Founders wanted a government that would give rise to virtue; they wanted to create a nation that would cultivate it. Modern Liberals have summarily dismissed this and want the government to rid humans of *insecurity*; they want the government to give guarantees. In our founding era, these attributes took care of themselves because the institutions and their underlying beliefs were sound. These institutions were respected and part of the communities. These are the institutions that Modern Liberals seek to undermine and eradicate.

Conservatives know that liberty is not just the freedom to pursue our desires, but that our Founders intended liberty to free us from our slavery to them. Liberty is the ability to direct oneself toward individual and communal fulfillment without trampling on others' well-being, but Modern Liberals presume it means license to pursue hedonistic pleasure.

We Americans know that there are *honorable* actions. This is not an old-fashioned and outmoded concept; a sense of honor provides a guide to virtue and morality. But honor is antithetical to Modern Liberal thought. Modern Liberals envision history as moving in a predetermined course, toward a utopia, and they say that Conservatives are reactionaries, simply slowing down the inevitable. As James Bowman put it, "Honor was…not the agent of change…Honor was important not because it was a way to make a better world but because it guided us in our interactions with the world as it is." Modern Liberals live in a vision of the future, and honor has no place because honor deals "with the world as it is," forcing us to stay in the past, according to Modern Liberals, and preventing the realization of their dream.[15]

We Americans respect the sanctity of property; to violate this is to undermine the very fabric of our liberty. When Modern Liberals aspire to impose minimums and limits on the acquisition of property so they can redistribute wealth, it is a direct attack on that liberty. Americans know that private property is sacrosanct and its protection is essential for liberty and prosperity. DiLorenzo, in *How Capitalism Saved America*, cogently outlined some reasons:

> Protection of private property at the very least will minimize political conflict, for the political allocation of resources…is primarily legal plunder…Private property establishes the supremacy of consumer sovereignty…[It] also creates a wide dispersal of economic power. No matter how wealthy any one person becomes, his power is severely limited by the fact that he is just one of millions of property owners.[16]

Modern Liberals assume that they know what is best for the people, so they insist on establishing the ends and the outcomes. This ultimately is against individual choice, which equates to being against freedom. We Americans know that the free market is inextricably tied to the emphasis on individuals as opposed to the collective; it implies that the individual is the highest good because it defers to individuals' free and voluntary choices in the marketplace. Modern Liberals, in their desire to plan for the entire society, assume that there is a higher good than this, one that is superior to this focus on the individual. But the free market is a manifestation of the individualism toward which Western civilization has been striving for centuries by releasing people from the yoke of feudal lords, Church and kings. In other words, by limiting government, people are freer to make their own choices and mistakes, even if their choices displease Modern Liberals. This is the glory and genius of Western civilization. Modern Liberals would basically reverse this progress, bringing us a regression to a more primitive past. Modern Liberalism is a return to rule by authority, by diktat, when those in charge were considered gods, were all-powerful, or were getting direction from what was assumed to be a higher authority. In contrast, Conservatives would set up the rules of the road, enforce these rules, and let people go where they decide. Modern Liberals' adherence to the rules of the road would be arbitrary and they would decide where the drivers will go.

Conservatives know that the free market is necessary to keep power with the people and minimize government power. A basic fact about free-market capitalism is that excess is produced—an amount that is more than necessary to simply sustain the population—and the reinvestment of this leads to advances in technology and prosperity. This reinvestment cannot occur without private property rights. Ludwig von Mises explained this over a half-century ago:

> The accumulation of new capital, the maintenance of previously accumulated capital and the utilization of capital for raising the productivity of human effort are the fruits of purposive human action.[17]

Our history is unique in the world. It gave birth to, and nurtured, our beliefs and values. John Harmon McElroy, in *American Beliefs*, described American cultural beliefs, which align with Conservatism directly conflict with Modern Liberalism. McElroy likens cultural habits and beliefs to a situation in which someone first came to a place where nobody had been before. This person started a path, and those after him generally conformed to that same path and made some variations. Others came and followed—they went along the same general way. Soon the path through the woods became the norm. Without this, there would be no guidelines, no stability. These are the beliefs that guide the people. And Americans' guiding cultural beliefs and its traditions have obviously worked.

Even before independence, Americans in the colonies developed systems of government. In this new land, the idea of classes simply could not apply, especially on the ever-changing frontier. In *American Beliefs*, John McElroy highlighted this by comparing the American colonies' political structure and life with those of Spain, France, and Portugal during this crucial period of development. The Spanish, French, and Portuguese inhabitants in the New World primarily *took* what was of value to bring back to the homeland, such as furs from Indian traders in the French colonies and gold in the Spanish and Portuguese colonies. In contrast, America was a set of colonies where the profits mainly were created by building farms, ranches, and lumber mills.

Another major factor during this period was that the "benign neglect" of the American colonies necessitated the development of self-rule, while the other colonies were ruled and supervised directly by their home countries. All of this resulted in—outside of the slave owners—an end of privilege, increased participation in government, building of local wealth, motivation to strike out on one's own, a sense of independence, and the taking advantage of and creating opportunities.[18]

McElroy divided American beliefs into four general categories:

1. Primary Beliefs—these are all related to work:
    a. Everyone must work.
    b. Persons must benefit from their work.
    c. Manual work is respectable.

2. Immigrant Beliefs—these are the ones that most immigrants had about America and which motivated them to come here. These beliefs helped to shape America:
    a. Improvement is possible.
    b. Opportunities must be imagined.
    c. Freedom of movement is needed for success.

3. Frontier Beliefs—these were really extensions of our original colonies as we pushed west:
    a. What has to be done will teach you how to do it.
    b. Each person is responsible for his own well-being.
    c. Helping others helps oneself.
    d. Progress requires organization.

4. Religious and Moral Beliefs—Americans emphasize spiritual values, not only in their personal lives but in the life of the polity:

    a. God created nature and human beings.
    b. God created a law of right and wrong.
    c. Doing what is right is necessary for happiness.
    d. God gave men the same birthright.
    e. America is a chosen country.

We can see that American beliefs can be considered "Conservative" overall, even though that sobriquet is not necessary. What is essential, however, is to see how these fundamental beliefs—from the sense of independence and the desire to be effective with minimal government, to self-reliance and believing that individuals are responsible for their own lives and families—are anathema to the weltanschauung of Modern Liberals, who want a central authority regulating and organizing our society, experts determining what is "best" for the rest of us, and the power of the federal government enforcing conformity for what they allege is the "common good."

Modern Liberals, in contrast to the rest of Americans, generally become quite agitated and even hysterical when anyone alludes to the place of religion in our founding and early history. Michael Medved described this:

> The people who inhabited the New World always placed a higher priority on religious practice and Biblical beliefs than the communities they left behind in Europe…For conservatives, the religious character of our past and our people stands as a point of pride; for [Modern L]iberals, it's one more reason for embarrassment and apology.[19]

Religious freedom and high church attendance is generally a source of pride in America for Conservatives, but it embarrasses Modern Liberals. An irrefutable reality is that people have a religious impulse. Modern Liberals want to suppress religious expression, and distort the meaning of the "establishment clause." Conservatives know that the "free exercise" clause is part of our heritage, and this includes allowing more free expression in the public venue.

Conservatives see mystery and variety in traditions, while Modern Liberals see repression and inhibition. Modern Liberalism actually demands conformity and uniformity. Conservatives know that we must—as Paul Rahe wrote in *Soft Despotism, Democracy's Drift*—"be what we once were," otherwise we will "settle for a gradual, gentle descent into servitude."[20]

Typical Americans are independent and take for granted that they can strike out and create the lives they desire; this attitude usually seems naïve, foolish, and even haughty to Modern Liberals. But to those living in poverty or oppression, it still holds possibilities and stirs the imagination. Modern Liberals, in their quest for absolute equality and security, would strive to destroy this sense of independence and self-reliance. Modern Liberals prefer guarantees, they are fearful of uncertain outcomes, and the possibility of failure terrifies them.

Modern Liberals and Conservatives view America's history quite differently. Modern Liberals create a story of America's sin of slavery, mistreatment of Native Americans, and more than a century of imperialist adventures oppressing nations around the world. Conservatives focus on the way that America introduced ideals of liberty to all of humanity, gave rise to the planet's first anti-slavery society, and rescued the earth from two world wars and the dangers of international Communism.

Michael Medved, in an article for *Townhall Magazine* entitled "The Real Political Divide: Attitudes toward America," wrote the following:

> The left stresses America's failures, shortcomings, hypocrisies, and embarrassments while the right trumpets the nation's achievements, blessings, and distinctive advantages. Nothing enrages liberals more than the conservative tendency for jingoistic flag-waving and super-patriotism; nothing bothers conservatives more than the liberal habit of blaming America first and concentrating on historic guilt and present problems.[21]

Reminding us of our history, Michael Medved continued:

> [Conservatives focus] on the way that America introduced ideals of liberty to all of humanity, gave rise to the planets first anti-slavery society, and rescued the earth from two world wars and the danger of international communism, [but Modern Liberals] stress U.S. guilt for slavery, mistreatment of Native Americans, and more than a century of imperialist adventures oppressing nations around the world.

Along the same lines, Norman Podhoretz wrote this:

> The great issue between the two political communities is how they feel about the nature of American society. With all exceptions duly noted, I think it fair to say that what liberals mainly see when they look at this country is injustice and oppression of every kind—economic, social and political. By sharp contrast, conservatives see a nation shaped by a complex of traditions, principles and institutions that has afforded more freedom and, even factoring in periodic economic downturns, more prosperity to more of its citizens than in any society in human history. It follows that

what liberals believe needs to be changed or discarded—and apologized to other nations—is precisely what conservatives are dedicated to preserving, reinvigorating and proudly defending against attack.[22]

Modern Liberals insist on applying fanciful standards or benchmarks to *judge* America. Referring again to Michael Medved in "The Real Political Divide: Attitudes toward America":

> The contrast couldn't be more clear: Some partisans on the left…will [insist] they love the United States just as much as any right winger. The distinction, progressives regularly aver, involves their affection for a perfected America that might, through hope and change, come into existence sometime in the future, or else their nostalgic reverence for an America that once was, but ceased to exist through some malevolent influence (greedy businessmen, the religious right, conniving conservatives, take your pick).[23]

Modern Liberals do not just denounce America and its traditions; they revile its Western heritage. They ignore the fact that Western civilization was the first in which people could make independent moral decisions based on their own dispositions. Kenneth Minogue, in *The Servile Mind*, wrote that in Western civilization "the moral aspect of things has been uniquely able to disentangle itself from both religion and custom,"[24] and, as Diana Schaub wrote in her review of his book, "This moral freedom has been secured and protected by political freedom—essentially rule of law. Liberty of the individual and equality before the law are linked concepts."[25] But Modern Liberals want political correctness to take the place of morals, and this requires the central authority, not the individual, to determine what construes the morality of the citizens. Minogue described this:

> What the politico-moral makes politically correct has often been covered in the moral life by the precepts of good manners, which require the treating of all human beings with appropriate consideration…[This] politico-moral [fuses] together moral and political criteria…[and Modern Liberals live under] the illusion that our vices can be reformed if governments send the right "messages."[26]

Conservatives respect the accumulated wisdom of the past. Conservatives are not pretentious like Modern Liberals because Conservatives know that the millions of others before us have had the same fundamental problems, hopes, and dreams. In their accumulated wisdom, those before us developed ways to cope, and we do not want to destroy them with the social experiments of Modern Liberals. As David Horowitz wrote about this Conservative perspective in *The Politics of Bad Faith: The Radical Assault on America's Future*:

> [The Conservative perspective is] respect for the accumulated wisdom of human traditions; regard for the ordinary realities of human lives; distrust of optimism based on human reason; caution in the face of tragedies past.[27]

If, like Modern Liberals, we only look at the future and surmise that we will march to perfection, we are compelled to ignore the past. Modern Liberals reject the past because it informs the future. Modern Liberals think that those in the past are inferior and unenlightened compared to people today, and they actually posit that our ancestors were not as virtuous, moral, or wise as people today; their struggles are taken for granted by Modern Liberals. In contrast, Conservatives know it is incumbent on us to learn from the past.

Conservatives never sever their links to the past. Modern Liberals imagine that humanity is progressing toward an earthly paradise, and they insist that institutions such as the free market, traditions, and organized religions impede its realization. Modern Liberals' desire to strive toward, and to believe in, the perfectibility of man *sounds* wonderful, but it actually is not only flawed, it is dangerous: It is dangerous because it denies human nature which is bounded by limitations, and it disconnects us from the past. Mark T. Mitchell wrote about this for the *Intercollegiate Studies Institute* in "Why I am a Conservative":

> If...humanity is marching upward out of the benighted past toward a bright and happy future, there is precious little need or incentive to be grateful to those who have preceded us...[O]ur ancestors were...not our equals.[28]

Mitchell continues, explaining that Conservatives know that the Founders *were* our equals, describing *why* Conservatives appreciate that the link to our past is necessary:

The benefits of civilization [were] bought at such a high price...If we ignore the past, if we fail to grasp the invaluable and delicate gift we have received, then civilization itself is in jeopardy...[Our] sense of indebtedness should induce in us a sense of gratitude and our gratitude should give birth to love and our love will manifest itself in responsible action... A proper love of the past induces both a love for the present as well as a sense of duty to the future.[28]

Modern Liberals choose to ignore and belittle our past because if they recognize and respect the wisdom of the past, it confers responsibility to the gifts of civilization they have received. Conservatives accept and respect ordinary realities. They distrust those who declare that they have new answers to resolve problems for once and for all.

We Americans accept human nature and know that a paradise is not possible. There will always be struggle and conflict among humans; it is part of our nature. Our Founders understood this and set up a framework that works with human society because they recognized and accepted human nature. Madison wrote that "if men were angels, no government would be necessary," and he knew, unlike Modern Liberals, that "if angels were to govern men, neither external nor internal controls on government would be necessary."[29] Modern Liberals have inherited the legacy of a faith that man himself could be changed if the society could be *scientifically organized*. In other words, they fancy that humans are a "blank slate" upon which new human nature can be created. Modern Liberals suppose that we only need the experts organizing our society along scientific lines to create this new human nature. Centuries ago, our Founders knew the futility of this, but the utopians of every type tried—and failed miserably. But now, the very science they exalt is proving them wrong. Steven Pinker's book *The Blank Slate: The Modern Denial of Human Nature* summarizes a plethora of research studies in anthropology, psychology, genetics, and biology: Modern science itself is showing that the Founders were right, after all.

Conservatives see how unaided human reason and people who attempt to create fantasies and reject our nature have created horrible tragedies. This makes Conservatives cautious of change. Patrick Allitt wrote about this in *The Conservatives: Ideas and Personalities throughout American History*:

Conservatism is, first of all, an *attitude* to political and social change that looks for support to the ideas, beliefs, and habits of the past and puts more faith in the lessons of history than in the abstractions of political philosophy…Conservatives were skeptical and anti-utopian. They doubted the possibility of human, social, or political perfection…Planned societies are therefore impossible, and the attempt to create them will probably lead to chaos or tyranny.[30]

Human nature being flawed, Conservatives acknowledge that there is such a thing as the human condition and that life is unfair: Some people get good genes and some get bad ones, some are born in wealth and others into poverty, and some children have loving parents and some have abusive ones. Only smug and pretentious Modern Liberals presume to be able to sort out and then rectify the infinitesimal number of "unfair" things which people inherit. In *The Quest for Cosmic Justice*, Thomas Sowell pointed out the reality that refutes basic assumptions of Modern Liberalism:

> We have no generally applicable way to know how much of each individual's success or failure was due to such windfall gains as innate ability, a favorable upbringing, family wealth, or simply being in the right place at the right time, and how much was due to such personal merits as hard work and sacrifice. Moreover, even the latter virtues are often to some extent a consequence of upbringing.[31]

Rather than presuming to be able to sort out what is "fair" and dole out rewards according to arbitrary Modern Liberal ideas of "merit," Conservatives want to reward productivity. Rewarding productivity shifts power to the common people because they decide what to reward, not "experts" in the central government. Thomas Sowell continued:

> [W]e reward productivity rather than merit for the perfectly valid reason that we know how to do it. Moreover, since rewards represent not merely retrospective judgments but prospective incentives as well, a society can become more productive by rewarding productivity.[32]

Conservatives look at *actual* productivity, contributions, and efforts; Modern Liberals look primarily at failures and assert that they are from past injustices or oppression. Thomas Sowell wrote that these people cite disparities "as evidence that the injustices of the past are persisting into the present as discrimination against the groups in question."[33]

We know that values affect behaviors, but Modern Liberals refuse to accept that the values *they* promote are detrimental to both individuals and society. Instead, Modern Liberals blame American society itself for destructive behaviors. Conservatives want to foster traditional American values as described by John McElroy earlier in this chapter, such as doing hard work, trying to improve, and being responsible. In contrast, Modern Liberals promote destructive ideas such as crime being an inevitable result of oppression and going on welfare being a reasonable choice in an oppressive society. Before the Great Society programs, the "working poor" took pride in staying off of the welfare rolls, but the values promoted by the New Left encouraged these working poor to look at themselves as dupes, oppressed, victims, and fools, and these Leftists advised the poor to get government assistance. Myron Magnet pointed out the results of the values promoted by the New Left:

> Mainstream society withdrew "status rewards" from hardworking poor people who resisted the "incentives to fail" [offering welfare]...by erasing the distinction between the respectable poor and the irresponsible, disorderly, dependent poor. Once society began to see the poor who didn't work and who neglected their families as "victims" of the system rather than as personally responsible for their fate and actions, then how could these poor be seen as morally inferior to the industrious poor?[34]

This robbed the responsible poor of the rectitude they had in society and was devastating for them. Conservatives know that man is in charge of his destiny and life because man makes choices voluntarily. Modern Liberals, in contrast, hypothesize that man is a passive and powerless entity, moved by material forces beyond his control. This Modern Liberal idea deprives man of moral significance, individuality, and dignity.

Human nature is flawed, so humans are sometimes inclined to do wrong. But Modern Liberals have an imperative of consulting the "inner self" as a standard for behavior, and this is misguided. In direct opposition to this Modern Liberal prescription, Conservatives know that this focus on the self has to be overcome! If there is confidence in the existing moral order then the motivation is not to focus on the self, but on one's family and one's local community. The

Modern Liberals' aim is to destroy this order. "Self-fulfillment" is really selfishness, wrapped up in a nice-sounding terms to make it look like the opposite of what it is.

Conservatives know that civil order in society dignifies the lives of America's citizens. In contrast, Modern Liberals claim that promoting and encouraging public propriety is an infringement on freedom. Modern Liberals contend that people who are obscene, dirty, and nasty in public have a "right" to express and show themselves in the very places where ordinary people have built a "social order," such as in public parks, beaches and libraries. We see this in the Modern Liberal Occupy Wall Street Movement where *each month* there have been hundreds of arrests for rapes, property destruction, obscenities, attacks on the police, and even participants exposing themselves to children. Conservatives know that the "toleration" of disorder, obscenity, and filth in such places destroys the "civil society" that reasonable, diligent, and hard-working people have done their utmost to create, and that it requires responsibility and *true* concern for the community at large to preserve it.

Conservatives know that the social order restrains violence and crime by imbuing, passing on, and teaching inhibitions that are needed to curb aggression. Conservatives know that crime is not a result of "oppression," but comes from not being adequately socialized. But Modern Liberals contend that rage and resentment are natural and predictable consequences of an America filled with oppression, racism, and cutthroat competition. The New Leftist icon Ramsey Clark, former Attorney General under Lyndon Johnson, said that crime results from "racism, poverty, and injustice." Conservatives know crime results from a lack of socialization and, most of all, individual choice.

Christina Sommers and Sally Satel, authors of *One Nation under Therapy*, reject "the assumption that vulnerability rather than strength characterizes the American psyche and that suffering is 'a pathology in need of a cure'":

> Human beings, including children, are best regarded as self-reliant, resilient, psychically sound moral agents responsible for their behavior. For, with few exceptions, that is what we are.[35]

We Americans know this, of course, despite the Modern Liberals' insistence that most of us need personal counseling and therapy for guidance and stability in our lives.

Conservatives know that the policies of Modern Liberals and their parents have harmed the culture at large. Affirmative Action, just to name one, overturns four principles in which Americans believe:

1.   All men are created equal and are equal in the eyes of the law.
2.   In a democracy, the individual is the unit, not a class, group, or race.
3.   Rights belong to individuals, not any group.
4.   Opportunity and progress are open to talent and ability, and the best person should benefit; rewards should be based on achievement and merit rather than on the group to which one was born.

Conservative recommendations for Americans are few: Each person is responsible for his own actions, there is freedom under Rule of Law, rights belong to individuals and not to classes of people, and we are free to shape our own fate.[36]

We Americans ascribe to our "dream" of equality of *opportunity*, not equality of *outcome*. When Modern Liberals manipulate the law, regulate the society, and change the rules to get their predetermined outcomes, they have destroyed equality of opportunity; they have destroyed *real* equality. We know that the only true equality, as Russell Kirk said, is "moral equality": We are all equal in a divine sense.[37]

We Americans believe in the American Dream. Modern Liberals endeavor to paint a picture of Americans as people who have given up on the American Dream and the free market, and that the mass of us are turning against traditional values. This shows that these Modern Liberals live in their own closed and self-reinforcing world. Even a rather Liberal source did not deny the truth; in 2009, almost two years after the recession began, *CBS/New York Times* reported the following:

> Most Americans (72%) still think it is possible to start out poor in this country, work hard and become rich. However, that number is down from two years ago, when 81% felt that was possible.

Of course, people get disheartened during a downturn. Modern Liberals want to take advantage of any situation and frighten people into thinking that this is permanent. When we take a longer view, we see the American Dream is very much alive, no matter how much Modern Liberals wish for its demise. The *CBS/New York Times* article also included the following:

44% of Americans say they have already achieved the American Dream—up 12 points from 2005. Another 31% say they will reach it in their lifetime.[38]

There was actually an increase in those who felt they had achieved the dream *after* the recession was in full swing. The American Dream is alive and well!

America is special in that *anybody* can be an American. Conservative writer and speaker Dinesh D'Souza was born in India and became an American citizen in 1991. He wrote about his experience in *What's So Great about America*:

> Over the years my identification with America has deepened to the point that I truly feel that I have "become an American." An American could come to India and stay for forty years, perhaps even taking Indian citizenship, but he could not "become Indian."...Being Indian, like being German, Swedish or Iranian, is entirely a matter of birth and blood...In America, by contrast, millions of people come from all over the world, and over time most of them come to think of themselves as Americans...Their experience suggests that becoming American is...a function of embracing a set of ideas.

He spoke of his daughter, who was born in America: "Her life is likely to have greater depth, meaning, and fulfillment in the United States than it would in any other country." Near the end of his book, D'Souza concluded that "America is the greatest, freest, and most decent society in existence."[39]

Conservatives are cognizant that our society and the world are not controlled by a few powerful people or cabals but by innumerable individuals acting independently. The Dow-Jones Industrial Average goes up and down not because someone planned it, but from millions upon millions of individual voluntary transactions.

Conservatives accept that there are costs to achieve things, and that nothing is free. Modern Liberals assert that there are no costs.

Conservatives want to preserve the autonomy and independence of the family, and Modern Liberals want to increase government management and dependence. For example, Conservatives favor big tax exemptions for families so they can use the extra income—*the income that they themselves earned*—completely independent of government influence. Modern Liberals, in contrast, prefer government programs such as public-funded day care services and social worker visits to homes.

Conservatives know that the "Pursuit of Happiness" *is not* something the government provides or guarantees: Happiness is a result of choices, individualism, responsibilities, achievement, and improvements. 2001 Nobel Prize winner Vidiahar Naipaul spoke about that particular phrase in an address to the Manhattan Institute:

> So much is contained in it: the idea of the individual, responsibility, choice, the life of the intellect, the idea of vocation and perfectibility and achievement. It is an immense human idea. It cannot be reduced to a fixed system. It cannot generate fanaticism.[40]

In Michael Medved's excellent article from which excepts have been selected several times, he wrote a clear contrast about some fundamental attitudes of Conservatives and Modern Liberals:

> Conservatives have an easier time connecting with the sentiments of everyday Americans because our love of country remains less complicated: we admire and relish and savor the United States just as it is, even with all its quirks and imperfections. For us, the sight of Old Glory in the autumn breeze inspires a sense of instant pride and exaltation, not the bittersweet ruminations of a guilty liberal who automatically evokes embarrassing episodes associated with the flag.[41]

10

Our Conservative Origins

That is what the Constitution is: a system of restraints against the natural tendency of the government to expand in the direction of absolutism.[1]

—BARRY GOLDWATER, *THE CONSCIENCE OF A CONSERVATIVE*

In America, the Federal Constitution has endured as the most sagacious conservative document in political history.[2]

—RUSSELL KIRK, *THE CONSERVATIVE MIND*

Conservative beliefs and values align with those of mainstream America.

In standard dictionary definitions of the generic term "conservatism," you will find commonalities: The drive to preserve what exists, the inclination to be cautious of change, and the desire to emphasize stability and permanence.

Conservatism has very old roots, but this book deals with today's Conservatives in America in contrast to Modern Liberals. Conservatism is not the Republican Party: Many Conservatives gravitate toward the Republican Party, simply because they would not be comfortable in the Democratic Party. So, one cannot say that because a person is a Republican that person necessarily is a Conservative any more than one could say all Democrats are Modern Liberals. Besides, countless Americans consider themselves independent of party affiliation. As of June 2011, more people considered themselves "independents" than either Democrat or Republican, and those two parties are similar in size.

Compared to the history of Modern Liberals, ours is not only a shorter story, it is a rather dull one. Ours deals with an adherence to an old document, the Constitution. Our principles are based on those established centuries ago. We strive to preserve the best of the past and endeavor to apply its enduring qualities to our 21st century society. We believe in compromising as long as we do not betray our founding principles, and these compromises entail a process of slow deliberation and consent. For example, there have been over 2,000 proposals to add amendments to our Constitution after it was ratified with the Bill of Rights, yet only 17 were added. (In effect, only 15 were, since the 21st amendment nullified the 18th.) Americans revere and respect our Constitution; despite its being over two centuries old, only 2 percent of Americans think we should have a new one, and this minority is dismissed as radical; no politician would have a chance at being elected if he ever proposed scrapping it (except perhaps in New York City or San Francisco).

In contrast, Modern Liberals and their predecessors have a more "exciting" history: They have tried to overthrow our government, held debilitating strikes, assassinated public officials and two presidents, fought to install a Communist government, held out promises of utopias, endeavored to revamp the culture, rioted and burned on our city streets, strove to nullify centuries of traditions, and fought for new sets of "morals."

And the history of Modern Liberals is twice as long: American Conservatism did not start as a coherent movement until after World War II; Conservatives can look back and identify people who had "Conservative" values and ideas, but these people did not characterize themselves as Conservatives in the sense of a unified philosophical or political movement. Some think that a starting point for American Conservatism was with Richard Weaver's classic *Ideas Have Consequences* in 1948. Some date it a bit earlier, around 1944 or 1945, when the University of Chicago Press published Fredrick Hayden's *Road to Serfdom*, or several years later when that work was abridged and published in the *Reader's Digest*. However, possibly the beginning was with William F. Buckley's 1951 *God and Man at Yale*, or with the first publication of his *National Review* in 1955. In any case, today's Conservatism is only about 60 years old.

The history of Modern Liberals began in the last two decades of the 19th century, making it twice as long as ours; Edward Bellamy's *Looking Backward*, published in 1888, could be a marker for its inception. From that point, Progressive ideas coalesced and reflected a "faith" that science could be applied to society and solve virtually any problems, and a centralized government run by experts would be necessary to engineer and manage this society for the benefit of all. These ideas spread among the population in an inchoate form, and politicians, academics, and Socialists of all kinds pandered to the hopes and fears of people: They said that the policies of laissez-faire would result in impoverishment and social chaos, and they told the people that only the very affluent would accumulate wealth, at the expense of the masses.

But around the turn of the century, prosperity spread throughout America. A number of powerful people—Carnegie, Melon, Vanderbilt, Rockefeller, Ford, and others—were becoming immensely wealthy, but they introduced new products and methods of production, lowered prices for consumers, improved transportation, created industries with jobs, and helped to develop the country. America became the wealthiest and most powerful nation on the planet.[3]

At that time of bourgeoning prosperity, the government was barely visible. But it became very visible in World War I. During the Great War, there was an incredible buildup of government power. After the Great War, the Progressives and emerging Old Left tried to seize the opportunity to expand federal power, advocating for more federal control of the economy through the takeover of industries, transportation, and energy. The leading magazine of these people, *Nation*, called for nationalization of industry and energy while it was possible. But it did not happen, Wilson's party was easily voted out of office, government shrank, and the Roaring Twenties was ushered in.

But a series of events occurred that changed Americans' attitudes toward the federal government's roles and turned them away from an emphasis on individual self-reliance and "hands off government": the Great Depression and World War II. FDR's policies—initially following Hoover's interventionist policies and machinations—actually prolonged and deepened the Great Depression, but it was not known at that time. Today's scholars and researchers estimate that FDR's policies resulted in the Great Depression's being protracted by as much as seven years.[4]

Neither Hoover nor FDR did this deliberately, of course; they were in unchartered waters. FDR had charisma and was a persuasive and inspiring speaker who was able to keep instilling hope in the American people during this economic crisis and World War II. Criticism of his policies—even though many of his policies were declared unconstitutional by the Supreme Court itself—was minimized and deliberately ignored by the press at the time and for decades after. Some considered criticism of FDR as bordering on treason.

However, something new came out of the 16 year period from 1929 until 1945: Americans began to deeply trust and depend on the government. The American people grew to believe that *government* had prevented a total collapse of the economy and then saved the world from malevolent forces. After the war, Americans felt the threat of Communism and wanted protection from the Soviet menace and its nuclear power—they wanted their government to protect them. For most Americans, our government could do no wrong, and there was scant hesitation to grant more and more power to it.

Conservatism, as a movement, responded to this growing trend, but not without internal conflict. During the early part of the Cold War era, the country was socially and culturally Conservative; politically it was Leftist. The first Conservative voices came from three areas: Anti-Communists, Libertarians, and Traditionalists.

The Anti-Communists began warning Americans about the spread of Totalitarianism and Communism. In 1947, James Burnham, a former Communist spokesman, wrote *The Struggle for the World*, in which he postulated that World War III had already started. Another voice was that of Whittaker Chambers; Chambers was a Communist agent until 1937, and he warned Americans of its dangers. Chambers exposed Russian agents, including Alger Hiss. Another was Elizabeth Bentley; she was a Soviet spy from 1937 to 1945. Bentley left the Communist Party and informed the FBI of numerous Soviet agents in the United States government. Bentley's testimony became public in 1948 but was largely ignored; later, it was found that virtually all of her testimony was accurate. (Two decades later, a scion of the Old Left, the Democratic candidate for president, George McGovern, gave a response typical of the New Left: As recently as 1996, McGovern said that Hiss was part of the "Red Scare.")

The Libertarians emphasized reducing government management of the economy and allowing the free market to do its magic. They also warned Americans about the encroachment and expansion of government. The first spokesmen came from Europe—Fredrick Hayek and Ludwig von Mises were two Austrians who saw the rise of totalitarianism there. Hayek and Mises were warning people as early as the 1940s about the dangers of the state getting power through control of the economy. They explained how government's controlling the economy invariably led to totalitarian states. Hayek emphasized that Nazism was an inevitable outcome of the central government's managing the economy and the lives of the people.

The most prominent spokesman of the Traditionalists—the person who likely launched the intellectual base of the Conservative movement—was the venerable Russell Kirk. In his seminal work, 1953's, *The Conservative Mind*, Kirk wrote that "the essence of social conservatism is the preservation of the ancient moral traditions of humanity." They looked at tradition as an unwritten law of social conduct, the established order of civilization. In fact, Traditionalists looked at the American War of Independence as a war that actually *prevented* a "revolution" because it was waged to defend the inherited rights of the colonists and to preserve local self-government against the encroachments of a centralizing state. In the same year, 1953, another Traditionalist, Robert Nisbet, was alerting people in *The Quest for Community* that the increase in the power of the central government was eroding the sources of communities: Family, neighborhood, and church were weakened, and this led people to turn even more to the government.

Two years before Kirk and Nisbet wrote their influential books, a young and brilliant upstart from Yale, William F. Buckley, wrote a book that became a bestseller and brought about a violent reaction from the Old Left: *God and Man at Yale*. Buckley, a Yale graduate and only 26 years of age, exposed Yale's dirty secret, one that dominated most prestigious universities throughout the country: Yale was not passing down American values, but promoting relativism, Socialism, and internationalism.

In the early 1950s, when Conservatism as a cohesive movement was at its incipient stage, the Old Left already had numerous publications, such as *The New Republic, Nation* magazine, the *New Masses, Reporter, The Daily Worker,* and *The Progressive.* Conservatives had very few with limited circulation—*Human Events* and the *Freeman* were about it. The latter had only about 12,000 subscribers, and the audience was mainly the intellectual part of the Conservative community, the few academics and economists who were writing only for one another.

Then came the Intercollegiate Society of Individualists (now the Intercollegiate Studies Institute) in 1953 and the *National Review* in 1955. Not long after, in 1960, William Buckley also created the Young Americans for Freedom, an organization of college-age Conservatives who even confronted and overwhelmed huge New Leftist demonstrations in front of the White House the next year. An observer of the scene wrote that "A flock of little Buckleys now torment social scientists in colleges large and small."[5]

In short, in the early 1950s, when Lionel Trilling could write that "at this time Liberalism is not only the dominant but even the sole intellectual tradition," and that the "impulses" to Conservatism "express themselves…in irritable mental gestures which seek to resemble ideas,"[6] Conservatism began to change and coalesce rapidly.

The political organizing did not emerge until a decade later. Taft was a social Conservative who ran for the Republican nomination for president in 1952, but he had no chance against the affable war hero, Eisenhower. In 1964 another Conservative appeared from Arizona—Barry Goldwater—and the American political scene hasn't been the same since. Goldwater was handily defeated by Lyndon Johnson, who used myriad underhanded tactics, but Goldwater's legacy is what is significant: He moved the base of the Republican Party from the rather liberal "Eastern Establishment" to the south and the west. Even more importantly, a grassroots movement across the country was formed. Finally, the person chosen to introduce him at the convention was presented to the country, and he electrified and inspired Americans: Ronald Reagan. Ronald Reagan is the bane, gadfly, and nemesis of the Old Left and the New Left. Today, even though more than two decades have passed since his presidency ended, he still haunts and enrages Modern Liberals. There will be more on this in another chapter.

Goldwater did not even seek the nomination of the Republican Party; rather, he hoped to rally Conservatives and take back the Grand Old Party. Despite the vicious, immoral, deceitful, and unethical campaigns against him—with the aid of a darling of Modern Liberals and the New Left, Bill Moyers—Goldwater got only six states and 38% of the popular vote.

From the formation of the Great Society in 1965, more aptly entitled the *Ungrateful* Society, the New Left had the support of the media, policymakers, and academics, so there was virtually no real examination of its devastating effects on American society. But by the late 1960s, when Conservatives were building their intellectual, grassroots, and political base, the public was already starting to see the results of the policies of the Leftists. Earlier, the Old Left that supported Stalin's USSR—those who apologized for and denied his every misadventure and horror—fell into oblivion: Nikita Khrushchev denounced Stalin's dictatorial rule and cult of personality at the Twentieth Party Congress of the Communist Party on February 25, 1956, and the Old Left could no longer escape the truth of the history of atrocities, starvation, forced movements of masses, and murders of millions in their Soviet dreamland. Later, the New Left would suffer the same disappointments when even worse events came out in the open about their beloved China and Southeast Asia, but for a time, the New Left enjoyed its dominance. A slew of New Leftist fatuous dreams—the ones of creating a new society, ending the "scourge" of capitalism, and forming a new consciousness—seemed possible for them, and they tried to use government to bring about their Shangri-La; the *Ungrateful* Society was one of their prominent vehicles of propaganda and influence.

What came to pass was not a dream but a nightmare. The New Left managed to convince enough of the public and politicians that with the *right* programs and plans, with the *right* education, and with the *right* funding, the "root" causes of crime, poverty, and illegitimate childbirths in America could be discovered and extirpated. And virtually all of these "root" causes, according to these New Leftists, were the same as those that the dreamers described a century and a half ago: oppression arising from religion, capitalism, and traditions such as marriage and patriotism. They insisted that these had to be weeded out and destroyed. Over a century earlier, the antebellum dreamers set up their visionary communities apart from mainstream society; these New Leftists—in line with their Progressive grandparents and Old Leftist parents—wanted the power of the federal government to organize the entire society—*for its own good*, they proclaimed. The New Leftists were convinced, just as their Progressive progenitors were, that the central government needed to carry out the plans and bring about true prosperity, equality, and fairness. The government had to regulate more, they claimed, create more laws, control education and spend more—then the dream could finally be realized.

Meanwhile, the more radical elements—realigning with the teachings of the dead Italian Communist Gramsci and the doctrines promoted by the refugees from the Frankfurt School such as Horkheimer, Fromm, Adorno, and Marcuse—said that Marx's idea of the proletarians forming a class consciousness would not be effective because religion and materialism stood in the way. Ipso facto, an attack on the culture was the way to go: Tear down the institutions, values, and traditions that maintained a resistance to what they designated as "critical consciousness"—the awareness of one's oppression—and the barriers to the dream would crumble.

So the culture war began. History was revised, minorities were told that they were excluded and victimized, Western civilization was presented as repressive and malevolent, America was taught to be the epitome of oppressive capitalist imperialism, women were indoctrinated to undermine the traditional family, and middle-class life was presented as stifling, inhibited, joyless, and hypocritical. Plays such as *The Death of a Salesman*, for example, were written as examples of the white middle-class workers leading a meaningless life of despair: In *Salesman*, the main character builds walls around himself and barriers to "genuine" human interaction, and this results in his suicide. This nonsense was considered to be something that provided insights into the true nature of our society, but it was pretentious claptrap designed to promote the agenda of the Left.

Americans saw the results of the ludicrous dogma and programs of the parents of the Modern Liberals: Drug use, apathy, welfare dependency, increased racial strife, riots in the streets, inflation, family breakups, abortions, destruction of university property, disparaging of veterans, and flag burning.

The New Left ushered in new demands. For example, they got "rights" for criminals in cases such as the notorious *Miranda*, which actually resulted in an increase in violent crime and a reduction of apprehensions and imprisonment. Confessions had accounted for solving over 24 percent of crimes: A study published in the *Stanford Law Review* showed that after *Miranda*, confessions went from 49 percent to 14 percent in New York City and dropped to 16 percent across the country; and there were not as many convictions—3.8 percent less overall—resulting in 28,000 fewer convictions for violent crimes and 80,000 fewer for property crimes. The fact was that coercive questioning had been dropping well before *Miranda*, and was almost nonexistent; in 1967, right around the time of *Miranda*, the President's Commission on Law Enforcement and the Administration of Justice concluded that "today the third degree is almost nonexistent," and it referred to "its virtual abandonment by the police."[7]

The New Left managed to get court-ordered busing forced on communities, and this resulted in a flight of the most important people—black and white—from the very places where they were most needed, and the resultant destruction of neighborhood schools was felt for generations and remains with us today. There were also strong reactions to the ending of school prayers and legalizing abortions at the Supreme Court level, twisting the meaning of the Constitution by claiming it is a "living document" in order to engineer society and "liberate" people according to the Leftist agenda. In 1965 alone, LBJ submitted 63 legislative proposals and spent more than any previous period in American history.

Johnson refused the nomination for president in 1968, and the resulting Democrat Convention exposed the degree to which the radical element had seized control of that party. Nixon then presented himself as a candidate who would end the war in Vietnam with honor, and he promised to stand up for the "silent majority." But Nixon was no Conservative, and his presidency, with its final Watergate scandal, wreaked havoc on the reputation of the Republican Party. In the next election, Carter easily defeated President Ford, Nixon's replacement after he resigned.

Meanwhile, grassroots Conservatism was building its base. The Equal Rights Amendment was defeated with the help of an anti-Communist Conservative, Phyllis Schlafly. Hayek's book, *The Road to Serfdom*, had been condensed into a Reader's Digest version and sold over a million copies in the 1960s. Conservative foundations and think tanks were being formed and growing; William Buckley had a television program, *Firing Line*, and it reached across America into the homes of average people. The Heritage Foundation and American Enterprise Institute—two of today's most influential think tanks—were getting started in helping Conservative policymakers and Congressmen.

More and more books and magazines came into circulation, disseminating ideas that countered decades of dominance by Progressives and the Left.

Milton Friedman, winner of the Nobel Prize in 1976, became the bane of Modern Liberals, next in line after Ronald Reagan and, possibly, William Buckley. Friedman informed Americans that having the market as free as possible is not mainly about increasing profits or prosperity (although it leads to this), but about freedom itself. Friedman taught us that without a free market—as free as it possibly can be—we would lose an essential pillar of our liberty and, without this pillar, the whole edifice would come crumbling down. He cogently explained how government simply cannot be as efficient and productive as the private sector; because of the nature of the market, government simply is not able to respond to the consumer and his needs as the private sector can. Milton Friedman, George Gilder, and others also disabused Americans of the myths perpetuated by the forerunners of Modern Liberals, the main one being that free-market capitalism promotes *greed*. Milton Friedman taught us how individual self-interest leads to progress and freedom, and George Gilder took us back in time and engaged our imagination by telling tales of how the market forces us to be altruistic in the sense that we must focus on the needs and wants of others, while for the government it is not necessary.

The coup de grace to the New Left came from Ronald Reagan: He pulled the disparate Conservative factions together and united them under the Republican umbrella. Ronald Reagan unabashedly reminded us of our unique roots, clearly and unequivocally stated the evils of Socialism, exposed the agenda of the New Left, and reinstilled the idea that the restoration of fundamental American values would bring us liberty and prosperity.

Under the watch of President Ronald Reagan, the idea of a "living Constitution" was fought by a new organization from 1982: The Federalist Society. This Society sought to influence law schools with the traditional idea based on Natural Rights that the role of courts is to say what the law *is* and not what it *should be*. Little more than a decade later, it had chapters in every major law school and over 25,000 members.

From not long after World War II, the Fairness [in Broadcasting] Doctrine (better thought of as the *Unfairness* in Broadcasting Act) had been in effect, essentially forcing radio stations to "balance" the presentation of political opinion. This was an obvious infringement to our fundamental right to free speech, and the upshot was to drive Conservative stations off the air: Station owners knew that Conservative broadcasts would attract listeners and thus sponsors, but they would also lose sponsors by "balancing" the opinion with Liberal programs because few people would listen to them. So they chose to simply have neither. Under the presidency of Ronald Reagan, the *Unfairness* in Broadcasting regulations ended in 1987, and Conservative hosts grew in prominence, the most notable being Rush Limbaugh. Limbaugh exerted such influence that once, during a debate on the House floor, Speaker Newt Gingrich stepped off the House Floor, called Limbaugh, and asked him to request support from his listeners: There were immediate responses to Congress, and he won over his proposal. By the mid-1990s, Limbaugh had 20 million listeners on 660 stations. And this extended into television: FOX News began in 1996, and within eight years it had the largest share of cable television news; as of February 29, 2012, FOX News had "the top 12 cable news programs" in America.[8] Other Conservative organizations gained strength and prominence as well: The Heritage Foundation, Cato Institute, the American Enterprise Institute, the Manhattan Institute, and the National Rifle Association were all now influential and powerful organizations, reaching into American's homes and consciousness.

Modern Liberals claim that America is a Liberal country, and Conservatives who propose restoring traditional values and founding principles are reactionaries, racists, and dupes of corporate interests. Modern Liberals present Europe as a shining example of the successes of Socialism and internationalism, and they insist that most Americans really want to be like them. But if we take a good look at our basic beliefs—in the previous chapter—and compare our fundamental differences with those of Europe—in the next chapter—we easily see that Conservatism is not a movement of any "far right" groups, but actually an expression of America itself.

The next two chapters are, in part, a continuation of this story of our origins. In the next chapter, the differences between America and Europe further show how conservative America really is; the chapter following it about Ronald Reagan describes the rout of the New Left and the recrudescence of Conservatism in America.

Conservative expressions in America now dominate our culture: Supreme Court decisions have been decided in favor of gun ownership; the term "Liberal" has become a pejorative; self-identified Conservatives now outnumber their Liberal counterpart by slightly over two to one; Conservative think tanks proliferate and grow; Conservative magazines and books are seen in every bookstore across the country; people have a renewed interest in our founding and its principles; and the Tea Party has become a formidable force in shaping American politics. Our radio and television now have Conservative stations on "24/7," and they attract far more listeners and viewers than any Modern Liberal ones do. And, most of all, to say one is a Conservative today is a badge of honor, unlike, only a generation ago, when Lionel Trilling defined Conservatives as people with "irritable mental gestures."

George Nash, in *Reappraising the Right: The Past and Future of American Conservatism*, wrote that Conservatives have accomplished in less than four decades:

> The creation of a veritable conservative counterculture, a burgeoning infrastructure of alternative media, foundations, research centers, think tanks publishing houses, law firms, homeschooling networks, and more.[9]

11

America And Europe

*Our unwavering faith in those traditions which have
made England and America countries of free and upright,
tolerant and independent, people is the thing that counts.*

—FREDRICK HAYEK

Our primary political and cultural origins are European, and most come
from England itself, where the system of government was fundamentally
different from that of the European Continent. Our Founders created
the Constitution from ideas originating in classical, Biblical, and European
sources. Carl Richard concluded that the Greek and Roman authors had the
dominant influence (*The Founders and the Classics*), but Bernard Bailyn (*The Ideological
Origins of the American Revolution*) wrote that much of the referencing of the writers
of antiquity was "window dressing," and that European Enlightenment thinkers
and Biblical sources—especially as evidenced in pamphlets that were widely
circulated—were the dominant sources. Donald Lutz (*The Origins of American*

Constitutionalism) attempted a quantification of the sources by analyzing over 10,000 documents written by the Founders to investigate how often sources were referenced: The Bible was the most frequent, cited 34 percent of the time; English Whigs and English Common Law, if combined (18 and 11 percent, respectively), came next with 29 percent. Enlightenment thinkers followed with 22 percent, then classical writers with nine percent.

Ever since America was a colony, Europeans immigrated to *our world* for a better life or to escape the limitations, prejudices, and oppressions of their own lands. At first, throngs came to seek religious freedom, and others came to improve their lives. Later generations of Europeans would leave their homelands and venture to America for those reasons and others.

Today, Modern Liberals, in their desire to create a centralized state, tell Americans that we should emulate Europeans. They often arbitrarily compare selected aspects of Europe to America, singling out policies and citing statistics from specific countries and ignoring historical backgrounds, cultural differences, and the larger picture. These Modern Liberals blithely brush aside the huge disparities in the attitudes toward the role of government and humanity itself. Modern Liberals profess that Europe is more advanced than we are; that America is bereft of culture; that Europeans are happier; that Europe enjoys more prosperity and security; that Europeans work less and have just as much or more; that Europe's welfare state "works"; that Europe is safer; and that Europe is not militaristic like America.

But could we become like Europeans, and do most Americans even want to? This is one of the most subtle and powerful appeals that Modern Liberals present in their drive to centralize power in the federal government: We need to be more like the Europeans who got things "right." In fact, these Modern Liberals claim that Americans who disagree and do not want to establish a European-style culture and political system are witless, uneducated, unsophisticated, reactionary, imperialist, and supporters of the so-called "military-industrial complex."

Therefore, it is important to take a good look at our differences and why we Americans seem "stubbornly resistant" to the Europeanization of our country.

Modern Liberals conveniently forget the centuries of the exodus from Europe when multitudes from there dreamed of going to America. Modern Liberals "cherry-pick" isolated pieces of information in different European countries—choosing only those that support their agenda for Statism—and ignore the "unintended" and accompanying consequences that invariably follow. British national health care, for example, has resulted in rationing, and the French system of health care requires its citizens to contribute almost one-fifth of their *gross incomes*. European homes are expensive to buy and maintain, so fewer buy their own homes; the houses that the middle class do own are stiflingly small by American standards and without the land and conveniences we enjoy. In Europe, when people move, they have to register with the state, and in most countries, it is unthinkable for an average person to own a gun.

A brief look at Europe itself since our colonial era shows a history of constantly moving borders, religious strife, changes in government, and persecution. From where did *all* of the radical ideas and philosophies—the ones resulting in death, misery, and poverty—originate? They originated in continental Europe. Continental Europe brought not only religious wars, but later the radical and murderous French Revolution, Napoleon, Fascism, Nazism, Anarchism, and the various forms of Marxism. And these spread to all corners of the world—from continental Europe.

But Modern Liberals ignore all of this history; instead, they say that the modern European state—the one that America twice rescued from itself in the 20th century, built back up, and now protects—is the model, the form that we should take as our guide to our future.

It can be difficult for most reasonable people to respond to Modern Liberals who fix upon selected European policies and programs without seeing the entire picture. It is easy for Modern Liberals to parrot the talking points that present an inaccurate, yet ostensibly favorable, picture of Europe. Few of them have actually lived there on the local economy and directly experienced life in the Old World. (This author has, however.)

Rather than just swallowing information delivered by ideologically-driven Modern Liberals, or trying to debate each of their cherry-picked items, let's consider how we differ from Europeans in our nature, character, values, and traditions. Let's have a closer look. And the closer we look, the more we come to understand how unique, special, and exceptional America truly is.

———◆———

Our Founders created a system that was decidedly and deliberately non-European. They looked at Europeans as people to be pitied because of the yoke of their political system. For example, the Founders saw that conflicting European states living next to one another was a significant factor in war, so they created a *union of states*. This also was to protect rights by having other centers of power—the individual states—as opposed to the European one that leads to the centralization of power within each nation-state. The system that the Founders wanted basically forces the government to control itself.

Europeans dwell on the past and their history is filled with grievances. For Americans, history is a source of pride, and it is considered the fountain of our greatness that is in constant renewal. Europeans want to get over their histories, but Americans want to preserve it and live it in the present.

We have had one civil war within our boundaries since our inception; Europe has had *ten* in the same period: 1796–1814, 1821, 1823, 1830, 1848, 1866, 1870, 1875–1878, 1914–1918, and 1939–1945. And war naturally brings about lingering resentments that last for generations, as did our Civil War. Imagine what this must have done in Europe.

America's state boundaries have been stable throughout its history. There have been some changes, but these were mainly voluntary and through compromise for mutual benefit. One look at an historical map of Europe shows a completely different story, and the centuries of ever-changing boundaries and borders were altered at the cost of blood.

America has the longest-existing written constitution in the world. In contrast, France has had fifteen constitutions since its revolution, which happened ten years *after* ours, and Italy has had too many to count.

Patriotism is not shared in Europe, but we Americans proudly wave our flags and do not hesitate to express our love of country. Americans have always been fiercely *American*, even in this age of globalization and internationalism; Europeans drift along with the times. As Mark Steyn wrote, "the German people became just as obnoxiously pacifist as they once were obnoxiously militarist, and as avowedly 'European' as they once were menacingly nationalist."[1] According to a Gallup poll, 76 percent of Americans consider themselves "very" or "extremely" patriotic, and another 19 percent consider themselves "somewhat" patriotic.[2]

Europe wants to dissolve national identities; We Americans are patriotic and would never relinquish ours. 60 percent of Americans believe that American culture is "superior," while only 30 percent of the French think that their own culture is superior and just 40 percent of the English and Germans think so of theirs.

Except for Modern Liberals, Americans do not want to defer to an international court as the Europeans do; Americans honor our supreme law, embodied in our Constitution.

Immigrants have much more difficulty integrating into European society: A person from Africa, India, or Thailand, for example, can never really be considered a *real* German, Italian, or Frenchman even if he gets legal status as such. In contrast, most Americans almost automatically think of people with citizenship—if he has learned English—as a fellow American; many will even get annoyed at the person who gets American citizenship but still refers to himself as an Australian, Indian, or Thai. Americans want people who get citizenship to *be* Americans, to *feel* American, and to *love* America.

America has had a history of those who create prosperity coming from outside of any kind of aristocracy of birth, wealth, or education. Unlike Europe, in America there has been no entrenched aristocracy, no class that denigrated labor, no elite coterie that denied the principle of equality and resisted the forces of social change. In America, people grew alike in attitudes toward work. In contrast, the workers in Europe were in a fixed class and understandably found identity struggling against the ancient regime.

Many primary values in America developed out of accessible land and the necessity of labor by almost everyone; in Europe, one's class and lineage were of the utmost importance. John Diggins wrote about our origins:

> What precluded the development of "proletarian" class consciousness…was not only the absence of huge concentrations of wealth and poverty characteristic of the Old World but also the absence of an entrenched aristocracy, which meant there was no class in America to denigrate the value of labor, deny the principle of equality, and resist the forces of social change. In America, where "every honest calling is honorable," the work ethic found universal recognition…and the people grew increasingly alike in their attitudes because there was no distinct separate class whose aristocratic

arrogance provoked opposing class mentalities based on genuinely different interests and ideals. In Europe both the middle class and the working class found their identity in struggling against the ancien regime, which preached the virtues of paternalism when confronted by the rights of labor.[3]

In dramatic contrast to the condition of the working man in Europe, in America it was easy for an individual to own land or a shop, leading to the idea of acquiring some property and working for oneself; achieving success was limited only by one's imagination. Americans' wages in its early years were two and three times as large as those in Europe, simply because of labor shortages. Americans could save some money and start out on their own; Europeans were stuck.

In Europe's rigid class structure, everyone knew his or her "place," but America was built on a tradition of mutual aid, especially in the frontier. People in early America could not have survived if they based contact and cooperation on the class to which one belonged. In America, families came and they were strangers to one another; to survive and prosper, they developed the spirit of cooperation, and this forced a leveling of social distinctions that remained in Europe. Any "distinctions" became to be based on success. Americans know that we are in control of our destinies and consequently do not resent the well-to-do; this appalls Europeans. Christopher Wolfe, emeritus professor at Marquette University, explained a difference in cultural emphasis with a historical comparison:

> European nations, even after the overthrow of the *ancien regime* in the French Revolution, never completely eliminated the old "culture of deference" to the "higher orders"—which still lingers...Americans, by contrast, never lived in a feudal society, and they experienced substantial social equality from their beginnings...Americans have many more additional opportunities for participating directly in politics, for example on school boards, in town-council meetings, at state legislative hearings, and so on.[4]

As part of this history of class structure, Europe has "society." In this society, intellectuals have status and power. In Europe, far more than in America, the intellectual class mixes with those in the aristocracy and in high levels of business and government. This is not so in America, where the successful *entrepreneurs* gain better access than intellectuals. The American intellectuals compare themselves to their European counterparts and imagine how wonderful it could be there. This accounts for much of the resentment and envy of American intellectuals in our universities, and it gives rise to their attacks on the free market, our traditions and institutions, and even the founding itself.

Europeans had negative attitudes toward work and this was related to one's class: The desired condition, attainable or not, was to be a person of leisure; work was something in which the lower classes occupied themselves. Americans value work and Europeans value leisure. This, too, stems from our respective histories: In America, people gained prestige and status by *building* something. Europeans, in contrast, respected the classes that already were established, had old money, and enjoyed leisure. Matthew Spalding wrote about these differences in our values:

> [I]n Europe, work, especially physical labor and commerce, was looked down upon. The social ideal in Europe had been the leisured life…The Founders' ideal American citizen was to be very different.[5]

In stark contrast, Americans had attitudes that were antithetical to a culture of aristocracy. In America, the only way to reach success and respect was to work and build. Unlike Europeans, Americans developed the beliefs that *everyone* must work, that people benefit from work, and that manual work is respectable. The European system with fixed classes was even tried in our first colonies, but it failed miserably: In the first settlement at Jamestown there were 12 "laborers," 12 "skilled laborers," and 81 "gentlemen," and the property was communal. When the company finally gave most of the colonists their own property and expected everyone to work, they prospered. (Essentially the same thing happened in Plymouth.) Later, Europeans who came to America were shocked to see landowners working with hired hands and eating at the same table; it was obvious that Americans did not look at one another in terms of rigid classes.

Unlike Europeans, Americans did not exempt any class from work and rewarded people based on skill and efforts. Americans made little value distinction between physical and mental work; the *results* were what counted. This is why a plumber can make more than a professor, and Modern Liberal "Elites," aligning with European thoughts and values, resent this. In America, people are actually expected to attain some level of economic success via their own efforts in order to have some degree of respect, both from others and oneself. In Europe, however, tradition and culture tell the people that they should "know their place." As John McElroy noted in *American Beliefs*, "living in America, one cannot avoid recognizing that achieving and maintaining a certain level of success is not only possible but required to retain one's self-respect."[6]

Americans volunteer and have huge numbers of associations and clubs. From our colonial era, Americans have had to rely on neighbors in carving out a life in the New World. This gave rise to a spirit of volunteerism. America has the highest volunteer rate in the world. For example, in 1990, Americans volunteered four times as much as people in Great Britain. Europeans expect the state to fulfill such functions.[7]

Charitable giving in Europe is far less than that of America because Europeans have come to believe that it is a government, not personal, responsibility. Americans, in fact, give more on a private basis than Europeans give in government welfare. This is simply a leftover artifact of their history in which only those of the upper classes were indeed capable of, and duty-bound, to give charity as they saw fit. Hence, Europeans became used to the idea—developed over many centuries—that the central power provides for the masses.

Because of our frontier history, centuries of governing ourselves, traditions of volunteering, and lack of class distinctions, Americans greet and speak to complete strangers. In contrast, most Europeans find this gauche and barbaric. We refuse to "know our proper place" as Europeans do. One observer from Europe was shocked to find that he could go to an upscale restaurant or simple diner and not know the "status" of those who sat next to him.

We Americans support our religious organizations by individual donations and have the largest church attendance among advanced nations. In most of Europe, the state supports the churches, they have the *lowest* attendance, and religious beliefs are mocked. In fact, Europe relegates religious denominations to the authority of the central governments. Former member of the Senate Foreign Relations Committee and assistant Secretary of State Jeff Bergner wrote about it:

> [Churches are] controlled and leveled under government registration, affiliation, support and power. Europe has little experience with truly free religious expression apart from and unauthorized by the central government; Europe reconciles religious freedom and equality by subordinating religion to the state…Europe has marginalized its growing Muslim communities…Europe knows how to tolerate religious expression only by subordinating it, not by protecting its free expression.[8]

Tocqueville, the great French observer of early 19th century America, knew that Europeans were simply used to being controlled by their governments for centuries. The ideals of equality spread in the 17th and 18th centuries. In Europe, however, one form of centralized government simply replaced another; in essence, nothing has changed. Monarchies were simply replaced by the centrally administered state, and this central control is natural to Europeans today. In their parliamentary systems, for example, the party in power automatically possesses both the executive and legislative branches.

Americans ask government to stay out of our lives and insist on limiting its power; we accept that human rights are inherent, not created or granted by the State. In contrast, Europeans ask the government not only to grant rights, but to give more—jobs, welfare, social security, medical care, unemployment benefits, and vacations. Mark Steyn, commenting about the "anti-collectivism" of those involved with the Tea Party notices the Europeans always asking "Why don't you, the government, do more for me?" and contrasts this to America:

> This is the only country in the developed world where hundreds of thousands of people take to the streets to tell the state: I could do just fine if only you'd get the hell out of my life.[9]

Americans are noted for running *from* government help. Many planned communities in America have their own schools, hospitals, and libraries, and the home-school movement has sprouted and spread throughout the country. These are unthinkable to Europeans.

And taxes? In a poll in Britain in 2002, 62 percent of the respondents agreed on having higher taxes for better services. In America, it was *one percent*.[10]

Because Americans have acquired the habits of self-governance, we are more involved and active in politics than almost any other nation. In America, there are more elections for more offices than in other countries, and we even often elect judges and law-enforcement officials.

The European Union's philosophy of governance is unlike America's, where we want to *preserve liberty*; the European's is to *enforce equality*. Their government is not restricted by the limits we impose on our government, and this reveals not only the concept of the government, but the expectations of the governed. Their Lisbon Treaty does not speak to liberty but explains the power of the state. Americans revere our Constitution, written over two centuries in the past; it is a short, ten-page document, easily understood by the citizens. The European

Union has created a document that was initially almost 50 times as long as ours. They "reduced" it, and now it is only about 30 times as long. Unlike our Constitution, the European counterpart is essentially inaccessible to the common man.

In Europe, the far Leftists aligned themselves with the "workers" to get the vote. This was not needed in America, where mass democracy developed along with, as the Leftists called it, "bourgeois capitalism." So, in Europe, the struggle for democracy expanded with the struggle for socialism. In America, the spread of democracy never posed a threat to capitalism, simply because throughout our history—from colonial times—many people owned property. In *The Rise and Fall of the American Left*, John Diggins contrasted the conditions that Americans and Europeans inherited after Marxism began to spread:

> [M]ass democracy developed at the same time as bourgeois capitalism. The "specter" of a democratic class war against capitalism and property that haunted European conservatives turned out to be more shadow than substance in America...In contrast to Europe, where the struggle for democracy often accompanied the struggle for socialism, democracy in America never posed a direct threat to capitalism, since many Americans owned some property, and even those who did not could dream of doing so.[11]

Since Europe had fixed classes and property, when free-market capitalism put pressures to spread property rights and for individuals to acquire wealth, the entrenched interests in Europe resisted. In America, no majority has ever risen up against another class, but Europe's history is filled with that very pattern. America never had European-style "class warfare," even though Modern Liberals have tried to create it. In America, no such classes existed, property was available, work was needed, and there were places to go. So Socialism—as an organized struggle against the entrenched interests—never took hold in America as in Europe. Rather, the idea of creating something, buying a piece of the pie, and going to where there were opportunities not only took hold of the American mind, but were the primary incentives for those who wanted to come.

America's universities compete; Europe's do not compete because they are mostly run by the government: Salaries are fixed, and there is essentially no competition for many staff positions.

Americans value home ownership much more than Europeans, and this is undoubtedly due to our emphasis on private property. The average American house has more rooms per person, is larger, and has more bathrooms. Europeans had a history of the masses not owning land, whereas Americans had the opposite: Even an indentured servant in America—after a decade or so—could, and usually did, own his own land.

For Europeans in general, life is devoid of purpose that can transcend the satisfactions of the appetite, and humans are nothing more than complicated machines for the fulfillment of sensations. Theodore Dalrymple wrote in his review of *Reflections on the Revolution in Europe: Immigration, Islam, and the West*:

> For many young Europeans, Western civilization comprises little more than pop music, soccer, a sexual free-for-all, social-security programs, and five-week holidays to exotic places; to Europeans the past is a mere distraction from the most fundamental question of human existence: "Is it Goa or Bali this year?"[12]

In his own book, *The New Vichy Syndrome: Why European Intellectuals Surrender to Barbarism*, Dalrymple describes the self-doubts European intellectuals have about their civilization, stressing a history of failings and catastrophes and discounting its incredible achievements. We Americans know that the children are the future, and our belief and hope in the future becomes clear when we yell about the budget deficit: The main concern is for our children, not us. In contrast, Dalrymple wrote, Europeans "see children not as the inheritors of what they themselves inherited…but as obstructions to the enjoyment of life, as a drain on resources, an obstacle to next year's holiday."[13]

Charles Murray described the general mentality of Europeans concerning human existence and its inevitable consequences:

> Human beings are a collection of chemicals that activate and, after a period of time, deactivate. The purpose of life is to while away the intervening time as pleasantly as possible…If that's the purpose of life, then work is not a vocation, but something that interferes with the higher good of leisure. If that's the purpose of life, why have a child, when children are so much trouble—and, after all, what good are they, really? If that's the purpose of life, why spend it worrying about neighbors?[14]

Americans know that doing what is moral and right will lead to happiness. Europeans think that leisure and pleasure bring happiness. Americans know that happiness is from successful and virtuous engagement with life.

Morals are very important to Americans. Abortion is a very controversial and hot issue in America, reflecting moral concerns; Europeans do not even discuss the issue. Americans see international conflicts in terms of morals—which country is upright and on the side of goodness. Europeans see them in practical and pragmatic terms; morality has no place in their worldview.

Europeans think that money can solve the world's problems, and Americans assume that ideals and democracy are more important.

American's population is young, and Europe's is old. In the next 50 years, the median age in America is projected to be 35; in Europe, 53.

Older Europeans fear and loathe popular culture and Americans embrace it.

Americans respect and admire the self-made man of action, one who builds a business, starts a company, and uses his own brains and brawn to succeed: Europeans are people of "credentials" who live in a society dominated by government officials who promote this. In Europe, "credentials" give position, authority, and money to those who get the education and certificates, not the ones who actually *create* something.

Europeans talk and philosophize and "reflect," but Americans *act*. Americans are action and results-oriented. We learn by doing. We believe that what has to be done will be done, and this is how we will learn. Europeans are shocked and even offended by the American attitude of confidently jumping in to "fix problems." Over two-thirds of Germans believe that "success in life is pretty much determined by forces outside our control," but less than one-third of Americans think so. This predisposition to act stems from our pioneering spirit, action-orientation, and what Europeans disparagingly refer to as a "cowboy" mentality. Americans respect cowboys, the rugged individualists of action and courage in the American mind; Europeans mock and disparage the "cowboy mentality" as benighted, simplistic, and barbaric. Ultimately, Europeans sneer at us for our "action" orientation, but resent and are envious of us for being what they could or should be. The eminent historian Henry Steele Commager said that no country in the world ever succeeded like America, and everyone knows it. In *their* resentments, we see *our* strengths and exceptionalism.

Americas are always "on the move," and we have the idea that if one place is not satisfactory, we can always move to another. Moving is often associated with upward mobility. Europeans basically "stay put" in their jobs and where they live. All of the immigrants—the people who made up the country—moved. Even virtually all of the original inhabitants—the Native Americans—roamed the fields, the plains, and the forests. America is filled with highways, motels, vans, and service stations—all to accommodate the ever "on the move" Americans.

Americans like guns and feel that our ownership expresses fundamental rights. According to the Department of Justice, 35 to 43 percent of households had at least one gun in the 1990s.[15] American universities have been notoriously anti-gun and liberal, but things are changing: Harvard, the bastion of Modern Liberalism, now has a gun club, and Mount Holyoke has the Second Amendment Sisters. Oxford-educated Micklethwait and Wooldridge, authors of *The Right Nation: Conservative Power in America* postulate that one reason for the university-based gun clubs "is a desire to tweak the noses of America's leftish academic establishment…One form of professor baiting has been to set up gun clubs."[16] Europeans think this is a reflection of a barbaric and violent nation.

Americans in many areas of the county have supported an increase in punishment for crime: Felons are banned from jobs; schools have a "zero tolerance" policy for weapons of any kind; and there are mandatory sentencing rules for many crimes. In contrast, criminals are "rehabilitated" in Europe, and no European country has the death penalty. In fact, to join the European Union, countries are required to renounce it. Outside of America, the only advanced nation in the world to have the death penalty is Japan.

Referring again to Charles Murray's speech, let us remember that the "real stuff of life" takes place in the family, community, work, and faith, and the European model enfeebles each of these by taking the effort out of things, stripping each of its vitality.

American exceptionalism is not just something that Americans claim for themselves. Historically, Americans have been different as a people, even peculiar, and everyone around the world has recognized it. I'm thinking of qualities such as American optimism even when there doesn't seem to be any good reason for it. That's quite uncommon among the peoples of the world. There is the striking lack of class envy in America—by and large, Americans celebrate others' success instead of resenting it. That's just about unique, certainly compared to European countries, and something that drives European intellectuals crazy. And then there is perhaps the most important symptom of all, the signature of American exceptionalism—the assumption by most Americans that they are in control of their own destinies. It is hard to think of a more inspiriting quality for a population to possess, and the American population still possesses it to an astonishing degree. No other country comes close.[17]

12

Ronald Reagan

You don't understand, Dave. Ronald Reagan was elected president. We're all conservatives now.
—PRESCOTT BUSH, GEORGE'S OLDER
BROTHER, TO DAVID KEENE

This chapter deals with a single subject: Ronald Reagan. Today, Ronald Reagan continues to inspire and give guidance to our leaders and is loved by more Americans than ever. Ronald Reagan is also the nemesis, the nightmare, the torment, and the bête noire of Modern Liberals, and remains so more than two decades after the end of his presidency. If one merely mentions his name to Modern Liberals, they will rant and rave, trying to dredge up anything to vilify and discredit not only Ronald Reagan's presidency, but the man himself.

In order to understand the key reasons Ronald Reagan is so reviled by Modern Liberals, we need to consider the next two questions:

1. What specifically do Modern Liberals *hate* about Ronald Reagan? They will point to some policy or issue of economics, but this does not account for the irrational and hysterical paroxysms of rage that ensue at the mere mention of his name.

2. Why does Ronald Reagan remain a fond memory in the hearts of Americans? Why does he grow in stature, despite the constant Modern Liberal hostility and revisionist histories denouncing him? In a February 2011 national poll by Gallup, the public was asked, "Who do you regard as the greatest United States president?" Reagan received the highest percentage, followed by Lincoln.[1] In February 2012 he received the highest percentage again.[2] In addition, the percentage of people who chose him as our greatest president actually *increased* for the third year in a row. Why is this? Modern Liberals will never consider this question; the very idea terrifies them.

Modern Liberals get apoplectic when, despite their unified invective hurled against him, Reagan not only remains one of the most beloved presidents in our history, but the public's fondness for him grows and grows. President Obama, during his Christmas vacation in Hawaii in 2010, made sure that the reporters knew that he was reading a biography of Ronald Reagan; this led one of Reagan's most esteemed biographers to draw the obvious conclusion:

> The news that President Obama decided to read a biography of Ronald Reagan during his Christmas holiday in Hawaii might be taken as a sign that Reagan's triumph over liberals is complete.[3]

A national poll was taken just before Barack Obama assumed the office of the presidency in 2009. A news report of the results was entitled "Obama Should Emulate Ronald Reagan, Voters Tell Pollster." Following is a summary statement:

> When given the choice of Abraham Lincoln, FDR, George Washington, Andrew Jackson, JFK, Dwight Eisenhower, Theodore Roosevelt, Harry Truman and Ronald Reagan—registered voters overwhelmingly said

they want the new Democratic president to emulate the late conservative Republican president, who held office in the 1980's.[4]

Scholars were also queried: In 2000, a study was conducted in which 78 scholars from the fields of law, political science, and history—"explicitly balanced [to have] approximately equal numbers of experts on the left and the right"—rated Ronald Reagan as our eighth greatest president.[5] In 2005, the Federalist Society and the *Wall Street Journal* asked 130 prominent professors of history, law, political science, and economics—ideologically balanced—to rate our presidents. Reagan was ranked sixth in our entire history.[6]

Ronald Reagan not only changed America, but the world: Before Reagan took office, interest rates hit 21 percent, Ted Kennedy bellowed for gas rationing, and there were fuel shortages. Capitalism and democracy were in retreat, the Third World was opting for Marxism and Socialism, and the Soviet nuclear arsenal surpassed that of the United States for first time. After Reagan, there was no inflation to speak of, we had normal interest rates, housing starts were up, gas prices went down, the oil crisis ended, 20 million new jobs were created, the stock market doubled, the poverty rate declined, and the United States became the vanguard of technology in the world. Not only that, but soon after, the Soviet Union collapsed and Socialism was in disrepute. The American economy went into high gear, and the technological revolution took off; young people wanted to be entrepreneurs and not Peace Corps volunteers. The Founders gained a new status: People began to look at our Constitution and founding principles. The welfare state stopped growing, and the idea of wanting "bigger government" came to an end. Ronald Reagan's defense buildup restored morale to the military and built respect for our armed forces in the public mind. When Ronald Reagan built up our military, recruitment and retention increased, and the quality of new soldiers improved. Even GI Joe Action Figures were selling like hotcakes, and the antiwar TV program *M*A*S*H** ended in 1983 after 11 years.

The Liberals' aspirations for more tax increases were dashed—permanently. Steven Hayward wrote about it in *The Age of Reagan*:

> The 1986 tax reform foreclosed the possibility of using the income tax code for purposes of punishing the rich or redistributing wealth in any significant way. The liberal principle of progressivity was not completely

banished, but no longer would the tax code be seen as a plaything for changing society wholesale.[7]

In 1987, under Ronald Reagan's presidency, the Federal Communications Commission repealed the "Fairness [in Broadcasting] Doctrine." This "Doctrine" mandated that broadcasters present opposing political viewpoints. In other words, prior to this point, the stations were not free to present opinions or views unless opposing ones were also presented. The Democrats tried to choke the repeal by codifying the "Doctrine," and Reagan vetoed it. The Liberals tried to restore it again in 1989 and 1990 but failed. They tried again is 2007, 2008, and 2009 but continued to fail.

Despite the bombardment by the Left-wing press in 1984, Ronald Reagan was reelected in a landslide: he won 49 states and got 59 percent of popular vote, the fourth largest in history, and we have not seen such a victory since.

Reagan was well-liked by the young: He got three-quarters of first time voters and an 82 percent approval rating from people under the age of 24. Liberal Pat Moynihan said, "I'll tell you what chills the blood of liberals. It was always thought that the old bastards were the conservatives. Now the young people are becoming the conservatives and we're the old bastards."

Ronald Reagan left office with the highest approval rating in the modern era—70 percent—surpassing Dwight Eisenhower and John Kennedy. Today, people refer to "Reaganism," but we never hear of "Clintonism" or "Obamaism."

Reagan was inspiring because he was able to build upon the American character, reminding Americans of where we came from, but not wanting to regress to the past. He was a different kind of Conservative who believed in the future. In the first edition of *National Review*, William F. Buckley said this of Conservatism: "It stands athwart history, yelling Stop." Reagan stood athwart history, embraced the founding, but yelled, "Go!"

Modern Liberals, who refuse any contradictions or acceptance of facts that do not fit, do not see the larger picture, the one in which Ronald Reagan renewed hope and pride at a time when Americans were despairing of it. He did it with something near and dear to the hearts of virtually all Americans: Ronald Reagan was the modern embodiment of our Founding Fathers. The American people saw their Founders living in this man; they saw American exceptionalism, virtue, the American dream, liberty, and the "shining city on a hill." In short, when they saw and listened to Ronald Reagan, they saw what made America great. The "Reagan Revolution" is everyday parlance now, but Ronald Reagan conceived of his presidency not as any kind of revolution, but as a restoration of the founding principles. Steven Hayward wrote in The *Age of Reagan: The Conservative Counterrevolution, 1980–1989*:

> Reagan has so fully internalized the thought of so many of his political forebears such as Jefferson, Lincoln, and Roosevelt that it is not clear whether he knew he was paraphrasing them.

Ronald Reagan's central idea was anathema to the New Left of his time and to the Modern Liberals of today. Steven F. Hayward continued:

> Lincoln once wrote that all nations have a central idea, from which all its minor thoughts radiate. The same can be said of leading statesmen. Reagan's central idea can be summarized as the view that unlimited government is inimical to liberty, both in its vicious forms such as Communism or socialism, but also in its supposedly benign forms, such as bureaucracy.[8]

Ronald Reagan was not against the growth of government because of problems with efficiency or effectiveness, but because it went against the Constitutional grounds of consent. Ronald Reagan had faith in America and its Constitution.

Why Modern Liberals are Hostile to Ronald Reagan

So what did Ronald Reagan bequeath that Modern Liberals detest so much?

First of all, Ronald Reagan put Conservative ideas in the mainstream; this may be his greatest enduring legacy. Modern Liberals abhor this, and it is the main reason that they want to discredit him and defile his memory. Ronald Reagan's victories meant the defeat of the New Left, and today's Modern Liberals are well aware of this. They loathe him for it. Harvey Mansfield, Professor of Government at Harvard University, concluded that Reagan's overwhelming victory in 1980 was "a general repudiation of the values of the 1960s."[9] Today, the word "Liberal" is often an aspersion, a pejorative; in fact, many Modern Liberals have abandoned the term and now identify themselves as "Progressives." In 1988, William Schneider of the *New Republic* explained this: "Why has liberalism become such a scare word? The reason is that Reagan has changed the shape of American politics."[10] Later, in 1996, Richard Reeves, author of *The Reagan Detour*, wrote, "I was no fan of Ronald Reagan, but...he was a man of conservative principle and he damned near destroyed American liberalism."[11] In 1999 Reeves wrote that "Reagan, in fact, is still running the country. President Clinton is governing in his shadow."[12]

Ironically, Ronald Reagan told us that Conservatives were really the new Classic Liberals of the past!

> The Classic Liberal used to be the man who believed the individual was, and should be forever, the master of his destiny. That is now the conservative position. The liberal used to believe in freedom under law. He now takes the ancient feudal position that power is everything. He believes in a stronger and stronger central government, in the philosophy that control is better than freedom. The conservative now quotes Thomas Paine, a long-time refuge of the liberals: "Government is a necessary evil; let us have as little of it as possible."[13]

During Ronald Reagan's presidency, the idea of the "Original Intent" in our Constitution gained momentum from the efforts of Attorney General Edwin Meese, the man who had called the American Civil Liberties Union "the criminals' lobby." This reopened a fundamental quarrel with the New Left and today's Modern Liberals that no prominent politician had advanced since the Coolidge era. In itself, it was a de-facto declaration of war on the New Left that continues with today's Modern Liberals. As Steve Hayward wrote in *The Age of Reagan*, "original intent...is incendiary for liberals—the idea of a restrained or limited constitutionalism strikes at the heart of any liberal agenda for political intervention into social affairs."[14]

Ronald Reagan and Communism

As we saw on the maps in Chapter 6, the growth of Communism throughout the world cannot be denied. Communism was proliferating rapidly after World War II. The policy toward Communism was "containment," but it was not being contained. In 1964, James Burnham, in *Suicide of the West*, wrote that "if Communism continues to advance at the rate it has in fact maintained...it will achieve its goal of world power before the end of the century."[15] Up until the era of Ronald Reagan, the consensus of the Old Left and the New Left was that Communism in the world was permanent—we had to accept and live with it. The best we could hope for was to limit its expansion.

But Ronald Reagan thought differently: "Here's my strategy on the Cold War: *We win,* they lose." At a speech in Notre Dame in 1981, Ronald Reagan said: "The West won't contain Communism. It will transcend communism. It will dismiss it as some bizarre chapter in human history whose last pages are even now being written."

Ronald Reagan not only labeled the Soviet Union the familiar "Evil Empire," but he also said that it was "the very heart of darkness." On March 8, 1983, Ronald Reagan said that the Soviet Union was "the focus of evil in the world." Earlier, in an interview with Walter Cronkite of CBS News on March 3, Ronald Reagan was asked about his strong statement concerning the USSR in an earlier press conference. Reagan replied:

> I said, "I don't have to offer my opinion. They have told us where they're going over and over again. They have told us that their goal is the Marxian philosophy of world revolution and a single, one-world Communist state and that they're dedicated to that."…[T]heir statement about morality is that nothing is immoral if it furthers their cause, which means they can resort to lying or stealing or cheating or even murder if it furthers their cause, and that is not immoral…And I've noticed that with their own state-ments about me [since then]…they have never denied the truth of what I said.[16]

With the help of Prime Minister Margaret Thatcher (the Iron Lady) of England, Pope John Paul II, and others, the Evil Empire was brought down. As Martin and Annelise Anderson thoroughly chronicled from primary sources in *Reagan's Secret War: The Untold Story of His Fight to Save the World from Nuclear Disaster,* and as Peter Schweizer documented in *Reagan's War: The Epic Story of His Forty-Year Struggle and Final Triumph Over Communism,* Ronald Reagan formed convic-tions about Communism before he ever held office. His initial dealings with Communists occurred when he was head of the Screen Actors' Guild and saw them infiltrating Hollywood. Later, as vice-president of public relations for General Electric, he outsmarted the Communists in the electrical work-ers' unions.[17] Ronald Reagan wrote in his autobiography, *An American Life,* that "Stalin had set out to make Hollywood an instrument of propaganda [and] aimed at communizing the world."[18] At that time, the Communists threatened to throw acid in Reagan's face, and the FBI gave him 24 hour surveillance and a gun. According to FBI files released in 1985, Ronald Reagan worked with the FBI from 1941 and even had the code name "T-10." He helped lead Congress to the infamous "Hollywood Ten" and challenged Truman's "containment" policy. Sterling Hayden had been a member of the Communist Party; he said that the Communists' efforts to gain support from film stars failed because of "a one-man battalion named Ronald Reagan."[19]

In the decade before his presidency, Ronald Reagan warned about the growing strength of the Soviet Union. He protested when Carter proposed to withdraw all US ground forces and nuclear weapons from South Korea without trying to force North Korean concessions, and he spoke out against Carter's plan to cut $57 billion from the seven-year defense spending plan. When Carter suspended the development of the neutron bomb, planned to halt the building of the Trident nuclear submarine, and canceled the B-1 bomber, Ronald Reagan openly stood against it. Ronald Reagan opposed the treaties to turn over the Panama Canal to Panama as compromising the defense perimeter of the United States. Above all, he opposed the idea of détente. He opposed the Helsinki Accords because he thought they codified the captive status of Moscow's East European satellites, and he believed détente conferred a false legitimacy upon states whose governments were not installed by the consent of the governed. Ronald Reagan looked at the arms race as a symptom, not a cause, of international tensions, and he correctly maintained—contrary to the New Left—that the cause was the Communists' expansionist tendencies. Ronald Reagan agreed with Churchill and with the Democrats' mid-century presidents that the best way to avoid a war was to be ready to fight one, and in one of his radio addresses repeated the phrase, "No nation ever saved its freedom by disarming itself in the hope of placating an enemy."

After the Communists consolidated power from the 1917 Russian Revolution, the Old Left was in thralls of ecstasy and their dream continued for over three decades. But the Soviet Union became discredited after its tyrannies in Eastern Europe, mass movements of populations in the USSR, the deliberate starvation of millions of peasants, and the notorious Stalin "Show Trials" could no longer be denied. The Old Left tried hard to disclaim, excuse, and apologize. The America people were naturally frightened by this empire acquiring an atomic bomb, especially after hearing Winston Churchill's famous Iron Curtain Speech in America on March 5, 1946: "From Stettin in the Baltic to Trieste in the Adriatic an iron curtain has descended across the Continent." Just under a decade later, Khrushchev would utter his well-known declaration to the West: "We will bury you." (He actually said, "We will dig you in," but the effect was quite the same.)

But with Ronald Reagan's presidency, Communist countries began to become free for the first time in the 20th century. Not a single country fell to Communism while Reagan was in office.

Ronald Reagan and the Demise of Communism

Communism came to an end in the Soviet Union; that is irrefutable. But Modern Liberals refuse to acknowledge the existence of an essential element: Ronald Reagan played a pivotal role in its demise. Modern Liberals deny the undeniable by asserting that other factors brought the change and that Reagan played no role in its denouement. Instead, they have their own absurd explanations:

1. Gorbachev brought about the needed changes.
2. Communism had simply evolved into its inevitable democratic form.
3. The Russian economy was rapidly deteriorating because of its own internal difficulties, and they were not exacerbated or generated by Ronald Reagan.

The truth that Modern Liberals deplore is that the dissolution of the Soviet Union and the end of Communism were brought about—or at least dramatically hastened—from external pressures. It is possible that the USSR would have eventually dissolved, but it would have been much later, and who knows at what cost? Would another war have started? Would the Soviets have tried—in their usual brutal fashion—to take direct control of Eastern Europe? Would the USSR have formed other dangerous alliances? We can never know the answers to such questions, but we *can* know for certain that it ended peacefully, and that it was a result of the policies that accompanied the leadership, guidance, will, and courage of Ronald Reagan. Even Gorbachev recognized Reagan's role, saying "I am not sure what happened would have happened had he [Ronald Reagan] not been there."[20] While giving Gorbachev his due for not sending in the tanks into Poland—at least in part because he wasn't sure he could—it was Reagan who fatally undermined the confidence of the entire Communist bloc. Gorbachev's very appointment was due to Reagan: The Soviets felt they needed a younger, more modern leader to deal with Reagan. If the Soviets had still felt confident about an inevitable triumph of Communism, not only would they never have gambled with Gorbachev, they certainly would not have allowed the Perestroika movement.

Ronald Reagan actually *did* something: He installed Pershing missiles in Europe; he invaded Grenada; and he supported anti-Communist forces around the world—in Angola, Afghanistan, Ethiopia, Poland, and Nicaragua. Reagan formed a compact with Pope John Paul II which was credited as being "one of the great secret alliances of all time."[21]

Most of us are very aware of the American defense buildup that aimed at making it too costly for the Soviets to compete militarily: Reagan's Strategic Defense Initiative—Star Wars—became a crucial part of the strategy. But there were also the covert operations aimed at encouraging reform movements in Hungary, Czechoslovakia, and Poland, and anti-Communist forces around the world—in Afghanistan, Angola, Poland, and Ethiopia—were openly supported. And there was the financial aid to Warsaw Pact nations to support their willingness to protect human rights and undertake political and free-market reforms. Reagan also began an economic isolation of the Soviet Union: Western and Japanese technology were withheld from Moscow, many world markets were cut off from the Soviets, a trade embargo was put on Russian goods, and oil was deregulated. In addition, he convinced the Saudis to *triple* oil production to get the prices down even further, from 30 dollars a barrel to 13 dollars a barrel; this dramatically hampered Soviet cash inflow from their oil exports. The Reagan Administration focused on denying the Soviet Union its principal source of hard currency: profits from a pipeline to supply natural gas to Western Europe. The Reagan administration also collaborated with the French so that the Russians thought that they had "stolen" computerized technology that would regulate pressures in gas walls and pipelines: After it was installed, it blew up in one of the biggest nonnuclear explosions in history. Less well known, or forgotten, is the increased use of Radio Liberty, the Voice of America, and Radio Free Europe to transmit the messages of freedom to the peoples of Eastern Europe.

There is no need to even debate and discuss each action; just look at the results:

1982: Grenada was free. It was the first time a Communist nation had been rolled back in over six decades.

1989: Soviet troops were out of Afghanistan.

1989: The Berlin Wall was torn down.

1990: NATO announced that the Soviet Union was no longer an adversary after almost 45 years.

1990: The republics of the Soviet Union declared their independence one by one.

1991: The day after Christmas, the Soviet Union was officially dissolved.

And Ronald Reagan lived to see his victory in less than three years after his presidency ended.

The causes of the fall of the Soviet Union are still being debated, and Modern Liberals stubbornly refuse to give Ronald Reagan credit, of course. Modern Liberals say everyone knew at the time that the USSR was weakening. This is another example of Modern Liberals' use of "presentism"—applying standards of the present to the past. Reason and common sense—of which they are bereft—unequivocally tell us that the president and others worked with the prevailing wisdom and consensus *at that time*. And here are some statements from politicians and pundits *at that time*:

"We cannot prevent the growth of Soviet power" and we must adhere to the "imperative of coexistence."

- Henry Kissinger, during the Carter presidency.

"The Soviet Union is not now nor will it be during the next decade in the throes of a true systemic crisis, for it boasts enormous unused reserves of political and social stability."

-Sovietologist Seweryn Bialer, 1982, Foreign Affairs

"Those in the United States who think the Soviet Union is on the verge of economic and social collapse [are] wishful thinkers who are only kidding themselves."

-Arthur Schlesinger, Jr., 1982

"That the Soviet system has made great material progress in recent years is evident both from the statistics and from the general urban scene...One sees it in the appearance of solid well-being of the people on the streets...and the general aspect of restaurants, theaters, and shops...Partly, the Russian system

succeeds because, in contrast with the Western industrial economies, it makes full use of its manpower."
-John Kenneth Galbraith, 1984

"[T]here can be no doubt that the Soviet planning system has been a powerful engine for economic growth...The Soviet model has surely demonstrated that a command economy is capable of mobilizing resources for rapid growth."
-Paul Samuelson, Nobel Prize winner, 1985

"Can economic command significantly...accelerate the growth process? The remarkable performance of the Soviet Union suggests that it can...Today the Soviet Union is a country whose economic achievements bear comparison with those of the United States."
-Lester Thurow, MIT economist, 1988

In response to the Modern Liberals' insistence that the USSR was on its way out anyway, Jeane Kirkpatrick, former member of Ronald Reagan's Cabinet and Ambassador to the United Nations, pointed out that in just the decade before Ronald Reagan came into office, the Soviets had expanded influence and control in the following countries. (Refer to the maps in Chapter 6):

Aden
Afghanistan
Cambodia
Ethiopia
Grenada
Laos
Libya
Madagascar
Mozambique
Nicaragua
South Vietnam
South Yemen
Syria
The Congo
The Seychelles

But Kirkpatrick left out the countries that embraced Marxism or Socialism during that decade:

Algeria
Benin
Cape Verde
Guinea-Bissau
San Tome
Tanzania
Zambia

And let's add the other countries through which the Soviets had previously marched:

Albania
Angola
Armenia
Azerbaijan
Bulgaria
Cuba
Czechoslovakia
East Germany
Estonia
Georgia
Hungary
Kirgizia
Latvia
Lithuania
Moldavia
Mongolia
North Korea
North Vietnam
Poland
Romania
Tajikistan
Turkmen
Uzbekistan
Yugoslavia

Modern Liberals cannot accept the truth that the methods on which Ronald Reagan based his resolution to bring about the demise of Communism actually did so: decentralization of government, lower taxes, free-market capitalism, and our founding principles. Maybe the Soviets would have eventually collapsed on their own, but it would have taken much longer, and in truth, it wasn't really an economic or military collapse that did them in: It was a collapse in their confidence in the Communist system, and Ronald Reagan contributed more to *that* than any other man alive. Modern Liberals refuse to acknowledge that Ronald Reagan helped to win the Cold War because, if it were true, it would mean that they were monumentally wrong on the matter of America's security and their view of the Communist world. But some honest people among Modern Liberals realize that it can no longer be denied; Sean Wilentz, a Liberal historian (*The Age of Reagan: A History, 1974–2008*) wrote about it:

> His success in helping finally to end the Cold War is one of the greatest achievement by any president of the United States—and arguably the greatest single presidential achievement since 1945.[22]

Several times, Margaret Thatcher said that under Ronald Reagan's leadership we "won the Cold War without firing a single shot." Even the prominent far-Left Senator Ted Kennedy said: "On foreign policy, he [Ronald Reagan] will be honored as the president who won the Cold War." Thatcher helped Reagan of course: In 1982, not long after Reagan completed the first rollback ever of Communism in Grenada, Margaret Thatcher retook the Falkland Islands. Thatcher did this partly to show the Communists that the free world had the will to not only resist tyranny, but to roll it back.

Today, revolutionary Communism as an ideal and as a threat to the world is over. This is another reason that the New Leftists and Modern Liberals revile Ronald Reagan: He ended the illusion that there could be a utopian Communist state. Ronald Reagan was clear in his convictions about Communism: "Communism…is a form of insanity…It is contrary to human nature,"[23] and he knew that "communists use lies, deceit, violence, or any other tactic."[24] William F. Buckley said that with Ronald Reagan, "the countdown for communism began."[25] Margaret Thatcher said "We were not to know it at the time, but 1981 was the last year of the West's retreat from the axis of convenience between the Soviet Union and the Third World,"[26] and "There is new leadership in America, which gives confidence and hope to all in the free world."[27]

Only last year, in November 2011, a statue of Ronald Reagan was unveiled in Warsaw, Poland, by Lech Walesa, leader of the movement against the Communists. It was dedicated "to former US president Ronald Reagan who is highly respected in Poland for having helped hasten the fall of the Iron Curtain."[28]

The Reagan Wealth-Creating Machine

Modern Liberals cannot accept that the Reagan era ushered in under his policies a wealth-creating machine such as the world had never seen.

The Modern Liberals' attempts to deprecate the Ronald Reagan economic record provide an excellent example of how they distort and manipulate data for their purposes. It requires some time for policies to go into effect, but Modern Liberals begin an analysis from the day Ronald Reagan took office (actually from three weeks *before*), not from when the results of his policies started to be felt. If we analyze data *after* Reagan's policies had time to go into effect, the information changes dramatically: Real economic growth averaged 3.2 percent during the Reagan years versus 2.8 percent during the Ford-Carter years and 2.1 percent during the Bush-Clinton years; real median family income grew by $4,000 during the Reagan period after experiencing no growth in the pre-Reagan years, and it experienced a loss of almost $1,500 in the post-Reagan years; and interest rates, inflation, and unemployment fell faster under Reagan than they did immediately before or after his presidency. When Jimmy Carter's economic policies were in place, family incomes plummeted by 9 percent, but after Reagan's economic policies took effect (1982–89), family incomes rose by 11 percent. By the end of the Reagan years, the American economy was almost one-third larger than it was when it began. GDP growth per adults age 20-64 in the Reagan years grew twice as rapidly, on average, as it did in the pre- and post-Reagan years. From 1982 through 1989, the US economy produced over 17 million new jobs, well over two million new jobs each year: Contrary to the Clinton administration's claims of vast job gains in the 1990s, the United States has averaged only 1.3 million new jobs per year in the post-Reagan years.

Over the past 30 years there has been a downward trend in US productivity growth. Under Reagan, productivity grew at a 1.5 percent annual rate. This was lower than in the 1950s, 1960s, and 1970s, but much higher than in the post-Reagan years. Under Clinton, productivity increased at an annual rate of just 0.3 percent per year. Domestic spending grew at a slower real rate under Reagan than under all other recent presidents. Five-year tax and spending projections under President Carter's last year would have seen taxes and spending rise from about

21 percent of GDP to 24 percent by 1984. Domestic outlays as a share of GDP fell from 15.3 to 12.9 percent from 1981 to 1989. If defense spending had been held to the rate of inflation from 1981 to 1989, the total real deficit would have fallen in the 1980s rather than risen; however, the decline in the military budget accounts for almost the entire fall in the deficit from 1988 to 1996.

Not long ago, Steven Forbes wrote the following:

> Between the early 1980s and 2007 we lived in an economic Golden Age. Never before have so many people advanced so far economically in so short a period of time as they have during the last 25 years. Until the credit crisis, 70 million people a year were joining the middle class. The U.S. kicked off this long boom with the economic reforms of *Ronald Reagan*, particularly his enormous income tax cuts. We burst from the economic stagnation of the 1970s into a dynamic, innovative, high-tech-oriented economy.[29]

Lee Iacocca, the man known for engineering the Mustang and successfully reviving the Chrysler Corporation, said "Reagan rolled up his sleeves, got inflation down to almost nothing, and cut taxes." Jack Kemp, the architect of the Economic Recovery Tax Act of 1981, known as the Kemp-Roth tax cut, said that Ronald Reagan's "programs led to the fastest growth without inflation, 21 million new jobs and 4 million new businesses."

Robert Barro of the Wall Street Journal concluded that from 1949 until 1992, on the conditions of unemployment, changes in inflation and long-term interest rates, Reagan's first and second terms were number one among all administrations.[30]

But possibly most of all, it exasperates Modern Liberals that nearly all other industrialized countries *emulated and followed* the Reagan tax plan!

> Norway cut its top tax rate from 75 percent to 54 percent, Finland cut rates from 71 percent to 54 percent...New Zealand from 60 percent to 33 percent...Canada, from 58 percent to 45 percent; Austria, from 62 percent to 40 percent; Japan, from 75 percent to 50 percent.[31]

Ronald Reagan United Americans

Modern Liberals cannot accept that the American people can be inspired by a restoration of our founding principles. It is antithesis of their credo of the formation and management of a visionary new society controlled by the central government. They are hostile to the idea of the embodiment of our Founders and deem it to be antiquated and unenlightened. But the people voted and gave Ronald Reagan one of the greatest electoral victories in our history, and he remains one of the most popular presidents ever.

Modern Liberals will never forgive Ronald Reagan for elevating William Rehnquist to the highest position in the Supreme Court and for putting Antonin Scalia there, followed by his vice president, George H. W. Bush, nominating the conservative justice Clarence Thomas.

From the standpoint of the New Left and Modern Liberals, one of Ronald Reagan's greatest sins was uniting Conservatives. He moved Conservatism from the fringes to the mainstream. As Alfred Regnery wrote in *Upstream: The Ascendance of American Conservatism*:

> Reagan took the [conservative] movement's ideas, communicated them to the American people in understandable terms, and applied them to practical politics. His political march moved the conservative cause from the fringes to the mainstream...He pulled the anti-Communists, libertarians, economic conservatives, traditionalists, the Christian right, and even neoconservatives into a powerful coalition.[32]

Ronald Reagan welcomed all and was the person who took action. Among Conservatives, there are, and have been, free-market economists, traditionalists, social conservatives, anti-communists, isolationists, libertarians, and the religious right. Ronald Reagan made a home for them and encouraged all to find common ground. Ronald Reagan *embodied* America.

Ronald Reagan possessed a clear vision. He understood something in the world anathema to our founding principles—Communism—and called it what it was without reservation: *evil*. He saw similar forces at home and brought America's attention to it without fomenting hate. After Ronald Reagan welcomed all Americans under his broad umbrella and exposed the Left for what it was, many deserted that camp and united under Reagan. The most notable of these were the "Neoconservatives." Jeane Kirkpatrick, for instance, was one of the Left who came to the Reagan Conservative camp and became Ambassador to the United Nations. Something Kirkpatrick said demonstrated how far these people had come from the New Leftist mentality that had constantly disparaged, attacked, and vilified America: "Americans need to face the truth about themselves, no matter how pleasant it is."

Four things stand out about how Ronald Reagan dealt with America and its people:

1. Ronald Reagan focused on large, central themes.
2. Ronald Reagan's tone was unfailingly gracious and civil; he was concerned mainly with issues, not men. Reagan did not oppose for the sake of opposing. For example, he criticized Carter's ideas but seldom criticized the man, and he almost never uttered the president's name.
3. Ronald Reagan was an optimist.
4. Ronald Reagan succeeded in setting out a coherent and principled message while forming and leading a diverse coalition.

There were two main ways that Ronald Reagan behaved toward the Old and New Leftists, and we can be inspired to respond in the same vein:

1. Ronald Reagan did not proclaim he was a Conservative. He used attractive policies and ideas to get individuals to look at his Conservatism.
2. The Founding Fathers were important to Ronald Reagan. They provided unity and roots in American traditions and nobility.

Ronald Reagan was a man of the people. When he worked for General Electric he traveled the country as a motivational speaker where he discovered America in the factories and in the cafeterias. What he actually heard in those conversations formed the basis of a philosophy that was in touch with mainstream America, and opposed to the conventional wisdom of the elites. In 1986, five and one-half years after he first became president and one reelection later, Ronald Reagan's picture was on the cover of *Time Magazine*. Next to his picture was the question: "Why is this man so popular?" Some reasons were explained in the magazine's lead article:

> [Ronald Reagan] has restored the authority of the American presidency. He has given the Americans optimism and pride in themselves and in their country that they have not possessed since the death of John Kennedy. And he is the first President since F.D.R. to alter the debate over what the role of government should be. As one keeps score in the art of the possible, that is not bad at all...Reagan seems to derive his strength from the fact that he does exactly what he says he will do...All that has a tonic effect. It may give Americans the idea that they are getting what they pay for.[33]

The *Washington Post* cited Ronald Reagan for "one of the most remarkable demonstrations of presidential leadership in modern history." The Liberal Senator from Massachusetts, John Kerry, said that "Ronald Reagan's love of country was infectious." Tip O'Neill, Reagan's arch-rival, said, "In my fifty years of public life, I have never seen a man more popular with the American people."[34]

———————◆———————

Ronald Reagan started the conversation about Liberalism, and it has not finished. The conversation really started on a national scale with him, and he horrified the Old Left and the New Left when he spoke about government being the problem. No president had ever done that in the 20th century. Ronald Reagan spoke against enlarged government, the welfare state, and socialized medicine. Before Reagan, people thought that more limited government was simply impossible in the modern age: People started to give up on the idea of government by the people, one comprised of ordinary citizens. Americans were falling into the mindset that experts in government should provide and think for the people, and that huge bureaucracies are necessary. Reagan believed in the people and renewed our spirit when he spoke about them:

> They are not "the masses," or as the elitists would have it, "the common man." They are very uncommon. Individuals, each with his or her own hopes and dreams, plans and problems, and the kind of quiet courage that makes this whole country run better than just about any other place on earth.[35]

Reagan's supply-side economics brought about debates that will never be fully resolved, getting lost in a morass of economic numerology and jargon. This argument usually centers on the supply-siders belief that tax cuts were most effective on the supply side (as opposed to the consumption side), and that tax cuts might increase revenue—depending on whether is it applied to earned income or unearned income—and so on. The real issue here is liberal ideology, not economics per se. Supply side really means that the private market is more powerful and effective than government intervention. By implication, supply-side economics represented a rebuke to the premises of activist government, and hence to Modern Liberalism itself. Steven Hayward explained why it irks Modern Liberals so much:

> The most significant of the challenge to liberal orthodoxy was…its premise that the decisions and actions of the private market were more powerful than government intervention. By implication, supply-side economics represented a rebuke to the premises of activist government, and therefore of liberalism.[36]

Steven Hayward, in *The Age of Reagan*, made an appeal to Americans in the last paragraph of his 753-page book: "If the Reagan Revolution is finally to be consummated, the movement that cherishes his name will need to return to this mode of constitutional thinking and press to achieve the reforms that Reagan could only dream of."[37]

But let's end this chapter with a statement by the great Ronald Reagan that reflects his attitude toward us—the American people:

> We can and will resolve the problems which now confront us. And after all, why shouldn't we believe that? We are Americans!

13

Taking America Back

*Every child in America should be acquainted with his
own country. As soon as he opens his lips, he should...
lisp the praise of liberty and of those illustrious heroes and
statesmen who have wrought a revolution in her favor.*
—NOAH WEBSTER

*Freedom is a fragile thing and is never more than one
generation away from extinction. It is not ours by
inheritance; it must be fought for and defended constantly
by each generation.*
—RONALD REAGAN, 1961

Most of us know—primarily at an intuitive level—that something is wrong, and that there is a destructive force in our presence. Modern Liberals have contrived to arouse a sense of needless guilt in countless Americans, instilled a fear of being branded as "cold-hearted" or "bigoted," and compelled us to want to show that we have "compassion" and "care" *as Modern Liberals define it.*

Modern Liberals—whether they push their agenda for power, the dream of utopia, sheer opportunism, or out of their own fears—can be seen everywhere: They are in our schools, the media, the workplace, and our neighborhoods and towns. They are the "squeaky wheel" whose noise draws attention and energy, the one that is quite impossible to ignore, the one which we often feel compelled to appease if only to get a respite from their incessant demands. Sometimes this "squeaky wheel" manages to raise doubts that maybe *our* attitudes and proposals have wrought economic problems, racial tensions, poverty, and unnecessary war upon the nation. Modern Liberalism is destructive, and we must not—we *cannot*—remain silent, hoping that it will go away, or believing that it does not really matter. We must not conclude that by appeasing Modern Liberals "just this one last time," they will be satisfied because they never will. Maggie Gallagher, President of the National Organization for Marriage, wrote about the malevolence we face:

> Culture consists of ideas. Ideas, like civilizations, can die out. They die when no one is willing to defend them out loud…In the marketplace of ideas, not all Americans are equal. Culture is created by "elites"; the culture war we are in with the Modern Liberals ends when one side's will to fight is broken…A culture shift is complete only when an idea becomes uncontested (and uncontestable) by good, decent, law-abiding, "normal" citizens.[1]

But she offers hope: "But here is *our* edge: The truth is easier to represent when reality is on your side."

The primary purpose of this book is to help prepare individuals to stand up to, and deal with, Modern Liberals in their everyday lives. Hopefully, readers will encourage others in these endeavors. If we refuse to back down from these Modern Liberal ideologues and instead go on the offensive, fellow Americans will join in: As our numbers grow, Modern Liberals will be driven out of the mainstream and relegated to the fringes of society. The media, our children's schools, and elected officials will respond as our voices grow.

———◆———

Modern Liberals are active in a multitude of arenas, including environmental issues, race relations, economics, education, sex, family, taxation, culture, and the media. Most Modern Liberals, as described in Chapter 3, do not feel that they are part of a unified and overall pattern of the centralization of power, but they have become convinced that the solutions for all problems lie in uniformity, organization, and regulation of which only a central power is capable. They suppose that if, for example, educational policies were left up to local communities or even to state governments, the result would be chaos, discrimination, and a lowering of standards. These Modern Liberals are therefore participating, willy-nilly, in the drive to centralize power in the federal government. Each may be in his or her own little bailiwick, demanding that the federal government increase taxes, regulate, manage, or bureaucratize. Some do not even see that they are participating in this drive to centralize power.

The "data battle" with Modern Liberals is rarely winnable; statistics and numbers can be manipulated in various ways, social and economic variables can be cherry-picked and presented as typical, and evidence can be distorted and have various interpretations. For example, Modern Liberals use selected "happiness" scales to praise Europe, but ignore that Europeans have a poor work ethic; Modern Liberals will pay homage to the long vacations of Europeans, but not mention the corruption that their Socialism has engendered. A favorite Modern Liberal distortion in economics is to pick and compare extreme low and high points on a moving scale and present this as something fixed: For example, the Dow hit a high of about 14,000 in October 2007 and a low of about 6,600 in March 2009; the Modern Liberal media said that people had lost over half of their savings in March. This was a deliberate distortion for the purpose of turning people against the free market and advocating for massive federal government control.[2]

Thomas Sowell documents how people whom he designates the "anointed" deliberately distort, fabricate, and misrepresent data in order to push their agenda.[3] Bill O'Reilly identifies these people as "Secular-Progressives (S-Ps)," and he is very clear, but rather cynical, about what we are up against:

> There is no reasoning with most of these people, no way to debate them...They are committed, determined, and live in a permanent "no traditionalist zone." You will not persuade, convince, or mollify them. If you are on the traditional side, the S-Ps will reject you and perhaps try to inflict pain upon your person. *Of that there is no question.*[4] (Emphasis added)

Harry Stein wrote that "anyone who believes that a liberal can be straightened out if only reality is explained to him, simply and clearly, is doomed to fail."[5] He quoted John Leo, a syndicated columnist and senior fellow at the Manhattan Institute, who said, "You can go your whole life and not hear a liberal take seriously any conservative argument—they just yell 'racist' or 'fascist' and think they've won."[6]

So, how do we respond to Modern Liberals when they distort data, revise history, play on people's fears, make personal attacks, and refuse to accept or acknowledge *anything* that contravenes their ideology? How do we fight back? Most of us, like my friend whom I described in the Introduction, prefer to simply remain silent because Modern Liberals can be aggressive, vicious, relentless, uncompromising, and overwhelming. And we Americans, unlike Modern Liberals, do not politicize every aspect of our lives; we prefer to devote our energy and time to our families, work, church, and communities. Modern Liberals vilify the private sphere because they know it gives rise to differences of opinion, varied success, and disparate values; in other words, it weakens the collective. Ergo, Modern Liberals strive to politicize—make public—every aspect of our lives. This limits true freedom and it is incumbent on us to resist. We must refuse to politicize our personal lives. And remember, as described in Chapter 7, "Tactics and Propaganda of the Modern Liberals," they will never—repeat *never*—accept or recognize research, information, concepts, or logic that do not align with their dogma and programs.

Robert Bork described four things that would halt the onslaught of Modern Liberalism on our culture:

1. A religious revival.
2. A renewal of public discourse about morality.

3. A war.
4. A deep economic recession.[7]

Of course, the last two are basically out of our hands, but Bork pointed to two things that we can do to fight Modern Liberals in everyday life:

1. Be aware.
2. Resist them in every area of our culture.[8]

There are some simple ways in which we—as Howard Beale in the movie *Network* said, "I'm mad as hell, and I'm not going to take it anymore"—can stand up to Modern Liberals. Modern Liberals—the representatives of the lust to centralize power—can never be totally defeated, but they can be minimized and rendered impotent. In confronting them, keep the following two points foremost in your mind:

1. Always focus on fundamental principles.
2. Always stay on the offensive.

If we can manage to advert the "conversation" with Modern Liberals (Modern Liberals do not discuss or converse; they vilify, intimidate, distort, and badger) around to one of the fundamental principles on which each idea is based, it will *have to* boil down to a contrast of individual liberty versus a centrally organized and engineered society. For example, Harvey Mansfield, professor of government at Harvard, points to an example of the Modern Liberals' avoidance of principles when discussing ObamaCare:

> Obama wanted…to put health care beyond politics…Once the bill is enacted, health care need only be administered by experts…The principle will have been decided. It becomes an entitlement that is no longer open to political controversy…But what about the principle?…There is one: Should the government take over health care or should it be left to the private sphere?…Instead of raising the issue of government vs. private control, this nonpartisan strategy made government control appear to be another option in the health insurance market rather than regulator of the market.[9]

More about going on the offensive follows.

GENERAL PRINCIPLES AND SPECIFIC ISSUES

Our Fundamental Beliefs

Of course, we need government, even a central (federal) government. The stance that most Americans take is simply to limit it so it stays within the boundaries that are specified in our Constitution. Modern Liberals will say that our society has changed and that the Founders could not even imagine today's world. At this point, most Americans will attempt to *defend* our founding principles when they should instead go on the *attack* against Modern Liberals. This is the time to point out the enduring principles of our founding, such as Natural Rights and the protections of property, and to accuse Modern Liberals of going against and undermining our basic liberties. When a Modern Liberal asserts that some people have too much wealth—implying that the State has a right to seize it—a patriot should ask the Modern Liberal to clearly quantify what is "too much," who determines this, and specifically how his proposal will be enforced in a practical sense. When such a Modern Liberal contends that some people have "too much," he is undermining the very essence of our basic rights of private property free of government control and interference; and private property rights are essential to our freedom. The Modern Liberal should be told this very clearly and in no uncertain terms.

A country with individual liberty is not a utopia by any means, even though Modern Liberals sometimes accuse Conservatives of portraying this kind of America as one. A society with a strong sense of individual liberty is one that necessitates hard work and self-reliance, and it means that people live with the consequences that are likely to occur if one is not conscientious and hardworking. A society with individual liberty is one in which we can never be sure of the results of our efforts, and it is a society in which we accept the results of our own actions and even bad luck. This can seem daunting at times and leave us with uncertainty and apprehension, and Modern Liberals play on those worries, aiming to convince us that without a powerful central government, rapacious capitalists, racists, and "big business" will drive us into poverty and helplessness, all to get cheap labor, preserve a docile population, and preserve power and control. Modern Liberals will paint a picture of a society of destitute elderly, polluted air and water, children in sweatshops, and people unable to get basic medical care, food, and housing—they deem all these things inevitable unless the federal government manages our economy, education, and society. In short, Modern Liberals will endeavor to convince us that a more powerful central authority is the only way to protect ourselves from what we most fear.

Our strength lies in our founding principles, and this is where Modern Liberals approach with trepidation. Much of Ronald Reagan's appeal was his embodiment of our Founders and their principles. This is our bulwark against the onslaught of Modern Liberals' drive toward the centralization of power in the federal government. If we stand firmly on this rock of Gibraltar and bring the conversation back to this edifice, Modern Liberals are lost, for their principles—the centralization and enlargement of government power—are anathema to ours, which are embodied in our Constitution. At heart, Modern Liberals have no reverence or respect for our founding principles. For Modern Liberals, people of today are superior to our Founders, simply because they believe that humans have "progressed" beyond them over the past two centuries. But this is where Modern Liberals catch themselves in their own trap: By asserting this, they are implying that there are no enduring principles; it would mean that morality, justice and even truth are not possible, but they are things that simply change with the times. For Modern Liberals, concepts such as Rule of Law, the sanctity of private property, consent of the governed, and the limitation of government can have no eternal qualities. For these Modern Liberals, the concept of "Natural Rights"—the idea that our human rights come from our very being and are inalienable—is not a permanent truth because, according to them, there are no permanent truths but only evolving ones. For these people, our rights and our freedoms are to be dictated by the times in which we live and to be decided by experts in the government.

Our Constitution, in typed book-sized print, is only about ten pages long. As Americans, we have a duty to read our Constitution, and it can be obtained free on the Internet. There are several excellent books that summarize and explain our principles very well. One of the best introductions is *We Still Hold These Truths: Rediscovering Our Principles, Reclaiming Our Future*, by Matthew Spalding.[10] For the more ambitious among our readers, the near 500-page *The Heritage Guide to the Constitution*, edited by Edwin Meese, is not only a guide to our Constitution, but is a clause-by-clause analysis of the document by over 100 scholars from prestigious universities and think tanks; it includes descriptions of each amendment, summarizes relevant court cases, and reviews the sources that served as the foundation of this great creation. For example, do you know about the word "secure" that was used in relation to our inalienable rights in our Constitution *and* Declaration of Independence? This very word is significant: Our Founders knew that our rights were not granted, bestowed, created, or given by the government. They knew that our rights were always there, inalienable, but that not all governments "secure" them. They created a written constitution that does, of course.[11]

Never Compromise

We want to get along with others and have harmony, but there never can be any compromise with Modern Liberals. Like a voracious two-year old, Modern Liberals will *always* demand more, more, more. For example, Modern Liberals had the name of George Washington removed from a school in Louisiana because he was a slave owner; statues of Robert E. Lee were torn down; flags of the Old South were never to be put up for public display again; a Ten Commandments monument was removed from the rotunda of Alabama's state judicial building; and the song "Dixie" must never be sung. This is a "Zero-Sum Game" that actually applies: Every time that we concede a bit to Modern Liberals, we lose some of our liberty and independence. And they will be emboldened to demand more, more, more yet again. Remember, the ultimate outcome of a Modern Liberal victory over our political and cultural life would be the overthrow of our order and nothing less.

Modern Liberals would focus on destroying—even without evidence— institutions that they imagine result in oppression. Conservatives want to focus on what has brought prosperity and develop that. When you confront a Modern Liberal who clamors for the dismantling of "oppressive" forces, ask him what has brought prosperity; he will not be able to tell you. As Myron Magnet wrote in *The Dream and the Nightmare*, "Poverty is no mystery...The real wonder is how societies became rich in the first place."[12]

Rule of Law

Modern Liberals profess to have discovered, or that we need to find, the "root causes" of poverty and other social ills. By insisting that there are "root causes" of societal problems, Modern Liberals are denying the realities of human nature because they think that human behavior can be fundamentally changed by structuring an ideal environment. Our Founders knew better; they understood and accepted human nature. In *Federalist 51*, Madison wrote that "there is a degree of depravity in mankind which requires a certain degree of circumspection and distrust," and "the latent causes of faction are *sown in the nature of man*," factions being groups of citizens with interests contrary to the rights or others or to the interests of the whole community (emphasis added). John Adams wisely stated that with human beings, "reason holds the helm, but passions are the gales." In *Federalist 78*, Alexander Hamilton recommended "making deductions for the *ordinary depravity of human nature*" (emphasis added). Our Founders also noted the positive aspects of our natures, of course. In *Federalist 51*, this was written: "there are other qualities in human nature, which justify a certain portion of esteem and confidence."

Our Founders understood and accepted human nature; Modern Liberals neither understand it, nor do they accept its realities. Conservatives know that we need to study and focus on what brings prosperity and liberty, not on aspiring to alter human nature to fit some vacuous and chimerical visions.

Knowing that factions will always exist when there is liberty, James Madison wrote about these factions and said that there are two ways to deal with them: (1) Remove the cause or (2) control the effects. Madison warned about trying to remove causes, but this is precisely what Modern Liberals choose. Madison said this is dangerous because there are only two ways to remove causes: (1) destroy liberty, and (2) make all citizens the same, aligning with Rousseau's statement that it is necessary to "force men to be free." In other words, if a society tried to remove causes of faction as Modern Liberals propose, an all-powerful government would have to force all citizens to behave certain ways and conform to specifications—all for our "own good." In contrast, Conservatives choose Madison's second option: control factions' *effects*. This is accomplished via Rule of Law: Our courts, in upholding the laws prescribed in our national and state constitutions, and as enacted by our legislatures, provide *consequences* for those who willfully violate the laws enacted by our elected representatives. In other words, they dole out appropriate punishment for unlawful behaviors *after* they have been committed; they do not seek to restrain liberty or punish people *before* the fact in a nightmarish version of *Minority Report*, in which Tom Cruise plays the role of a policeman of the future who arrests people for crimes *before* they commit them.

Modern Liberals pervert the law and justice. Modern Liberals routinely try to bend the law, encouraging judges to modify outcomes and decisions to attain specific social goals. This subverts Rule of Law and destroys true justice.

As Matthew Spalding pointed out in *We Still Hold These Truths*, Rule of Law has four essential components:

1. It is a formal or regular process of enforcement and adjudication.
2. Rule of Law is binding on *all*. John Adams, for example, demonstrated this when he defended the British soldiers who were involved with the Boston Massacre.
3. Rule of Law—to exist—has to acknowledge generally understood standards to which specific laws and lawmaking conform, such as not making laws *after* a crime occurs, punishment without a trial, due process, habeas corpus, and double jeopardy.
4. Rule of Law ultimately keeps a restraint on government.[13]

Conservatives know that real justice comes from Rule of Law, and that the "social justice" of Modern Liberalism undermines it. Rule of Law protects against the arbitrary exercise of power: Government's role is to establish the general rules, then leave things up to individuals. This can be compared to a highway: The laws and rules are established for everyone. The Conservatives want to enforce these laws *as they have been decided*, and let people go where they choose; Modern Liberals want to tell people where to go. Rule of Law and "social justice" are incompatible because the latter requires (1) defining groups and (2) taking special care of the selected groups. When Modern Liberals start screaming that they want "social justice," tell them that it entails *group* rights, and that in America, *individual* rights are essential for true justice. Press them to describe the actual cost of achieving "social justice." Modern Liberals will typically speak in generalities, but badger them for specifics. Thomas Sowell wrote about their sloppy and superficial thinking about "social justice" in *The Vision of the Anointed*:

> [A]nyone can be in favor of "social justice" without further ado. In short, the ideas of the so-called "thinking people" often require much less thinking. Indeed, the less thinking there is about definitions, means, and consequences, the more attractive "social justice" seems.[14]

Point out to Modern Liberals that they believe in *positive* rights, and Conservatives believe in *negative* rights. Positive rights are the ones that the government *gives* us; negative rights are those rights that *cannot be taken* from us by the government. For example, a Modern Liberal *positive* right would be a right to "decent" housing or a job. A *negative* right, in contrast, restricts government: The government *cannot stop us* from getting a house or seeking a job. Modern Liberals contend that the government *creates* and *grants* rights, and Conservatives know that our rights are part of our human nature—they are *inalienable*. Conservatives know that a government may or may not *secure* our inborn Natural Rights while Modern Liberals think that the government decides what rights *are*.

Never Defend Yourself

[Ronald Reagan] was always at his best when on offense against liberalism, and seldom worse when he assumed a defensive posture.[15]

–STEVEN HAYWOOD

Refusing to be defensive and actually fighting back, that's what really drives 'em nuts.

–VICKI MCKENNA, CONSERVATIVE TALK SHOW RADIO HOST, MADISON, WISCONSIN

One of the most potent weapons of Modern Liberals is to put Americans on the defensive with their attacks: If you recommend recognition of states' rights, Modern Liberals brand you as a racist who wants a return to Jim Crow; if you want lower taxes, they characterize you as a dupe of the wealthy; if you even *question* gay marriage, you are deemed a homophobe or a religious fanatic and bigot; if you endorse home schooling, vouchers, or school choice,

Modern Liberals assume you are undermining public education and abandoning handicapped children and the poor; if you encourage welfare reform, you are denounced as lacking compassion for the impoverished; and if you praise the founding, they condescendingly allege that you are whitewashing a history that is steeped in racism, sexism and genocide. The list is endless, but the purpose of their accusations is simple: to put you on the defensive. The Modern Liberals actually *want* you to say, "No, I am not a racist," "No, I am not *for* the rich," or "No, I acknowledge that our Founders were all white males and many owned slaves."

Once we respond defensively, once we attempt to deny the accusations of Modern Liberals, once we attempt to explain why we are not what they say we are, we have lost. We have joined *their* game, and we are playing by *their* rules. The ideas, especially fundamental principles, get pulled into the Modern Liberal sewer of accusations, insults, and distortions. We wind up defining what we are *not*, and they position themselves on a high moral ground, condescendingly looking down at us. In our attempts to assure them that we are not what they say we are, we are really demeaning ourselves and actually granting Modern Liberals that they *are* on that higher moral ground. In this way, we lose. Looking at it another way, would you bother to exert any effort to defend yourself in this manner from attacks by pornographers, thieves, pimps, or scam artists? Of course not.

So, why do we lower and demean ourselves to Modern Liberals? Why do we allow this? Why do we give in?

It is quite simple: Modern Liberals know a major weakness we have: We want to be considered fair, even-handed, kind, and upright. When we are accused of not being so, many of us may feel a sense of desperation to prove otherwise. Modern Liberals have no compunction, no sense of fair play, and no conscience in contriving to bring us around to that position; Modern Liberals will not hesitate to use shame, intimidation, badgering, rejection, isolation, or mockery. Modern Liberals are relentless: Lower taxes? Modern Liberals will say that you not care if the poor suffer while the rich get richer. Fewer regulations? You are typecast as someone aligned with the "despoilers and polluters" of our environment. Advocating for states' rights? You do not care if women die from back-alley abortions.

Never defend yourselves by attempting to prove you are *not* what a Modern Liberal claims you are. Go on the offensive and tell the Modern Liberal that *he* is the racist, that *he* is advocating the centralization of power that will rob our liberties, that *he* harms his neighbors—the "little capitalists"—by increasing government power over the economy, that *he* is a hypocrite in advocating liberty while telling others what is best, that *he* disdains his fellow citizens by implying that people are too stupid and irresponsible to plan and make choices, that *he* thinks productive members of society should assume responsibility for the slackers, that *he* is restricting choice in our personal lives, that *he* is intolerant, and that *he* has perverted the sense of our being an overall decent and upright nation. Point out that *he* proposes that the federal government should supervise, regulate, control, and/or fund anything *he* deems of importance in society, and that *he* believes that nothing of importance should be the bailiwick of local control or simply "let alone." Assert that *he* is advocating for the central government to interfere with every aspect of our lives. Ask *him* to articulate the bases of the premises on which *he* bases his ideology.

Going on the Offensive

A plethora of Modern Liberal tactics are described in Chapter 7. Let's take one of the most commonly used—the charges of racism—to provide an example of how to respond by staying on the offensive and referring to our principles. This charge has less power than it did decades ago, simply because people are sick of the constant and unnecessary barrage from Modern Liberals, and Americans are tired of being in fear of these charges. However, it is still a somewhat effective Modern Liberal technique.

As with all such encounters with Modern Liberals, never defend yourself and explain why or how you are not what they say you are; rather, use the opportunity to thus prove—without hesitation, reservation, or impunity—such attacks divulge what the Modern Liberal really is; in this case, it reveals the Modern Liberal for the racist that he or she is. Our laws protecting equal access and opportunities are in place, of course; therefore, the Modern Liberal who is making these claims has brought to light his or her deep-seated racism:

1. The Modern Liberal, by virtue of his assertion that any "minorities" need special help is implying that they are inferior. Unless people are inferior in some way, they do not need help, but Modern Liberals believe that they do, and this reveals one aspect of their racism.
2. The Modern Liberal is refusing to look at the individual and instead looks at people as members of groups defined by skin color; that is

what racists do. Their very ideology and psyche virtually necessitates their looking at people as part of some category, and that is a tell-tale mark of a racist.

3. The Modern Liberal, by revising history, assumes certain races and ethnicities want more representation. Again, he assumes—by virtue of race—that people of certain skin colors *must feel inferior* because, the Modern Liberal assumes again, they need to have history revised to raise their self-esteem. This is about as condescending as it gets: How would *you* like someone to assume you must feel inferior to the "rest of us" by virtue of your skin pigmentation?

4. The Modern Liberal is actually destroying lives of people whom he teaches are victims or oppressed. When a person becomes convinced that he is a victim or a member of an "oppressed" class, it permanently changes him—for the worse.

5. The Modern Liberal is using various groups to enhance his own status and sense of superiority. By claiming he knows what is best for Group X, the Modern Liberal attempts to elevate his status as both an authority and a savior of a group that he deems inferior and in need of help.

6. The Modern Liberal undermines Rule of Law by not treating people as individuals. The law is not perfect, but to change it to meet outcomes or treat members of a group differently is to pervert the law and seize the rights of others.

In sum, always stay on the offensive and avoid the following two major errors:

1. Trying to provide evidence that you are *not* what Modern Liberals assert you to be: Stay away from that trap.

2. Getting into the "name game" of enumerating how many people of the other's persuasions or political party are corrupt, adulterous, racists, or who voted for and against civil rights laws, and so on. That is a Modern Liberal game that you cannot win. Get back to fundamental principles.

Demand that Modern Liberals Define Their Terms

In general, get a Modern Liberal to define terms. This is especially useful when there are the typically mindless charges of your being a Nazi or a Fascist. Simply ask the Modern Liberal to prove his charges. If he typecasts people who attend

Tea Party gatherings "astroturfers" or "racists," ask him if he has ever attended one. Most certainly he has not, so invite him to one or provide the address of the local chapter so he can learn. Jay Nordlinger wrote about this in the *National Review*:

> [Modern Liberals] seem not to accept conservative protest as legitimate at all. They seem practically offended at the very idea of conservative protest: because activism, energy, passion, and all that are not supposed to figure in conservative soil.[16]

When you are called a Nazi or a Fascist by a Modern Liberal, you can have fun by telling him that he is actually following a script of the Communist Party: In 1943, the Moscow Central Committee told its members that they should "continually embarrass, discredit and degrade our critics. When obstructionists become too irritating, label them as fascist, or Nazi."

Modern Liberals never question whether the goals they promote and advocate are truly achievable, or even the degree to which they can be accomplished in reality. Ask them to specify what they hope to bring about and *insist on specifics*.

One big weakness with Modern Liberals is that they rarely look at the processes, only at the goals. For example, Modern Liberals insist that medical treatment or college tuitions should be "free" or at minimal cost. Ask them from where the funds will come; they will almost always revert to claims of being "compassionate," say you do not "care," or say that the Europeans do it. But press on: Ask them to delineate processes needed to achieve their goals and demand real answers.

The "I Care" and "I'm Tolerant" Modern Liberals

One of the most exasperating Modern Liberal techniques with which to deal can be their appeals to "compassion," "caring," and "fairness." In virtually every case, however, they are shallow and meretricious claptrap that can be easily exposed: Modern Liberals demonstrate this "compassion" by advocating the commandeering and redistribution of *other people's* property. Modern Liberals will actually have the effrontery to proclaim they are righteous because they propose repressive and prohibitive tax structures that confiscate and redistribute what *they* deem is "excessive wealth." When a Modern Liberal uses this approach, get him to speak to *personal* morality, and invoke Jesus, Buddha, or Gandhi. Also bring up morality itself and its meaning: Morality is a *personal* choice; it is not forcing certain behaviors by law and regulations on *others*. If there is no choice, there can be no virtue or rectitude. The man who donates money because someone holds a gun to his head has not shown virtue, but the man who has voluntarily given of his possessions or time certainly has.

Then consider dropping the bombshell: Ask the Modern Liberal specifically what *he* has done for the groups in question. In most cases, it is never more than demanding something from others. However, in the rare instances one meets a Modern Liberal who has actually made some sacrifices, at least one can steer the conversation in the direction of how morality and virtue are personal attributes and that the central government cannot make others upright and virtuous. At the most, the central government could possibly provide some incentives—deductions, for example—to encourage individual donations. Remind the Modern Liberal that in the era of supposed "greed"—the 1980s—charitable giving increased, as both totals and percentage of incomes, and this was beyond the expected projections.[17] This had nothing to do with government.

Preempt Modern Liberals. They like to declare they have "compassion" and that they are "caring." *You* preempt this by pointing out how you want to help people who work and have families. Remind them that there is proof that Conservatives "care" more than they do, as evinced by how they prefer to spend their time, the amount they give to charities, and the time they spend volunteering. Be sure to tell them that Conservatives even give blood more often than Modern Liberals. (Refer to chapters 8 and 9.)

Another powerful tactic of Modern Liberals is insisting on "tolerance," and proclaiming that any dissent indicates *a lack of tolerance*. Once again, people will typically attempt to defend themselves by offering examples of how they are tolerant, falling into the Modern Liberal trap. But the Modern Liberals' comprehension of this is so manifestly flawed that it is nonsensical. "Tolerance" is *putting up with something* of which one does not approve or one does not like. If I do not like cats and my brother has one, I "tolerate" his cat while in his home; if I like dogs and he has one, there is no "tolerance" involved. However, with Modern Liberals, even if a person maintains that homosexual sex is a sin but otherwise does not attack, insult, slander, socially exclude, or badger any gay person, the Modern Liberals will say that his attitude shows "intolerance." What Modern Liberals are *really* doing is demanding an acceptance—and even celebration—of what they value, and they are rejecting and vilifying what they deem unacceptable. Tolerance is really restraining oneself from openly attacking what one does not approve, in adherence to the law or civil order. Tell Modern Liberals how they are *really* demanding complete conformity to *their* values. Accuse them of being like a selfish child, showing the worst kind of *in*tolerance and hypocrisy. Roger Kimball cogently exposes the inherent contradiction in Modern Liberalism and its promulgation of complete "openness" and "tolerance," referring to it as the "disease of liberalism":

> In attempting to create the maximally tolerant society, we also give scope to those who would prefer to create the maximally intolerant society…Liberalism implies openness to other points of view, even those… whose success would destroy liberalism…It is a prescription for suicide… The escape from this disease of liberalism lies in understanding that tolerance and "openness" must be limited by positive values if they are not to be vacuous…Our society…is founded on particular positive values—the rule of law, for example.[18]

Sometimes, and as a desperate last measure, Modern Liberals will profess that their intentions are pure, and they must therefore not only be excused but actually revered for their displays of virtue. Remind the Modern Liberals that this silly and immature idea has the following manifest flaw: It shows a simple refusal to accept responsibility for one's actions. It reminds us of a child asking a parent not to be angry because he broke the lamp while he was playing with the dog.

Emotional Problems

University of Chicago-trained forensic psychiatrist Lyle Rossiter, author of *The Liberal Mind*, explains the psychology of people who choose the more radical forms of Modern Liberalism. His book is excellent for understanding the more die-hard Modern Liberals. He describes psychological pathologies that drive some of them to push their agendas and contrasts this with the normal and healthy adult who strives to be autonomous, enterprising, and industrious:

> [A]ll competent adults know that actions have consequences. For the competent man to act freely is to assume risk and accept responsibility, [but] in the liberal agenda, we have a society of literally care-free persons,

each of whom is falsely held to be responsible for everyone else, and none of whom is properly held to be responsible for himself.[19]

The contrast with the mentally healthy adult is quite dramatic:

> The liberal agenda's invasive social policies foster economic irresponsibility, pathological dependency and social conflict [and] the modern liberal agenda's welfare statism and moral relativism [are] pathological distortions of normal social instincts...Instead of promoting a rational society of competent adults who solve the problems of living through voluntary cooperation, [it] creates an irrational society of child-like adults who depend upon governments to take care of them...The liberal agenda undermines the character traits essential for individual liberty, material security, voluntary cooperation and social order.[20]

Rossiter further explains the development of this pathology:

> [It] is the result of early trauma [from] a personal history of neglect, deprivation and abuse, including early deficits in attachment, attention, affection, empathy, validation, direction and discipline [that] lead him to fear freedom itself: the prospect of genuine autonomy arouses primitive fears of aloneness and danger. The challenge of self-reliance reactivates primitive fears of inadequacy.[21]

Looking at this lack of normal emotional development mainly from an Eriksonian perspective, we see that there is a failure in the development of basic trust:

> [The Modern Liberal has a] basic mistrust of relationships between persons who act by mutual consent...The modern liberal is unable to believe that human beings can make good lives for themselves through individual initiative and voluntary cooperation. He believes that ordinary citizens cannot relate effectively to each other without extensive regulation by the state.[22]

Modern Liberals scream that they want to "help" others, they "care" and are "compassionate." Rossiter contrasts the hypocrisy and pathology of Modern Liberals with the sincerity and the moral sense of the rest of us:

There are only two basic methods by which human beings can aid each other: voluntarily through individual and joint efforts...or coercively through the power of government. Because they operate only by the consent of those who organize them, voluntary methods preserve all of the basic rights that ensure individual liberty and social order...[and] it also channels charitable motives...through persons who can be held accountable for their actions. In contrast, the government-run welfare program attacks all of the basic rights that protect individual liberty and social order while it disconnects the charitable motives of the citizen from the kinds of distributions the programs makes [and has] destructive effects on individuals, families and the culture...distortions of incentives...and endless bureaucracy.[23]

When Modern Liberals start saying that dissent with their views is a manifestation of some unfavorable personality characteristic—such as repression, anger, inhibitions or sociopathy—tell them about the Soviet Union's Serbsky Institute that was used to classify as insane those who disagreed with the "politically correct" line. Also, present them with Dr. Rossiter's cogent analysis of why *their* ideology reveals severe emotional problems. Remember: Attack *them*, never defend yourself.

Modern Liberals Who Attack America

The hostility Modern Liberals have toward America came to national attention with September 11. Their contempt and enmity toward America have carried forward from their predecessors, the Old Left and New Left, and this stood out during the terrorist attacks in September 2001. With these attacks, Modern Liberals faced a dilemma: They were loathe to defend America, and their adherence to "political correctness" prevented them from condemning jihadism. Modern Liberals were impotent in the aftermath of the attack, and Americans saw this.

Modern Liberals disparage America, and much of their enmity focuses on our founding. Most Americans—especially when there are international conflicts—proceed from the assumption that America is virtuous. Modern Liberals proceed from the assumption that America has malevolent intent. Modern Liberals fathom that our very beginnings are fundamentally flawed and based on the racism, greed, and genocide of white Europeans. Modern Liberals insist that any attempt to prove otherwise is to whitewash history and deny the truth.

For example, Modern Liberals are wont to say that the Founders started the American Revolution to increase their own opulence and power. When they state that nonsense, remind them of the Founders who lost everything: For starters, Robert Morris subsidized the Revolution with his personal funds and wound up in debtors' prison; Richard Stockton lost everything to the British and later became a beggar; Thomas Hayward was shot in battle; George Walton was shot in battle; Francis Lewis lost his home and belongings to the British; and Thomas Nelson wound up destitute.

When you talk about our founding principles and the Original Intent of our Constitution, Modern Liberals often say that your ideas are antiquated and that you want to return to some idyllic past that never was. Remind these Modern Liberals that wanting to preserve individual rights, free markets, and democratic institutions is not any "longing for the past," and ask them why they abhor and revile those things. Consider referring to Conservatives as "reactionary" forces and "counter-revolutionaries"; use those terms sarcastically because it shows that you are aware of Modern Liberals' Marxist-Communist roots and legacies.

Modern Liberals insist that the Founders disagreed, and they present this as the prevailing atmosphere among them. Tell these Modern Liberals they are distorting history and that they lack fundamental understanding. Our Founders concurred on fundamental principles: People have inalienable rights, there is a permanent human nature, a written constitution needs to be created, republican self-government is necessary, and we will live by Rule of Law, not Rule of Man.

When Modern Liberals start bellowing that the Constitution does not apply to society today because it was created over two centuries ago, you may wish to remind them of what Calvin Coolidge said and ask if they disagree:

> About the Declaration of Independence there is a finality that is exceedingly restful....If all men are created equal, that is final...No advance, no progress can be made beyond these propositions.[24]

David Horowitz wrote about the origins of the struggle that we see today between those who would preserve our founding principles and Modern Liberals who would regress us to a state controlled by a central power:

> Looking back on the two-hundred-year history now past, we can see that it is not simply a unitary conflict between revolution and *ancien regime*...

It is the conflict of two distinct revolutionary traditions. The struggle that has shaped our age has not been between the old order and the new revolution, but between two revolutionary paths to the modern world…The radical ethos of the French Revolution became the wellspring of a socialist revolt against bourgeois order that has culminated in the creation of the Soviet empire…the libertarian ethos of the American Revolution inspired the conservative opponents of the Soviet tyranny, a *counter*revolution based on individual rights, free markets and democratic constitutions.[25]

Try this experiment with a Modern Liberal and watch him foam at the mouth: First ask, "Do you believe that the concept of universal rights, natural rights—basically that all humans are equal—is valid, important, and basically good?" (The Modern Liberal will be forced to agree, of course.) Next, ask him if he accepts that the concept iterated above is primarily of Western origin, and press for a definitive answer. (He will not be able to demonstrate another culture where this originated.) Then, hit him with this: If he fancies that Europeans in the New World are to be judged on the standards in the first question—all humans are equal—then he has only two choices: (1) He believes that not only Europeans but everyone should be judged by these standards, or (2) he believes that only Europeans should be held to these standards. If the Modern Liberal chooses the first one, he bears the onus of applying these standards to the Native Americans in the same way that he applied them to Europeans. He is obliged to judge them in their wars, ritual sacrifices, often brutal treatment of women, and slave ownership of other Native Americans. If he goes with the second option—the one illustrative of a higher moral order—he is saying that the Native Americans' society or civilization is inferior in this regard, and that only Europeans can be held to this standard. He is saying that European civilization is morally superior. Modern Liberals want to have it both ways in order to attack the foundations of our civilization, so remind them of their hypocrisy.

In general, when engaging Modern Liberals who vilify our country, keep two points in mind:

1. Press for the ultimate meaning of their assertions.
2. Maintain balance.

Press Modern Liberals to articulate what they surmise is the premise of America, what is its meaning, what is its foundation? Howard Zinn is a hero of many Modern

Liberals, and many ascribe to the tripe and hate he wrote about our country. Zinn wrote the infamous *A People's History of the United States*, in which he describes our history as a series of endless oppression. If our history is based on what Modern Liberals presume, then we should scrap our Constitution and founding principles: Press for a response to that. The Modern Liberal will deny he wants to trash our Constitution, so get him to say why he wants to preserve it. By doing this, you will force him to make statements about limited government and the wisdom of the Founders. Also, when he impugns America as fundamentally racist and oppressive, ask him if we should then tell our children that we live in a country based on evil.

"Balance" is important because Modern Liberals will present examples of a utopia, a fantasy that is not possible. Then Modern Liberals will point out our country's failures to live up to this impossible fairyland that has never existed anywhere in the history of the world. When hearing the Modern Liberals blast and demean the United States over and over, point out that they are like children, believing in Shangri La and Santa Claus.

Modern Liberals never say anything favorable about America without qualifying it: "America is great, *but...*" "The United States saved the world from tyranny, *but...*" Modern Liberals declare that they are just presenting the truth, of course. They will say that it is necessary to point out flaws in order to improve the situation, and they will insist that it is best not to hide any problems. These absurd assertions can be put to rest by drawing an analogy to their families: Would they always tell their spouse or children about their flaws without expressing unconditional love? Would they not envisage their family members primarily in a positive light of love and affection, and put problems and needed improvements in that context? Would not the very foundation with their children be primarily one of trust and affection? Also, isn't it necessary to have this base in order to get improvements? Could we really expect our children or spouses to be better people by constantly finding fault and criticizing them? Most of all, what would such behavior uncover about our true feelings toward them? Ask them to make a positive statement about America without any qualifiers or excuses—It is virtually impossible for a Modern Liberal to do this! You may even be shocked at the extent they will go to avoid giving unqualified praise. Modern Liberals will use any trick in their repertoire to avoid it.

Modern Liberals make comparisons to specific and isolated programs and policies in different countries, holding them up as examples of how America is inferior and not up to the so-called "modern standards," especially those of Europe. In response to that, remind the Modern Liberal of the incredible number of vast differences between our two ways of life, beliefs, and histories as outlined in Chapter 11. In addition, ask these Modern Liberals two simple questions:

1. Why did—and still do—multitudes choose to come to the United States?
2. Why don't we see Americans moving en masse to the European paradise? More to the point, why don't the complaining and criticizing Modern Liberals themselves move? Press this second point and do not let up on a Modern Liberal. This response flummoxes them to no end because it exposes their hypocrisy and brings out the positive aspects of America.

Modern Liberals constantly bash America on the international scene. Ask them how they got their membership in the BAF Club—the "Blame America First" Club. Remind them that America is the oldest republic in existence, has had free elections for centuries, has trial by jury, maintains Rule of Law, and promotes upward mobility. Despite being the most powerful military force in the world, we have not "ruled" any other countries but have used our power to roll back, weaken, and defeat the most murderous regimes in history: Nazis, Fascists, and Communists.

Modern Liberals say that America is impoverishing the Third World, so ask them why these people want capitalism and American stuff. Daniel Flynn provides some reasons:

> America is an island of freedom...Americans can say what they want, worship any god they fancy, and associate with any motley crew they care to...This successful venture in self-government sparked many imitators... No country has ever come close to matching America's generosity... Anywhere on Earth, whenever someone turns on a light, surfs the Internet, watches television, goes to the movies, or talks on the telephone, America receives a tacit endorsement. American doctors and scientists have shielded mankind from tuberculosis, polio, yellow fever, and numerous other debilitating and deadly illnesses. Humans live happier, healthier, and longer lives because of Americans. The American story is an uplifting narrative.[26]

Modern Liberals contend America is imperialist; ask them to name the "colonies." If we are imperialist, why have we not expanded our territory in over 70 years? They will often say it is "corporate" or "economic" imperialism, but ask them why people all over the world welcome it. After the USSR ended

Communism, people in Moscow lined up to get a McDonalds hamburger. Also, remind them of the words of the great philosopher, George Santayana, who cogently compared the Soviet approach to America's:

> What the Russians are trying to impose is not only their form of government…but their own government as it exists in Moscow…The American system cannot be imposed in this way because it conceives "democracy" to mean government by the majority, and respects elections fairly carried on.[27]

Ask these Modern Liberals if the world would be better off now if America had lost—or not participated in—World War II, the Korean War, and the Cold War. They do not like that question because it forces them to acknowledge that the United States has used its military power for good in the world. They find this question to be very disturbing because it obliges them to praise America or to say that they prefer Nazis and Fascists to be in power.

Modern Liberals detest being reminded that Americans give far more to charity than Europeans do. Remind them often.

Our legislative process frustrates Modern Liberals because of its lack of speed in implementing their radical agenda. For example, since 1789 there have been over 5,000 bills proposed to amend the Constitution, and only 17 made it. Our form of government requires much debate and it takes time to get bills and proposals through the House and the Senate, and then past the president. When things do not move quickly—according to the Modern Liberal agenda—they say "progress is being obstructed." Abraham Lincoln was against "progress" in government; to Lincoln, the Founders stood for *fixed principles*, so American statesmen look *backward*, not *forward*, for direction. If a Modern Liberal insists that we look forward, remind him that he is essentially denying that there are any permanent truths. It must be remembered that democracy in our republic is not a process to get to some ends; democracy is the end. We may need to refine and improve some areas, but *we have arrived.*

You're a Dupe of Corporations, Talk Radio, and FOX News!

Modern Liberals have had considerable success—mainly through constant repetition—in creating associations that listening and viewing certain "talk radio" and TV stations indicate that the person is ignorant, racist, and close-minded. None of us wants to feel or be considered "ignorant," so we may sometimes cringe and even deny we listen to these sources. However, rather than denying or disclaiming that you watch or listen to those media outlets, try a different response: Just ask the Modern Liberal for the facts. When a Modern Liberal criticizes a television or radio host, ask him specifically how this person has distorted, prevaricated, or spun information. The Modern Liberal's responses invariably will be vague and general: "Everyone knows that," for example. They will allege that "x" is a liar; when this happens, simply ask for examples. In virtually every case, the Modern Liberal will be unable to provide one. This is when the condescending "oh" with a slight tilt of the head, looking down a bit at him, is very effective. Then, if you want to completely humiliate and embarrass the Modern Liberal, remind him of the essence of *prejudice*: Judging someone or something about which one does not have information. Confront him with a truth: If a Modern Liberal traduces someone, then he either has watched and listened to the person and thus can express an informed position (this is the extremely rare bird), or he is spouting conclusions without knowing much at all, and that is bigotry. So, either he has listened to the person and can present an informed position and point out the falsehoods and distortions, or he is prejudiced. And prejudice is bad—a Modern Liberal should know *that*, of course. When one demonstrates how Modern Liberals are really bigots, it invariably sets them off into sputtering fits and rages more than almost anything else. Enjoy it!

Modern Liberals equate any donations from organizations that they deem "Conservative" as arms of corporate interests. They are quick to say that Conservative organizations are pouring money into propaganda machines of corporate interests and the affluent. However, if we make recent comparisons of the twelve largest Modern Liberal foundations with their twelve largest Conservative counterparts, we see that the Liberal ones had $109 billion in assets, while the Conservative ones had $1.7 billion. As far as donations go, these Modern Liberal organizations gave away $6 *billion* while the Conservatives ones gave away $85 *million*. In addition, if we look at the sources and amount of contributions candidates for political offices received, the results are quite startling: Among the top *eighteen* contributors, all but *four* were to Democrats, and those four were nonpartisan in that they contributed to both Democrats and Republicans. In addition, among those top 14 contributors to Democrat candidates for political office, all but three were unions in the public or private sector![28]

Since Modern Liberals believe that government does not *secure* our rights but that it *grants* them, the Tea Party movement is for them, as Charles R. Kesler sarcastically put it, "inherently reactionary…because it doesn't grasp that Big Government, far from being a threat to liberty, is freedom's greatest achievement."[29]

Modern Liberals proclaim that people's ideas and values are shaped by various kinds of propaganda from advertisers, the media, the environment, and the upper classes. They postulate that since much of this propaganda has deleterious effects on the society, we (i.e., the government) need to ensure they get the *right* ideas. When you hear this inanity, remind the Modern Liberal that in a free society, people should be allowed to pursue any truth and debate any idea or cause. Even though few people will actually take the time and make this effort, this does not mean that the *State* should decide which ideas will be presented to them, or who is capable of deciding the best values. As F. A. Hayek wrote, "what is essential [for intellectual freedom] is not that everybody may be able to think or write anything but that any cause or idea may be argued by somebody."[30]

Modern Liberals—in their opprobrious style—will declare that anyone who advocates for fewer regulations wants to deregulate *everything*, and that he does not care about pollution, dangerous products, accidents and deaths in the workplace, and children being poisoned. In reality, when reasonable people call for fewer regulations, it signifies recognition that regulations are burdensome and costly to businesses, and we should keep them to a minimum and have only those that are necessary to protect consumers and workers.

Take the High Road

Be positive. Do not complain about "how awful" Modern Liberals are. When you do confront their hypocrisies, inconsistencies, and distortions, always give positive suggestions and make references to the greatness of American's history, traditions, liberties, opportunities, and people. This serves two purposes:

1. It robs Modern Liberals of their ability to criticize America; they will sound negative, cynical, and destructive.
2. It will keep you and others in a positive frame of mind, and it will encourage others to join.

Keep the image of Ronald Reagan in mind: State your convictions with pride and confidence, be aware of your underlying premises, stay with ideas, do not personalize, come down as hard on a Modern Liberal as needed, be optimistic about America and its future, and let others know you love your country.

Remember to support and encourage other Conservatives. Some feel very isolated and even under siege; remind them that they speak for most Americans, and that they are on the side of those who want to preserve our founding principles and the traditions and values that made us the most prosperous and free nation in the history of the world.

Modern Liberals emphasize "liberation," "finding the self" and "loving oneself." Almost 3,000 years ago, Taoist philosophers on the other side of the world told people that selfishness destroys compassion for one's fellow human beings and leads to greed and mistrust. The Conservatives know that the Modern Liberals' focusing on personal gratification, self-love, and "self-fulfillment" leads to destructive narcissism; Conservatives value *helping others* first.

Conservatives know that shame plays a role in the socialization of humans, but Modern Liberals want to shift the focus from individual responsibility as a social being to one centering on the "inner self" as the locus of responsibility and morality. In other words, the New Leftists and Modern Liberals have promoted the idea that the primary—responsibility and duty one has is to *self-fulfillment* and *one's own* happiness rather than to the people around oneself. For Modern Liberals, this is the modern, educated, and "sophisticated" way to think, but in reality it is imposing *their* worldview and demanding it take precedence over true morality and virtue, which require fulfilling roles in society and assuming responsibility for how one's actions affect others. Remind them how they are promoting egoism, selfishness, and narcissism, and that Conservatives know that our primary duties and responsibilities are to others, not ourselves.

Socialism and Freedom

Ask any Modern Liberal if he would openly reject Socialism or even consent to limit it. A typical Modern Liberal invariably characterizes public schools, the military, or the police and firemen as examples of Socialism. A Modern Liberal will engage in this distortion in order to make it appear that we all want and need Socialism, and that we are already benefiting from it. But it is a lie: Remind him that Socialism is the government management, regulation, organization, or ownership of the *means of production*, and that he has simply described *services* that any group or society can request, as in a condo association or a golf club. Ask him again about Socialism, and get him to refer to the control of the *means of production*. This infuriates Modern Liberals because they are forced to admit that they want a government takeover of our industries, transportation, communications, and resources.

A typical Modern Liberal invokes "free speech" and the First Amendment in defending the rights of such things as pornography and obscenities. First, remind him why the First Amendment was actually written: To ensure that the citizens could criticize—in speech and in writing—their government without fear of reprisals. Next, ask the Modern Liberal if he believes that America is worth fighting for and what would motivate people to sacrifice for the country. Then ask him if it would be for the rights of pornographers and abortionists, or would it be to preserve the founding principles. If you corner a Modern Liberal with this, the silence or outrage will be deafening.

Modern Liberals should be asked why people fled Socialism and came to America where there is this alleged racism and oppression. Smile or snicker as your see the Modern Liberal stutter and stammer.

When Modern Liberals say that people need security—in jobs, housing, health care, and so on—ask them if they would be willing to give up their own goods and share their incomes with those who are not getting guarantees. They will respond by saying that the government should provide for the "needy" by taking money from the so-called affluent, but not them, of course. Point out that what these Modern Liberals are really asking for is another type of security: They want to preserve their own standard of living, the one to which they and their cohorts feel entitled.

When Modern Liberals push for Socialism and its accompanying central government control, ask them if government "diktats"—using Communist jargon irks them to no end——were responsible for the practical application of electricity, the development of air conditioning, synthetic rubber, DNA discoveries, mapping the genome, entertainment, music, and skyscrapers.

Modern Liberals tell people that they are *entitled* to many things such as "free" post-secondary education, health care, or housing; they assert that people deserve these and mock the idea of being grateful or thankful for receiving any such benefits. Be sure to tell these Modern Liberals that they not only have destroyed a sense of morality and independence, but their programs are harmful to the health: Research has shown that being grateful actually leads to more health, success, and a longer life. Gratitude leads to happiness, but Modern Liberals are against this because they want people to focus on the self and not feel indebtedness to others.[31]

Responsibility and Success

The very values and habits that lead to liberty and prosperity are those that Modern Liberals disdain: those of the bourgeois. David Horowitz wrote about this disdain of Modern Liberals:

> For two hundred years, the leftist counterrevolution against liberal democracy has meant permanent war against bourgeois society—against the culture of individual rights and political pluralism, against the private property foundations of the liberal state. To have been on the left is to have been at war with the only democratic and free societies the world has ever known.[32]

One tactic that many Modern Liberals use to attack our valuing bourgeois habits and behaviors is to say that all lifestyles, cultures, and values are equal. By insisting that no set of habits and behaviors is better than any others, Modern Liberals hope to undermine bourgeois values in our culture. If they are successful, it will result in a weakening of behaviors, values and standards that lead to social harmony, family cohesion, lower crime rates and productivity. Conservatives know that there are habits that promote these desirable outcomes. Thomas Sowell wrote about this in *The Quest for Cosmic Justice*:

> Cultures have consequences. Ignoring those consequences while proclaiming equality as a self-justifying ideal does nothing to benefit the less fortunate, and in fact tends to freeze them into their backward position while the rest of the world moves forward…The equal-respect "identity" promoters would have each group paint itself into its own little corner, with its own insular culture, thus presenting over all a static tableau of "diversity," rather than the dynamic process of competition on which the progress of the human race has been based for thousands of years.[33]

If you ask Modern Liberals what specific behaviors lead to success in a free society, they will usually mouth Socialist-style platitudes and denounce moneyed people. But hold your ground and *insist* that they describe individual *behaviors* that lead to personal success.

Remind Modern Liberals that we can really only reward productivity—the results that we actually see. If we undertake to compensate for some *perceived* unfairness, we are making individuals pay who are not responsible. After all, the "compensation" will come from others who have become successful. In contrast, Conservatives want to use personal achievement as a criterion for the natural distribution of rewards. Remind Modern Liberals that a powerful state will be necessary to constrain the real achievers from getting their due rewards. Therefore, they are recommending that the State should take over the functions of tradition, authority, and the free market.

Modern Liberals blame society for the condition of individuals, and this is a rejection of the idea that individuals are responsible for their own happiness. It is really a kind of infantile mentality in which responsibility is not accepted. Ask Modern Liberals how they conceptualize personal responsibility—its role and meaning. This makes Modern Liberals squirm because they *cannot* dismiss it. If a Modern Liberal acknowledges it, it annihilates his doctrine of society being responsible for how people behave. Remind Modern Liberals that just as we do not accept credit for others' achievements, we have no right to assume credit for their failures—to do so is arrogance and narcissism. Another reason that Modern Liberals avoid discussing the idea of personal responsibility is that it eliminates their special role and status. You should tell them about what Charles Murray, author of the acclaimed *Losing Ground: American Social Policy, 1950–1980*, stated in a speech at the American Enterprise Institute:

> Almost anything that government does in social policy can be characterized as taking some of the trouble out of things. Sometimes, taking the trouble out of things is a good idea. Having an effective police force takes some of the trouble out of walking home safely at night...The problem is this: Every time the government takes some of the trouble out of performing the functions of family, community, vocation, and faith, it also strips those institutions of some of their vitality—it drains some of the life from them. It's inevitable. Families are not vital because the day-to-day tasks of raising children and being a good spouse are so much fun, but because the family has responsibility for doing important things that won't get done unless the family does them. Communities are not vital because it's so much fun to respond to our neighbors' needs, but because the community has

the responsibility for doing important things that won't get done unless the community does them. Once that imperative has been met—family and community really do have the action—then an elaborate web of social norms, expectations, rewards, and punishments evolves over time that supports families and communities in performing their functions. When the government says it will take some of the trouble out of doing the things that families and communities evolved to do, it inevitably takes some of the action away from families and communities, and the web frays, and eventually disintegrates…If we knew that leaving these functions in the hands of families and communities led to legions of neglected children and neglected neighbors, and taking them away from families and communities led to happy children and happy neighbors, then it would be possible to say that the cost is worth it. But that's not what happened when the U.S. welfare state expanded. We have seen growing legions of children raised in unimaginably awful circumstances, not because of material poverty but because of dysfunctional families, and the collapse of functioning neighborhoods.[34]

Modern Liberal Social Engineering, Crises, and Root Causes

Ask Modern Liberals about families that make decisions that are not in congruence with their agenda. When the family (or any) unit is independent of the State, different values and standards will emerge. For example, some parents may teach their children that God created the world, homosexuality is sinful, or sex education is not the responsibility of the school. Modern Liberals want to prevent families from teaching their own children such ideas. The rejection of such independence means that their agenda requires limiting and eventually destroying the family as a decision-making unit. Modern Liberals seek to prevent individual decision-making because the results may not be in conformity with the agenda set by the federal government. Get a Modern Liberal to admit or recognize this, and tell them that they simply want the family to conform to *their* agenda.

Modern Liberals thrive on crises, and they will contrive to create them where none exist. Thomas Sowell documents the creation of nonexistent crises that the "anointed" used to increase government power and spending in the 1960s. In fact, as Sowell pointed out, many of the so-called crises in crime, illegitimacy, racism, and poverty were not crises at all, and these problems were actually *improving*. For example, violent crime was decreasing, the income of blacks was rising, and rates of illegitimate births and venereal diseases were declining. But the "anointed" claimed that these were crises that needed immediate government intervention.[35] And when there are real, but obviously temporary, problems, Modern Liberals have a predilection to scream "crisis!" Modern Liberals present our society as one of increasing impoverishment, oppression, and deterioration which can only be ameliorated, they claim, by implementing their federal government programs as quickly as possible. When one simply takes a longer view, the Modern Liberals' deceptions and distortions become clear: In *The Progress Paradox* and his following book, *Sonic Boom*, Gregg Easterbrook presents a plethora of information about how virtually every aspect of our lives has improved over the past century, half-century, and even over the past couple of decades:

> Before the economic downturn that became apparent in 2008, the larger global economic trend for three decades was rising prosperity for almost everyone, accelerating growth, higher living standards for average people, better education, increased ease of communication, low inflation, few shortages, and more personal freedom *across most of the family of nations...* [Even] IQ scores have risen about 3 percent per decade in almost all nations (emphasis added).[36, 37]

Easterbrook points out that in 2000, for example, 13 percent of home purchases were of second homes; a century before, less than 1 percent were of such homes. From 1950 to 2000, the square footage of new home construction doubled from about 1,100 square feet to 2,250 square feet. Only 15 percent of our grandparents had central heating, and today over 95 percent of us do. The costs of virtually everything—per unit cost—have dropped; even the same medical treatment and cost of medicine have dropped when we take inflation into account. The only reason that costs for education and medicine have increased—the only two things that have increased in real cost—is that we have demanded much more of these. In terms of such things as longevity and the gap between the rich and poor, things are better: In 1900, the difference between the life spans of the "rich" and the poor was 15 years; today it is only four. The rich and the poor have the same levels of basic education, use the same roads, see the same television shows, and have access to the same cultural experiences.

These improvements—due to the free market—can be seen internationally as well. Modern Liberals scream that globalization, capitalism, and American imperialism impoverish other countries, but a Brooking Institute study showed otherwise: In 1950, the developing world had 72 percent of the population but only 28.8 percent of global income; in 2000, their population had increased by only 9 percent, but their share of income went up to 42.2 percent. According to a United Nations study, the mean income in these countries almost doubled since 1975. Freedom has also spread. In 1980, only one-third of nations had free elections; by 2005, it increased to two-thirds. In Latin America, 40 percent of children under five were underweight; by 2004, this dropped to *five* percent. In the 1960s, nobody believed India could ever even feed itself. However, it has dropped most of its Socialist programs, welcomed globalization (capitalism), and is now rapidly becoming a world economic powerhouse. Jimmie Carter said that there would be mass global starvation by 2000.[38] In a 2009 report about world poverty by the National Bureau of Economic Research, the findings were summarized:

> Using the official $1/day line, we estimate that world poverty rates have fallen by 80% from 0.268 in 1970 to 0.054 in 2006. The corresponding total number of poor has fallen from 403 million in 1970 to 152 million in 2006. Our estimates of the global poverty count in 2006 are much smaller than found by other researchers. We also find similar reductions in poverty if we use other poverty lines. We find that various measures of global inequality have declined substantially and measures of global welfare increased by somewhere between 128% and 145%.[39]

Modern Liberals like to predict crises from coming shortages of energy, food and commodities. These apparent "states of emergency" are declared in order to help the central planners gain more control over our lives and economy. However, Modern Liberals conveniently deny or ignore the past: In 1909, for example, it was predicted that our oil supply would be depleted by 1935; in 1922, it was predicted that it would be gone by 1942; and in 1932, it was forecast that the oil would be gone by 1952. In 1885, it was concluded that no oil could be found in California, and in 1891, none in Texas. Hysterical predictions like these have led to "solutions" such as speed limits across the country and price controls; Modern Liberals have even proposed the regulation and control of home heating.

Modern Liberals claim that we need to search out the "root causes" of crime, implying that it stems from our social structures and not individuals choosing to violate the law. Modern Liberals need to be reminded that the "Get Tough" laws have helped to reduce crime.[40]

Modern Liberals refuse to recognize human nature; they are convinced that they can change it by creating new institutions, the right education, and new laws. Modern Liberals assume that if experts engineer society with the federal government enforcing their dictums, we will all live in harmony and become "caring" and "compassionate." In contrast, as previously pointed out, our Founders were well aware of the realities of human nature over two centuries ago: In the *Federal Papers*, faction was described as a group of citizens united by an interested motive against the common good. The "latent causes of factions are thus sown into the *nature of man*,"[41] and "the accumulated experience of the ages [teaches that] men are ambitious, vindictive and rapacious" (emphasis added).[42] The Constitution aimed at hindering the formation of factions because "there is a degree of depravity in mankind,"[43] and due to "the ordinary depravity of human nature."[44]

In order to establish programs of social justice, Modern Liberals want people to believe that only specific types of people do wrong, such as racists, capitalists, religious zealots, and sexists. Conservatives know *all* people are capable of wrongdoing, and it is part of human nature. Remember that when we say that *all* people are capable of evil, the responsibility then shifts from society to the individual; this view results in not demonizing or punishing any one type of citizen as Modern Liberals do. The Modern Liberals' position not only condemns certain citizens, but it also exonerates their chosen ones from wrongdoing. Moreover, it opens the door for the persecution of the ones that Modern Liberals labeled as the "wrongdoers."

Diversity and Unity

Modern Liberals profess that they want unity and cohesiveness. Jonah Goldberg, author of *Liberal Fascism*, wrote about what these people would do if they *really* wanted unity:

> [They] would pine for the 1950s or even the 1920s. But the left didn't thrive in these decades, so any unity enjoyed by Americans was illegitimate. In other words, it is not unity the left longs for but victory…

In the 1930s and 1960s, the left's popular-front approach yielded real power—and that is the true object of liberal nostalgia; nothing more, nothing less.[45]

When Modern Liberals say they want diversity, remind them of their implacable resistance to real diversity of *thought*. Modern Liberals insist that we all must have the same values and attitudes. This dogma has driven Modern Liberals to attack the independence of the family, religious institutions, home schooling, and communities, especially via enforcing Political Correctness and speech codes.

When Modern Liberals say that specific groups do not have "access," it really means that the people have not learned to behave to meet the standards to *get* "access." The expression "denied access" preempts any questions about why things *really* turned out as they did. Ask Modern Liberals to specify *who* is denied access and precisely how it is denied.

Tell Modern Liberals that Conservatives envision themselves in terms of being Americans, not as members of a particular race or ethnicity. It is likely that you will be branded intolerant, benighted, or bigoted for this, but remind them that you are looking at people as individuals and they are not. Modern Liberal doctrines prevent them from seeing people as individuals instead of as members of a particular race or class. Their agenda compels them to view people in terms of race, class ethnicity, and a host of other groups; their programs prevent them from seeing other Americans as individuals. Modern Liberals say that Conservatives see Communists under every bed; Modern Liberals see *racists* everywhere. This is because Modern Liberals view everyone in terms of the race to which he or she belongs. It can be fun to pull out some quotes by Ann Coulter; try these: "With their infernal racial set-asides, racial quotas, and race norming, liberals share many of the Klan's premises. The Klan sees the world in terms of race and ethnicity. So do liberals!"[46] "Democrats don't care about race discrimination: They are the party of race discrimination! George Wallace, Bull Connor, Bob Byrd—all Democrats!"[47]

The Evil Rich

Modern Liberals say the so-called rich invariably impoverish the masses and desire a permanent underclass. If a Modern Liberal blurts out such drivel, remind him that if this absurdity were true, countries with the most wealth should have the most people in poverty. Also, ask him how the "rich" people are supposed to make their fortunes if everyone around them is poor.

The anti-capitalism and hypocrisy of Modern Liberals can be readily demonstrated by asking them a hypothetical question: Modern Liberals profess to want more money for the poor, so suppose wealth in real terms doubled, but the so-called "disparities of income" remained the same—would that be okay with them? Modern Liberals will try not to answer it, and the few who do will declare it is still "unfair," despite the fact that real purchasing power in this scenario has doubled for everyone. There can be really only one explanation: envy. Remind them that many Modern Liberals promote their socialist agenda out of envy. Personal failure is another reason, of course. Telling Modern Liberals that their ideology and agenda originate from envy and personal failures irks them to no end. Enjoy the show that they will provide.

Modern Liberals often use the phrase, "undeserved income"—get them to define and clarify it. There are serious flaws in their reasoning that can be pointed out. First, there is the Modern Liberal assumption that the "undeserved income" is coming from a source for which the person did not work hard to get. So, would they consider the dividends a teacher gets from some good stock purchases "underserved?" Modern Liberals usually answer by saying that this only applies to people in higher income brackets, but that is the second flaw: It necessitates a relationship between the total income and this so-called "underserved income," and they know nothing about this distribution of the latter income, of course. They are obliged to assume that all persons with huge incomes have the same proportions of this "undeserved" income. Their irrational assumptions are thus exposed. Also, tell them you are well-aware of their purpose in classifying income as "undeserved": It supplies a rationale for its confiscation by the federal government. Ask them why they are not more honest, and simply state that they want any excuse to seize the wealth of private citizens.

When a Modern Liberal supports redistribution of wealth, ask how it supports liberty. Remind him that redistribution requires a centralized state to put it into effect and carry it out, of course.

Miscellaneous Modern Liberal Nonsense

Conservatives know that some recognition of authority is essential for learning and cohesion in society, but Modern Liberals declare that this supports power structures and fosters oppression. Conservatives understand that a sensible and proper amount of deference to traditional and established authority is essential to maintain our independence and civilization. It forms the basis of much of our culture, manners, and civility. Modern Liberals inherited the New Left's absurd notion of insisting on informality in dress, address, and action, and they claim that this is being "liberated" and fostering "fairness" and "equality." The result is that instead of good manners and civility, we now have *political correctness*; in place of respect, we confess our vulnerabilities even on television; and rather than looking at life as a place where we seek success and adhere to rules to achieve this, we look at life as an endless filling of expanding wants. Modern Liberals must be confronted with how this destroys structures necessary for success and prosperity, and that it weakens the edifices for holding our civilization together and giving it meaning. Modern Liberals' visionary delusions are tearing apart the foundation of mutual respect between parents and children, between husbands and wives, and between teachers and students.

Modern Liberals reflexively (and mindlessly) use the term "McCarthyism." When they do, ask them how many people went to prison because of McCarthy's actions. The reality is nobody did. Around 200 people were merely blacklisted from the movie industry and completely free to do anything else, even though they openly supported a mass murderer and an avowed enemy of America. Hubert Humphrey himself said that Liberals hated McCarthy because "he has immobilized the Liberal movement."[48]

Have Fun!

We know Modern Liberals well—what they are like and how they will respond—but they know little about us. We have this element of surprise—use it. They do not know America, nor do they identify with its people and its values. Modern Liberals isolate and stay among themselves. This is one of the reasons that they assume others think as they do. Modern Liberals are never challenged, so when they are, they become helpless and enraged. Harry Stein describes Viki McKenna, a broadcaster in Madison, Wisconsin, one of the three most Modern Liberal towns in America. Viki tells her audience that she is "broadcasting from occupied territory" or from "the city that lost its collective mind." Viki reminds her audience that "refusing to be defensive drives Liberals nuts."[49]

Remember a fundamental weakness of Modern Liberals: They know what they *should* think and what they are *supposed* to think, and this makes it easy to create cognitive dissonance in them. Harry Stein, in a chapter of his book entitled, "Dinner Party Mischief," offers suggestions about how to create this dissonance in Modern Liberals: Ask them, for instance, what they think about the rape-murder by a parolee, the results of affirmative action, welfare promoting dysfunction, or Asian-Americans being discriminated against when applying for entrance to universities. Stein's favorite is to ask them whether they would prefer their children to be heterosexuals or not.[50]

ECONOMICS

Socialism has never and nowhere at first been a working-class movement[51]

—FREDRICK HAYEK

The people of the United States are more prosperous. . . because their government embarked later than other governments. . .upon the policy of obstructing business.[52]

—LUDWIG VON MISES

Abraham Lincoln frequently spoke about looking to our founding for inspiration and guidance, and he also spoke about the free market in America. In a speech in New Haven, Connecticut, on March 6, 1860, just a year before he became president, Abraham Lincoln said this:

> When one starts poor, as most do in the race of life, free society is such that he knows he can better his condition; he knows that there is no fixed condition of labor, for his whole life. I am not ashamed to confess that twenty-five years ago I was a hired laborer. . .I want every man to have

his chance…when he may look forward and hope to be a hired laborer this year and the next, work for himself afterward, and finally to hire men to work for him!

Economics is a separate section of this chapter. Much of the "debate" with Modern Liberals (we discuss and they scream) centers on economics. These debates can become burdened with detail, formulas, and statistics: Should we control the money supply? Do tariffs really help or hinder industry? Are we over or under regulated?

Modern Liberals insist that we should and can organize and control the economy, but Hayek warned us of its consequences:

> [This] is not only the path to totalitarianism but the part to the destruction of our civilization and a certain way to block future progress…[The] mere preservation of what we have so far achieved depends on the coordination of individual efforts by impersonal forces.[53]

Trying to master economics can be a full-time endeavor, and there are forces beyond our control—terrorism, natural disasters, wars, crop yields, innovations, and discoveries—that can dramatically affect any economy. If we look at history, we see countless developments, such as the discovery of oil, electricity lighting homes, cars replacing horses, and trucks transporting goods instead of trains. These led to the creation of innumerable new industries and jobs. Inevitably, these were followed by economic or geographical sectors going boom and bust, large transfers of wealth, and changes in demands for certain goods and services.

Basic Principles

Rather than attempting to master the myriad economic theories and concepts, let's review some basic principles that clearly demonstrate how Modern Liberalism is a threat to our liberty and way of life.

First of all, do we want to reduce the discussion of America to simply one about which policy will result in a better economic situation? Would this not imply that we view our country solely in terms of a place to be prosperous? Is the only attraction to America simply a good place to make money? Are we willing to accept any system only to get more income? It that it? Let's hope not.

The Nobel Prize winner Milton Friedman—possibly the most widely known "free market" advocate, writer of Goldwater's speeches, advisor to Ronald Reagan, and bane of Modern Liberals—was asked if he were a Conservative. Friedman replied that he was not and simply said he was for freedom. His two most widely read books contain that very word: *Capitalism and* Freedom and Free *to Choose* (emphasis added). In a FOX News interview in May 2004, Friedman presented simple realities of human nature. When Modern Liberals are told about these, they fly into paroxysms of rage. Friedman explained that there really are only four ways to spend money, and humans respond to each in a predictable way:

1. Spend one's own money on oneself—the person will be careful of the cost and also of value and quality of the purchase.
2. Spend one's own money on someone else—the person will be careful about the cost, but less about the quality.
3. Spend someone else's money on oneself—the person will spend a lot.
4. Spend someone else's money on someone else—the person doesn't care about the cost or the quality.

Friedman said of the fourth option: "That's government."[54] Conservatives want to emphasize the efficiency, productivity, and freedom in the first two options; Modern Liberals—want the fourth one.

Modern Liberals attack free-market capitalism at every opportunity. They want a planned economy administered by a central authority, and one quickly sees that Modern Liberals always do the following:

1. Avoid the expression "free-market" and only use the term "capitalism" in a sarcastic, condescending, and sneering manner. Modern Liberals do not want listeners to think of the actual freedom we have in our day-to-day voluntary exchanges; rather, they want to create an impression that capitalism leads to destructive greed and that capitalists are "predators."
2. Use the term "corporatism"—business colluding with government— over and over, saying that this is really what the market is all about.

Let's have a look at some basic and irrefutable principles in economics with which we can confront the tyranny of the enemies of free-market capitalism, the Modern Liberals:

1. Those in the private sector who seek to provide a product or a service have to put the needs and wants of individuals first. If people do not want what they provide, they simply cannot exist. Modern Liberals will scream "greed" and ascribe other negative motives to entrepreneurs, but the motives are not relevant at all; what is relevant is that these entrepreneurs have to focus on providing something that people choose to buy.

2. Those outside of the private sector—government employees—do not have to be concerned with what people want as those in the private sector *are compelled to be*. Some certainly go into "public service" (Modern Liberals like to use that endearing term to imply that they "serve" the public) for that purpose, but their work does not necessitate concern. As previously mentioned, even if the public at large rejects and is inconvenienced by these bureaucrats, government employees are pressed to convince themselves and others that they are providing something needed. Modern Liberals insist that citizens can control government employees through their elected officials, but this is absurd: Government employees are hired and appointed, not elected, and the process of eliminating or even reducing the size of a bureaucracy is cumbersome and nearly impossible. Ask a Modern Liberal to name some that have been eliminated. Remind them that agencies such as the Environmental Protection Agency have been given independent power to create new regulations and to punish transgressors.

3. Every day, citizens "vote" for and against those in the private sector—with their wallets. With the free market, the citizens are in control, not the "experts." For Modern Liberals, the fact that the free market is really in the hands of citizens is probably its most repugnant aspect. This is because Modern Liberals want to allocate rewards to those *they* consider worthy. A free market shifts the allocation of rewards from the hands of government and puts it into the hands of ordinary people, the American citizens. These people choose the radio and television shows, the types of restaurants, the kinds of cars, and the style of furniture and clothing that they prefer. Every day, millions of citizens "vote" by changing television channels, choosing where to go on the weekend, and buying what they like in grocery and department stores. In a free market, these citizens are the ones who determine which stations will stay on the air, which restaurants will succeed, which line of clothes

and cereal will be popular, and which car companies will prosper or go bankrupt, not the government.

4. The free market exerts a countervailing force to the government. If the government controls most of the economy, the experts—consisting primarily of Modern Liberals, of course—can decide prices and how we will use our resources.

5. Modern Liberals presume that "rich capitalists" are a threat to our freedom. Modern Liberals get apoplectic if they are asked for specific examples of when any CEO or corporation forced them to do something. Ask them how any major company threatened their liberty in the past year. But government officials—from the surly clerk at the Department of Motor Vehicles and the punctilious bureaucrat regulating your business, to the Environmental Protection Agency minions telling you how to use your own land—hover over us every day and have the power to force us to follow government regulations and rules.

6. Modern Liberals fancy that Socialism is more in tune with human nature, but the opposite is true. Their dogma is awash with fallacies: Modern Liberals consider simple sharing to be a form of Socialism, and they even declare that a community choosing to tax itself to pay for police, garbage collection, and parks to be Socialism! This is just cooperation. In fact, if we look at what always happens among individuals in a highly controlled and regulated economy, it reveals humans' natural inclination toward voluntary exchanges of a free market type: A black market emerges. In *Cannibals and Kings,* Marvin Harris noted that in tribal societies, leaders were "capitalists" of a sort who vied with one another in giving feasts—gifts were given with an expectation of a return.[55] In *Fighting with Property,* Helen Codere described the "free-market capitalist" system of pot latching with Native Americans—a system of work, saving, capital accumulation, and feasting.[56] In fact, in the free market, the provider of goods or services *must* consider others; he has to cater to their needs and desires in order to succeed. The person beginning a private enterprise may be motivated by personal gain, but this does not negate the fact that he must provide what others want. Another aspect of the free market is that trust is implicit in every transaction. We take this for granted, but it is there, all the same. If one receives a check from another, he *trusts* that it is good; if one gets dental treatment, he *trusts* that the dentist did what should be done;

and if one signs a contract for a payment with someone, both *trust* each other to fulfill the responsibilities. The free market necessitates trust and cooperation.

7. Modern Liberals scream that monopolies get control and raise prices, but—as long as the companies are not colluding with government—with "monopolies" real prices usually drop. In 1980, Julian Simon, professor of business, made a wager with Paul Ehrlich, author of *The Population Bomb*: Ehrlich insisted that resources will become scarcer and scarcer, driving up prices, thus trying to make a case for government control and management of our resources. However, Simon posited that the human mind is the "ultimate resource," and prices would not go up. Simon let Ehrlich pick five metals and agreed to check their prices in ten years. Well, not only did the prices not go up, but the prices went down for every metal. There is not a single recorded instance of private companies—ones not colluding with the government—controlling the market and driving up prices. In *Antitrust and Monopoly: Anatomy of a Policy Failure*, Dominick T. Armentano and Yale Brozen document this in 55 antitrust suits[57], and the record of the so-called Robber Barons allegedly creating monopolies to fleece the public is clarified: Private companies *lowered* prices, while the ones that increased prices *always colluded with the government*.[58] The absurdities of the claims of monopolies being harmful were clearly stated in the Warren Court: Justice Warren himself said that product improvement and lower prices were unfair. These antitrust suits were simply based on a company getting a large control of the market and not on having raised prices or harmed consumers in any way. These potential antitrust lawsuits terrified some industries: General Motors, for example, so feared attacks that from 1937 to 1956, it never let its market share to get too high, and this led the way to the Japanese and German dominance of the market. According to Thomas DiLorenzo, "the company so feared prosecution that its official policy from 1937 until 1956 was never to let its market share top 45 percent...This fear of antitrust prosecution made GM a less competitive company, and it therefore was incapable of effectively competing when Japanese and German automakers began dominating the US auto market in the 1970s."[59]

8. So-called government "protections" often have had harmful effects: Zoning has sometimes led to more crime; rent controls have reduced

available units; seatbelts have resulted in more deaths when bicyclists and pedestrians are included in the calculations; airbags have killed small women and children; and where welfare programs have been implemented on a large scale, the number of illegitimate children, poverty, and crime have increased. Over-regulating drugs has led to higher prices and less choice. From 1959–1964, when the New Left, the parents of Modern Liberals, said that there was a poverty "crisis," the poverty rate had been *decreasing*; when the money started pouring in, the decline stopped and then poverty (and crime) rates steadily increased.[60]

9. An economic fact that Modern Liberals conveniently refuse to acknowledge is that if any industry needs government help to survive, it really means that it is not productive or the public is simply not willing to pay for it without being forced to. The government cannot pay for anything. When the government subsidizes something, it is really the tax-paying citizens giving the subsidized entity their money via the government, so the people are really paying a higher cost—directly or indirectly.[61]

10. Free-market capitalism not only *necessitates* cooperation, it forces us to improve and to learn. In the past, new articles were initially made for royalty. Later, with the advent of technologies, efficiency, and methods of mass production engendered by the free market, production served virtually everyone. When automobiles first came out, they were playthings of the well-to-do. Within a couple of decades, they became affordable for practically everyone, not just the well-heeled. Today, virtually every adult has a car. At the turn of the century, refrigerators were only for the affluent; today we see them in the most modest of homes. Because of the free market, production changed from making things and providing services for an elite few to producing for the general population, and this did not come about from central government plans.

Go on the Offensive

When Modern Liberals start their denunciations of free-market capitalism, here are some ways to go on the offense and put them on the defense:

1. Keep using the expression "*free* market" and do not refer to the loaded term "capitalism" in isolation. Modern Liberals are counting on any

unfavorable associations that people may have with the terms "capitalism" and "capitalists." Modern Liberals will claim that there is no perfectly "free" market: That is the tactic described in Chapter 7, "If it is not 100 percent perfect in 100 percent of all situations, then it cannot be considered." In that way, Modern Liberals try to nullify the existence of the free market in order to introduce the Modern Liberal alternative—an economy managed and controlled by their beloved government. So, never seek to provide examples of "perfectly free" markets. Rather, remind Modern Liberals that freedom requires laws and protections; remind them that they engage in voluntary transactions without government coercion practically every day; inquire if they have ever shopped around for better prices; and ask them if they have ever negotiated the price of a used car, a house, or any payment of a service—examples of the "free" market allowing prices to be decided by individuals. Tell the Modern Liberals that we must strive to make the market as free as possible and to get the government out of colluding with business. Ask them if they are against it being free and watch them stutter and stammer.

2. Compare the power over our daily lives—in practical, real-life terms—of the free market or even of corporations as opposed to the government. When a Modern Liberal contends that capitalists are controlling our lives, ask him when businesses or companies of any sort have coerced him into behaving any way he did not choose? Ask the Modern Liberal for concrete examples and specifics; he will not be able to provide any. Tell the Modern Liberal to consider the government in the same sense: The power of the State is used to tell us how to use our land, whether we can drive a car, and if we can marry. A Modern Liberal will often allege that the companies and businesses manipulate our desires, but ask him if he feels that he has no free will. If he does not, how can he even make such a statement?

3. When a Modern Liberal asserts that capitalism promotes greed, selfishness, and rapacity, ask him to consider something: If he wants to start any business—and all have some beginning—what is the *first* question he must ask at the very start without which he could never succeed? The answer is simple: What do people want? What service or product is in demand, how can I make an improvement on existing ones, or can I create something new that others will want? The individual's

motive is not the issue at all. The motive may be to amass wealth, to buy more objects, to give to a charity, to get a big house, to buy fast cars, to feel economically secure, or to attain status. No matter what the motives are, an entrepreneur has to supply what others want; he has to take their needs and desires into account. In contrast, the government worker focuses on what his or her employer wants. In addition, if the government employee wants to get ahead, he usually does this by amassing more certificates and educational credits, by currying favor, and by staying on the job. The government worker has to anticipate what the government and his immediate employer wants, and the entrepreneur in the free market must anticipate what the consumers want.

4. Modern Liberals forget what wealth creation in the free market really is: Essentially, it is producing more than one needs for one's minimum sustenance, and then reinvesting the excess in one's own or another's business, learning a new skill, buying stocks, or even helping one's own children. But Modern Liberals have created and propagated an image—one that they rarely, if ever, see in reality—of some huge corporations controlling our lives. The reality is quite different: Small businesses are the ones creating jobs and wealth. Get Modern Liberals to look around at their own town, friends, and family and see these "capitalists" (call them that sarcastically) at work. Ask Modern Liberals to look at a dentist, an owner of a restaurant or gas station, a carpenter, and a plumber; they are all free-market capitalists who have learned a skill and taken risk to provide a product or service and offer voluntary exchanges in the "free market" of everyday life. Point out that many are also *incorporated* and see their faces flush with an admixture of embarrassment, exasperation, and outrage.

5. Press Modern Liberals for alternatives to the free market. Modern Liberals and their forefathers have been claiming that corporations are out of control for over a century, but what has *actually* happened to our standard of living? Modern Liberals will contend that without government intervention, there would be child labor, sweat shops, and other horrors, but remind them that prosperity from capitalism itself was necessary for the advancements that allowed children to attend schools, workers to press for higher wages, and producers to provide better conditions in the places of work. With increased prosperity came increased demands. It was precisely as prosperity came—with its

accompanying increase in education, income, and leisure—that these demands were heard and met. Remind Modern Liberals of the "Asian Tigers"—Malaysia, South Korea, and Taiwan—and their very recent boom through industrialization: After the *free market* raised their standard of living and brought them out of poverty, the children in these countries left the factories and went to school, the hours of necessary labor decreased, and workplace safety improved.

Modern Liberals scream that anyone who is not in agreement with their agenda of government controlling, managing and regulating the economy is a radical ideologue, and that he is a proponent of a "laissez faire" economy who wants the rich to become even richer. First of all, these Modern Liberals need to be made aware that *they are the ideologues* and that Conservatism is anti-ideology. Next, they should be told how fatuous their presumption is that any typical American would promote policies designed specifically to make the rich even richer. Most of all, they should be reminded that providing a legal framework in which people are as free as possible to pursue voluntary exchanges with a minimum of government interference not only supports liberty but also give us the following:

1. We get efficiency from the private sector and competition. In the private sector, businesses continuously aim to provide either superior products for similar prices, lower their prices, or both. Tell Modern Liberals to remember that they choose products *voluntarily*; if they and other consumers do not choose a product, that company loses business and *must* provide better products or lower prices to get customers back.
2. The market—consumers as well as producers and service providers— gives *true* feedback about what is important and how things are valued. True feedback focuses on what *consumers* want (what they actually buy), not what *government experts* deem valuable. Prices provide reliable feedback only when they fluctuate freely, and they give needed information to the producers and service-providers: When people like a product, the demand goes up. If something becomes scarce for any reason— from huge demands or even war, strikes, or depletion of resources—the prices rise, either for the producer or the consumer. If the government forcibly holds down prices at which goods sell, producers and service providers lose incentives because their costs rose but the government

prohibited them from charging accordingly. In that way they suffer losses, incentives are gone, and they make fewer things or quit working—the result is scarcity and even unemployment. This is detrimental to consumers, producers, labor, and service providers.

3. The free market in the hands of citizens is a countervailing force to the power of government. With an economy mostly in the hands of private citizens, the power remains with the people. In contrast, if the economy is completely, or almost completely, in the hands of the government, the government dominates our economic lives.

The Free Market, Not Government Plans, Improved Our Lives

Modern Liberals claim that capitalists impoverish workers and government intervention is needed. In the early 19th century, before such intervention, wages rose (in real terms) 60 percent from 1820 to 1860. In an even shorter period, from 1869 to 1890—still with almost no government intervention—real wages went up 50 percent, and the work week grew shorter. The work week grew shorter because employers needed to compete, and this was due to increasing prosperity. Employers had to offer higher wages and/or shorter work hours. This was the same with child labor: People began to be able to keep their children in school and out of the factory because of increased incomes. Modern Liberals profess that early 20th century Progressive policies got children out of the labor force, but their assertions ring hollow when we look at child labor in agriculture. These "caring" and "concerned" Progressives did not try to help children working on farms; they worked primarily with unions. Farms were not unionized at all. Despite this, fewer children in farms were working, and more were going to school. This was not a result of Progressive policies and laws, but because mechanization led to higher profits and demanded more skilled adult labor. Thomas DiLorenzo documents this:

> [There] was never an organized propaganda campaign against child labor in agriculture...The most likely reason for this is that labor unions were the driving force behind anti-child labor crusades, and unions were concerned...because it represented competition for union labor.[62]

In other words, the real reason that child labor laws were enacted was not because Progressives "cared" about the children, but they simply wanted to keep or increase the high level of wages that union members were enjoying. It was not to "protect" children—they did not apply this to nonunion farm work—but to protect *union workers* from any competition.

Because of free-market capitalism, not the policies of Modern Liberals and their predecessors, child labor was eliminated, the aged did not have to work, and women could be "homemakers" and out of the labor force. Overall prosperity from the free market formed the foundation from which we could reduce the necessity of children, mothers, and the aged from having to work. Modern Liberals attack the very foundation upon which *they* claim *they* have created with *their* compassionate policies.

Modern Liberals present a picture of the poor being stuck in the lower rungs in order to rationalize the case for redistribution. The facts show that their data are flagrantly distorted: Within eight to 15 years, from 86 to 95 percent of people in the lowest one-fifth moved into a higher income level.[63] These Modern Liberal distort information by reporting the percent of people at the poverty level as if it were static; they willfully ignore the mobility data because it would render bogus their proclamations of a permanent underclass stuck in poverty. At any time, new people—especially young people and immigrants—temporarily move into the "poverty level" then get out as they finish schooling, learn English, and gain job experience. Some others have temporary setbacks from which they generally recover. And Modern Liberals further distort the picture by including retired people who are "officially" at the poverty level but who have paid off their homes and are living comfortably on savings and social security. These Modern Liberal prevaricators do not tell us that these older people are classified as being at the "poverty" level based on their Adjusted Gross Incomes on their tax forms, and that much of their income—social security and savings, for example—is simply not reported there. Modern Liberals will never draw a full picture of what is really happening and what the data mean.

The "free market"—a market in which people voluntarily participate with a minimum of government intervention—centers on the individual as opposed to the collective. Modern Liberals—in their desire to plan and regulate the economy—are ultimately demanding the government to decide what is best for the entire populace, and that the government bureaucrats, not individual citizens, make choices. In other words, Modern Liberals are saying that the government knows best. In *The Road to Serfdom*, F. A. Hayek wrote about true liberty under Rule of Law; it is anathema to the position of Modern Liberals:

> [The] individual's system of ends should be supreme…It is this recognition of the individual as the ultimate judge of his ends, the belief that as far as possible his own views ought to govern his actions, that forms the essence of the individualist position.[64]

Modern Liberals postulate that we can keep prices down through wage and price controls. In *Four Centuries of Wage and Price Controls*, Robert Schuettinger documents 4,000 years of governments attempting such controls in China, Europe, Colonial and Modern America, and even in ancient Egypt. He concluded that the result was *always* the same: Sooner or later there were higher prices and/or shortages. Nobel Laureate Ronald Coase concluded that these controls *always* did more harm than good.[65]

Modern Liberals have three consistent and patently obvious fallacies in their view of economics:

1. They look only at the immediate effects of their policies.
2. They look only at its effects on isolated sectors of the economy.
3. They do not look at the *long-term effects* on the sector in question and on *all* citizens. Henry Hazlitt describes it as the "fallacy of overlooking secondary consequences."[66]

Myths Surrounding the Tennessee Valley Authority

The Tennessee Valley Authority (TVA) is an excellent example that demonstrates the three fallacies above. The TVA is extolled by Modern Liberals as a munificent government blessing of the Great Depression, bringing jobs and utilities to thousands of people. Its reality is quite different. As Burton Folsom points out in *New Deal or Raw Deal?*, "the concentrating of benefits among the 2 percent of the population living in the Tennessee Valley had to be done by taxing away wealth from the other 98 percent," and he referred to research done by William Chandler in *The Myth of the TVA*. It is worth quoting at length:

> [The] state of Tennessee in the fifty years after the 1930s actually lagged behind nearby states in economic development…Chandler compared

income levels of Tennessee with Georgia, where the TVA is absent. [They] started with roughly the same per capita incomes in 1933, but in the next two decades Georgia began inching ahead...Among the nine states of the southeastern United States, there has been essentially an inverse relationship between income per capita and the extent to which the state was served by the TVA...[S]ubsidized power gave many people in Tennessee...incentives to stay on small farms, not to change their way of life. In Georgia... more people were willing to move and start business...with the non-TVA states industrializing faster, that created larger incomes and a larger market for electricity in the cities...The TVA flooded hundreds of thousands of acres...Those acres, when flooded, had to be removed from the tax rolls, and that reduced economic development.[67]

Jim Powell, in *FDR's Folly*, points more serious problems with the TVA:

[It] is exempt from more than 130 federal laws, including workplace safety law...and hundreds of laws in the states where it operates...it is immune from civil liability lawsuits...Many environmentalists consider the TVA to be America's most notorious polluter...[It is] the biggest U.S. violator of the Clean Air Act...One of the worst nuclear power accidents occurred at the TVA's Browns Ferry Unit #1.[68]

Citing authorities, Powell pointed out that taxpayers in the Midwest and Northeast subsidize it while paying more for their electricity. In essence, the government appropriates money from A and gives it to B; Modern Liberals highlight and sensationalize the effects on B, but the effects on A are hidden and forgotten. The TVA is but one of a multitude of government "projects" to which Modern Liberals offer panegyrics.

Other Modern Liberal Myths, Fallacies, and Disasters

Rent controls provide another excellent example of disastrous results from a Modern Liberal plan: Rent controls encourage a waste of space, discourage new building, foist disincentives on people to move, inflate rents in the noncontrolled areas, reduce the desire of landlords to repair their properties, make tenants angry at negligent landlords, and result in slums. Rent controlled buildings have been abandoned, and desperate owners have committed arson; the surrounding property values decrease and tax revenues fall. All of this happens from Modern Liberal "plans."

Remind Modern Liberals that private property is better maintained than property owned by the government. Ask them to use common sense and compare a public housing project to any homes owned by citizens.

There is a simple and commonsensical fact with which Modern Liberals refuse to deal: If government investments actually created wealth, the citizens would applaud and not complain, of course. The fact is that the only way to improve the American economy—any economy—is to increase its production, and government does not *increase* the productivity of the nation, it *hamstrings* it.

Modern Liberals have a fallacious reasoning process that many people believe because it *sounds* good: The assertion is that government spending puts money in the hands of people, the people spend this money, it goes around and prosperity increases. This nonsense is easy to refute with a simple analogy: If a thief robs someone, according to this Modern Liberal notion, he is helping the economy; after all, he now has purchasing power that he did not previously have and he starts spending it quickly, stimulating different sectors of the economy where he spends. The fallacy, of course, is that the victim's purchasing power has declined! When the government says a program of government job creation is to increase people's purchasing power, it is a sure sign that the program should be stopped. Modern Liberals present "full employment" bills, but they do not present full *production* ones. Primitive societies have full employment. If employment is separated from the real source of a country's wealth—full production—then full employment is easier. Progress in a capitalist society actually can result in less employment. When the government creates a job, it simply means paying more than the open market would because the people are not demanding it.

When Modern Liberals disagree with the above—and they will—remind them of something very basic and simple: We cannot distribute more wealth than is created.

Modern Liberals abhor profits in the private sector and want to limit what they disparagingly describe as "excess profits." But these Modern Liberals never acknowledge the entrepreneurs' risks and how often they fail. If we adhere to the Modern Liberal idea and limit profits, what happens to what gave us prosperity: *incentives?* The misguided and histrionic ideologues—Modern Liberals—somehow assume production will continue, even when they attack incentives.

Free-market capitalism consists in providing first and getting back later; in addition, money confers freedom. In the Socialist world of Modern Liberals, things are fixed: The present status quo is preserved, and that destroys creativity because experts decide what to produce and what their value will be. George Gilder wrote about this in *Wealth and Poverty*:

> Money bears a presumption of faith and a grant of freedom. Without money all exchanges must be partly predetermined. It is the willingness of man to give—or work—without a specific reward that allows liberty. Money in a planned economy tends to be a deceit or false promise because the purchases are mostly preordained. In a capitalist economy every worker and businessmen...goes to the store and buys this book, not in essence with money, but with work transmuted into money...He values his money because his expenditure of funds is psychologically rooted in his earlier expenditure of effort...Capitalist production entails faith—n one's neighbors, in one's society, and in the compensatory logic of the cosmos.[69]

The Free Market and Creativity

Modern Liberals say affluence is due to "luck." Modern Liberals do not understand the complex variables that lead to success, nor do they want to understand, so they chalk success up to "luck" or "chance" in order to imply that these people did not really work for, or otherwise deserve, their success. Modern Liberals strive to present economic success as something akin to winning the local lottery. These assertions are simply an attempt to render successful people as unworthy and provide a rationale to confiscate their earnings. In contrast, Conservatives know that this "luck" or "chance" is really unique to freedom and that freedom leads to creativity, a willingness to take risk, and incentives to become successful and generate prosperity.

The following question—especially to more imperious and patronizing Modern Liberals—outrages them to no end, and the responses usually provide good entertainment: "If you are so smart, why aren't you rich?" Before you ask this, check whether the Modern Liberal has any heart or blood pressure problems.

In the free-market world, an admiration of achievers—people who created a lifestyle or business from their own motivation, industriousness and creativity—provides incentives for upward mobility and prosperity. In the centralized government and bureaucratic world of Modern Liberals, education and credentials—certificates and licenses—are the usual ways to climb the ladder in their bureaucracies. In the world that Modern Liberals strive to create, one is promoted by taking courses, getting certificates, and waiting for seniority; promotions are not for producing and meeting the needs of consumers as decided by the consumers.

Government regulations rely on current knowledge; the government planners *have to* live in the past and maintain the status quo. The economic policy of central planners is always to stimulate demand for existing stuff, not something new because new is unpredictable. If we look at periods of rapid growth—late 19th and early 20th centuries America, or the more recent Asian Tigers like South Korea, Malaysia, Taiwan, and Thailand—we see they were not a result of detailed plans and predictable processes, but of individuals, initiative, and creativity. The regulators we have today would never have permitted the launching of an airplane or the industrial revolution. F. A. Hayek pointed this out:

> It was men's submission to the impersonal forces of the market that in the past has made possible the growth of a civilization which without this could not have been developed...[U]nless this complex society is to be destroyed, the only alternative to submission to the impersonal and seemingly irrational forces of the market is submission to an equally uncontrollable and therefore arbitrary power of other men.[70]

———— ◆ ————

Progress, liberty, and prosperity come with some risks. Modern Liberals seem unable to comprehend what George Gilder pointed out:

> [No] nation can grow, adapt to change except to the extent that it is capitalist, except to the extent, in other words, that its productive wealth is diversely controlled and can be freely risked in new causes, flexibly applied to new purposes, steadily transformed into new shapes and systems.[71]

But Gilder's message is not new; a century and a half ago, Lincoln spoke about the work ethic and capitalism:

> [If] he works industriously, he behaves soberly, and the result of a year or two's labor is a surplus of capital...and in course of time he too has enough capital to hire some new beginner...If any continue through life in the condition of the hired laborer it is not the fault of the system, but because either a dependent nature which prefers it, or improvidence, folly, or singular misfortune.

14

Conclusions

I t is imperative—for our own liberty and prosperity as well as for that of our children—to understand the nature of two opposing forces struggling against each other, and that our country is again on the front lines. It is a centuries-old struggle that will, unfortunately, never end. It is fundamentally a fight between lovers of liberty who want a government "of, by and for the people," and forces that strive for a central power that controls, manages, and directs the people—their lives, their incomes, and their own children—for their "own good," they profess. This never-ending struggle is between those who want to keep self-government close to home—in their communities, their towns, and their states—and those who seek to transfer local control to a central power. This is not limited to our country; it is a world-wide struggle.

The federal government is not inherently evil or an "enemy." Our Founders knew it was necessary, but that its power must be limited. Our Founders drew from eons of history, the wisdom of the ancients, the Holy Bible, and what led to more freedoms in England. They also saw what was happening right in their own backyards with self-governing counties, town meetings, people own-ing land, independent tradesmen, and the bounties and freedoms that accom-panied the end of a rigid social class structure. Our Founders also understood and accepted the realities of human nature: Rather than trying to change it, they wrote a document that took it into account, separating and balancing powers, and giving each the authority to defend itself while also limiting it. This document—the *Constitution of the United States of America*—is still with us after more than two centuries. It has lasted longer than any other constitution in the history of the world, and each president of the United States swears on a Bible that it is his primary duty to uphold this Constitution—*So help me God.*

But our Constitution is not invulnerable. It is fragile and needs protection. And there are forces at work that seek to undermine it for an obvious reason: to centralize power. They have always been there. In the past, there were kings with divine rights, churches, emperors, and demagogues and tyrants. In our era, it is those who "wish us well" and claim to want the best for the people: They propose fairness, security, safety; they say they can give guarantees of a "decent standard of living," health care, housing, a job, and a clean environment—if only we hand over the reins of power to the central authority. Their proposals are very seductive and appeal to our most base instincts and fears: Envy, greed, dependency, security, comfort, and resentment. They say they will make society "fair," that they have "compassion," and that they "care about the children." They declare that the wealth to accomplish all of this is available, but that reactionary forces only want to hold us to an outmoded past of inequality, oppression, poverty, and racism.

In today's America, "they" are the Modern Liberals and what remains of the aging New Left. The French Revolution and revolutions of the 20th century that strove to set up a central power to usher in a new era and new man all ended up as abject failures with starvation, poverty, and death. But the dream—unbelievable as it seems—still continues. In the United States, it is with the Modern Liberals. Modern Liberals have learned that they cannot achieve their vision with an outward cry to overthrow the existing system and establish a new one, so they now take one issue at a time, one idea at a time, one sector of the economy at a time. They revise history to undermine our principles and belief in our order; they work to rid the public sector of all expressions of religious belief because religion places allegiance to God above the central government; they propose federal programs to "take care" of the sick, the abandoned children, and the elderly, saying it is the only entity capable of handling these huge, complex, and overwhelming problems; and they paint pictures of a country overtaken by greedy capitalists with people living in poverty, children in factories, and the sick and the elderly abandoned and dying—unless we turn over the economy and the running of our states and local communities to the federal government.

In our daily lives, we meet the Modern Liberal "foot soldiers," the ones who have learned the basic party lines to parrot. The phrases of "compassion," "fairness," and "caring" glibly roll off their tongues, implying that unless you agree with them, you lack those qualities. We meet them every day in our neighborhoods, in our places of work, and even in our churches, temples, and synagogues.

This book is dedicated to you, the American people, the ones who are on the front lines with Modern Liberals every day. With your resistance and refusal to yield to their relentless and daily attacks on our values, our economy, our Constitution, and our children, *you* will be the ones who preserve our way of life. Ronald Reagan was congratulated for bringing back prosperity and renewing the American spirit, but he said it was not him but the American people, so "thank them."

Right now, Modern Liberals are on the run everywhere, but they will never be completely defeated. We have already lost some ground: They and their predecessors have managed to enlarge government, make many dependent on federal programs, and convince others that we need guarantees from the State to have a decent life. Modern Liberals and their parents—the New Left—have partially succeeded in eroding the work ethic of many, revising our glorious history, and casting doubt about our noble role in the world.

Resolve not to compromise with Modern Liberals—at any place or for anything. Do not give an inch; we have given them too much already. The American people are the most generous and moral people in the world, and Modern Liberals have preyed on us and taken advantage of our benevolent nature for decades. We had hoped to appease them and have even come to doubt ourselves. Sometimes, we thought that maybe we could compromise with the New Left and Modern Liberals and reach a peace, but they have betrayed us on every front. When we give in, they only ask for more. That stops now—with you.

Never back down from a Modern Liberal. Get others to join you. Be the inspiration—and *you will inspire others* when you stand up to these people who have turned against our country. Study and learn. Listen to talk radio. Join groups like Freedomworks and your local Tea Party. In the Appendix, there are lists of organizations, books, and Internet sources for news and information. Get yourself a pocket Constitution, underline specific parts of interest, then pull it out and quote it to Modern Liberals who seek to render obsolete that grand creation.

Go to forums that Modern Liberals inhabit, join, and give them hell. Modern Liberals are a vainglorious, insular, and bumptious group, and they are easily discomfited by those who would stand up to them; you will get thrown off forums for challenging them, but you will rattle their cages and cause them to lose confidence.

Above all, stay optimistic about America—our founding, our history, and our people. Never doubt that you are one of the fortunate and blessed few for being a citizen of the greatest country in the history of the world. Your optimism and love of country will encourage and embolden others. Do not forget to support others who love our country; many feel isolated and besieged. Never apologize for your love of country; your country deserves it. Display it openly and without reservation. You will be surprised how many others feel exactly the same. Be the person who yells that the king has no clothes on: Expose the Modern Liberals for what they are.

Look at what is important to other Americans: Some are concerned with their businesses, some worry about what their children are learning in school and what kind of a country they will inherit, some have sons and daughters fighting abroad to preserve our—and the world's—liberty, and some want to see our founding principles restored. Do not only look at what you see as important in the preservation of our way of life—listen to your fellow Americans.

As unpleasant and hateful as it seems, *it is possible* that we could lose the country to Modern Liberals. Ronald Reagan said that liberty can be lost in a single generation. It is the unthinkable, and it would reduce us to misery and barbarism. Even so, this possibility changes nothing for us. Bill O'Reilly wrote that "even if I'm wrong and the unthinkable happens - that is the United States 'evolves' into a secular-progressive country - I'll know that I have fought on the side of the angels."[1]

Ronald Reagan said:

> [T]he real friends of the conservative movement aren't those entrenched in the capital city for 50 years; the real friends of the conservative movement are an entity that gets heard from in a big way every four years and who, I promise you, are going to be heard from this year. I'm talking about those who, if the case is aggressively put before them, will vote for limited government, family values, and a tough, strong foreign policy every single

time. I'm talking about those believers in common sense and sound values, your friends and mine, the American people. You see, those who underestimate the conservative movement are the same people who always underestimate the American people.

Ronald Reagan spoke at Normandy on the 40th anniversary of the day when the noblest fighting force in the world—the Americans—hit the beaches to bring liberty and freedom to a besieged Europe. When Reagan described the courage and sacrifices of these brave men, even the Secret Service agents had tears in their eyes. Ronald Reagan told the story about a diary that was found on the dead body of an American soldier:

> We are told that on his body was found a diary. On the flyleaf under the heading, "My Pledge," he had written these words: "America must win this war. Therefore, I will work, I will save, I will sacrifice, I will endure, I will fight cheerfully and do my utmost, as if the issue of the whole struggle depended on me alone."

Appendix A

Suggestions
For Further Reading

The major sources for this book are cited in the notes. Recommended readings are presented here in several categories which are not necessarily mutually exclusive. In each category, the books are presented from introductions and general surveys to more in-depth analyses requiring some familiarity or background with the subject matter.

AMERICAN HISTORY

Paul Johnson, *A History of the American People* (New York: HarperPerennial, 1999). Larry Schweikart and Michael Allen, *A Patriot's History of the United States* (New York: Sentinel, 2007). Both of these readable narratives of America are complete histories and pleasures to read. The authors have the deepest respect and love of America, and it shows.

Matthew Spalding, *We Still Hold These Truths: Rediscovering Our Principles, Reclaiming Our Future* (Wilmington, DE: Intercollegiate Studies Institute, 2009).

A readable book that describes ten core principles that made our nation great and the need to renew them.

Richard Brookhiser, *What Would the Founders Do?* (New York: Basic Books, 2007). Just as the title indicates, the book presents a number of our major concerns today—such as abortion, trade, a taxes, and the legalization of drugs, —and discusses them from the Founders' viewpoints, always reminding us about how our leaders have consistently looked to these men in times of crisis.

John Harmon McElroy, *American Beliefs: What Keeps a Big Country and a Diverse People United,* (Chicago: I. R. Dee, 1999). An excellent explanation of the origins of the fundamental beliefs and values that are unique to America and that made us great.

Bernard Bailyn, *The Ideological Origins of the American Revolution* (Harvard University Press, 1992). A scholarly and somewhat demanding read, this is a definitive work on the creation of our Constitution in which our core founding principles are articulated and documented.

Edwin Meese, Matthew Spalding and David Forte, editors, *The Heritage Guide to the Constitution* (DC: Regnery Publishing, 2005). This almost 500-page tome is a compilation of the writings of over 100 scholars, taking every clause and even word in our Constitution and analyzing them with accompanying histories and court cases. An excellent reference tool.

ECONOMICS

Robert P. Murphy, *The Politically Incorrect Guide to Capitalism* (Washington, DC: Regnery Publishing, 2007). Any book of the *Politically Incorrect Guide* series is recommended. This is an excellent introduction to free-market capitalism and good for those who want to review and brush up on what they already know.

Henry Hazlitt, *Economics in One Lesson* (New York: Crown, 1979). An excellent introduction—very readable—to free-market concepts and how government policies wind up costing us more in the long run.

Thomas DiLorenzo, *How Capitalism Saved America: The Untold History of Our Country, from the Pilgrims to the Present* (NY: Three Rivers Press, 2004). The author takes on the myths of the anti-capitalists who have revised our history. Historical examples—from the Pilgrims to Microsoft—are presented to show how free-market capitalism helped to propel America into the most prosperous nation in the world in a short time.

Milton Friedman, *Capitalism and Freedom* (University of Chicago, 2002), and Milton Friedman and Rose Friedman, *Free to Choose: A Personal Statement* (New York: Harcourt Brace Jovanovich, 1990). The Nobel Prize winning economist and his wife describe how our liberty is inextricably tied to the free market. The first book was originally published in 1962.

George Gilder, *Wealth and Poverty* (New York: Basic Books, 1981). Gilder makes an excellent case for the morality of the free market. Government planning destroys the source of wealth, but the private market brings wealth through encouraging creativity, courage, and technological adventure.

Charles Wheelan and Burton Maikiel, *Naked Economics* (New York: W. W. Norton, 2010). Tim Harford, *The Undercover Economist* (New York: Oxford University Press, 2006). Fun and readable nonpartisan books that look at our everyday economic life. After you read one of these, your shopping habits will never be the same!

Gregg Easterbrook, *The Progress Paradox* and *Sonic Boom* (New York: Random House, 2004 and 2009, respectively). Both of these books let us know how well off we really are; the progress and prosperity we have achieved is quite unbelievable when put in the historical perspective.

Robert P. Murphy, *The Politically Incorrect Guide to the Depression and the New Deal* (Washington, DC: Regnery Publishing, 2009). Another excellent book from the *Politically Incorrect Guide* series, this one thoroughly debunks the myth that the New Deal brought us out of the Great Depression. Good ammunition for those who fight with Modern Liberals on a regular basis.

Burton Folsom, *The Myth of the Robber Barons* (Washington, DC: Young America's Foundation, 2010). Another debunker of the "robber baron" myths of the titans of industry whose efforts resulted in prosperity for all.

Robert Schuettinger and Eamonn Butler, *Forty Centuries of Wage and Price Controls: How Not to Fight Inflation,* (Auburn, AL: Ludwig von Mises Institute, 1979). Historical examples from ancient Egypt to today about how government intervention of prices and production have always resulted in inflation and shortages.

MARXISM, COMMUNISM, AND SOCIALISM

Kevin Williamson, *The Politically Incorrect Guide to Socialism* (D. C.: Regnery Publishing, 2011). An excellent summary—with plenty of references—of Socialism. Williamson approaches it historically and theoretically and connects the dots to answer the question we all ask: How are Socialism and Communism different or the same?

Richard Pipes, *Communism: A History* (New York: Random House, 2001). Probably the best brief survey of Communism available; very readable and interesting.

Thomas Sowell, *Marxism: Philosophy and Economics* (New York: William Morrow and Company, 1985). An excellent introduction to the basic principles and thinking of Marxism.

David Conway, *A Farewell to Marx: An Outline and Appraisal of His Theories* (New York: Penguin Books, 1987). An excellent analysis of the failures of Marxism and how some of the ideas persist today, despite its gross failures. Some background required.

PROGRESSIVISM, THE OLD LEFT, THE NEW LEFT, AND MODERN LIBERALISM

John Diggins, *The Rise and Fall of the American Left* (New York: W. W. Norton, 1992). Daniel Flynn, *A Conservative History of the American Left* (New York: Crown Forum, 2008). Both examine the origins of the Left in America from the 19th century and trace its evolution to today.

Thomas Sowell, *The Vision of the Anointed: Self-Congratulation as Social Policy* (New York: Basic Books, 1995). The policies and gross failures of the New Left and Modern Liberals, the "anointed," are analyzed with an emphasis on how these people think and view the world and their place in it.

Jonah Goldberg, *Liberal Fascism* (New York: Penguin, 2009). The author traces the roots of the horrific movements of the 20th century, including today's Modern Liberalism that is a new kind of fascism: One that comes with a smile.

Ludwig von Mises, *The Anti-Capitalistic Mentality* (Mansfield Centre, CT: Martino Publishing, 2009). Originally published in 1956, it is still timely. The author explains the irrational fears, envy, and illogical thinking of anti-capitalists who promote Socialism.

Ronald J. Pestritto, *Woodrow Wilson and the Roots of Modern Liberalism* (Lanham, MD: Rowman & Littlefield Publishers, 2005). Possibly the best book explaining the ideological origins of Modern Liberalism that started with their predecessors' turn from our founding principles.

Myron Magnet, *The Dream and the Nightmare: the sixties' legacy to the underclass* (New York: Encounter Books, 2000). The author explains how the lifestyle experimentation and Liberal values foisted upon the poor in the 1960s counter-culture dramatically changed the face of our society for the worse.

Jonathan Leaf, *The Politically Incorrect Guide to the Sixties* (D. C.: Regnery Publishing, 2009). A good book to accompany the one above. The myths of the era are exposed, along with the failures of the programs.

Robert Bork, *Slouching Towards Gomorrah: Modern Liberalism and American Decline* (New York: HarperCollins, 2003). Another great book describing the thinking and values that were foisted on our culture by the New Left.

Daniel Flynn, *Why the Left Hates America: Exposing the Lies that Have Obscured Our Nation's Greatness* (New York: Three Rivers Press, 2004). The attacks and distortions on America by Modern Liberals are dissected and exposed in this book.

John McElroy, *Divided We Stand: The Rejection of American Culture since the 1960s* (Lanham, MD: The Rowman & Littlefield Publishing Group, 2006). A devastating attack on the counter-culture of the 1960s.

Lyle Rossiter, *The Liberal Mind: The Psychological Causes of Political Madness* (Chicago: Free World Books, 2006). This book provides excellent insights into the psychopathology of the more radical Modern Liberals.

CONSERVATISM

Dinesh D'Souza, *Letters to a Young Conservative* (New York: Basic Books, 2002). An easy read, explaining Conservatism to young budding Conservatives. Can be viewed as a recruiting brochure.

Dinesh D'Souza, *What's So Great About America* (D. C.: Regnery Publishing, 2002). A defense and explanation of the greatness of our country.

Mark Levin, *Liberty and Tyranny: A Conservative Manifesto* (New York: Threshold Editions, 2009). A series of essays about practical programs for today's Conservatives from the outspoken and erudite radio host.

Alfred S. Regnery, *Upstream: The Ascendance of American Conservatism*, (New York: Threshold Editions, 2008). George H. Nash, *Reappraising the Right: The Past and Future of American Conservatism* (Wilmington, DE: Intercollegiate Studies Institute, 2009). Both are comprehensive histories of the rise of American Conservatism.

Russell Kirk, *The Conservative Mind* (D. C.: Regnery Publishing, 1986). Originally published in 1953, this seminal work deals with the roots of the

Conservative thinking. It emphasizes tradition and historical sources rather than economics in most other works about Conservatism.

Bruce Caldwell, ed., *The Collected Works of F. A. Hayek, Volume II: The Road to Serfdom: Text and Documents* (University of Chicago Press, 2007). The seminal work, written in 1943, to warn the West about the dangers of the central government managing the economy. A demanding read but well worth it.

RONALD REAGAN

Dinesh D'Souza, *Ronald Reagan: How an Ordinary Man Became an Extraordinary Leader* (New York: Simon & Schuster, 1999). An informal history showing how Ronald Reagan was a man of the people, and permanently changed the way we look at government.

Steven Hayward, *The Age of Reagan: The Conservative Counterrevolution, 1980–1989* (New York: Crown Forum, 2009). An in-depth and comprehensive history of the decade of Ronald Reagan.

Martin Anderson and Annelise Anderson, *Reagan's Secret War: The Untold Story of His Fight to Save the World from Nuclear Disaster* (New York: Crown Forum, 2010). A fascinating story about Ronald Reagan's lifetime determination to rid the world of Communism.

Appendix B

Online Information, Organizations And News

To "fight the good fight" for America, we must stay informed. Most news in the popular media is limited in scope and depth. By finding some sources of online news and information that fit *your* interests and needs, you can stay up-to-date, focus on your area of interest, choose the depth and breadth, and become involved with discussion groups or organizations.

As in the suggested readings, sites are presented in categories, beginning with the ones most highly recommended in each.

THINK TANKS AND IN-DEPTH ESSAYS

http://www.american.com/
http://www.aei.org/
http://www.cato.org/
http://www.heritage.org/
http://www.conservative.org/

http://www.hoover.org
http://www.claremont.org/

MISCELLANEOUS ESSAYS

http://reason.com/
http://biggovernment.com/
http://www.newcriterion.com/
http://www.manhattan-institute.org/

IN-DEPTH ARTICLES

http://www.hillsdale.edu/news/imprimis/archive/date.asp#2008
http://www.chroniclesmagazine.org/
http://www.theamericancause.org/

FREE-MARKET CAPITALISM

http://www.freetochoose.tv/
http://www.campaignforliberty.com
http://www.fee.org/
http://www.taxfoundation.org/

ACADEMIC FREEDOM AND CONSERVATISM ON AMERICAN CAMPUSES

http://www.thefire.org/
http://www.isi.org
http://www.studentsforacademicfreedom.org/

SELF-EDUCATION: VIDEO LECTURES

http://www.freetochoose.tv/
http://mises.org/periodical.aspx

TEA PARTY AND RELATED SITES

http://www.teapartypatriots.org/
http://connect.freedomworks.org/
http://www.theteaparty.net/

THE RESPONSE TO THE ACLU

http://www.theacru.org
http://www.alliancedefensefund.org/About

DAILY NEWS SOURCES WITH OPINION AND ANALYSIS

http://spectator.org/
http://townhall.com/
http://www.humanevents.com/
http://www.realclearpolitics.com/
http://cnsnews.com/
http://www.nypost.com/

WEEKLY AND MONTHLY NEWS AND COMMENTARY

http://www.nationalreview.com/
http://www.weeklystandard.com/

DAILY NEWS SOURCES EMPHASIZING EXPOSING MODERN LIBERAL LIES AND DISTORTIONS

http://newsbusters.org/
http://www.mrc.org
http://www.aim.org/

http://www.drudgereport.com/
http://www.humanevents.com/

KEEPING OUR SENSE OF HUMOR ABOUT MODERN LIBERALISM

http://www.boycottliberalism.com/
http://www.zombietime.com/

MODERN LIBERAL SITES: KNOW WHAT THE ENEMY IS DOING

http://www.huffingtonpost.com
http://www.thenation.com/
http://www.americanprogress.org/
http://www.alan.com/
http://www.democracynow.org/

GUIDE TO MODERN LIBERAL SITES

http://www.discoverthenetworks.org/

NONPARTISAN SITES THAT CHECK VALIDITY OF REPORTS

http://factcheck.org/
http://www.publicagenda.org/

FIND OUT WHAT IS HAPPENING IN YOUR STATE

http://www.stateline.org

References

Chapter 1

1. Bill O'Reilly, *Cultural Warrior* (New York: Broadway Books, 2006).
2. John P. Diggins, *The Rise and Fall of the American Left* (New York: W. W. Norton, 1992).
3. Thomas Sowell, *The Vision of the Anointed: Self-Congratulation as Social Policy* (New York: Basic Books, 1995).
4. Mark Levin, *Liberty and Tyranny: A Conservative Manifesto* (New York: Threshold Editions, 2009), 3.
5. O'Reilly, *Cultural Warrior*, 124.
6. William Voegeli, *Never Enough: America's Limitless Welfare State* (New York: Encounter Books, 2010), 148.
7. Richard Hudelson, *Modern Political Philosophy* (Armonk, New York: M. E. Sharpe, 1999), 37.
8. William Novak, "The Not-So-Strange Birth of the Modern American State: A Comment on James A. Henretta's 'Charles Evans Hughes and the Strange Death of Liberal America,'" *Law and History Review* 24, no. 1 (Spring 2005):193–200.
9. Caldwell, Bruce ed.,. *The Collected Works of F. A. Hayek, Volume II: The Road to Serfdom: Text and Documents* (Chicago: University of Chicago Press, 2007), 260.
10. O'Reilly, *Cultural Warrior*, 69.
11. Patrick J. Buchanan, Patrick J., *The Death of the West* (New York: St. Martin's Press, 2002), 52.
12. Jonah Goldberg, "Obama's Playbook, in Paperback: Liberal Fascism and its critics," *National Review*, June 22, 2009, 35.
13. Christopher Lasch, *The Culture of Narcissism: American Life in an Age of Diminishing Expectations* (New York: W. W. Norton & Company, 1971).
14. George Gilder, *Wealth and Poverty* (New York: Basic Books, 1981), 129.
15. On March 27, 2008, George F. Will wrote a column for the *Washington Post*:

Arthur C. Brooks, a professor at Syracuse University, published "Who Really Cares: The Surprising Truth About Compassionate Conservatism." The surprise is that liberals are markedly less charitable than conservatives.

If many conservatives are liberals who have been mugged by reality, Brooks, a registered independent, is, as a reviewer of his book said, a social scientist who has been mugged by data. They include these findings:

- Although liberal families' incomes average 6 percent higher than those of conservative families, conservative-headed households give, on average, 30 percent *more* to charity than the average liberal-headed household ($1,600 per year vs. $1,227).

- Conservatives also donate more time and give more blood.

- Residents of the states that voted for John Kerry in 2004 gave smaller percentages of their incomes to charity than did residents of states that voted for George Bush.

- Bush carried 24 of the 25 states where charitable giving was above average.

- In the 10 reddest states, in which Bush got more than 60 percent majorities, the average percentage of personal income donated to charity was 3.5. Residents of the bluest states, which gave Bush less than 40 percent, donated just 1.9 percent.

- People who reject the idea that "government has a responsibility to reduce income inequality" give an average of *four times more* than people who accept that proposition. Brooks demonstrates a correlation between charitable behavior and "the values that lie beneath" liberal and conservative labels. Two influences on charitable behavior are religion and attitudes about the proper role of government.

    http://www.washingtonpost.com/wp-dyn/content/article/2008/03/26/AR2008032602916.html

16. James Burnam, *Suicide of the West* (Washington, DC: Regnery Books, 1985), 84.

Chapter 2

1. John Hawkins, "Seven Flaws in the Way Liberals Think," *Townhall*, February 2, 2010.

2. William Voegeli, *Never Enough: America's Limitless Welfare State* (New York: Encounter Books, 2010), 212.

3. John McElroy, *Divided We Stand: The Rejection of American Culture since the 1960s* (Lanham, MD: The Rowman & Littlefield Publishing Group, 2006), 62–63.

4. Lyle Rossiter, *The Liberal Mind: The Psychological Causes of Political Madness* (Chicago: Free World Books, 2006), 328–329.

5. Milton Friedman and Rose Friedman, *Free to Choose: A Personal Statement* (New York: Harcourt Brace Jovanovich, 1990), 97.

6. Richard Hofstadter, *The Age of Reform* (New York, Knopf, 1955).

7. Jean-Jacques Rousseau, translated by G. D. H. Cole, *The Social Contract* (New York: Cosimo, Inc., 2008), 27.

8. John Dewey, *Reconstruction in Philosophy* (New York: Cosimo, Inc., 2008), 194.

9. Mark Kramer ed., translated by Jonathan Murphy, Nicolas Werthet al., *The Black Book of Communism: Terror, Repression* (Cambridge: Harvard University Press, 1999), 4.

10. James W. Ceaser, "Conserving Liberalism? Conservatism, modern liberalism, and classical liberalism: a symposium," *National Review*, December 7, 2009, 49.

11. George Gilder, *Wealth and Poverty* (New York: Basic Books, 1981), 98–99.

12. Naomi Klein, "'America's Teacher': A Conversation with Michael Moore about Capitalism: A Love Story," *Nation*, October 12, 2009, 14.

13. Matthew Continetti "Obama's Tax Evasion," *The Weekly Standard*, September 27, 2010, 7.

14. Peter Wehner, "Class Warfare: The last refuge of a Democrat," *The Weekly Standard*, December 27, 2010, 10–11.

15. Steven Pinker, *The Blank Slate: The Modern Denial of Human Nature* (New York: Penguin, 2003), 245–247.

16. Ralph Nader, *The Ralph Nader Reader* (New York: Seven Stories Press, 2000), 270.

17. Jim Manzi, "Unbundle the Welfare State," *National Review*, December 20, 2010, 30–38.

18. Jonah Goldberg, "Mortal Remains: The wisdom and folly in Albert Jay Nock's anti-statism," *National Review*, May 4, 2009, 38.
19. Quoted in Thomas G. West, *Vindicating the Founders* (Lanham, MD: Roman & Littlefield, 1997), 59.
20. Ronald Grigor Suny, "Empire Falls," *Nation*, November 16, 2009, 26–28.
21. John D. Skrentny, *The Ironies of Affirmative Action: Politics, Culture, and Justice in America* (Chicago: University of Chicago Press, 1996), 153.
22. Harry V. Jaffa, "God Bless America," *Claremont Institute*, April 18, 2008. http://www.claremont.org/publications/crb/id.1540/article_detail.asp#
23. Walter Mosley, "Get Happy: Americans deserve a government agency charged with fostering the pursuit of happiness," *Nation*, October 5, 2009, 23–24.
24. George Lakoff, *Don't Think of an Elephant* (White River Junction, Vermont: Chelseagreen Publishing), 91.
25. Quoted in Matthew Continetti "Obama's Tax Evasion," *The Weekly Standard*, September 27, 2010, 7.
26. Thomas Frank, *What's the Matter with Kansas?: How Conservatives Won the Heart of America* (New York: Henry Holt, 2005).
27. Robert Lindsay Schuettinger and Eamonn F. Butler, *Forty Centuries of Wage and price Controls: How Not to Fight Inflation* (Washington, DC: Heritage Foundation, 1979).
28. Jonah Goldberg, "Obama's Playbook, in Paperback: Liberal Fascism and its critics," *National Review*, June 22, 2009, 35.
29. Albert Jay Nock, *A journal of these days, June 1932–December 1933* (New York: W. Morrow & Company, 1934), 232.
30. Myron Magnet, *The Dream and the Nightmare* (San Francisco: Encounter Books, 2000), 27.
31. Thomas Sowell, *The Quest for Cosmic Justice* (New York: The Free Press, 1999).
32. Sowell, *The Quest for Cosmic Justice*, 149–150.
33. Thomas Sowell, *The Vision of the Anointed: Self-Congratulation as Social Policy* (New York: Basic Books, 1995), 110.
34. Barry Loberfeld, "Social Justice: Code for Communism," *FrontPageMagazine.com*, February 27, 2004.

http://www.discoverthenetworks.org/guides/Z-Social%20Justice-Code%20for%20Communism.htm

35. Thomas Sowell, "The Quest for Cosmic Justice." http://www.tsowell.com/spquestc.html

36. Michael Novak, "Defining Social Justice," *First Things*, December 2000. http://www.firstthings.com/article/2007/01/defining-social-justice-29

37. Balint Vazsonyi, *America's 30 Years War* (Washington, DC: Regnery Publishing, 1998), 53.

38. Gara LaMarche, "Repairing Our Broken Justice System," *Nation*, October 5, 2009, 21.

39. Bill O'Reilly, *Cultural Warrior* (New York: Broadway Books, 2006), 128–129.

40. Akiva Gottlieb, "Last Man Standing: On Clint Eastwood," *Nation*, June 1, 2009.

41. Paul G. Cassell and Richard Fowles, "Handcuffing the Cops? A Thirty-Year Perspective on Miranda's Harmful Effects on Law Enforcement," *Stanford Law Review*, Volume 50, April 1998, 1055–1172. This study reported the results of an extensive investigation into the effects of the Miranda decision. In the Executive Summary, it was concluded that after the Miranda decision, the following resulted:

    The fraction of suspects questioned who confessed dropped from 49 percent to 14 percent in New York.

- In Pittsburgh, the confession rate fell from 48 percent to 29 percent.

- An estimate from the best available studies is that, across the country, confession rates fell by about 16 percentage points.

- With fewer confessions, the police found it more difficult to solve crimes.

- Following the decision, the rates of violent crimes solved by police fell dramatically, from 60 percent or more to about 45 percent, where they have remained.

- The rates of property crimes solved by police also dropped.

- With fewer confessions and fewer crimes solved, there were also fewer convictions.

- Given that a confession is needed to get a conviction in about one of every four cases, a rough estimate is that there are 3.8 percent fewer convictions every year because of Miranda.

- This means that each year there are 28,000 fewer convictions for violent crimes, 79,000 fewer for property crimes and 500,000 fewer for other crimes.

Some defenders of the decision argue that fewer crimes were solved after *Miranda* for a good reason: the police were forced to abandon unconstitutionally coercive questioning techniques. However, coercive questioning methods had begun to decline in the 1930s and 1940s, and even the Court agreed that genuinely coerced confessions were rare at the time of *Miranda*.

Defenders of *Miranda* also might argue that there is no causal link between the drop in crime clearance rates and the Supreme Court's new rules. However, when the percent of crimes solved (the clearance rate) is subjected to standard statistical techniques, with controls for other influences, the findings are that *Miranda* had a statistically significant effect on clearance rates for both violent and property crimes. Specifically:

- Between 8,000 and 36,000 more robberies would have been solved in 1995 in the absence of the *Miranda* ruling.

- Between 17,000 and 82,000 more burglaries, between 6,000 and 163,000 more larcenies, and between 23,000 and 78,000 more vehicle thefts would have been solved.

- The ruling had a minimal impact on the solving of homicides, rapes, and assaults.

42. Sowell, *The Quest for Cosmic Justice*, 149–171.
Alan Charles Kors, "The Betrayal of Liberty on American Campuses," Bradley Lecture Series, Heritage Foundation, October 5, 1998. http://www.aei.org/speech/16634.

43. Ryszard Legutko, "What's Wrong with Liberalism?," *ISI Web Journal, First Principles*, May 15, 2008.
http://www.firstprinciplesjournal.com/articles.aspx?article=733&theme=home&page=1&loc=b&type=ctbf.

44. Kors, "The Betrayal of Liberty on American Campuses."

45. Jonah Goldberg "U. Topia: Liberals envision a perfect world, and it looks a lot like campus," *National Review*, October 18, 2010, 38.

46. Copyright 1988 by Peggy McIntosh. Available for $6.00 from the address below. The paper includes a longer list of privileges. Permission to excerpt or reprint must be obtained from Peggy McIntosh, Wellesley College Center for Research on Women, Wellesley, MA 02181 Ph.: 781- 283-2520 Fax: 781-283-2504.

47. Christina Hoff Sommers and Sally Satel, "The Tyranny of Therapism," *Signet House*, June 21, 2005.
http://www.spiked-online.com/articles/0000000CABF8.htm.

48. Christina Hoff Sommers and Sally Satel, *One Nation Under Therapy* (New York: St. Martin's Press, 2006), 5.

49. Jay Nordlinger, quoted in "Critic-in-Chief: Obama's hour is also Charles Krauthammer's," *National Review*, November 23, 2009, 30.

50. Sowell, *The Quest for Cosmic Justice*, 122–123.

51. Roger Morris, *Partners in Power: The Clintons and Their America* (Washington, DC: Regnery Publishing, 1996), 135.

52. Dinesh D'Souza, *Letters to a Young Conservative* (New York: Basic Books, 2002), 49.

53. Ceaser, "Conserving Liberalism?," 49.

54. Patrick M. Garry summarizes the data in "The Cultural Hostility to Religion," *First Principles: ISI Web Journal*, November 28, 2008:
    ...in February of 2004, a study by the John Jay College of Criminal Justice reported that only 4 percent of Catholic priests had even been accused of such abuse, and more than half of the accusations had been made against just seven priests. In addition, the majority of abuse incidents had occurred prior to 1982, twenty years before the scandal erupted on the front pages. What the study also found was that the Church had made steady progress over nearly three decades in eliminating this problem. The percentage of priests accused each year of abuse had been consistently declining ever since the mid-1970s, and the number

of alleged abuses had fallen dramatically from the 1970s to the 1990s.[22]For instance, the number of boys aged 8 to 10 alleged to have been abused dropped well over 90 percent during that time period. Another study of the sexual abuse scandal revealed that less than one percent of all contemporary priests had charges pending against them. http://www.firstprinciplesjournal.com/articles.aspx?article=786&theme=home&page=4&loc=b&type=ctbf.

55. *United States Catholic Conference and National Conference of Catholic Bishops v. Abortion Rights Mobilization*, 487 US 72 (1988).

56. Patrick M. Garry, "The Cultural Hostility to Religion," *ISI Web Journal, First Principles*, November 28, 2008. http://www.firstprinciplesjournal.com/print.aspx?article=786&loc=b&type=cbtp.

57. Ronald J. Pestritto, *Woodrow Wilson and the roots of modern liberalism* (Lanham, MD: Rowman and Littlefield, 2005), 6.

58. Richard Hofstadter, *The American Political Tradition and the Men Who Made It* (New York: Vintage Books, 1974), 20–21.

59. David Horowitz, *The Politics of Bad Faith: The Radical Assault on America's Future* (New York: Simon and Schuster, 2000), 57.

60. Ceaser, "Conserving Liberalism?," 48.

61. Jess Bergner, "Can Republicans Govern? Not unless they change The Narrative," *The Weekly Standard*, February 8, 2010, 23–24.

62. Patrick J. Buchanan, *The Death of the West* (New York: St. Martin's Press, 2002), 52.

63. Greg Grandin, "Off Dead Center: William Appleman Williams," *Nation*, July 20, 2009, 25–32.

64. Tamara K. Nopper, "The White Anti-Racist Is an Oxymoron: An Open Letter to 'White Anti-Racists,'" *Race Traitor: Journal of the New Abolitionism.* (Not dated; retrieved January 10, 2012.) http://racetraitor.org/.

65. Reported by D. Wilson in "Income Mobility and the Fallacy of Class-Warfare Arguments Against Tax Relief," *Heritage Foundation*, March 8, 2001.

66. Introduction to F. A. Hayek, *The Road to Serfdom*, by Milton Friedman. http://www.word-gems.com/wealth.hayek.preface.milton.html.

Chapter 3

1. Irving Kristol, "My Cold War," *The National Interest,* Spring 1993, 141.
2. "Sweden: Something Souring in Utopia," *Time Magazine*, July 19, 1976, 32-33.
3. John P. Diggins, *The Rise and Fall of the American Left* (New York: W. W. Norton, 1992), 40–41.
4. Daniel J. Flynn, *A Conservative History of the American Left* (New York: Crown Forum, 2008), 2.
5. Flynn, *A Conservative History of the American Left*, 274.
6. Flynn, *A Conservative History of the American Left*, 26.
7. Flynn, *A Conservative History of the American Left*, 27.
8. Hugh Gough, *The Terror in the French Revolution* (New York: MacMillan, 1998), 77.
9. Diggins, *The Rise and Fall of the American Left*, 34.
10. "The Omaha Platform," *The World Almanac*, 1893 (New York: 1893), 83–85.
11. Theodore Roosevelt and Elting Morison, *The Letters of Theodore Roosevelt: 1914–1919* (Harvard University Press, 1954), 1018.
12. Ronald J. Pestritto, *Woodrow Wilson and the roots of modern liberalism* (Lanham, MD: Rowman and Littlefield, 2005), 8, 90.
13. Jean O. Pasco, "Sinclair Letter Turns Out to Be Another Expose," *Los Angeles Times*, December 25, 2005
14. David A. Shannon, *The Socialist Party of America: A History* (New York: Quadrangle Books, 1967), 48–49.
15. Pestritto, *Woodrow Wilson and the roots of modern liberalism*, 122.
16. Herbert Croly, *Progressive Democracy* (New York: MacMillan, 1914), 421.
17. John Reed, *Ten Days that Shook the World* (Lawrence, KS: Digireads.com, January 1, 2007), 144.
18. Chase, Stuart, *The Road We are Traveling, 1914–1942: Guide lines to America's Future* (The Twentieth Century Fund, 1942), 95.
19. Roger Nash Baldwin, *Liberty under the Soviets* (New York: Vanguard, 1928), 187.
20. Baldwin, *Liberty under the Soviets*, 24.
21. Rexford Tugwell, Thomas Munro, and Roy Stryker, *American Economic Life and the Means of Its Improvement* (NY: Harcourt, Brace and Company, 1930), 711.

22. Thomas Sugrue, "The Hundred Days War," *Nation*, April 27, 2009, 25.

23. Karl Marx and Allen Wood ed., *Marx Selections* (New York: MacMillan, 1988), 54.

24. Fraiser Harbutt, *Frasier, Yalta 1945: Europe and America at the Crossroads* (Cambridge University Press, 2010), 241.

25. Diggins, *The Rise and Fall of the American Left*, 152–153.

26. Ronald Radosh, "Hinge of History," *National Review*, May 25, 2009, 50.

27. Lewis Mumford, *The City in History* (New York: Harcourt, Brace & World, 1961), 486.

28. Myron Magnet, *The Dream and the Nightmare* (San Francisco: Encounter Books, 2000), 16–17.

29. James Seaton, "The Critical Trio," *The Weekly Standard*, May 24, 2010, 34.

30. Thomas Wheatland, *The Frankfurt School in Exile* (University of Minnesota Press, 2009), 292.

31. Christina Hoff Sommers and Sally Satel, "The Tyranny of Therapism," *Signet House*, June 21, 2005.
   http://www.spiked-online.com/articles/0000000CABF8.htm.

32. John D. Mayer, reported in *Psychology Today*, August 9, 2009, from *Fact Magazine*, September/October 1964.
   http://www.psychologytoday.com/blog/the-personality-analyst/200908/libel-in-factthe-1189-psychiatrists.

33. Diggins, *The Rise and Fall of the American Left*, 264.

34. *United States Government Printing office*, 1970: Social Security and Welfare Proposals, Hearings, Ninety-First Congress, first session, Volume 3, 1022.

35. *United States Government Printing office*, 1967: Social Security amendments of 1967, Volume 2, 1465.

36. John R. Hall, *Gone from the Promised Land: Jonestown in American Cultural History* (New Brunswick, New Jersey: Transaction Publishers, 1987), 132.

37. Theodore Roszak, "Skeptics and True Believers," *Nation*, February 10, 1979, 137.

38. Critical Studies refers to the study of "critical theory" which was developed by the Marxist Frankfurt School in 1930s Europe. They are considered a revisionist school of Marxism by classical Marxists. Essentially, they purport to analyze power structures in society

instead of the classical Marxist position of analyzing society in terms of only economic structures and classes.

39. Aaron Goldstein, "Why Do Liberals Throw Things at Conservatives?" *American Spectator*, July 19, 2011.

40. Diggins, *The Rise and Fall of the American Left*, 296.

41. John Derbyshire, "The Husks of Dead Theories," *National Review*, April 24, 2009. http://www.nationalreview.com/articles/227355/husks-dead-theories/john-derbyshire.

42. Harry Stein, *I Can't Believe I'm Sitting Next to a Republican* (New York: Encounter Books, 2009), xv.

43. Pascal Bruckner, *The Tyranny of Guilt: An Essay on Western Masochism* (Princeton University Press, 2010), 26.

Chapter 4

1. Nancy Morgan, "I wish I were a liberal," *American Thinker*, May 19, 2009. http://www.americanthinker.com/2009/05/i_wish_i_were_a_liberal.html.

2. Robert Bork, *Slouching Towards Gomorrah: Modern Liberalism and American Decline* (New York: HarperCollins, 2003), 51.

3. Caldwell, Bruce ed.,. *The Collected Works of F. A. Hayek, Volume II: The Road to Serfdom: Text and Documents* (University of Chicago Press, 2007), 160.

4. Lyle Rossiter, *The Liberal Mind: The Psychological Causes of Political Madness* (Chicago: Free World Books, 2006), 4.

5. "You Don't Need a Weatherman to Know Which Way the Wind Blows," Document 5, *Revolutionary Youth Movement* (1969). http://martinrealm.org/documents/radical/sixties1.html.

6. Lucinda Franks, "U.S. Inquiry Finds 37 in Weather Underground," *The New York Times*, March 3, 1975.

7. Interview of Todd Gitlin in "The Weather Underground." http://www.youtube.com/watch?v-6I_5mAqBUko &feature=related.

8. Dinesh D'Souza, *Letters to a Young Conservative* (New York: Basic Books, 2002), 25.

9. Jonah Goldberg, "U. Topia: Liberals envision a perfect world, and it looks a lot like campus," *National Review*, October 18, 2010, 38.

10. Barton Swaim, "Mill of the Gods," *Weekly Standard*, June 15, 2009, 32–33.

11. Thomas Sowell, *The Quest for Cosmic Justice* (New York: The Free Press, 1999), 150.

12. Thomas Sowell, "Morality vs. Sanctimoniousness." http://www.tsowell.com/spmorali.html.

13. Ron Radosh, "The Zinning of America: How to Watch 'The People Speak'," *The History Channel*, December 12, 2009. http://pajamasmedia.com/ronradosh/2009/12/12/the-zinning-of-america-how-to-watch-the   -people-speak-on-the-history-channel-on-sunday-night/?singlepage=true

14. Roger Kimball, "Professor of Contempt: The legacy of Howard Zinn," *National Review*, February 22, 2010, 29–30.

15. "Howard Zinn, Historian, Dies at 87," *Associated Press*, January 28, 2010. http://query.nytimes.com/gst/fullpage.html?res=940DE0D7133CF93BA15752C0A9669D8B63

16. Michael C. Moynihan, "The People's Historian?," From *American Scholar*, quoted in *Reason.com*, February 3, 2010. http://reason.com/archives/2010/02/03/the-peoples-historian.

17. Michael Kazin, "Howard Zinn's History Lessons," *Dissent*, Spring, 2004 http://www.dissentmagazine.org/article/?article=385

18. David Horowitz, *The Politics of Bad Faith: The Radical Assault on America's Future* (New York: Simon and Schuster, 2000), 46.

19. Thomas J. DiLorenzo, *How Capitalism Saved America: The Untold History of Our Country, from the Pilgrims to the Present* (New York: Three Rivers Press, 2004).

20. Steven Pinker, *The Blank Slate: The Modern Denial of Human Nature* (New York: Penguin Books, 2002), 260–266. According to research referenced by Pinker, since individuals are attuned to others' emotional states, the more one actually believes one's own presentation of the self, the better the chances are to convince the other: In a potential fight, for example, all else being equal, the person who *actually believes* that he is stronger is more intimidating than the one who is unsure, and thus increases his chances of defeating the other or avoiding the fight.

21. William Ayers, Therese Quinn, and David Stovall, eds., *Handbook of Social Justice in Education* (New York: Routledge, 2009), 1.

22. Ayers et al, *Handbook of Social Justice in Education,* 24

23. Ayers et al, *Handbook of Social Justice in Education,* 212.

24. William Ayers and Bernardine Dohrn, *Race Course: Against White Supremacy* (Chicago: Third World Press, 2009).

25. In Thomas Frank, *What's the Matter with Kansas?: How Conservatives Won the Heart of America* (New York: Henry Holt, 2005), the Modern Liberal viewpoint is that Conservatives vote against their own limited interests. The author appears unaware that people often vote for the interests of the country at large.

26. Maurice Isserman, "Afterimages," *Nation,* June 29, 2009, 33–36.

27. Greg Granden, "Off Dead Center: William Appleman Williams," *Nation,* July 20, 2009, 25–32.

28. "Ten Things the Past Can Teach Us Today," *Nation,* September 20, 2010, 8.

29. Peter Dreier, "The Fifty Most Influential Progressives of the Twentieth Century," *Nation,* October 4, 2010, 11–21.

30. Robert Bork, *Slouching Towards Gomorrah: Modern Liberalism and American Decline* (New York: HarperCollins, 2003), 334.

Chapter 5

1. Ludwig von Mises, *The Anti-Capitalistic Mentality* (Mansfield Centre, CT: Martino Publishing, 2009), 82.

2. Kevin D. Williamson, *The Politically Incorrect Guide to Socialism* (D. C.: Regnery Publishing, 2011), 45–46.

3. John Jay Simon, "Leo Huberman Radical Agitator, Socialist Teacher," *Monthly Review: An Independent Socialist Magazine,* August 23, 2011.

4. Paul Sweeny and Leo Huberman, "Critical of Capitalism," in *Introduction to Socialism,* retrieved December 18, 2010.
http://www.skeptically.org/socialism/id18.html.

5. Williamson, *The Politically Incorrect Guide to Socialism,* 50.

6. Adam Shaw, "Obama's Socialism," *American Thinker,* February 25, 2010.
http://www.americanthinker.com/2010/02/obamas_socialism.html.

7. David Conway, *A Farewell to Marx: An Outline and Appraisal of His Theories* (New York: Penguin Books, 1987), 10.

8. Michael Lowy and George Lukacs, *From Romanticism to Bolshevism* (NLB, 1979), 130.

9. Myron Magnet, *The Dream and the Nightmare* (San Francisco: Encounter Books, 2000), 122.

10. Thomas Sowell, *Marxism: Philosophy and Economics* (New York: William Morrow and Company, 1985).

11. David Conway, *A Farewell to Marx: An Outline and Appraisal of His Theories* (London: Penguin Books, 1987).

12. Leszek Kolakowshi, *Main Currents of Marxism* (New York: W. W. Norton, 2007).

13. Marx claimed that it was the enclosures of common land in Britain from the 15th century, and especially in the 18th that deprived peasants of subsistence and drove them to the factories where they became the industrial proletariat. But this was not true at all: Small land owners were increasing in late 18th century, and the poor squatters had more work from these small landowners. There was no general exodus to the factories. The increase in the factories in cities was due to an enormous increase in overall population. The labor force increased faster than agriculture could absorb it. Improved technology from capitalism actually improved the standard of living and resulted in more dependable work. Rondo E. Cameron, in *Banking in the Early Stages of Industrialization* (Oxford University Press, 1967), used the example of Richard Arkwright, who has been credited with inventing the water frame and the engine to convert raw cotton into yarn, was a "self-made man" whom many consider as the founder of the modern factory system. He was the youngest of 13 children, and his father—a tailor—could not afford to send him to school; he apprenticed for a barber. He and a partner set up a small horse-driven factory at Nottingham and later a factory in Albion. "The Albion steam flour mill, 'the most highly mechanized unit of its kind,' had less capital sunk in plant and equipment than in inventories and other forms of working capital" (page 38).

14. Karl Marx, *Capital, Volume I* (Knopf Doubleday Publishing Group, 1977), 874.

15. Marx, *Capital, Volume I*, 326.

16. Marx, *Capital, Volume I*, 784.

17. Marx, *Capital, Volume I*, 799.

18. Marx, *Capital, Volume I*, 789.

19. Marx, *Capital, Volume I*, 480.

20. Marx, *Capital, Volume I*, 739.
21. Conway, *A Farewell to Marx*, 14.
22. Karl Marx, *Capital, Volume I*, 96.
23. If we look at the census data in a limited way, it appears that there is a large income gap that is increasing. This is completely invalid as attested to by university and government data. First of all, the data only reveals *group* differences. What is important is whether people are getting ahead. This has, in fact, been tracked by the government and the University of Michigan: http://psidonline.isr.umich.edu/.

    This study has collected information on over 50,000 Americans. The facts revealed:

    Only 5 percent of the bottom fifth (lowest quintile) in 1975 were still there sixteen years later; most actually made it into the top three quintiles. The study found that being in the lowest quintile was usually transitory. In the first year of the study, about 25 percent moved up and never returned to it. Over the total period of the study, *less than 1 percent remained in the bottom quintile every year!*

    Since only one third of those classified as poor by the Census Bureau stayed there for twenty-four months or more, this means that the long-term poverty rate is only 3 percent!

    The US Treasury Dept. used a similar income-tracking study. This study used a different sample. It covered only nine years. During those nine years, 86 percent of those in the lowest quintile moved to a higher one; 66 percent reached the middle; and 15 percent made it to the top! http://www0.gsb.columbia.edu/faculty/ghubbard/Articles%20for%20Web%20Site/Household%20Income%20Changes%20Over%20Time_Some%20Basic%20Questions%20and%20Facts.pdf.

    Another study summarizes the likely reasons for this real mobility: http://www.dallasfed.org/fed/annual/1999p/ar95.cfm.

    Basically, it is a result of new workers, and they are mostly young people. It is that simple. If lifetime earning patterns are viewed at different periods in our recent history, it then becomes obvious:

    In 1951, the peak earning years were ages 35-44, and their earnings were 1.6 times those in the 20-24 age bracket. In 1973, the peak was the same, but it became 2.4 times as much. By 1993, the peak years rose to the 45-54 age bracket, and they earned 3.2 times more than the youngsters.

What accounts for this? In the 1950s, there was more industry and blue collar work; bodily strength was important. In 1993, brains were more important. Today, earnings continue to rise as people gain experience and learn. Marx, *Capital, Volume III,* 929.

24. Marx, *Capital, Volume III,* 959.
25. Marx, *Capital, Volume III,* 959.
26. Marx *Capital Volume I,* 135.
27. Marx, "Economic and Philosophical Manuscripts (1844)," *Early Writings,* (Middlesex: Harmondsworth Publishers, 1975) 359.
28. Karl Marx, "On the Jewish Question (1843)," *Early Writings,* 240.
29. Marx, "Excerpts from James Mill's 'Elements of Political Economy (1844),'" in *Early Writings,* 265.
30. Marx, "Economic and Philosophical Manuscripts (1844)," *Early Writings,* 361.

Chapter 6

1. Charles Krauthammer, "Decline is a Choice: The New Liberalism and the End of American Ascendancy," *The Weekly Standard,* October 19, 2009, 16.
2. Krauthammer, ibid., 17.
3. Daniel J. Flynn, *A Conservative History of the American Left* (New York: Crown Forum, 2008), 209–210.
4. David Horowitz, *The Politics of Bad Faith: The Radical Assault on America's Future* (New York: Simon and Schuster, 2000), 51.
5. John Earl Haynes and Harvey Klehr, *In Denial: Historians, Communism & Espionage* (San Francisco: Encounter Books, 2003).
6. John Earl Haynes and Harvey Klehr, *Venona: Decoding Soviet Espionage in America* (New Haven: Yale University Press, 2000).
7. Paul Hollander, ed., *Understanding Anti-Americanism* (Chicago: Ivan R. Dee, 2004), 240–241.
8. Hollander, *Understanding Anti-Americanism,* 242.
9. Hollander, *Understanding Anti-Americanism,* 350–351.

10. William Ayers and Bernardine Dohrn, *Race Course: Against White Supremacy* (Chicago: Third World Press, 2009), 5.

11. James W. Ceaser, *Reconstructing America: The Symbol of America in Modern Thought* (New Haven: Yale University Press, 2000).

12. James Seaton, "The Liberal Paradox," *The Weekly Standard*, August 31, 2009, 35.

13. D. D. Guttenplan, "The Secret History of Izzy," *Nation*, June 1, 2009, 26.

14. John Earl Haynes and Harvey Klehr, *In Denial: Historians, Communism & Espionage* (San Francisco: Encounter Books, 2003).

15. Alexander Cockburn, "The 'Rogue Nation' Contest," *Nation*, June 29, 2009, 9.

16. Robert Bork, *Slouching Towards Gomorrah: Modern Liberalism and American Decline* (New York: HarperCollins, 2003), 88.

17. John McElroy, *Divided We Stand: The Rejection of American Culture since the 1960s* (Lanham, MD: The Rowman & Littlefield Publishing Group, 2006), 213–214.

Chapter 7

1. Patrick J. Buchanan, *The Death of the West* (New York: St. Martin's Press, 2002), 51–52.

2. Steven F. Hayward, *The Age of Reagan: The Conservative Counterrevolution, 1980–1989* (New York: Crown Publishing, 2010), 221.

3. Myron Magnet, *The Dream and the Nightmare* (San Francisco: Encounter Books, 2000), 233–234.

4. Allan David Bloom, *The Closing of the American Mind* (New York: Simon and Schuster, 1988), 331.

5. Thomas Sowell, "Morality vs. Sanctimoniousness," retrieved on November 22, 2011.
   http://www.tsowell.com/spmorali.html.

6. Lionel Trilling, *The Liberal Imagination* (Oxford University Press, 1981), 84.

7. J. Budziszewski, "The Problem With Liberalism," *First Things* (March 1996): 20–26.

8. *Ibid.*

9. Sharon Basco, "Dissent In Pursuit Of Equality, Life, Liberty and Happiness: An Interview with Historian Howard Zinn," *Tompaine.com*, July 3, 2002.
http://www.tompaine.com/Archive/scontent/5908.html.

10. Daniel J. Flynn, *Why the Left Hates America: Exposing the Lies that Have Obscured Our Nation's Greatness* (New York: Three Rivers Press, 2004), 115–116.

11. Daniel J. Flynn, *A Conservative History of the American Left* (New York: Crown Forum, 2008), 72.

12. Lisa Fabrizio, "The limits of self-hate," *American Spectator*, September 9, 2009.
http://spectator.org/archives/2009/09/09/the-limits-of-self-hate.

13. J. Budziszewski, "The Problem With Liberalism," *First Things* (March 1996): 20–26.

14. *Ibid.*

15. Caldwell, Bruce ed.,. *The Collected Works of F. A. Hayek, Volume II: The Road to Serfdom: Text and Documents* (Chicago: University of Chicago Press, 2007), 153.

16. Jonah Goldberg, *Liberal Fascism* (New York: Penguin, 2009), 359.

17. Ellis, *The Dark Side of the Left: Illiberal Egalitarianism in America*, 253.

18. David Horowitz, *The Politics of Bad Faith: The Radical Assault on America's Future* (New York: Simon and Schuster, 2000), 81.

19. Ludwig von Mises, *The Anti-Capitalistic Mentality* (Mansfield Centre, CT: Martino Publishing, 2009), 11.

20. Sowell, *The Vision of the Anointed*, 199–200.

21. Thomas Sowell, *The Vision of the Anointed: Self-Congratulation as Social Policy* (New York: Basic Books, 1995), 183.

22. *Ibid.* Sowell referred to studies showing that "fertility rates among teenage girls had been *declining* for more than a decade since 1957, and the rate of syphilis infection was, by 1960, less than half of what it had been in 1950," and that these rates *increased* after the programs went into effect (17–19). With crime, "the number of murders committed…in 1960 was less than in 1950, 1940, or 1930—even though the population was growing…The murder rate, in proportion to population, was in 1960 just under half of what it had been in 1934," and after the programs had had their effect, "crime rates skyrocketed. Murder rates suddenly shot up

until the murder rate in 1974 was more than twice as high as in 1961" (pp. 21, 27).

23. Robert Bork, *Slouching Towards Gomorrah: Modern Liberalism and American Decline* (New York: HarperCollins, 2003), 29.

24. As early as 1931, the US Congress was alarmed by the ACLU's devotion to communism. A report by the Special House Committee to Investigate Communist Activities stated the following:

> The American Civil Liberties Union is closely affiliated with the communist movement in the United States, and fully 90 percent of its efforts are on behalf of communists who have come into conflict with the law. It claims to stand for free speech, free press and free assembly, but it is quite apparent that the main function of the ACLU is an attempt to protect the communists.

> Roger Baldwin and Crystal Eastman founded the ACLU in 1920 along with three other organizations dedicated to the most leftist of causes. The histories of these two individuals belie their claims of patriotism and respect for the Constitution. Baldwin openly sought the utter destruction of American society. Fifteen years after the founding of the ACLU, Baldwin wrote:

> I am for Socialism, disarmament and ultimately, for the abolishing of the State itself...I seek the social ownership of property, the abolition of the propertied class and sole control of those who produce wealth. Communism is the goal.

> Earl Browder, the general secretary of the Communist Party of the United States, admitted that the ACLU served as a "transmission belt" for the party. Baldwin agreed, claiming, "I don't regret being a part of the communist tactic which increased the effectiveness of a good cause."

http://www.wnd.com/news/article.asp?ARTICLE_ID=45959#ixzz1PMmZIPSU.

25. *Goss v. Lopez*, 419 US 565, 1975. Nine students were suspended from Marion-Franklin High School for ten days for destroying school property and disruptive behavior. One's name was Dwight Lopez. A three-judge District Court struck down the state law—Ohio Law #3313.66 that empowered the school principal to suspend a student for up to 10 days—saying that it violated the students' right to due process of law. The school appealed to the Supreme Court. The court

was split five to four, but concluded that the state had violated due process by removing the process of a hearing. The Supreme Court deemed that a public school must conduct a hearing before suspending a student, and that a suspension without a hearing actually violated the due process clause of the Fourteenth Amendment of our Constitution. Justice Powell wrote the court's dissent in which he said that the court was interfering for the first time in how schools ran their own classrooms. But precedent had been set six years earlier in *Tinker v. Des Moines Independent Community School District*, 393 US 503 1969. This was a decision by the Supreme Court that defined the constitutional rights of students in U. S. public schools. In December 1965, in Des Moines, Iowa, three siblings of the Tinker family and a friend wore black armbands to their schools in protest of the Vietnam War and supporting the Christmas Truce. The principals had adopted a policy banning the wearing of armbands to school, and violating students were to be suspended, but allowed to return to school when they agreed to comply with the policy. The three Tinker siblings deliberately violated the policy and were suspended. The radical ACLU got involved. Suit was filed in US District Court, and the decision of the school was upheld. It went to the US Court of Appeals where there was a tie vote. Then, with the help of the radical ACLU, they appealed to the Supreme Court. The Court held that the First Amendment applied to public schools. Two Justices, Hugo Black and John Marshall Harlan II, dissented. Black wrote the following:

If the time has come when pupils of state-supported schools, kindergartens, grammar schools, or high schools, can defy and flout orders of school officials to keep their minds on their own schoolwork, it is the beginning of a new revolutionary era of permissiveness in this country fostered by the judiciary.

26. Magnet, *The Dream and the Nightmare*, 143.
27. Jonah Goldberg, *Liberal Fascism* (New York: Penguin, 2009), 254.
28. Sowell, *The Vision of the Anointed*, 96–97.
29. *World Almanac and Book of Facts*, 2003, 74.
30. Quoted in Buchanan, *The Death of the West*, 193.
31. Sowell, *The Vision of the Anointed*, 102.

32. Richard J. Ellis, *The Dark Side of the Left: Illiberal Egalitarianism in America* (Lawrence, KS: University Press of Kansas, 1998), 7.

33. Magnet, *The Dream and the Nightmare*, 3.

34. Thomas Sowell, *The Quest for Cosmic Justice* (New York: The Free Press, 1999), 135-136.

35. F. Scott Fitzgerald, Wilson Edmund, ed., *The Crack-Up* (New York: New Directions Publishing, 2009), 290.

36. Noemie Emery, "Secondhand Hate: Another step downhill for modern liberalism," *The Weekly Standard*, January 4/January11, 2010, 27.

37. Matthew Continrlli, "'The Palin Persuasion' A case for the new populism," *The Weekly Standard*, November 16, 2009, 19–20.

38. Irving Kristol, *Neoconservatism: the Autobiography of an Idea* (New York: Ivan R. D., Publisher, 1999), 134.

39. David Barton is an American history scholar and the founder of Wallbuilders. His organization and historical writings emphasize our constitutional heritage, our moral foundations and forgotten history. Barton is a bugbear to Modern Liberals because of his emphasis on our founding principles, Christian heritage and American traditions. His works include *America's Godly Heritage* (2009), *Original Intent: The Courts, the Constitution and Religion* (2008), *Separation of Church and State: What the Founders Meant* (2007), *Celebrate History! Famous American Speeches and* Sermons (2003), and many more. His organization is located at the following website:
http://www.wallbuilders.com/.

40. Gary Younge, "A Method to Their Madness," *Nation*, September 29, 2009, 11.

41. Thomas Sowell, *The Vision of the Anointed: Self-Congratulation as Social Policy* (New York: Basic Books, 1995), 183.

Chapter 8

1. "In 2010, Conservatives Still Outnumber Moderates, Liberals," *Gallup*, June 25, 2010:

    Conservatives have maintained their leading position among US ideological groups in the first half of 2010. Gallup finds 42 percent of Americans describing themselves as either very conservative

or conservative. This is up slightly from the 40percent seen for all of 2009 and contrasts with the 20 percent calling themselves liberal or very liberal.
http://www.gallup.com/poll/141032/2010-conservatives-outnum-ber-moderates-liberals.aspx.

2. "Are We Happy Yet?," *Pew Research Center*, February 13, 2006.
http://pewresearch.org/pubs/301/are-we-happy-yet.

3. Peter Schweizer, *Makers and Takers: Why Conservatives Work Harder, Feel Happier, Have Closer Families, Take Fewer Drugs, Give More Generously, Value Honesty More, Are Less Materialistic and Envious, Whine Less...and Even Hug Their Children More Than Liberals* (New York: Doubleday, 2008).

4. Retrieved on July 20, 2011 from the "Catalogue for Philanthropy, 2004 Generosity Index."
http://www.catalogueforphilanthropy.org/cfp/db/generosity.php?year=2004&orderby=generosity_index.

5. David Horowitz, *The Politics of Bad Faith: The Radical Assault on America's Future* (New York: Simon and Schuster, 2000), 180–181.

6. Ryszard Legutko, "What's Wrong With Liberalism?," *ISI First Principles*, May 15, 2008.
http://www.firstprinciplesjournal.com/articles.aspx?article=733&theme=home&page=1&loc=b&type=ctbf.

7. Bill O'Reilly, *Cultural Warrior* (New York: Broadway Books, 2006), 66.

8. Text of *House Resolution 579*, 105th US Congress, December 17, 2005.
http://www.govtrack.us/congress/billtext.xpd?bill=hr109-579.

Chapter 9

1. Russell Kirk, "Ten Conservative Principles," The Russell Kirk Center for Cultural Renewal, adapted from *The Politics of Prudence* (Wilmington, DE: ISI Books, 1993).
http://www.kirkcenter.org/index.php/detail/ten-conservative-principles/.

2. *Ibid.*

3. Jonah Goldberg, *Liberal Fascism* (New York: Penguin, 2009), 402–403.

4. Patrick Allitt, *The Conservatives: Ideas and Personalities Throughout American History* (Yale University Press, 2010), 7.

5. Thomas West and William Schambra, "The Progressive Movement and the Transformation of American Politics," *Heritage Foundation*, July 18, 2007.

6. West and Schambra, *Ibid.*

7. Charles R. Kesler, "The Constitution, at Last: Let us return from a regime of arbitrary power to one of self-government," *National Review*, May 17, 2010, 26.

8. Edwin Meese, Matthew Spalding and David Forte, eds., *The Heritage Guide to the Constitution* (Washington, DC: Regnery Publishing, 2005), 13.

9. Caldwell, Bruce ed,. *The Collected Works of F. A. Hayek, Volume II: The Road to Serfdom: Text and Documents (*Chicago: University of Chicago Press, 2007), 112–113.

10. Hayek, *The Road to Serfdom*, 117.

11. Mark Levin, *Liberty and Tyranny: A Conservative Manifesto* (New York: Threshold Editions, 2009), 67.

12. Kesler, Ibid., 26.

13. Ronald J. Pestritto, *Woodrow Wilson and the roots of modern liberalism* (Lanham, MD: Rowman and Littlefield, 2005), 72.

14. Hayek, *The Road to Serfdom*, 74.

15. James Bowman, "The Right Thing," *The Weekly Standard*, January 17, 2011, 37–38.

16. Thomas DiLorenzo, *How Capitalism Saved America: The Untold History of Our Country, from the Pilgrims to the Present* (NY: Three Rivers Press, 2004), 15.

17. Ludwig von Mises, *The Anti-Capitalistic Mentality* (Mansfield Centre, CT: Martino Publishing, 2009), 85.

18. John Harmon McElroy, *American Beliefs: What Keeps a Big Country and a Diverse People United* (Chicago: Ivan R. Dee, 1999).

19. Michael Medved, "The Real Political Divide: Attitudes Toward America," *Townhall*, September 16, 2009.

20. Rahe, *Soft Despotism*, 280.

21. Medved, **"The** Real Political Divide."

22. Norman Podhoretz, "Why are Jews Liberals?," *Wall Street Journal*, September 10, 2009.

23. Medved, "The Real Political Divide."

24. Kenneth Minogue, *The Servile Mind: How Democracy Erodes the Moral Life* (New York: Encounter Books, 2010), 147.

25. Diana Schaub, "The Souls of Free Men," *National Review*, September 20, 2010, 46.

26. Minogue, *The Servile Mind*, 107, 317, 13.

27. David Horowitz, *The Politics of Bad Faith: The Radical Assault on America's Future* (New York: Simon and Schuster, 2000), 72.

28. Mark T. Mitchell, "Why I Am a Conservative," *ISI Web Journal, First Principles*, December 30, 2008. http://www.firstprinciplesjournal.com/articles.aspx?article=183&theme=home&loc=b.

29. James Madison, *The Federalist*, #51, February 6, 1788.

30. Allitt, *The Conservatives*, 2–3

31. Thomas Sowell, *The Quest for Cosmic Justice* (New York: The Free Press, 1999), 23.

32. Sowell, *The Quest for Cosmic Justice*, 23.

33. Sowell, *The Quest for Cosmic Justice*, 23.

34. Myron Magnet, *The Dream and the Nightmare* (San Francisco: Encounter Books, 2000), 58.

35. Christina Hoff Sommers and Sally Satel, "The Tyranny of Therapism," *Signet House*, June 21, 2005. http://www.spiked-online.com/articles/0000000CABF8.htm.

36. Myron Magnet, *The Dream and the Nightmare*, 238.

37. Russell Kirk, *The Conservative Mind* (D. C.: Regnery Publishing, 1986), 181.

38. "The American Dream," *CBS/New York Times Poll*, May 4, 2009. http://www.cbsnews.com/htdocs/pdf/poll_050409americandream.pdf.

39. Dinesh D'Souza, *What's So Great about America* (NY: Penguin Books, 2003), 193.

40. Vidiahar Naipaul, "Our Universal Civilization," Wriston Lecture at the *Manhattan Institute for Policy Research*, October 30, 1990.

41. Medved, "The Real Political Divide."

Chapter 10

1. Barry Goldwater, *The Conscience of a Conservative* (Princeton University Press, 2007), 10.

2. Russell Kirk, *The Conservative Mind* (Washington, DC: Regnery Publishing, 1986), 459.

3. Burton W. Folsom, *The Myth of the Robber Barons* (Herndon, VA: Young America's Foundation, 2010).

4. Meg Sullivan, "FDR's policies prolonged Depression by 7 years, UCLA economists calculate," *UCLA Newsroom*, August 10, 2004.

5. Rick Perlstein, *Before the Storm: Barry Goldwater and the Unmaking of the American Consensus* (New York: Nation Books, 2009), 108.

6. Lionell Trilling, *The Liberal Imagination* (Oxford University Press, 1981), ix.

7. Paul G. Cassell and Richard Fowles, "Handcuffing the Cops? A Thirty-Year Perspective on Miranda's Harmful Effects on Law Enforcement," *Stanford Law Review*, Volume 50, April 1998, 1055–1172.

8. Don Irving, "February Cable TV News Ratings: Fox News Continues Dominance," *Accuracy in Media*, February 29, 2012.

9. George H. Nash, *Reappraising the Right: The Past and Future of American Conservatism* (Wilmington, DE: Intercollegiate Studies Institute, 2009), 361.

Chapter 11

1. Mark Steyn, "Welcome to Rome: Commit National Suicide, shall We?," *National Review*, January 25, 2010, 36.

2. "One in Three Americans 'Extremely Patriotic,'" *Gallup Poll*, July 2, 2010.
   http://www.gallup.com/poll/141110/One-Three-Americans-Extremely-Patriotic.a

3. John Diggins, *The Rise and Fall of the American Left* (New York: W. W. Norton, 1992), 338–339.

4. Christopher Wolfe, "The Cultural Preconditions of American Liberty," *National Review*, May 17, 2010, 45.

5. Matthew Spalding, *We Still Hold These Truths: Rediscovering Our Principles, Reclaiming Our Future* (Wilmington, DE: Intercollegiate Studies Institute, 2009), 140.

6. John Harmon McElroy, *American Beliefs: What Keeps a Big Country and a Diverse People United* (Chicago: Ivan R. Dee, 1999), 68.

7. John Micklethwait and Adrian Wooldridge, *The Right Nation: Conservative Power in America* (New York: Penguin Books, 2004), 280.

8. Jeff Bergner, "Europe is No Model," *The Weekly Standard*, May 17, 2010, 28.
9. Mark Steyn, "Right Turn on Main Street: Thank goodness for the tea-party crowd and their collective anti-collectivism," *National Review*, October 5, 2009, 29.
10. John Micklethwait and Adrian Wooldridge, *The Right Nation: Conservative Power in America* (New York: Penguin Books, 2004), 303.
11. Diggins, *The Rise and Fall of the American Left*, 33.
12. Theodore Dalrymple, "Struggle for a Continent," *National Review*, August 10, 2009, 42–44.
13. Theodore Dalrymple, *The New Vichy Syndrome: Why European Intellectuals Surrender to Barbarism* (New York: Encounter Books), 149.
14. Charles Murray, "The Happiness of the People," Irving Kristol Lecture, *American Enterprise Institute for Public Policy Research*, March 11, 2009.
15. "Guns in America: National Survey on Private Ownership and Use of Firearms," *United States Department of Justice*, 1997. https://www.ncjrs.gov/pdffiles/165476.pdf.
16. Micklethwait and Wooldridge, *The Right Nation*, 280.
17. Murray, "The Happiness of the People."

Chapter 12

1. "Americans Say Reagan Is the Greatest U.S. President," *Gallup*, February 18, 2011.
2. "Americans Judge Reagan, Clinton, Best of Recent Presidents," *Gallup*, February 17, 2012.
3. Steven F. Hayward, "Reagan Reclaimed: Against the Liberal Revised Standard Version of our 40th President," *National Review*, February 7, 2011, 34.
4. Pete Winn, "Obama Should Emulate Ronald Reagan, Voters Tell Pollster" *CBS News*, Tuesday, January 20, 2009. http://www.cnsnews.com/node/42244
5. "Rating the Presidents," *International World History Project*, November 16, 2000. http://history-world.org/pres.pdf.
6. "The Rankings," *Wall Street Journal*, September 12, 2005. http://online.wsj.com/article/SB122633869449214207.html

7. Steven F. Hayward, *The Age of Reagan: The Conservative Counterrevolution, 1980–1989* (New York: Crown Publishing, 2010), 477.

8. Steven F. Hayward, "The Reagan Revolution and Its Discontents," Bradley Lecture, *American Enterprise Institute*, April 13, 2009.

9. Harvey Mansfield, *America's Constitutional Soul* (Baltimore: The Johns Hopkins University Press, 1991), 23.

10. Schneider, William, "Tough Liberals Win, Weak Liberals Lose," *New Republic*, December 5, 1988.

11. Richard Reeves, "Historians Undervalue the Reagan Presidency," *The Seattle Times*, December 19, 1996.

12. Richard Reeves, "Shaping Reagan's Legacy," *The Baltimore Sun*, February 9, 1999.

13. Steven F. Hayward, *Greatness: Reagan, Churchill, and the Making of Extraordinary Leaders* (New York: Crown Forum, 2005), 99.

14. Hayward, *The Age of Reagan*, 413.

15. James Burnham, *Suicide of the West* (Washington, DC: Regnery Books, 1985), 288.

16. "Excerpts from an Interview with Walter Cronkite of CBS News," *The American Presidency Project*, March 3, 1981.

17. Martin Anderson and Annelise Anderson, *Reagan's Secret War: The Untold Story of His Fight to Save the World from Nuclear Disaster* (New York: Crown, 2009).

18. Ronald Reagan, *An American Life* (New York: Simon and Schuster, 1990), 110.

19. Alfred S. Regnery, *Upstream: The Ascendance of American Conservatism* (New York: Threshold Editions, 2008), 289.

20. Steven Hayward, "A Lion Like Churchill," *American Enterprise Institute*, June 28, 2004.
http://www.aei.org/article/20895.

21. Statement by National Security Advisor Richard Allen, *Congressional Record*, November 18, 2003, page 29537.

22. Sean Wilentz, *The Age of Reagan: A History, 1974–2008* (New York: HarperCollins, 2009), 281.

23. Kiron K. Skinner, et al.,, *Reagan, in His Own Hand: The Writings of Ronald Reagan that Reveal His Revolutionary Vision for America* (New York: A Touchstone Book, 2001), 8.

24. Reagan, *An American Life*, 237.

25. William F. Buckley, Jr., *Let Us Talk of Many Things: The Collected Speeches with New Commentary by the Author* (New York: Basic Books, 2008), 361.

26. Margaret Thatcher, *The Downing Street Years* (New York: HarperPerennial, 1995), 156.

27. Thatcher, *The Downing Street Years*, 160.

28. "Ronald Reagan Statue Unveiled in Warsaw," *The Telegraph*, February 22, 2012

29. Steve Forbes, "How Capitalism Will Save Us," *Forbes Magazine*, October 22, 2008.

30. Robert Barrow, "A Gentleman's B-minus on Bush for Economics," *Wall Street Journal*, September 30, 1992, A16.

31. Hayward, *The Age of Reagan*, 166, 659.

32. Regnery, *Upstream*, 284.

33. Laurence Barrett and Barrett Seaman, "Ronald Reagan: Yankee Doodle Magic," *Time Magazine*, Volume 128, Number 1, July 07, 1986.

34. Walter LaFebe, Richard Polenberg and Nancy Woloch, *The American Century: A History of the United States since the 1890s* (Armonk, NY: M. E. Sharpe, 2008, 6th edition), 474.

35. Skinner, et al., *Reagan, In His Own Hand*, 20.

36. Hayward, *The Age of Reagan*, 79.

37. Hayward, *The Age of Reagan*, 639.

Chapter 13

1. Maggie Gallagher, "The Carrie Effect: Notes from the frontlines of the Marriage War," *National Review*, August 10, 2009, 28–34.

2. Modern Liberals obfuscated the truth that almost all people who invest in stocks for retirement do it over a period of two to four decades; therefore, if a longer view is taken—the average of any two 10-year periods, for example—we see that the value of the Dow has always increased since World War II.

3. Thomas Sowell, *The Vision of the Anointed: Self-Congratulation as Social Policy* (New York: Basic Books, 1995).

4. Bill O'Reilly, *Cultural Warrior* (New York: Broadway Books, 2006), 168.

5. Harry Stein, *I Can't Believe I'm Sitting Next to a Republican* (New York: Encounter Books, 2009), xvi.

6. Stein, *I Can't Believe I'm Sitting Next to a Republican*, 17.

7. Robert Bork, *Slouching Towards Gomorrah: Modern Liberalism and American Decline* (New York: HarperCollins, 2003), 336.

8. Bork, *Slouching Towards Gomorrah*, 342.

9. Harvey Mansfield, "What Obama Isn't Saying: The apolitical politics of progressivism," *The Weekly Standard*, February 8, 2010, 8–9.

10. Matthew Spalding, *We Still Hold These Truths: Rediscovering Our Principles, Reclaiming Our Future* (Wilmington, DE: Intercollegiate Studies Institute, 2009).

11. Edwin Meese, Matthew Spalding and David Forte, eds., *The Heritage Guide to the Constitution* (DC: Regnery Publishing, 2005).

12. Myron Magnet, *The Dream and the Nightmare* (San Francisco: Encounter Books, 2000), 133.

13. Spalding, *We Still Hold These Truths*, 84–86.

14. Sowell, *The Vision of the Anointed*, 191.

15. Steven F. Hayward, *The Age of Reagan: The Conservative Counterrevolution, 1980–1989* (New York: Crown Publishing, 2010), 376.

16. Jay Nordlinger, "All Wee-Weed Up: Protests on the right, hypocrisy on the left," *National Review*, September 21, 2009, 42.

17. Richard B. McKenzie, *What went Right in the 1980s* (San Francisco: Pacific Research for Public Policy, 1994). McKenzie presents the results of voluminous research showing that charitable giving not only increased in total amount, but also as a proportion of income and more than projected based on previous increases.

    - [Giving] by individuals and corporations jumped dramatically in the 1980s….measured not just in absolute current dollar terms but also in total read dollars contributed…per capita, and…relative to national income. (p. 57)

    - The annual rate of growth in total real giving in the 1980s was nearly 55 percent higher than in the previous twenty-five years. (p. 58)

    - [Giving] in the 1980s was more than two-thirds higher than in the prior two and a half decades. (p. 59)

    - [In] the 1980s the growth in private giving exceeded the growth of expenditures on a variety of goods and services that might be considered extravagances. (p. 60)

18. Roger Kimball, "Marxism's Main Critic: Leszek Kolakowski, 1927–2009," *The Weekly Standard*, August 3, 2009, 12.

19. Rossiter, *The Liberal Mind: The Psychological Causes of Political Madness* (Chicago: Free World Books, 2006), 320–321.

20. Rossiter, *The Liberal Mind*, 12.

21. Rossiter, *The Liberal Mind*, 336–337.

22. Rossiter, *The Liberal Mind*, 340–341.

23. Lyle Rossiter, *The Liberal Mind*, 314–315.

24. Quoted in Spalding, *We Still Hold These Truths*, 220.

25. David Horowitz, *The Politics of Bad Faith: The Radical Assault on America's Future* (New York: Simon and Schuster, 2000), 142.

26. Daniel J. Flynn, *A Conservative History of the American Left* (New York: Crown Forum, 2008), 111–112.

27. William G. Holzberger, Herman J. Saatkamp, Jr., and Marianne S. Wokeck, eds., *The Letters of George Santayana, Book Eight, 1948–1952: The Works of George Santayana, Volume 5* (Cambridge: MIT Press, 2008), 294.

28. "All-Time Donors, 1989-2012." *Open Secrets.org: Center for Responsive Politics*, April 25, 2011.
    http://www.opensecrets.org/orgs/list.php.

29. Charles R. Kesler, "The Constitution, at Last: Let us return from a regime of arbitrary power to one of self-government," *National Review*, May 17, 2010, 26.

30. Caldwell, Bruce, ed., *The Collected Works of F. A. Hayek, Volume II: The Road to Serfdom: Text and Documents* (Chicago: University of Chicago Press, 2007), 179.

31. There is a multitude of well-documented university research demonstrating that gratitude can lead to happiness and success:
    http://www.ca.uky.edu/hes/fcs/possibilities/Media_Articles/29-Benefits_of_Gratitude.htm
    http://www.umassd.edu/counseling/forparents/reccomendedreadings/theimportanceofgratitude/.

32. Horowitz, *The Politics of Bad Faith*, 143.

33. Sowell, *The Quest for Cosmic Justice*, 75.

34. Charles Murray, "The Happiness of the People," Irving Kristol Lecture, *American Enterprise Institute for Public Policy Research*, March 11, 2009.

35. Thomas Sowell, in *The Vision of the Anointed: Self-Congratulation as Social Policy* (New York: Basic Books, 1995), writes that "a very distinct

pattern has emerged repeatedly when policies favored by the anointed [Modern Liberals] turn out to fail." (p. 8) The four stages are the "crisis," the "solution," the "results," and the "response." In the crisis, "evidence is seldom asked or given to show how the situation at hand is either uniquely bad or threatening to get worse. Sometimes the situation described as a 'crisis' has in fact already been getting better for years." (p. 8) For example, poverty was lessening, illegitimate births were decreasing, and venereal diseases were on the decline, yet the "anointed" claimed we were in a "crisis."

36. Gregg Easterbrook, *Sonic Boom: Globalization at Mach Speed* (New York: Random House, 2009), xi.

37. Easterbrook, *Sonic Boom*, 187.

38. Easterbrook, *The Progress Paradox* (New York: Random House, 2004), 289.

39. Maxim Pinkovskiy and Xavier Sala-i-Martin, "Parametric Estimations of the World Distribution of Income," *National Bureau of Economic Research*, Working Paper 15433, October 2009. http://www.nber.org/papers/w15433.

40. Easterbrook, *The Progress Paradox*, 74.

41. Charles R. Kesler (contributor), Alexander Hamilton, James Madison, John Jay, and Clinton Lawrence Rossiter, *The Federalist Papers*, Part 2 (New York: Mentor, 1999), 47.

42. Kesler, *The Federalist Papers*, 22.

43. Kesler, *The Federalist Papers*, xx.

44. Kesler, *The Federalist Papers*, 439.

45. Jonah Goldberg, *Liberal Fascism* (New York: Penguin, 2009), 171–172.

46. Ann Coulter, *Slander: Liberal Lies about the American Right* (New York: Three Rivers Press, 2002), 26.

47. Ann Coulter, *Godless: The Church of Liberalism* (New York: Crown, 2007), 94.

48. Quoted in Ann Coulter, *Treason: Liberal Treachery from the Cold War to the War on Terrorism* (NY: Three Rivers Press, 2003), 119.

49. Stein, *I Can't Believe I'm Sitting Next to a Republican*, 124–126.

50. Stein, *I Can't Believe I'm Sitting Next to a Republican*, 25–28.

51. Fredrick Hayek, "The Intellectuals and Socialism," *University of Chicago Law Review*, Volume 16, 417.

52. Ludwig von Mises, *The Anti-Capitalistic Mentality* (Mansfield Centre, CT: Martino Publishing, 2009), v.

53. Hayek, *The Road to Serfdom*, 212–213.
54. Transcript from David Asman's May 15, 2004 interview with economist Milton Friedman, from "'Your World' Interview With Economist Milton Friedman," *Fox News*, November 16, 2006.
55. Marvin Harris, *Cannibals and Kings: Origins of Cultures* (New York: Knopf Doubleday Publishing, 2011).
56. Helen Codere, *Fighting with Property* (Seattle: University of Washington Press, 1966).
57. Dominick T. Armentano and Yale Brozen, *Antitrust and Monopoly: Anatomy of a Policy Failure* (Washington, DC: Independent Institute, 1996).
58. Burton W. Folsom, *The Myth of the Robber Barons* (Herndon, VA: Young America's Foundation, 2010).
59. Thomas DiLorenzo, *How Capitalism Saved America: The Untold History of Our Country, from the Pilgrims to the Present* (New York: Three Rivers Press, 2004), 154.
60. Sowell, *The Vision of the Anointed*.
61. Henry Hazlitt, *Economics in One Lesson* (New York: Crown, 1979).
62. DiLorenzo, *How Capitalism Saved America*, 101.
63. Michael Cox and Richard Alm, *Myths of Rich and Poor: Why We're Better off than We Think* (New York: Basic Books, 2000), 76.
64. Hayek, *The Road to Serfdom*, 63.
65. Quoted in Locay, Alex, *Unveiling the Left* (Townhall Press, 2008), 140.
66. Hazlitt, *Economics in One Lesson*, 16.
67. Burton Folsom, *New Deal or Raw Deal? How FDR's Economic Legacy has Damaged America* (New York: Threshold Editions, 2008), 101–v102.
68. Jim Powell, *FDR's Folly: How Roosevelt and His New Deal Prolonged the Great Depression* (New York: Three Rivers Press, 2003), 257–260.
69. George Gilder, *Wealth and Poverty* (New York: Basic Books, 1981), 23–4.
70. Hayek, *The Road to Serfdom*, 212–213.
71. Gilder, *Wealth and Poverty*, 6.

Chapter 14

1. Bill O'Reilly, *Cultural Warrior* (New York: Broadway Books, 2006), 208.

Index

www.ingramcontent.com/pod-product-compliance
Lightning Source LLC
Chambersburg PA
CBHW072345290526
45794CB00001B/20